Juan de Segovia and the Fight for Peace

Juan de Segovia
and the Fight
for Peace

Christians and Muslims in the Fifteenth Century

ANNE MARIE WOLF

University of Notre Dame Press
Notre Dame, Indiana

Copyright © 2014 by University of Notre Dame
Notre Dame, Indiana 46556
www.undpress.nd.edu
All Rights Reserved

Manufactured in the United States of America

Library of Congress Cataloging-in-Publication Data

Wolf, Anne Marie.
Juan de Segovia and the fight for peace : Christians and Muslims
in the fifteenth century / Anne Marie Wolf.
    pages   cm. — (History, languages, and cultures of the
Spanish and Portuguese world)
Includes bibliographical references and index.
ISBN 978-0-268-04425-1 (pbk. : alk. paper) —
ISBN 0-268-04425-2 (pbk. : alk. paper)
1. Segovia, Juan de, 1393–1458.   2. Christian biography.
3. Church history—Middle Ages, 600–1500.   4. Christianity and
other religions—Islam—History—To 1500.   5. Islam—Relations—
Christianity—History—To 1500.   I. Title.
BR1725.S4265W65   2014
282.092—dc23
                                                    2014001705

Contents ⟜𝔪⟝

Abbreviations   vii

Acknowledgments   ix

Introduction   1

Chapter One   The Years at the University of Salamanca   13

Chapter Two   Contact, Conversations, and Conversion:
                   Early Thought on Islam   61

Chapter Three   The Basel Years   95

Chapter Four   Converting Fellow Christians   129

Chapter Five   Converting Muslims   175

Epilogue   223

Appendix 1: Excerpt from Juan de Segovia,
Repetitio de fide catholica   232

Appendix 2: Excerpt from Juan de Segovia,
De mittendo gladio divini Spiritus in corda sarracenorum   238

Appendix 3: Excerpt from Juan de Segovia,
Letter to Nicholas of Cusa, December 2, 1454   252

Notes   262

Bibliography   349

Index   367

Abbreviations ⟶〜〜⟵

AGS	Archivo General de Simancas (Spain)
ASV	Archivio Segreto Vaticano
BAV	Biblioteca Apostolica Vaticana
BN	Biblioteca Nacional (Madrid)
BSC	Biblioteca de Santa Cruz (Valladolid, Spain)
Bulario	*Bulario de la Universidad de Salamanca (1219–1549)*. Vols. 1–3. Edited by Vicente Beltrán de Heredia. Salamanca: Universidad de Salamanca, 1966.
BUS	Biblioteca Universitaria de Salamanca (Spain)
Cartulario	*Cartulario de la Universidad de Salamanca (1218–1600)*. 6 vols. Edited by Vicente Beltrán de Heredia. Salamanca: Universidad de Salamanca, 1970.
MC	*Monumenta Conciliorum Generalium*, s. XV (Vienna, 1857–96).
RAH	Real Academia de Historia (Madrid)
Reg. Avin.	Registra Avinionensia: registers of papal letters from the Avignon popes, in the Archivio Segreto Vaticano
Reg. Vat.	Registra Vaticana: registers of papal letters in the Archivio Segreto Vaticano
Vat. Lat.	Codex Vaticanus latinus (in Biblioteca Apostolica Vaticana)

Acknowledgments —∞—

C ompleting this project has put me in a reflective mode, awed at the way life's disparate threads meet. Although this endeavor began as a dissertation at the University of Minnesota, my interest in Spain had its roots in my superb Spanish classes at the Academy of the Holy Cross in Kensington, Maryland, with Victoria Thompson, a proud native of Burgos who told us (jokingly . . . I think) that Spanish was the language of God and that proper use of the imperfect subjunctive was simply not optional. The college year in Sevilla transformed a high school interest into a lifelong one, thanks to all the many sevillanos whose spirit keeps their city so enchanting. The interest in Christian-Muslim dialogue in the Middle Ages I owe to an independent study in medieval philosophy and theology that David Burrell for some reason generously agreed to direct during my senior year at the University of Notre Dame. David has been a cheerleader for me in many ways since and has enthusiastically supported this project, even spending a certain long afternoon over cookies and tea and some tortured Latin helping me unravel the meaning and significance of some of Juan de Segovia's comments on Islamic theology. And of course, my parents, Michael and Kathleen Wolf, made possible, through their priorities and sacrifices, the educational opportunities that put Mrs. Thompson, Sevilla, and David in my path.

At the University of Minnesota, I was even luckier than I then knew to be a student of William Phillips and Carla Rahn Phillips, whose wise guidance and solid support I still value and call upon, and whose circles were blessedly free of the drama that I later learned can plague one's graduate school years. The university also supported my work through a fellowship for my first year, a Graduate School Dissertation Fellowship, a Humanities Institute Fellowship, and summer grants for archive forays.

The taxpayers of the United States and Spain funded a Fulbright grant to me for a dissertation research year, during which the congenial Árabe department of the Consejo Superior de Investigaciones Científicas in Madrid graciously gave me desk space and library access. Special thanks to Mercedes García Arenal, Manuela Marín, and Cristina de la Puente for their interest, support, and good cheer. José María Soto Rábanos, downstairs with the medievalists, became almost a third advisor through his generous leads, questions, and encouragement. My thanks to Adeline Rucquoi for her helpful suggestions early on and for introducing me to the Consejo crowd. Ana Echevarría offered leads and ánimo. Fellow becarias Ana Carballeira Debasa and Elisa Mesa provided a social component to the research day and remain good friends.

Klaus Reinhardt took an early interest in this project and provided a very welcome transcription of Juan de Segovia's 1426 *repetitio*. Tom Burman has encouraged my studies since early grad school years, read chapters, and helped with Qur'ānic citations from Latin manuscripts. And then some. Jesse Mann and I exchanged e-mails for years about Juan de Segovia matters before meeting in person. His comments on this manuscript improved it significantly.

Frank Mantello went far beyond the normal in his passionate preparations for our Latin and paleography classes over two summers I spent at Notre Dame's Medieval Institute and in his availability to students for help. His teaching made it possible for me to work with the manuscripts that are the foundation of this book, and his student Damon Smith later provided invaluable assistance ironing out many confusing sentences. Obviously, any errors here remain mine.

The following people helped me to keep body and soul together over these research and writing years: Janet Wheelock in Minneapolis and beyond, Mary Louise Gude from South Bend years on, Allegra Grawer for our frequent walks in Retiro, Norah Martin and Anissa

Rogers during the UP years, Julie Lawrence and Tonya Garreaud in Portland, and Deb Salata and Anne Huebel from Minnesota years and since.

Finally, this project benefited from funding provided by the following sources not already mentioned: Saint Louis University's Mellon grant program to work at the Vatican Microfilm Library, the Butine fund at the University of Portland, and the Programa de Cooperación Cultural. My thanks to all.

Juan de Segovia and the Fight for Peace

Introduction

At the end of a research year in Spain in 2000–2001, which produced the bulk of the research for this book, I spent some time in the archives in Rome and then Turin. While in Turin, I discovered that a trip to Chambery's archive was also in order. This put me a short drive from Aiton, about thirty kilometers, and I could not resist a trip to see the village in the French Alps where Juan de Segovia had written so copiously in response to the dire news from Constantinople in 1453 and where he received a Muslim scholar to help him translate the Qur'ān. Aiton cannot have expanded much since then. It consists of two parts, a lower Aiton, at the valley level not far from two parallel highways and the high-speed rail line rushing passengers through numerous tunnels on their way to Italy, and upper Aiton, which is high up a mountain. Each has only a few buildings. The priory, in Benedictine hands by the time Segovia was there, stood in upper Aiton. The 1451 bull of Nicholas V that arranged for Juan de Segovia to live there noted that there were only two monks there at the time.[1] In July of 2001, a structure on the site was in deteriorated condition and showed vestiges of multiple expansions and alterations in the intervening centuries. The building was abandoned except for the workers engaged in some type of restoration or reconstruction.

The workers directed me to a house not far away where there lived an older couple who had the keys to the small church. I managed to communicate that I was interested in Juan de Segovia, and the friendly woman brightened and rushed to fetch her keys. She seemed honored and delighted by my visit, and she took me directly to a plaque in the wall reading "Cardinal Jean de Segovie" marking the site within the wall where his remains are kept. There was no sculpture or monument, but nearby, on a sheet of paper taped to the wall, was a description of Juan's life and activities. It proclaimed that, having been persecuted by the cardinals of Rome, Juan de Segovia had lived in the priory there patiently as if in exile and later was esteemed for miracles he performed. Modern visitors are further advised that a tunic and two hats of his were preserved as relics, and that one of the hats can be viewed in nearby St. Jean Maurienne. I saw one of the hats that day at the museum at the Grand Seminaire de Maurienne, formerly the bishop's palace in St. Jean Maurienne.

That Juan de Segovia is remembered with reverence by the tiny population of Aiton and the modest museum in St. Jean Maurienne seems a fitting reflection of the trajectory of his ideas after his death. The legacy of Juan de Segovia is not as far-reaching as might be suggested by the vigor of his thought or the esteem accorded him by great thinkers and leaders of his day. Over the centuries, the people in Savoy have been most active in preserving the memory of the illustrious retiree who lived for a few years among them. In fact, the paper I saw taped to the wall in Aiton's church bore a French translation of a Latin inscription composed centuries earlier. In September of 1592, an ecclesiastical visitor to Aiton, Antonius Cortailius, described a tomb decorated by many candles and bearing a bold inscription, which he recorded in his report: "B. Cardinal of Calixtus and prior of this place: who for the sake of the truth suffered persecution from the very cardinals of Rome and lived in this priory with utmost patience as if an exile and later was distinguished [*claruit*] by miracles." He also added that locals could readily direct a visitor to the tomb, and knew under which pope the man had lived and the date of his death.[2]

Juan Alfonso de Segovia, more commonly known as Juan de Segovia, died far from home. Perhaps in his waning years his thoughts returned to his youth and his roots in one of the Spanish kingdom of Castile's most prominent cities. Decades before he arrived in Aiton, he had studied and then taught at the University of Salamanca, spending a total of over twenty years there, and then represented the university at the Council of Basel (1431–49). There he became an outspoken proponent of church reform, especially reform that involved placing limits on papal authority. Unlike many of his colleagues at Basel, he never abandoned the conciliar cause or transferred his loyalty to the pope. He persisted in Basel's reform agenda despite the loss of his position at Salamanca and of several ecclesiastical benefices. This did not endear him to the pope or the Roman curia. When the Council of Basel adjourned after recognizing Nicholas V as pope, he was the only cardinal appointed by Felix V (previously Amadeus VIII, duke of Savoy), the pope elected by the council, who was not later confirmed in this dignity by Nicholas V. Surely Segovia's strained relationship with the leading churchmen of his day was at least part of the reason that he spent the last five years of his life in tiny Aiton, in the French Alps in the duchy of Savoy.

In Aiton he received word of the fall of Constantinople to the Ottomans in 1453. This devastating news prompted him to dedicate his remaining years to promoting dialogue with Muslims as a strategy for achieving peace. He hoped to convert them to Christianity, and to convert his fellow Christians to a nonmilitary response to the events. Juan articulated these positions in several works that he sent to various contemporaries. He also welcomed the prominent Muslim jurist and scholar Yça Gidelli to his mountaintop priory and paid him to help produce a new translation of the Qur'ān. This translation was trilingual (Arabic, Latin, Castilian), and it is no longer extant, although its fascinating prologue survived.[3] We can only wonder how much the villagers of Aiton knew about the various endeavors of the prolific and outspoken Castilian theologian in their midst.[4]

To the people of Aiton, where Juan de Segovia retired to a life of quiet and study, must go some ironic recognition for having most persistently perpetuated his memory. In his native land, by the time of that 1592 visitor's report on Aiton, he had long since slipped into virtual obscurity. Perhaps this is not surprising, given that he had spent over two decades of his adult life far beyond the borders of Castile. With papal power more firmly consolidated, it could hardly be expected that in the exalted circles of church politics in which Segovia had moved there could be much interest in memorializing one who had spent much of his life trying to constrain papal authority.

Although he was one of Europe's leading intellectuals and a correspondent of thinkers as renowned as Nicholas of Cusa and Aeneas Sylvius Piccolomini (Pope Pius II), most modern scholars of this period have not heard of Juan de Segovia. There are two exceptions to this: those who study late medieval Christianity's discourse on Islam, and those who study conciliarism, especially the Council of Basel. He deserves to be more widely known, not only because he was a prolific and rigorous thinker in a dynamic period, but because his endeavors placed him at the nexus of the dominant and most far-reaching questions facing Europe at the time. His life and works present a prism through which students of the Middle Ages can observe these currents and crises refracted. In him we can see how one thinker, a thinker actively involved in the real-world demands of political negotiations, approached a range of issues and how the various sources of information coalesced in his thought.

There exist only three general studies of medieval Christians' perspectives on Islam, and Juan de Segovia makes at least a cameo appearance in all three. The most influential of these studies remains Norman Daniel's *Islam and the West: The Making of an Image* (1960, republished with minor revisions in 1993). Two years later, this was followed by the much less extensive *Western Views of Islam in the Middle Ages*, by Richard Southern. More recently, John V. Tolan published his *Saracens: Islam in the Medieval European Imagination* (2002) to fill a gap in Daniel's account, namely, that Daniel made no effort to explain why such an image of Islam was produced and promulgated. Ana Echevarría's *The Fortress of Faith: The Attitude towards Muslims in Fifteenth Century Spain* (1999), more limited in scope than these other three volumes, is an important contribution, even though it is still broad enough to preclude a sustained examination of Segovia's thought.

Although there have been some focused studies on a specific aspect of Christian-Muslim relations or perceptions of the other, the fact that the number of broader studies is so small is one sign of a field that is still ripe for exploration.[5] In fact, a striking disparity emerges when a reader compares the attention given to the question of Christian Europeans' encounters with and perceptions of Jews with the attention given to their perceptions of Muslims. The literature on Christian-Jewish relations is now vast, much of it focusing on uncovering the supposed medieval origins of modern anti-Semitism, while Christian-Muslim relations in this period have been relatively neglected by comparison. As John V. Tolan has noted, this is in spite of the fact that scholarship has energetically explored Christians' persecutions and demonization of many groups, including heretics, lepers, and homosexuals.[6]

Furthermore, general studies on this topic typically give little attention to the later medieval centuries. Daniel's study concentrates on the period through the thirteenth century, offering only a brief glimpse into later centuries. Tolan, too, decided to end his investigation with the thirteenth century, explaining that subsequent centuries merely recycled earlier ideas, images, and solutions.[7] Between 1300 and the Enlightenment, he wrote, Christians in Europe produced little new thought about Muslims.[8] A recent work by Nancy Bisaha examines the image of the Turk produced by Renaissance humanists, especially in Italy in the fifteenth century, and presents a serious challenge to that assessment. But she, too, laments a lacuna in the study of westerners' images of Muslims, noting that scholars until recently have neglected the writers of the fourteenth and fifteenth centuries, even though they produced a sizable body of writings on the "Turkish problem."[9] Margaret Meserve's *Empires of Islam in Renaissance Historical Thought* (2008) focuses on how fifteenth- and sixteenth-century intellectuals told the story of the rise and expansion of Islam and reveals much recycling of medieval material, but not without creative and deliberate reorganization and selection.

Invariably, Juan de Segovia is described as an exception, either to the drumbeat of crusading rhetoric in the Middle Ages or to the general rule that after the thirteenth century no one produced any new approaches to Islam for centuries to come.[10] Yet this is not quite accurate. Although Darío Cabanelas Rodríguez, in the only book-length study of Segovia's thought on Islam, portrayed him as striving tirelessly for peace with Muslims, Segovia nonetheless repeated much of the vitriolic language characteristic of the crusading era. Cabanelas downplayed this fact in his 1952 study, *Juan de Segovia y el problema islámico*, which the Universidad de Granada reprinted in 2008. Juan de Segovia's proposed dialogue with Muslims and his efforts to produce a trilingual study edition of the Qur'ān were, indeed, a fresh approach, yet his insistence that Muslims were lascivious and that Muhammad had been seduced by the devil, to mention just a couple examples, creates a paradox. Segovia is a valuable case study of someone inheriting a broad European tradition of anti-Islamic rhetoric but employing it selectively. He allows us to see what a fifteenth-century thinker did with a discourse that was produced by an earlier era and in different circumstances.

Of course, in Spain the encounter with Muslims was more than just a conversation among intellectuals who had never met any members of that faith tradition. This encounter had a long history by the time Juan de Segovia was born. In 711, Tāriq, lieutenant of the Arab governor of North Africa Musā ibn Nasayr, initiated an invasion across the strait of Gibraltar. The fragmented Visigothic kingdom presented feeble resistance, and within a year most of Iberia had fallen to his forces. When he learned of these events, the Umayyad caliph in Baghdad, Walid I, recalled both Tāriq and Musā. He had not authorized this campaign, and he did not think it was wise. Nevertheless, this misstep by his officials began a period of almost eight hundred years of Muslim rule in the peninsula. From 756 to 1031, the Umayyad dynasty reigned in Al-Andalus, the name for the part of Iberia that was under Muslim rule. In the tenth century, Abd al-Rahmān III (912–61) even took the title of caliph and established the Andalusian caliphate, with its capital in Córdoba, as a rival to the Abbasid caliphate in Baghdad. After the disintegration of the Umayyad caliphate, Al-Andalus fractured into multiple smaller kingdoms called the *taifa* kingdoms, a situation still in place when fresh invaders arrived from across the strait in the eleventh and twelfth centuries.[11]

For centuries, then, Christians and Muslims, as well as a sizable population of Jews, coexisted in Spain. Although it has been generally recognized that this is an important feature of Spanish history, it is a much harder task to decide exactly what impact it had.[12] The relations between Spain's different religious groups have been the subject of intense study by modern historians, who have produced some excellent works exploring these social dynamics. The flurry of scholarship has shown that important differences existed from one region to another in the situation of religious minorities, not to mention across time as well. The fates of both Jews and Muslims under Christian rule waxed and waned with local political and economic conditions, and circumstances were often vastly different on the Mediterranean coast than they were on the interior meseta.[13] Increasingly, historians question the centrality of religion as the key to identity or as an explanation for policies or loyalties. An important example is David Nirenberg's *Communities of Violence: Persecution of Minorities in the Middle Ages* (1996), which argued that violence in Aragon and southern France at the turn of the fourteenth century occurred more often within religious communities than between them.[14] Certainly violence and polemic against religious minorities existed, but relations between Christians and others were often casual and peaceful, as well. Once one accepts that the rosy picture of a tolerant society, which corresponds more to modern ideals of multiculturalism than to the historical record, and that of a doggedly militant and intolerant society are both distortions, a more nuanced investigation is possible. Increasingly, modern scholars are excited to explore the complicated context in which, as Lucy Pick put it, "potential cooperation and interdependence in economic, social, cultural, and intellectual spheres coexist with the continual threat of conflict and violence."[15] Her own study of Rodrigo Jiménez de Rada, archbishop of Toledo between 1209 and 1247, argues that religious polemic actually helped to stabilize relations with religious "others" and made it possible for the different groups to live side by side.

As early as the 1420s, when he was still in Salamanca, Juan de Segovia's writings indicate that he was mulling over the questions presented by the Jews and Muslims in his midst, and that he was encouraging efforts to convert them. These writings also reveal that he had quite different attitudes toward Jews and Muslims; they were not simply two different groups of "nonbelievers." In addition, he was curious about Islam and approached visiting dignitaries from Granada to learn more about it. It is tempting to attribute Segovia's more accommodating perspective toward Muslims, more fully articulated late in his life, to the intercultural context in which he spent his younger years, and indeed that context contributed significantly to his views. However, what he heard at Basel from Cardinal Guiliano Cesarini about the cardinal's experiences with the Hussites also played an important role in developing Segovia's mature thought on how to solve the problem of the Turkish threat. Segovia's polemical writings against Islam offer an opportunity to explore the multivalent functions of polemic, and to see how one person's ideas about dialogue and disputation that were sparked in the Spanish context were further developed at a pan-European church council and pressed into service on a larger, Mediterranean scale. In these works, denunciations occur alongside a certain respect and seemingly genuine desire for peace with those being denounced.

Juan de Segovia is also important to the study of conciliarism, particularly as articulated at the Council of Basel. Basel represented the maturity of a complex political and theological movement that historians have struggled to define adequately. Among its goals were the reform of the excesses of the late medieval church; the resolution of the Western Schism (1378–1417), which had produced two and then three rival popes; the subjection of the pope to the authority of an assembly (among other aims concerning church governance); peace with the Greek church; and reconciliation with the heretical Hussites. The origins and sources of this complex movement were vast, and different aims dominated as conciliarism evolved.[16] The first to explore Juan de Segovia's profound contributions to Basel conciliarism was Antony Black, who called him the "chief exponent" of Basel's political theory and ecclesiology, which was based on the precedent of the medieval guilds and other communal traditions. Black insisted that Segovia's significance in the history of political thought was comparable to that of Marsilius of Padua or Nicholas of Cusa, both of whom have long been recognized for their contributions.[17] Indeed, Segovia was one of the council's most active members. He served repeatedly as its envoy to assemblies in France and the Holy Roman Empire, and he held a number of administrative roles, particularly after 1436. His contributions to the council's more theoretical and intellectual endeavors were responsible for the forty-eight works he produced during the council, not including letters, extracts he compiled from other works, and collaborative works for which he was a minor contributor.[18] One of the goals of this book is to integrate an examination of his Basel work and activity with that of other periods of his life, so that the portrait of a thinker in his various contexts emerges.

It is not insignificant that Juan de Segovia appears both in Norman Daniel's study of medieval images of Muslims, especially those produced through the thirteenth century at that, and in Nancy Bisaha's study of Renaissance thought on the Turks, with its glance ahead at later centuries. Segovia can be claimed as both a medieval and a Renaissance figure, and not only for his views on Muslims. Both his endeavor to derive his translation of the Qur'ān from an Arabic copy and a curious work he produced while at Basel, a concordance of the indeclinable words in the Bible, have parallels in the Renaissance writers' focus on language, close textual study, and a return to the original sources for translations.[19] His comments on such issues as secular monarchy and the contingent nature of institutions of government anticipated later developments in political theory.[20] In many ways, Segovia's life and thought straddled two eras and remind us of the artificiality of the customary line between them. His approach to the Muslims, Jews, and Hussites allows us to glimpse what mental and textual resources a European thinker had available for thinking about "others" on the verge of Europe's expansion abroad.

Each chapter of this book accomplishes two goals: examining a phase in the life and thought of Juan Alfonso de Segovia and providing a window into significant events and conversations in his various circles. The area of Segovia's thought that receives the most attention is that of Islam and the proper Christian stance toward the Muslim world, and the discussion of this topic is set in the context of social and political developments as well as Europeans' images of Islam. My goal is to show how his approach to this subject intersected both with his other endeavors, especially church reform and the Council of Basel's discussions with the Hussites, and with cultural and intellectual movements at play in the fifteenth century. Unlike Segovia's contemporaries Nicholas of Cusa and Aeneas Sylvius Piccolomini, whose contradictory positions at different times in their lives have prompted much scholarly discussion about the reasons for their reversals, Juan de Segovia was remarkably consistent in his patterns of thought and the positions he argued.[21]

Chapter 1 lays the foundation for Segovia's adulthood by exploring life and learning at the University of Salamanca in the early fifteenth century, a time of political turmoil but also of growing prestige for the university. It was during this time that the Council of Constance (1414–18) infused fresh intellectual energy into Castile and elsewhere. In this chapter, I examine early influences on Segovia as well as his own career at Salamanca. This chapter includes an explanation for a lecture he delivered in 1426 that has puzzled scholars due to its strongly pro-papal argument, which contradicted the positions he took just a few years later at Basel. This discussion has implications for scholars' consternation at the inconsistency sometimes found in late medieval political theorists' works.

Chapter 2 discusses the interaction among different religious groups in Castile and considers the question of how extensive Segovia's acquaintance with Muslims would have been. It examines his earliest thought on Islam and Muslims and draws upon his later recollections of encounters with Muslims while he was in Castile, as well as a 1427 lecture in Salamanca that has received little attention from scholars. I argue that in these years, he had some contact with Muslims, but that it was not extensive. Information about Islam was not as forthcoming as one might think when reading some treatments of the intercultural Castilian society at this time. He was not familiar, for example, with longstanding objections that Muslims had to Christianity, despite his curiosity about this other faith tradition. Nevertheless, key elements of his later approach to Islam were in place by the time he left Salamanca in 1431.

Beginning with chapter 3, the context beyond Castile becomes more prominent. This chapter is devoted to the Council of Basel, with an emphasis on Segovia's arguments on behalf of the authority of a general council over a pope, what he learned from the council's dialogue with the Hussites, his diplomatic missions, and his interactions with leading European figures. I argue that Segovia was not, as some have stated, a "convert" to conciliarism, but a sympathizer even upon his arrival there; that strong continuities connected his thought from his Salamanca years through the Basel years and beyond; and that the council's overtures toward the Hussites made an important contribution to his later suggestions about how Christian Europe should approach the Muslim world. The general lines of his thought were consistent with the biblical orientation that is revealed in his earliest extant works, the two lectures at Salamanca. At Basel, too, he urged Christians to what he viewed as a closer faithfulness to the gospel and to the example of the early church. His positions earned him both respect and suspicion from powerful peers.

Chapter 4 turns to the years following the Council of Basel, most of which Juan de Segovia spent in Aiton. It was in this small alpine village that he heard the news of the Turks' capture of Constantinople in 1453, and from here that he began to write lengthy works advancing his ideas about how Christians should respond. These works contain two types of polemic: against his fellow Christians arguing for crusade, and against Islam. Focusing on the first of these polemics, this chapter introduces his interlocutors, explores his arguments against crusade as a strategy for dealing with these troubling events, and places these arguments in historical and contemporary context. I argue that his approach was distinctive, even though it shared some features with those of earlier thinkers. In these later works on the Turkish question, he continued to urge faithfulness to gospel norms of behavior, including even love of enemies.

Chapter 5 offers an account of Segovia's polemic against Islam, which he envisioned would take place in the context of an ongoing dialogue with Muslim leaders. This dialogue would be assisted by a more accurate translation of the Qur'ān, for which Segovia recruited a Muslim scholar from Spain to help him produce. I argue that his ideas about how to approach the Muslim world differed from others' in important ways, possibly because they were driven by his memories of the real Muslims he had spoken with in Castile in 1431 and inspired by Basel's success in negotiating with the Hussites. His polemic against

Islam, even as it echoed longstanding motifs from the Western polemical tradition, was genuinely aimed at converting Muslims, and not,
as was sometimes the case in polemical works, at shoring up Christian confessional identity. Unlike most writers of anti-Islamic polemic,
this endeavor was not associated in Segovia's works with any parallel
effort to convert Jews nor with any apocalyptic hopes.

This fascinating and creative thinker deserves more attention.
A study integrating his thoughts on Islam with other aspects of
his work is long overdue. I hope that this book does justice to his
thought and inspires more interest in him and in the complex world
he inhabited.

THE YEARS AT THE UNIVERSITY OF SALAMANCA

M edieval universities had their origin in the cathedral schools, or *studia*, of the central Middle Ages, and in the fourteenth and fifteenth centuries official documents still referred to them by this term. Whereas the earlier universities had drawn mostly clergy, by the fifteenth century students were more likely to be laymen preparing for a career in government, law, or medicine. In many cases it was not even necessary for them to complete a degree. Records indicate that between fifty and eighty percent of these aspiring professionals left before achieving that goal. Merely having spent time at the university was enough to give one connections and a certain status. Across Europe, and including in Spain, students tended to be neither from the uppermost nor the lowest classes. The poor could not afford university study, and nobles were not generally inclined toward it unless they were aspiring to a career in the church. This began to change in the fifteenth century, and by the early modern period attending the university became an expected phase in the life of a young nobleman.[1]

Nothing is known about the family or social origin of Juan Alfonso de Segovia. Elsewhere I have suggested that he likely came from a family connected with the rising urban oligarchies emerging in Castile in the late fourteenth and early fifteenth centuries.[2] Although "de Segovia" was a surname and does not in itself mean that its bearer came from this central Castilian city, in Juan's case it appears that this was, indeed, his native city. Vatican records identify him as a priest from the diocese of Segovia.[3] Although some have included the surname González among his name, giving his full name as Juan Alfonso González de Segovia, no extant contemporary documents support the inclusion of González in his name.[4] It is not clear what Juan de Segovia's goals were when he went to Salamanca to study, but about ten years after arriving there, as we will see, he was energetically pursuing appointments to church benefices around Castile. He also became a faculty member at this *studium* and traveled, including to the royal court, on university business. If he hoped to work as a university professor and also be engaged with the central issues and power circles of his day, he would not have been the first to combine these two activities. And he would have been well positioned to do so.

The purpose of this chapter is to explore Juan Alfonso de Segovia's formative years in the university community of Salamanca, one of Europe's oldest universities. Juan de Segovia spent over two decades of his young adulthood there, from 1407 to 1431, as a student and then professor of theology before he left Castile for the Council of Basel (1431–49). My aim is to show that aspects significant to his thought in later periods of his life were evident in these early years. These include a strong biblical orientation in his thinking, which he would carry with him to and beyond Basel as he considered Islam. In these early years at Salamanca, he also revealed concern for renewal in the church and for presenting the Christian faith credibly to non-Christians, a curiosity about Islam, and a willingness to stand in opposition to a powerful prelate. In addition, I argue that he was both exposed to the currents of conciliar thought and sympathetic to conciliarism's goal of collective governance. Contrary to what others have supposed,[5] I submit that Juan was no convert to conciliarism when he arrived in Basel in the early 1430s.

As a student arriving at the *studium* in Salamanca in the early fifteenth century, Juan Alfonso de Segovia surely already had benefited from some formal education. University students began their studies having already mastered certain fundamental skills such as literacy, although their preparation probably varied greatly from one student to the next. Almost no information survives concerning the instruction of Castilian children from the middle or lower nobility or the urban elite. Some of them might have had a private tutor, but most probably acquired their early training in the seigniorial household to which their family was tied by bonds of blood or clientage. Others may have attended one of the numerous grammar *studia* that were founded across the kingdom in the fourteenth and fifteenth centuries under the auspices of the cathedral, the municipal council (*concejo*), or both.[6] Segovia had a school of grammar as early as 1331,[7] and in the mid-fifteenth century the city's cathedral chapter included a *maestrescuela* (*scholasticus*, schoolmaster), who was in charge of supervising the instruction of clergy and choir boys, as well as dictating and authenticating official documents for the chapter.[8] It is possible that Juan de Segovia was a student at this school before going to Salamanca for higher study. In addition to the school in Segovia, other grammar *studia* existed by 1339 in Sahagún, 1368 in Jaén, 1369 in Atienza, 1387 in Sepúlveda, 1392 in Córdoba, 1394 in Zamora, and 1405 in Soria. In the early fifteenth century, Seville's cathedral chapter and city council together paid the salary of a master of grammar.[9] By one means or another, Juan Alfonso's early studies prepared him well enough to fare admirably at the University of Salamanca, where he arrived probably in 1407.[10]

If Juan entered the city of Salamanca from the south, he would have crossed the Tormes River via the Roman bridge, the only access to the city from the south side of the river.[11] Salamanca was a less prominent city than Segovia, but it was still fairly important. Its markets benefited from its location on a river and between a major grazing region and a rich agricultural region.[12] One indication of the city's stature and condition in the early fifteenth century is that the *infante* Don Juan ordered that Salamanca's main commercial streets be paved with stones because the animals pulling goods had a difficult time navigating the muddy thoroughfares.[13] During Juan de Segovia's time there, the cathedral itself (known today as the "old cathedral" because there is an adjoining, newer one) was still under construction. As late as

1392, its main tower was not yet complete.[14] The cathedral was closely tied to the nearby university. Many students and university personnel no doubt lived on the surrounding streets. Curiously, if they were renters, their rent was determined annually by a group of university officials, regardless of who owned the property.[15] Juan might well have called this area of the city home during this time there.

In any case, his association with the university was a long one. He spent twenty-four years there, from 1407 to 1431, interrupted only by two trips to Rome on university business in 1421–22 and 1427–28. Some years he was both student and professor, since he began teaching while still studying for his masters degree (*magister*). In Salamanca he received his training as a theologian and gained considerable leadership experience as well. He enjoyed the respect of his colleagues, who trusted him with embassies to the royal and papal courts on the university's behalf. It is reasonable to assume that a fair number of these colleagues were also friends. He undoubtedly made the acquaintance of a number of leading thinkers who passed through the *studium* during those years. By the end of his time there, he had also secured benefices for himself in prominent cathedrals. In short, during the Salamanca years of his life, Juan Alfonso de Segovia was well trained, well regarded, and well launched on a promising career.

The University of Salamanca in the Early Fifteenth Century

As an elderly man, Segovia wrote with pride of his alma mater. However, the university was struggling during his years there, enough to make one wonder if his praise of the university was prompted by feelings of defensiveness after having such long contact with intellectuals associated with fine universities across Europe. In the early fifteenth century, the *studium* in Salamanca was in a precarious but promising position. It had endured financial, staffing, and enrollment problems for several generations.[16] Its resources were lagging behind its French counterparts because the Avignon popes (1309–78) generally favored French universities in their patronage.[17] Vicente Beltrán de Heredia noted that the professoriate seemed to consist largely of part-time faculty, often only holding a bachelors degree, and that those few professors of renown who appear in the records left for another position without spending much time in Salamanca.[18] Benigno Hernández Montes suggested that Juan's impassioned call for easier access to libraries, which appears at the end of his *Donatio*, the testament in which he described the contents of his library and where he wanted items to go after his death, betrays his own memories of difficulties obtaining books while he was a student at Salamanca.[19] In any case, Juan clearly suspected that his alma mater, which he had not visited for decades, might still lack a suitable facility for storing the books he was donating. He specified that if the university had no such building or would not commission one, the books were to go to the cathedral library instead.[20] These indications do not suggest a thriving, prominent intellectual center. Nevertheless, Salamanca's fortunes were on the rise, partly because the Great Schism (1378–1417) favored the university, since patronage was a way for rival popes to seek legitimacy.[21] One sign of this reversal was that a university in danger of not surviving at the beginning of the fifteenth century had recovered enough to loan 100,000 *maravedis* to the Crown in 1475.[22]

In Juan's time there, the university's prestige and its support from Crown and curia were rising, and it was already a magnet that drew influential people to its halls.[23] Members of the urban oligarchies increasingly found that university training was a requisite preparation for a position of influence in the administrative machinery of Castile's Trastámara dynasty, which had come to power just a few decades earlier. In earlier generations, arms and wealth were sufficient to guarantee one's position in society. Prominent men were now expected to know certain things, especially things pertaining to the law, and if possible to possess a university degree.[24] Accordingly, Salamanca's graduates included people like the prolific scholar Alonso de Cartagena (ca. 1385–1456) of the prominent Burgalese *converso* family. He studied canon and civil law at Salamanca for about ten years, served as a judge in the royal court, represented Juan II at Basel, and was bishop of Burgos from 1435 to 1456.[25] Rodrigo Sánchez de Arévalo (1404–70) also studied law at Salamanca and went on to a career that included serving as an ambassador for both Juan II and Enrique IV.[26] The

Dominican Lope de Barrientos (1382–1469), one of the most influential men of his time, was at various times a professor of theology at Salamanca, confessor to Juan II, tutor for the heir prince Enrique IV, and chief chancellor under Enrique IV.[27] The founder of the house of Alba, Gutierre Gómez Álvarez de Toledo, was studying at Salamanca in 1393. At that time, he was the archdeacon of Guadalajara. Future promotions would make him the bishop of Palencia and the archbishop of Seville and later Toledo.[28] Along the way, the ambitious prelate arranged the murder of rival Juan Serrano.[29] In 1411, Pope Benedict XIII granted a request by Fernando Díaz de Toledo to be promoted to the doctorate in medicine at Salamanca without having finished his required courses for a Bachelor of Arts degree, provided he pass an exam. Probably the success of Díaz's request was at least partly due to the fact that he was the personal physician of Fernando de Antequera, coregent during the minority of Juan II and one of the most powerful men in the kingdom.[30] These five are representative of many more Salamanca men with close ties to the royal court and other powerful groups. The papal registers contain numerous petitions by faculty to be released temporarily from their duties in order to serve in the royal court or papal curia, and by students to retain their financial support while away on similar business.[31] The documents from the university's own *claustro*, which handled routine business and staffing issues, are extant only from 1464 on, but the records reveal that absences and substitutions continued to be frequent decades after Juan de Segovia's time in Salamanca.[32] But if the faculty was less stable at Salamanca than elsewhere, it was nevertheless drawn from a cadre of Castile's most influential men. Both the student body and the faculty counted among their ranks many of the kingdom's most powerful and prominent.

The University of Salamanca had a respectable profile internationally as well, which may have given Juan de Segovia a certain satisfaction when he traveled outside Castile. Years later, he proudly recalled that when he was incorporated at the Council of Basel, he was directed to a place of honor in the assembly, the place next to the delegation from the University of Paris.[33] About a century before Juan left for Basel, Pope John XXII granted universal validity to degrees from Salamanca. Its graduates were free to teach in any other university in Western Europe without submitting to an additional exam. Prior to this 1333 bull, they could teach everywhere except Paris or Bologna.[34] Pope Martin V's 1422 constitutions for the university referred to it as "one of four *studia generalia* under the apostolic order," thereby recognizing a status it shared only with Paris, Bologna, and Oxford.[35] Documents reveal a considerable contact between people at the Castilian university and other centers of learning. For example, by 1429 bachelor in theology Alvaro Martínez had studied in Oxford, Salamanca, and Lérida. He requested permission from the pope to receive his masters degree from the Roman curia.[36] In 1403 Salamanca's faculty included a professor of rhetoric, Bartolomé Sánchez, who came from Fermo, an Italian city on the Adriatic, despite his Spanish surname.[37] Juan Castellanos, a Dominican who was bishop of Salamanca from 1382 to 1385, held a masters in theology from Paris.[38] In the early fifteenth century, a Portuguese Augustinian named Juan de Santo Tomás was teaching theology at Salamanca.[39] Several faculty members at the *studium* participated actively in the Council of Constance (1414–18).[40] Even before leaving Salamanca, Juan de Segovia was exposed to international intellectual currents.

Further evidence of esteem for Salamanca's *studium* appears in scattered references in unexpected places, many related to aspirations to social ascent. Sometime during the pontificate of Eugene IV (1431–47), an anonymous graduate in canon law wrote a guidebook for use in confession in which he sometimes enlisted the fact that he heard a certain view taught at Salamanca as a support for its validity.[41] Toward the end of the fifteenth century, Pedro Sánchez de Berrío gave his son a sum of money in his will and specified that he could use it only for study at the University of Salamanca.[42] No doubt a degree from Salamanca was worth Pedro's money and his son's time. In the 1480s Segovia's cathedral chapter was engaged in a dispute over a seat on this body. The 1488 arbitration agreement stipulated that a chapter member's rank would correspond to how long he had been in the position, with the significant exception that if the canon had a doctorate or licentiate from either Salamanca or Valladolid, this would automatically place him above those with even the highest seniority.[43] Salamanca provided attractive advancement opportunities for the nobility, as well. A fascinating letter written in 1477 from the bishop of Coria to the duke of Alba details the machinations the bishop had recently undertaken in Rome on behalf of the duke's son, Don Gutierre Álvarez de Toledo, to secure for him the position of *maestrescuela* at Salamanca. He suggested that the duke persuade one contender to withdraw his bid for the position by offering him another benefice instead, since "those smaller benefices" added nothing to a man of his son's stature anyway, and the *maestrescuela* position was so valuable that it warranted such a measure.[44]

If the *studium*'s fortunes were on the rise, this was due at least in part to support from the papacy. Beginning with the Avignon pope Benedict XIII (1394–1417), who was Spanish and had numerous ties in Castile, popes were good to the University of Salamanca.[45] In an era in which the monarchy was weakened by succession disputes and restless nobles, and the papacy was weakened by the schism and its aftermath, the university benefited by both these powers' efforts to court its loyalties. Typically the pope's favors to the university were financial, as in 1416, when Benedict XIII conceded to the University of Salamanca two-thirds of the *rentas de fábrica* in the nearby towns of La Almuña, Baños, and Peña del Rey.[46] Sometimes a favor bestowed was both economic and political, as when Martin V exempted the Colegio de San Bartolomé and its personnel from the jurisdiction of the local bishop and also from the tributes imposed by the nuncios and apostolic legates.[47] Another university body to benefit directly from papal intervention on its behalf was its hospital, benefactors of which were assured indulgences in exchange for their generosity.[48] In addition, countless individuals either studying or teaching in Salamanca, including Juan de Segovia, relied for their income on benefices in cathedral and parish churches both within Castile and beyond its borders.

As powerful parties in the kingdom competed for influence, the *studium* was often caught in one power struggle or another. Studying in this atmosphere might have prompted Segovia to serious thought about issues of power and persuasion at an early age. As we shall see, his earliest extant work concerned control over the university. Some scholars have noted the growing power of the popes over the *studium* at Salamanca in the early fifteenth century and contrasted this with earlier times, in which the king's power was stronger.[49] Certainly Castilian king Juan II, whose reign was marked by armed conflicts between different factions of nobles, was concerned to retain some power over affairs at the *studium* in the face of an increasingly powerful pope. In 1411, following the issuance of new constitutions for the university by the pope, the king named *conservatores* of his own, charged with keeping the peace at the university and defending its interests. At the same time, he criticized the existing *conservatores* for not having done their job. In 1421, he ordered the royal *conservatores* to respond to the accusation of negligence. As María Isabel del Val Valdivieso has argued, king and pope struggled over whose officials had the authority to oversee and protect the university.[50]

Another incident occurred in 1432 in which the pope intervened in tensions among Castile's elite that were of great importance to the king. Although it did not directly involve the *studium*, the case serves to illustrate the high stakes power struggles between king and pope. This one unfolded because Juan II ordered the bishop of Palencia, Don Gutierre Álvarez de Toledo, imprisoned for threatening the peace and security of the kingdom. The bishop had participated in the military campaign against Granada a year earlier and had been entrusted with holding a defensive position. Instead, he and some allies decided to launch offensive campaigns. These failed, causing the bishop and his troops to need reinforcements and angering the powerful constable Álvaro de Luna. These tensions between Gutierre Álvarez de Toledo (and supporters) and Álvaro de Luna escalated until it was discovered that the bishop and his circle had conspired to murder Álvaro de Luna. The king was so concerned that this chaos in the upper ranks of his leadership would spell military disaster that he was forced to return to Castile to address the problem. Not unreasonably, he imprisoned Gutierre Álvarez de Toledo, who appealed to the pope to intervene.[51] Pope Eugene IV obligingly delegated to the archbishop of Santiago and the bishops of Plasencia and Astorga the responsibility of conducting an investigation. If the charges turned out to be true, they were to free him from jail, place him under ecclesiastical custody, and refer the case to the curia. If he was innocent, they were to see to it that he was freed.[52] If the plot against Álvaro de Luna had succeeded, it would not have been the first assassination orchestrated by the bishop of Palencia, who had a long history of being a menace to the peace of the kingdom.[53] What strikes the modern reader is that the pope chose to investigate and intervene in such a case. With a pope so willing to involve himself in high-level affairs within Castile, Juan II was prudent to show concern to protect his traditional authority, including over an important center like the *studium* at Salamanca.

Nevertheless, the increasing power of the pope over affairs at Salamanca did not always represent a challenge to the power of the king. Often enough, the popes acted to bolster royal authority. Along with the rest of the kingdom, the university sometimes benefited from the popes' support of the king against troublemaking prelates and general malefactors throughout the kingdom. In September of 1423, for example, Pope Martin V agreed to a request by Castilian king Juan II to appoint the bishops of León and Salamanca as judges in proceedings against prelates and other clergy who had occupied royal lands or seized royal rents or jurisdictions from the Crown.[54] Three years later the same pope gave the archbishop of Toledo the right to intervene in cases in which archbishops, bishops, and other ecclesiastical leaders had given controversial judgments in cases within the dominion of the Crown.[55] Apparently still struggling with the problem of unruly prelates, Juan II returned with another request to the pope in 1430, namely, that he be allowed to imprison any master, prior, commander, or other person from any of the military orders who acted against the king or the peace of the kingdom, or committed any crime that qualified as *lèse majesté*. The pope also granted the king the right to imprison anyone who had threatened the monarch or the peace and then hidden within the territorial jurisdiction of the military orders.[56] Chaos and lawlessness make normal affairs as difficult in a university as in the rest of society.[57] Popes often bolstered royal authority and thus helped to quell the disturbances in this tumultous era of Castilian history.

Apart from the political issues facing the wider kingdom, Salamanca's *studium* may have had its share of intrigues and power plays. In his *Sacramental*, a pastoral work on the sacraments that was written between 1421 and 1423 for priests, Clemente Sánchez de Vercial alerted his readers to the sins most commonly committed by various groups. A graduate of Salamanca, he asserted that the primary way in which professors sinned was by obtaining their degrees by means of bribes and entreaties (*ruegos*) to other doctors. Also, in their pride, they regarded their students and the simple with disdain. They cared less about saying helpful things than about saying subtle things that would earn them accolades, and thus they wasted their students' time. Furthermore, they taught things that were against their consciences in order to please others. They silenced the truth to avoid being held accountable for their wrongdoing. And for the right price, they gave false counsel.[58]

Juan de Segovia never commented on the political conflicts or dishonorable behavior by professors in Salamanca during his years there. Nonetheless, he later showed himself to be prepared to stand on principle, especially when it had to do with someone (such as the pope) overstepping the proper boundaries of his power. This early period of his life may have prompted him to think hard about how power is exercised and what good governance entailed. Quite possibly it left him wary regarding unchecked power invested in an individual, whether king, pope, or archbishop.

Juan de Segovia at Salamanca

In surveying Juan de Segovia's trajectory as a thinker, into the Basel years and beyond, it is clear that his endeavors reflected certain intellectual proclivities and social concerns that appear repeatedly throughout his work. For example, one of the major characteristics scholars have noted in his thought was a marked biblical orientation, especially in his works at Basel.[59] Another central aspect scholars have noticed was an affinity for Franciscan thinkers. Richard Southern, for example, simply assumed that Juan was, in fact, a Franciscan, and at least two scholars, Uta Fromherz and Ottokar Bonmann, considered the possibility strong enough to warrant careful attention.[60] Both concluded that he was not. Perhaps the strongest argument that Juan Alfonso de Segovia did not belong to the mendicant order is that papal documents routinely noted a person's affiliation with a religious order, if applicable, and none of the documents preserved concerning Segovia identify him as a Franciscan, or as a member of any other religious order, for that matter.[61] He was simply a secular priest who found much that was useful and interesting in texts by Franciscan authors.[62]

However, other themes in his later thought that were also present in his Salamanca years have received little attention from scholars. One of these is a commitment to collegial, collective governance, which was one of the main reforms that Basel conciliarists tried to implement in their efforts to curtail the power of the pope. This might surprise readers who know of Juan's *Repetitio de superioritate et excellentia supremae potestatis ecclesiasticae et spiritualis ad regiam temporalem* (1426), an unqualified defense of papal power, but I argue below that the context of this piece gives it a meaning that is not reflected in its title and literal content. Other themes nascent in these years at Salamanca that would emerge as pronounced elements in his later works were the need for church reform and an awareness of and reflections on the religious minorities in Castile. The latter will be the focus of the next chapter. The following study of these decades at Salamanca reveals a university undergoing change, even chaos, as it grew into a leading intellectual center. Segovia emerged from this environment a serious and careful thinker with keen political instincts, both features that would serve him well in his life beyond Castile.[63]

Three documents in the Vatican registers identify Juan de Segovia as a *magister in theologia et artibus*.[64] The degree in arts would have been pursued first, as preparation for theological study. As a student and then professor at Salamanca, Juan de Segovia learned the fine art of thoroughly expounding upon a question and defending a position in public disputation. His later career at the Council of Basel, in which a high number of university personnel participated,[65] surely called upon these skills, and this method of approaching a problem also could have influenced the solution he proposed to Christians' tensions with the Muslim Turks.

One of the sources to shed light on the program of study is Benedict XIII's bull *Sincerae devotionis*, issued in 1416, which reorganized the theology faculty into four autonomous *cátedras* or schools. Under the new course of study, a secular priest such as Juan de Segovia would have begun his theological study by attending classes for six years on the *Sentences*, during four of which he also attended lectures on the Bible. Then he would have delivered ten public lectures and completed the public disputation already described, after which he became a *baccalariatus* (bachelor). The higher degree required an additional four years on the *Sentences*, in which the candidate studied two books each year, reading all four books of the *Sentences* twice. During this time, he delivered a *principium*, a public exposition of a difficult theological problem, twice a year, at the beginning of his study of each book. He was then free to present himself for an *examen privatum*, successful completion of which would make him a *licenciatus* (licentiate). This exam had to precede the granting of the *magister* (masters) degree by at least one year. The next formal requirement was the delivery of two disputations in which the candidate responded to challenges from his peers. Next came the *quaestio ordinaria*, in which he argued a position against the *cátedra* masters other than the master under whom he had studied. If he acquitted himself well, there was the standard inquiry concerning his character (*vita et moribus*), after which he endured one more private exam and then received his *magister* title.[66]

It is not difficult to deduce from such a curriculum some of the skills and dispositions Juan de Segovia would have gained. Ruth Karras has argued that this entire process of a university education, especially the disputations, provided a model of masculinity no less important than knighthood or guild admission and membership. The university environment served to initiate young men into a subculture in which they proved themselves against others. The goal was to give the student "the skills to compete verbally against other educated men, and to prove his superiority over the uneducated."[67] Manhood was a matter of rationality, which was proven through disputation, as one took a stand and then defended it from attackers. Often the terms used for these exchanges were those of swordfighting—*impugnatio, adumbratio, evasio*. John of Salisbury compared the training of a logician to that of Roman and other soldiers, and Peter Abelard famously wrote, "I exchanged all other arms for these, and to the trophies of war I preferred the combat of disputation."[68]

This might help to explain a title Juan de Segovia gave to one of later works on how to convince Muslims of the truths of Christianity. His 1454 letter-treatise to Juan de Cervantes, archbishop of Seville, was entitled *De mittendo gladio divini Spiritus in corda sarracenorum*, or *On driving the sword of the divine Spirit into the hearts of the Saracens*.[69] It is a curious title because his purpose was to argue that war was not the answer, and that Christians should instead engage in dialogue with Muslims. He may have used this title ironically, but he also could have been envisioning academic debate as a model for the proposed discussions with Muslims. Certainly, as in the disputations he learned to do at Salamanca, his goal was to demonstrate superiority, in this case over those of a rival faith. Even with the martial language, however, if he was conceiving of Muslims as full interlocutors in a debate, in the same role as his fellow European academics, this seems a significant sign of respect for them as opponents. Karras noted that this culture of disputations at the universities served as a bonding mechanism as it gradually included the newest practitioners into a society formed by a specific form of discourse, with its own language, vocabulary, and conventions.[70] If Juan saw Muslims as worthy participants in such a dynamic, then in some way he must have seen them as peers.

Whatever skills the pedagogy at Salamanca would have conferred on him, it is not clear what Segovia's career aspirations were when he began his studies at Salamanca around 1407. At this time, theology was a relatively new discipline there, and it was taught in the mendicant schools of San Francisco and San Esteban, by Franciscan and Dominican faculty who were not part of the university.[71] When he began his studies, there would have been no possibility of teaching this subject, at least at Salamanca, without being a member of one of these orders. If his goal had been to teach theology, it is odd that no record exists of an affiliation with either of these orders. In addition, the study of theology was not required or expected of parish priests; it was a preparation for higher ecclesiastical and civil offices.[72] And yet, oddly, Segovia does not appear to have sought any church offices until 1418, about a decade after arriving at the *studium*. It is possible that he aspired to a position of political influence. Given the vagaries of

Castile's political scene in the early fifteenth century, this would suggest a certain fortitude, confidence, and maybe some naivete, or all three of those qualities. It is also possible that he pursued theological studies out of genuine interest in this area.

In any case, Benedict XIII's 1416 bull had a decided impact upon the future of theology at Salamanca and upon Juan's career opportunities. In it, the Aragonese pope established two new chairs or schools of theology at the university itself, the chairs of prime and vespers, and he made the existing mendicant schools at San Francisco and San Esteban formally part of the university, although their respective orders still staffed and administered them.[73] This effectively doubled the number of theology faculty in the city. It also created the possibility that a secular priest like Juan could teach theology at the university. Unless he was contemplating entry into one of the mendicant orders, Juan could not have aspired to such a position before this bull. So when he began his studies, his professional goals must have included other plans, possibly a career in church administration. Beginning in 1418, and especially throughout the 1420s, he submitted to Martin V a steady stream of petitions for various church offices. By the mid-thirties, he had succeeded in obtaining *canonicatos* (positions as cathedral canon) in Segovia, Toledo, Seville, Salamanca, and Palencia, and the position of archdean of Villaviciosa in Oviedo.[74] Juan de Segovia's ambitious pursuit of lucrative and prestigious cathedral offices during this period prompted Vicente Beltrán de Heredia to comment that if Juan's later calls for church reform were sincere, he should have started with himself and that Juan should have been content with his faculty salary and not sought further office and money.[75] Certainly his appeals for these positions, and for exemptions because their combined income exceeded the official limit, reveal a man with aspirations to power in the church. If he began his studies in theology out of pure interest, he was also determined to work the system.

But why did he apparently not begin to do that until 1418? If pure ambition drove him, it seems likely that he would have begun to accumulate benefices sooner. Perhaps in 1418 his family or patron lost a fortune and he found himself newly in need of funds, a prospect that seems especially plausible when we consider that 1418 was the year that the remaining regent, Queen Catalina de Lancaster, died and Juan II finally became king. His authority was immediately challenged by his meddlesome cousins, known as the princes (*infantes*) of Aragon, the sons of Fernando de Antequera, who was both coregent of Castile and king of Aragon until his death in 1416. With Juan II's accession, Castile became a battleground in which the *infantes*, and king, and the kingdom's various noble houses vied for dominance. In 1420, the infante Enrique even imprisoned the Castilian king and ruled on his behalf. The king was finally freed later that year by Alvaro de Luna.[76] It would have been easy in these years to lose family status, a fortune, or a patron, and prudent, in any case, to hedge one's bets and seek an independent income stream such as benefices just in case.

It is also possible that Juan de Segovia had aspired to civil offices, but reconsidered this plan as he watched the political dynamics unfold and found this career less attractive than he had originally thought. Or perhaps he was en route to entering one of the mendicant orders, which provided him with lodging and support while he was in formation, but then in 1418 decided not to follow that path. If he intended all along to pursue an ecclesiastical career and simply went to Salamanca to gain the requisite qualifications, he did not need the course of study that he chose. A degree in canon law would have taken less time and even been the more standard and expected training for most church offices. Theological study was never a required training for parish priests in the Middle Ages. Only university-trained and especially visionary bishops expected parish rectors to have such a background. The study of theology trained people to resolve ambiguities and recognize heresies, and it was an accepted preparation for higher ecclesiastical and civil offices.[77] If he did not intend to become a mendicant or a professor of theology, perhaps he aspired to these higher offices from the beginning of his studies.

It is also possible that he went to Salamanca to study the arts, a necessary prerequisite for any field, became interested in theology while there, and either considered joining the Franciscans or even actually joined for a time. Then with Benedict XIII's 1416 bull, perhaps he became excited at the prospect of an academic career in theology, and this made him consider other options in the church as well, including cathedral benefices. This possibility would have seemed especially attractive if, indeed, his financial situation changed around 1418. His Salamanca credentials might have not only prompted an interest in pursuing other roles in the church, but even made him a viable candidate for them. In August of 1432, he thought it necessary to ask Pope Eugene IV to reaffirm his right to the *canonicatos* in Seville and Salamanca. When he originally petitioned for them, he had said that he held the chair of prime in the faculty of theology at Salamanca, and he now admitted that this was not true, although he had since obtained this chair.[78] Clearly he sensed that having that chair strengthened his claim to the *canonicatos* in Seville and Salamanca.

Whatever Juan's aspirations were when he began his university studies, he was in no rush to leave academia for a position in civil or ecclesiastical administration after them. Over a period of thirteen to fifteen years, he held all three of the chairs in theology: Bible, prime, and vespers. The latter two took their names from the time of the daily lectures, the canonical hours of prime and vespers. The text for both was Peter Lombard's *Sentences*. Beltrán de Heredia suggested that Juan de Segovia might have occupied these chairs as substitutes for others who had to be absent from the university for a time. In a letter to Jean Germain written many years later, Juan wrote that for an unspecified length of time, he held two theology chairs simultaneously. It is impossible to know for certain which years or how many he spent in each chair.[79] Regardless, as a chair or even acting chair in any of these three positions, Juan would have been more than merely a professor. The holder of a chair position directed the activity of a number of *bachilleres* or *licenciados* who gave occasional and sometimes regular lectures, substituted for the master when he was away, and assisted the master in a variety of academic tasks.[80] Thus occupying a chair was similar to being the director of a small center for theological study. One who held such a position for nearly fifteen years, especially holding two simultaneously for a time, certainly would have been a prominent member of the university community. This would be all the more true if Beltrán de Heredia's observation concerning a high turnover rate for faculty was accurate. Juan Alfonso de Segovia might well have been one of the pillars of the university.

Segovia's opportunities at the *studium* were probably enhanced by the fact that faculty members were regularly absent on business related to the university or the court. This could have provided a young scholar with the chance to raise his profile by serving as a substitute for more senior professors. Among the significant events taking place during his time in Salamanca, one that required the attendance of university faculty was the Council of Constance (1414–18). This council met to resolve the crisis of the schism, which had by then produced three popes. This reform council, consisting of representatives from all over Europe, also declared that the highest authority in the church properly rested with a council and not a pope, and it resolved that in the future there would be regular councils. The next one would take place in five years, then seven years, and after that the interval would be ten years. The delegation appointed by Juan II included men active at Salamanca, most notably the bishop of Cuenca, Diego de Anaya y Maldonado (1357–1437), who had been a strong supporter of Benedict XIII. The University of Salamanca sent the Franciscan theologian Lope de San Román as its representative.[81] The Avignon pope Benedict XIII issued a document at his request reserving his faculty position for him while he was away at the council.[82] Lope de San Román, who held the chair in biblical studies, is one of the professors for whom Beltrán de Heredia speculated that perhaps Juan de Segovia substituted.[83]

The council's effects were pronounced at the university and beyond. It probably helped to bring this *studium*, still lagging behind French counterparts in prominence, into the currents of international debates and to raise its international profile. José Goñi Gaztambide wrote that, for many Spanish participants at Constance, their stay exposed them to a whole new world, which "captivated them with its charms." Many preferred to remain in this wider European milieu and sought positions in the papal curia in Rome. The presence of Spaniards there increased sharply following the council and continued to rise over the course of the fifteenth century. Diego de Anaya y Maldonado was among those who took advantage of their travels to Constance as an opportunity to acquire manuscripts. Anaya's book-buying energies resulted in a new infusion of texts available in Salamanca, since he donated them to the university's new Colegio de San Bartolomé, which he had founded.[84] According to Miguel Avilés, Constance thrust Spanish theologians into more sustained contact with the wider church and prompted them to deeper ecclesiological reflections, which resulted in the strengthening of both the conciliarists' and the anti-conciliarists' stances with regard to the crisis in church leadership.[85] For a young scholar at Salamanca, this must have been a heady and exhilarating time.

The issues at stake at Constance also had political implications, both within Castile and concerning the kingdom's relations with other Iberian kingdoms and other European nations. These high stakes were one reason that it is difficult to imagine that a university such as Salamanca, with its close connections to power, did not see intense discussion of the conflict. Similarly difficult to imagine is that Juan de Segovia, a rising star at the university, was unaffected by these discussions. As I argue below, he arrived at Basel already sympathetic to the conciliarists' arguments and having weighed in astutely to restrain the power of a prelate. At any rate, at least by the fall of 1439 he had come to admire Jean Gerson, chancellor of the university at Paris and one of the leading thinkers at Constance. He called him a "most outstanding doctor of theology" and a "most renowned doctor."[86]

Moreover, issues about papal power and its legitimacy, which would be central to Juan de Segovia's activities at Basel, did not begin when this council convened. It is likely that he was exposed to these questions from his earliest days at Salamanca. Discussions about which pope had the stronger claim on Castile's obedience had been under way for a while before Constance opened. Several important meetings on the topic had even taken place in Salamanca. In 1379, at the beginning of the schism, the king convened an assembly in Burgos to discuss the obedience question. At that meeting and at another the same year, which encompassed only the ecclesiastical province of Toledo, it was decided that Castile should declare itself neutral, at least for the time being. But Pedro Tenorio, the archbishop of Toledo, personally leaned toward obedience to Rome. At meetings in Medina del Campo (1380), Salamanca (1381), and Palencia (1388), those assembled voted to proclaim obedience to Avignon. Spanish prelate Pedro de Luna, later the Avignon pope Benedict XIII but then a delegate for the Avignon pope Clement VII, personally attended some of these meetings and was no doubt instrumental in making the case for Clement VII. Nevertheless, in 1397 an assembly of clergy meeting in Salamanca voted to support French efforts to persuade the Avignon pope, Benedict XIII, to cede his office. In 1398, an assembly of clergy meeting in Alcalá de Henares subtracted obedience from Benedict XIII. However, after the death of Pedro Tenorio the following year, the opinion shifted again, and in 1403 the restitution of Castile's obedience to Avignon was proclaimed in the Colegiata de Santa María la Mayor in Valladolid.

This shift of obedience back to Avignon was further reaffirmed in an assembly in Salamanca in 1410 or 1412, a few years after Segovia had begun his studies there. In Salamanca, royal delegates as well as the clergy of this diocese and the professoriate of the university declared Benedict XIII the sole pontiff of the universal church. Given the pope's enthusiastic financial support for the university and its personnel, it is not surprising that its faculty was inclined to endorse such a benefactor. One of those at the forefront of this shift toward declaring loyalty to Benedict XIII was the *converso* Pablo de Santa María, later one of Segovia's colleagues at Basel, who was rewarded for his support by the see of Cartagena. The influence of such powerful figures on behalf of a single legitimate pope could only have hardened the anticonciliarist line in Castile.[87]

As Segovia's studies progressed, this issue was still in play, and he would have continued to hear about developments. After Constance began, leaders of the Spanish church were forced to reconsider their position in the face of a pan-European council which sought to put an end to an Avignon papacy. In 1415, representatives from Aragon, Castile, Navarre, and Scotland met in Narbonne and reached an accord in which they agreed to support the conciliarists' efforts. The treaty was formally accepted by the kingdom of Castile on the first of January, 1416, but with strong opposition from the bishops of Toledo and Seville, both important and influential sees.[88] Hence the very participation at this council of a Castilian delegation, or one from the University of Salamanca, would have provoked opposition from certain powerful people in the kingdom.

Tne competing claims of loyalty advanced by the popes involved had international repercussions as well. This was the era of the Hundred Years War (1337–1453), during which Castile was usually allied with France and typically supported its interests abroad. However, Aragon and Portugal were normally allied with England. In the years immediately following Constance, Castile's support for the papacy (now in Rome alone) constituted an alliance with the pope against Aragon. This political configuration further strengthened the theological currents within Castile sympathetic to the primacy of the papacy.[89] Any support for constraints on papal power must have seemed dangerously close to questioning the power of a pope now tied to Castilian nationalism. During the Council of Pavia-Siena (1423–24), convened in accord with the decree of Constance stipulating that another council would meet in five years, Aragon's king Alfonso V further exacerbated the tensions by seizing Naples, advocating the resurrection of a papacy centered in Avignon, and ordering officials in his kingdom to retract obedience from Martin V.[90]

Surely all of these discussions about the right governance of the church, intertwined with both political and intellectual agendas and fueled by intense emotion, would have found expression in the streets and classrooms of Salamanca. Anyone studying or teaching there during these years would have learned of these events and probably formed opinions about them. Scholars such as Miguel Avilés have observed that the general direction was toward a hardening of the arguments for papal power, but that there was at the same time a stubborn residual support for the conciliarists' arguments among some thinkers. If Juan de Segovia was among them, as I argue, this would place him in what was likely a minority position in Castile. Also, this might be an early sign of a willingness on his part to go against the grain in his public positions. Later, he was one of a handful of leaders at Basel who did not abandon this council and declare loyalty to the pope after it became clear that the papacy would prevail in the power struggle. Certainly his call to reject an armed response to the 1453 fall of Constantinople was unconventional as well. Moreover, there is an uncanny conjunction between the end of Constance and the beginning of Segovia's quest for benefices. Both occurred in 1418. It is possible that whatever financial support Juan de Segovia had enjoyed before this had been endangered by the tensions and fallout surrounding positions taken at Constance. He might have been under the patronage of someone who lost money or authority in that struggle.

If church conflicts possibly induced Segovia to reflect about the proper governance of the church, political events closer to home could have given him a yearning for peace and reconciliation of differences. The 1420s were especially tumultous years in Castile because Juan II achieved majority in 1419, and this heightened the power struggles between nobility and monarchy, and among different powerful sectors of the nobility. Most of Juan II's reign, from 1419 until his 1454 death, was marked by a struggle to weaken the power of the *infantes*. Their father, Fernando de Antequara, was Juan II's uncle, and he was the regent, along with the mother of the young king, Catalina de Lancaster, until the new Castilian king came of age. Antequera became a powerful force in his own right, controlling many regions of the peninsula. After the throne of Aragon became vacant in 1410, he was asked to serve as king of this kingdom, so for the next four years, he continued as regent of Castile but was also king of Aragon. He remained highly involved in Castilian affairs and conspired, through his five sons and his daughter, to consolidate his control. Daughter María became queen of Castile by marrying Juan II, and Antequera's sons assumed control of various territories. Each of them was constantly trying to increase his authority, often by seeking alliances with and against other nobles and undermining the power of the other sons.[91] The 1420s were particularly active years for the *infantes* Juan and Enrique, and their various machinations threatened the stability of the kingdom.[92] This context probably explains a striking request to the pope in 1423 from Fernando Rodríguez Maldonado, who held a chair in law at Salamanca. The professor asked, and received, permission to be away from the university for a year without losing his faculty appointment. According to his request, he feared several magnates of the kingdom, and he could not enter the city without great danger.[93]

As for Juan de Segovia, there is reason to believe that he was not untouched by the violence sometimes threatening members of the university. In his 1914 history of the University of Salamanca, Enrique

Esperabé Arteaga transcribed a curious royal letter issued by Juan II on February 24, 1426. Unfortunately, he did not cite a source or location for this document, but the letter seems plausible and is consistent with other information we have about the personnel in and around Salamanca at the time. In his letter, the king took under his protection and guard Doctor Antón Ruíz, *maestrescuela* in Salamanca, and Juan Alfonso de Segovia, along with their respective dependents and companions. Apparently, the two had requested this safe passage declaration because they had been harrassed and threatened by Juan de Valencia, the king's own *corregidor* (appointed royal justice) as they traveled on university business. In this letter from the king, Juan de Valencia and his associates were specifically prohibited from injuring, killing, ordering killed, or robbing the goods of the two university men, and it was specified that this applied while they were travelling to and from the king's residence (*casa*), court, or chancery, as well as the cities of Salamanca, Zamora, Ciudad Rodrigo, or any other cities, towns, and places in the king's realm.[94] In addition to hinting that Juan de Segovia had somehow earned the unwelcome attention of powerful enemies, this document suggests that he was a regular associate of the *maestrescuela* of the university. This was a powerful position, and if he was traveling with this man on university business in 1426, he had earned the trust of his colleagues.

Other information concerning his activities at the university in the 1420s also suggests a high level of esteem from his peers. He was involved in an issue that lay at the heart of the university's governance and its future, a dispute over the immediate governance of the university, which had been simmering for some time. I believe this dispute provides the key to understanding Segovia's earliest extant work, a *repetitio* (required university lecture) written in 1426 in which he extolled the unlimited power invested in the papacy. The address warrants special discussion here because it reveals so much about his thought processes and activity at the university, and because of its close relationship with his subsequent activity at Basel. The work is entitled *Repetitio de superioritate et excellentia supremae potestatis ecclesiasticae et spiritualis ad regiam temporalem*, and only one manuscript exists. It is MS 89, fols. 130r–165v, in Valladolid's Biblioteca Universitaria de Santa

Cruz.[95] Since it has not been published, most scholars who know of the work know only its title. Not without reason, the document has been considered an unflinching defense of absolute papal authority. Throughout, the address was a reflection on the nature and exercise of power. Juan was faithful to the plan he announced near the beginning: to discuss first to which discipline it pertains to determine the "Catholic truths"; secondly, whether the faculty of dominium and leading derives from nature; thirdly, whether it can be proven from reason and from scripture that priesthood and supreme royal power existed in Christ; and, finally, whether it can be proven from the gospel message that Christ's fullness of power was passed to Peter.[96] After establishing that the power had, in fact, been conferred on Peter, he argued that it now rested on the pope as his successor.

In according extensive powers to the pope, Juan's language was extraordinarily strong. To the pontiff's supreme power, Juan argued, obedience must be shown in all things, since the high pontiff is the universal monarch of all Christians, and *de iure* of the whole world. Having the highest crown in both temporal and spiritual realms, he alone claims the fullness of power in both.[97] Juan wrote that the pope is under no one but God alone, even to the point that if he were to kill someone, it would not be "irregular" because Peter himself had cut off the ear of the soldier. The pope's power extended to non-Christians as well, since Christ said, "I have other sheep that are not of this flock, and it is fitting for me to lead them." Even if these outsiders were outside the law of nature, the pope could punish them when they violated that law.[98] The "breadth of extension to all worldly affairs, and the sublimity, dignity, and excellence and indeed the profundity of the influence and the strength of the supreme spiritual power" were such that there is no one who is outside its reach.[99]

This work presents a mystery for scholars because it stands in such contrast to Segovia's subsequent conciliarist position. In his descriptive inventory of Segovia's known works, Benigno Hernández Montes observed that Juan's position in this *repetitio* was similar to Boniface VIII's *Unam sanctam* and noted that this was all the more unusual because of the Castilian theologian's evolution, not that many years later, into one of the strongest advocates for conciliarism at the

Council of Basel.[100] Antony Black commented regarding this *repetitio* that except for Juan's interest in political theory, "There is little connection between this and his subsequent ecclesiology, except that he would always champion the principle of ecclesiastical autonomy."[101] One scholar writing about Juan's early positions at Basel wrote that he arrived there "with the fervor of a new convert."[102] James Biechler wrote of Juan de Segovia simply, "This Salamancan theologian had come to the Council of Basel in 1433 as a supporter of the papalist position but was 'converted' to the conciliarist cause and became one of its foremost theoreticians."[103]

Juan's apparent reversal of the views he held in 1426 serves as one more example of the type of ready change that prompted Antony Black to declare the political thinking of the later Middle Ages "intrinsically puzzling."[104] A disconcerting number of late medieval political thinkers espoused principles that flatly contradicted their own policies or their other writings and arguments. Black asked the question of what we should make of these reversals, which make modern readers uneasy with the suspicion that perhaps they do not truly understand what these theorists were saying. The medieval writers themselves, including Juan de Segovia, seem to have been untroubled by these shifts and offered no explanations. As Black articulated, "We are left asking: Did they really mean what they seem to us to have been saying? What exactly was their meaning in the more 'radical' sounding passages?"[105] Drawing from the work of John Pocock and Quentin Skinner, Black's own response was that these writers consciously employed different "languages" of political discourse in order to advance positions they embraced, with no particular loyalty to anything that we too readily call a "school" of thought.[106]

What exactly was the meaning, then, of Juan's arguments in his *Repetitio de superioritate*? Certainly this speech was no esoteric exercise for him. Near the beginning of his address, he told his listeners that the current circumstances urged a public discussion of the issue he was about to explore.[107] This raises the question of what those timely issues were that he thought would benefit from his address. It was the age of conciliarism, and the governance of the church was receiving more attention from scholars than it had in earlier centuries. Still, it had been several years since the Council of Constance had ended, the poorly attended Council of Pavia-Siena had ended two years earlier, and in 1426 there was only one pope, and he was in Rome. There was no open conflict between a council and a pope (or popes) and no immediately apparent reason for papal power to have been contested. If Juan was adding his voice to the pope vs. council discussion, it is odd that there is nothing in his *repetitio* that mentions councils or that seems to allude to them indirectly. Yet Juan de Segovia chose papal authority as the topic for his annual lecture and noted that it was a timely one. Looking more to the local circumstances, some have suggested that his apology for papal prerogatives was an attempt to defend the rights of the university against that troublesome *corregidor* (royal administrator) Juan de Valencia, or the still-new faculty of theology against the more established faculties of law.[108] And even in the absence of any such frictions, as I have already explained, the university had much to gain from being in the good graces of the pope. But if Juan de Segovia thought that his words had special relevance for his time, he probably did not compose this address simply because of the general benefits to come from ongoing papal support. Something had made papal authority an especially *timely* issue.

Other circumstances involving the university in 1426 provide the key to understanding Juan's insistence that the pope's power was absolute in a way that also accommodates the strongly conciliarist stance he took a few years later. I argue here that his aim was to limit the reach of the powerful archbishop of Santiago, Lope de Mendoza, and Salamanca's own cathedral in the governance of the university. When these dynamics are taken into account, it appears that Juan's defense of papal power was actually a reaction *against* a recent decision by Pope Martin V related to the university's governance. This was, furthermore, an issue in which Juan had more than a passing interest.

Traditionally, the diocese of Salamanca was under the jurisdiction of the archbishop of Santiago. Since the university was closely linked to the cathedral, Santiago's prelate exercised significant control over its affairs, an important fact in understanding the context of Juan's 1426 *repetitio*. In addition, a 1313 bull from Clement V, *Dudum oblata nobis*, gave the archbishop the authority to name, in consultation with his suffragans, the person in charge of administering the university's *rentas*. The *rentas* were the taxes from the surrounding towns and countryside; they constituted the university's most significant source of revenue. As Beltrán de Heredia explained, this was problematic because whenever the position became vacant, the university was forced to wait nervously until the next provincial council in Santiago before a replacement would come. An interim administrator often could not be as effective at collecting and distributing revenues, and the *studium*'s financial interests were thus regularly and severely jeopardized.[109]

The archbishop's involvement in the finances also interfered in the internal workings of the *studium* and placed him at odds with the *claustro*, the university's governing body, as an example from the early fifteenth century illustrates. To resolve a dispute between the university and Santiago's prelate, Benedict XIII issued a bull in 1413, at the university's request, entrusting the bishop of Segovia with the unenviable task of mediating between the two parties concerning the appointment of a new administrator of the *rentas*.[110] We do not know how the bishop of Segovia resolved the issue. We do know that the university leaders insisted that it was their right to appoint and dismiss the administrator of the salaries of the readers and officials in the *studium*, according to longstanding custom.[111] They charged the archbishop with "falsely asserting" that the appointments and dismissals were his to make.[112] The archbishop objected to this accusation and asserted that the *claustro* must have forgotten or ignored the bull of Clement V a century earlier. To this the *claustro* responded by requesting that Benedict XIII send them an authenticated copy of this bull, which arrived included in one dated to May 1415.[113]

In the early fifteenth century, the university faced a particularly formidable threat in the archbishop of Santiago, not just the longstanding and routine tussles with the holder of that office. The reason for the intensified hostilities was the long tenure of the ambitious Lope de Mendoza as archbishop of Santiago, a man whose aspirations I believe prompted Segovia's 1426 address to the university community. A member of a powerful family from the new Trastámara nobility, Lope de Mendoza occupied the see of Santiago de Compostela, and therefore exercised great influence over the bishop of Salamanca, from the first years of the fifteenth century until 1445. Until he died, the university managed the successive power struggles as best it could, seeking protection from Rome with varying results.[114]

To the dismay of the university community, the archbishop's power extended beyond the authority to name the *administrator* of *rentas*. The constitutions written when Pedro de Luna was the legate of Clement VII (1378–94) charged the archbishop of Santiago with their execution, which gave him and his local agents broad administrative authority over the university. The question arose of whether giving the archbishop of Santiago a hand in this diminished the authority of the *maestrescuela*, so in his 1411 constitutions the pope added that his intentions were not to do that, but rather that the archbishop was to aid the *maestrescuela* in this duty.[115] Obviously, this somewhat ambiguous provision gave an aggressive archbishop like Mendoza an excuse to involve himself in any number of affairs and disputes at the university. Apparently one such incident occurred in 1413. A papal bull that September entrusted an official in Segovia with the task of mediating between the university and Lope de Mendoza in a dispute over which party had the right to name the *administrator* of the university.[116]

In 1419, the university made a significant move toward autonomy and initiated a chain of events that provided the immediate context for Juan de Segovia's 1426 *repetitio*. It secured papal permission to form a commission to reform the constitutions of the university.[117] The commission included representatives of the archbishop of Santiago, but the majority of the members were from the university, and the momentum was certainly toward giving the university a freer hand in administering its affairs. Two key elements in their designs were a new definition of the powers of the *maestrescuela* and a new system for appointing a person to this office.

The committee members' decision to focus on the office of the *maestrescuela* was strategic. The 1411 constitutions of Benedict XIII had already made the *maestrescuela* (*scholasticus* or *escolasticus ecclesiae Salamantini*) the *iudex ordinarius dicti studii* with the authority to adjudicate all complaints against and among its members. He could also impose fines and punishments such as the loss of degrees, professorships, or offices, including perpetual ineligibility to hold them, on those who disturbed the good order of the university. For those unhappy with his decisions, the only recourse was an appeal to the pope. The *maestrescuela* also held apostolic authority to lift excommunications incurred by members of the university. He was one of the five to hold a key to the ark of the university, which housed its seal, constitutions, privileges, and money collected from fines.[118] Already invested with such broad powers, the *maestrescuela*'s position was a logical focus of attention for those who sought the means to end Lope de Mendoza's meddling. If they could clarify and expand the *maestrescuela*'s powers in such a way as to leave the archbishop without any, they would gain significant autonomy for the university.

This is precisely what they did in the constitutions they drafted.[119] They envisioned that the *maestrescuela* would retain all of his former powers, and in addition he would be the sole executor of the constitutions and other ordinances for the university and all its personnel.[120] The archbishop of Santiago and his subordinate, the bishop of Salamanca, would no longer have even an auxiliary role in ensuring that the pope's directives were followed.[121] Perhaps even more significantly, the proposed constitutions established a body of twenty *diffinitores*, ten with degrees or noble titles and ten holding salaried professorships. Elected annually, these twenty would direct the affairs of the university and would appoint the new *maestrescuela* when a vacancy occurred. They would elect someone to this office from the ranks of the professors in canon or civil law or theology, and the archbishop of Toledo or an apostolic nuncio would confirm the appointment. Furthermore, although the *maestrescuela* formally reported directly to the pope, before assuming office he would swear an oath that he would follow the directives given to him by the *diffinitores* or a majority of them, and that if he did anything contrary to their mandate, he would resign his position. All of this was to take effect "notwithstanding" (*non obstantibus*) the constitutions and previous statutes of the *studium*, and the archbishop was not to place anyone in an authority or intermediary position above the *maestrescuela*.[122] If the pope accepted these proposed constitutions, the university would be substantially free from interference by Mendoza or the bishop of Salamanca.

It was to Juan de Segovia and Ibo Moro, a doctor of laws, that the university entrusted the task of carrying the new constitutions to Rome and securing papal approval. Although both Julio González and Darío Rodríguez Cabanelas speculated that Juan might well have been among those who wrote the new constitutions, we simply do not know. However, as Benigno Hernández Montes argues, it seems at least logical that the university would have sent someone who knew the text and their interests well and who would be adept in explaining and arguing for their wishes. The constitutions were extremely important to the university. It is not an exaggeration to say, as Hernández Montes did, that it had probably been centuries since a delegation from Salamanca carried to Rome a matter of such importance.[123] Juan de Segovia and Ibo Moro left for this journey in 1421 and returned from their successful mission the following year.[124]

Approved by Martin V on February 20, 1422, the new constitutions met with predictable resistance. The *maestrescuela* position, after all, was still technically an office within Salamanca's cathedral chapter, even if appointments to it had long been a papal prerogative. The chapter was unwilling to accept that a body of electors from the university would choose the person to serve the cathedral in this capacity.[125] The bishop and cathedral chapter of Salamanca submitted a formal petition to the pope in May 1425, requesting that he return to them their traditional right to name the *maestrescuela*.[126] Martin V granted this request in January of 1426.[127] His accommodating bull was issued just six months before Juan delivered his *Repetitio de superioritate*. The pope had reversed his own decision to grant the university community, through its elected *diffinitores*, the right to name the *maestrescuela* and therefore also to determine the policies he would follow. This was a serious setback in the university's aspirations to autonomy from external control.

We are now in a better position to consider the question posed earlier in this discussion: What exactly was the meaning of Juan's arguments in his *Repetitio de superioritate*? It seems impossible that the circumstances outlined above were not on Segovia's mind as he planned this address. Given its immediate context, this *repetitio* was unavoidably, and probably quite intentionally, a commentary on the pope's reversal of this key element in the constitutions. Either Segovia was, indeed, defending the pope's right to reverse his earlier decision, or he was subtly challenging it.

The text of his *repetitio* might contain oblique references to the controversy and recent reversal by Martin V. In his conclusion to the section in which he presented theological arguments for papal power, he once again exalted the power and extension of papal authority and added, "So that concerning it, it can be said that according to his will he acts (*facit*) with the heavenly powers just as with the inhabitants of the earth, and there is none who resists his hand nor says to him, 'Why are you doing this?'; but his word is full of power and under it are bent all rectors who run (*comportant*) the world."[128] Even more striking is a passage later in the text:

> The power extends itself, therefore, to the mandates of discipline, under which fall only those things that are indifferent to salvation and to which we are not otherwise obliged than by the command of a superior. Such was the first command given to a man, that he not eat of the tree of the knowledge of good and evil, which otherwise was not bad, except that it had been prohibited. *And just so the supreme pontiff can make decrees* (praecipere) *in many temporal things that are not necessary and in themselves ordained to the eternal life, and we can not even ask of him the reason for his mandate, because no one can say to him, "Why are you doing this?"* Job 9.[129]

All were bent under the hand of the pope and should not even question his actions. Juan did not pioneer this creative use of Job 9. He was borrowing language the canonists used to defend the power of the pope.[130] Still, he chose to include and emphasize those strands of their arguments that insisted that no one should question the pope about his decisions.

In the summer of 1426, there were two groups in Salamanca who were actively questioning the pope's decisions: those distressed by the pope's restoration of the cathedral chapter's right to name the *maestrescuela*, and those distressed by the pope's decision to approve the earlier 1422 constitutions, which had given that right to the university.

The latter group is the more likely target audience for Juan's reminders that the pontiff's decisions were beyond question. Segovia had personally carried the proposed constitutions to Rome and argued for them before the pope. It is inconceivable that he would have greeted the revocation of the university's power to appoint its *maestrescuela* with satisfaction, let alone the enthusiasm toward a papal action that the text of his summer *repetitio* might lead one to expect. Presumably many in his audience, too, would have been dismayed to learn of the January revocation and hardly receptive to an impassioned defense of papal prerogatives, least of all from one of the two men to whom it had entrusted the delicate mission of securing papal sanction for its aspirations to greater autonomy. Indeed, despite the words he spoke, his listeners apparently did not understand him to be arguing for carte blanche authority for the pope and submission to his recent decision. If they had, they would not have sent him to Rome again in 1431, this time with Pedro Martínez de Covarrubias, to defend the constitutions.[131]

If Juan was adamant about unlimited power for the pope, he nevertheless carefully stipulated that local church officials did not share in it. The power that Christ conferred on Peter was over both heaven and earth. Temporal things were natural accessories to the spiritual, Juan explained, as Jesus indicated in Matthew 6: "Seek first the kingdom of God and his justice, and all these things, namely temporal things, will be added to you." The common distinction that people should obey secular power in civil matters and ecclesiastical power in spiritual ones applied to lower ecclesiastical officials, but not to the pope. He was the universal monarch of all Christians.[132] Juan might have included this stipulation as one more way to remind local prelates of their place. This is consistent with a comment that he made years later, in his 1457 *Donatio*. He reminded the Salamanca community that he had defended the 1422 constitutions, in particular the autonomy from local church control, again in 1435 before Pope Eugene IV.[133]

It is interesting to consider who would have been the intended audience for these remarks. *Repetitios* were addresses for the academic community, but the *studium* was closely tied to the cathedral chapter, so presumably Juan had chapter members in mind as he planned his talk. His comments must have been particularly directed at those with special loyalties to Mendoza. The timing of his speech invites further speculation about his intentions and his personality. He could not have hoped that the audience, having been duly reminded of the pope's authority, would stop questioning the pope's approval of the constitutions. The pope had already granted the petition to overturn the relevant aspects of the constitutions he had only recently approved. Persuasion probably was not Juan's goal here. Instead, he was registering a complaint and a public rebuke to the archbishop, seemingly just to make the point. This suggests that he was personally invested in ensuring the university's autonomy, as envisioned in the constitutions he had carried to Rome, and that this was not for him simply a routine matter concerning university administration.

The position the university took in proposing its 1422 constitutions was similar to the one that Castile's urban elites were claiming in the Cortes around the same time. As we have seen, the early fifteenth century was a bewildering time of political chaos, during which the power of the Trastámara dynasty was consolidated. Urban elites often allied themselves with the monarchy in order to fend off encroachments on their power by the kingdom's leading nobles. Since the king's own power was precarious, city leaders had some leverage with Juan II, at least toward the beginning of his reign, and they used it to press for measures that ensured municipal autonomy from local nobles.[134] If my reading of Juan's 1426 *repetitio* is accurate, this is similar to what he was doing on the university's behalf. He invoked papal authority to secure the university's autonomy from Archbishop Mendoza. Castile's chaotic political arena might have inspired Juan's speech.

In supporting constitutions that ensured communal, corporate governance for the university and bound the *maestrescuela* to follow the decisions of the body of *diffinitores*, he revealed goals consistent with the reform efforts of the conciliarists, goals he embraced enthusiastically just a few years later at the Council of Basel.[135] It appears that Juan de Segovia's vigorous arguments on behalf of papal power in 1426 should not be taken at face value, and that he was closer to conciliar ideals than has been recognized.

Segovia's 1426 address is an example of a thinker doing more than employing different languages to prove a point, with no particular loyalty to a school of thought. Here is a late medieval thinker using irony to advocate certain principles of governance, even a school of thought if conciliar principles can be described in this way, to which he *was* loyal. If this case does not exactly relieve the consternation experienced by scholars of late medieval political thought when they encounter apparent inconsistencies between thinkers' statements, it might nevertheless evoke admiration for the rhetorical and intellectual skill displayed. Segovia's argument was brilliant. Indeed, the approach he chose was the only one that could have allowed him to argue against a papal decision without appearing to oppose papal authority.

Juan de Segovia the Intellectual

This exploration of Juan de Segovia's career at Salamanca leaves us with the question of what were his interests and inclinations as an intellectual formed at the increasingly prestigious Castilian *studium*. Apart from the university governance issue described above, what kinds of issues interested him? Which texts resonated with him? These are questions that scholars have scarcely touched, and they are questions that cannot be addressed simply by identifying a prevailing school of thought and noting its presence in Segovia's works. In the early fifteenth century, competing schools of thought found a home in Salamanca. In theology, both the Dominican Convento de San Esteban and the Franciscan Convento de San Francisco enjoyed preeminence among the Castilian houses in their respective orders in the first decades of the fifteenth century.[136] In the field of law, traditionally the university's strongest field, scholars embraced a striking range of positions.[137] There simply was no "Salamanca man" whose perspectives were predictable given his alma mater. For this reason, the sources and methods Juan de Segovia preferred are that much more revelatory of the personality and intellectual instincts of the Castilian thinker. The question before us, then, is what sort of thinker the University of Salamanca chose as its representative to Basel.

Scholars have consistently noted in Segovia's work an affinity for Franciscan thinkers and themes. One Franciscan whose ideas he used, although not without some significant departures, was Duns Scotus (ca. 1265–1308). According to Rudolf Haubst, Juan's approach to the doctrine of the Trinity drew substantially from that articulated by Scotus and his disciples. Haubst reasoned that Segovia's attraction to Scotism originated during his years at Salamanca, and that this school of thought also heavily influenced his writings on the immaculate conception of Mary.[138] As a leading member of the theology commission at Basel, Juan wrote extensively on both these topics. The immaculate conception was a subject of controversy between the Franciscans and the Dominicans, and the doctrine of the Trinity received sustained attention at Basel because of the council's efforts to achieve union with the Greeks. If Juan did, indeed, draw heavily from Scotus in his treatment of these two important subjects, this would certainly give Scotus a prominent place in the thought of the Salamancan master. It is somewhat curious that, judging from his 1457 *Donatio*, Juan apparently did not own any works by Duns Scotus.

Jesse Mann has explored another aspect of Segovia's indebtedness to Scotus and presented a plausible account of how he might have become familiar with the earlier thinker's ideas even though he owned none of his books. In a letter of spiritual counsel written in 1456, Segovia discussed the sin of Lucifer in a way strikingly similar to Scotus's distinctive approach to this sin of the first angel. Mann argues that Juan probably learned of it by reading Franciscus de Mayronis's commentary on Lombard's *Sentences*. Mayronis was Scotus's most renowned student, and throughout this commentary, he cited his teacher often and explicitly. Segovia's letter to Guillaume d'Orlyé contains sections with almost exactly the same wording as Scotus's commentary on the *Sentences*.[139] Juan wrote his letter to Orlyé while in Aiton, where his access to books was presumably limited to his own library, which, as noted above, did not contain any works by Scotus. However, he did own a copy of Mayronis's commentary on the *Sentences*. This led Mann to suggest that Segovia borrowed the treatment of Lucifer's sin from Scotus via Mayronis, a hypothesis only strengthened by Mann's observation that another theme in Segovia's thought, the war in heaven described in Revelation 12:7–12, was more explicit in Mayronis than in Scotus.[140] Mayronis might well have been the conduit through which Juan discovered and admired the ideas of Scotus. If Hernández Montes was correct in including Mayronis's commentary among the works Juan acquired while still in Salamanca,[141] then Mann's work provides a clue on the sources Juan may have been working with as a student and faculty member at Salamanca.

We also owe to Mann the answer to another question concerning which texts Segovia knew while still in Salamanca. Hernández Montes had stated that we do not know whether Segovia was acquainted then with the *Dialogus inter magistrum et discipulum de imperatorum et pontificum potestate* by William of Ockham, another Franciscan (ca. 1280–1349).[142] Mann's convincing side-by-side comparison of Ockham's *Dialogus* and Segovia's *Repetitio de superioritate* has subsequently proven that the Castilian theologian did indeed use the *Dialogus*, and use it approvingly.[143] As he noted, this has implications for the question of whether the theologians at the Council of Basel were influenced by the works of Marsilius of Padua and William of Ockham.[144] It also has implications for the traditional assessment that nominalism and Ockham found a cool reception at Salamanca in the early fifteenth century.[145] While the questions surrounding the sources of the conciliarists' thought and the dominant schools in Salamanca at the time continue to hover and to demand attention, it is enough for our purposes to note yet another Franciscan thinker who had attracted Juan's interest at this early stage of his career. Furthermore, Segovia returned to Ockham's *Dialogus* in his later works, especially his *Explanatio de tribus veritatibus fidei* (August 1439).[146]

Nevertheless, Juan's decisions to cite or borrow from Franciscan thinkers does not necessarily place him within a Franciscan "school of thought." It is not clear that there was such a school in the late medieval period. Since the late nineteenth century, Franciscan scholars and scholars with Franciscan sympathies have written of a succession of Franciscan "schools," most with roots in Augustine. Modern scholars typically refer to an early or "old" school (centered on Alexander of Hales and especially Bonaventure) and a later or "new" school (centered on Scotus and Ockham). Due to Ockham's association with the decline of the scholastic synthesis and with antipapal positions, Franciscan scholars have tended to minimize the significance of Ockham's thought and to emphasize that of Hales, Bonaventure, and Scotus. The establishment of these thinkers as pinnacles of an alleged Franciscan schoo: has distorted the evaluation of their contemporaries, predecessors, and successors, who have been seen only in relation to the three recognized pinnacles. In addition, Bert Roest has recently explained, modern scholars hoping to identify the chief characteristics of Franciscan thought have given disproportionate attention to the writings of Franciscan university masters in the throes of intense controversy. They assume that the views expressed in these conflict situations were those of the order in general. Also, the polarized contexts themselves might have led the medieval writers to advance positions and authorities they would not normally have pushed, or to emphasize methods or ideas that they otherwise would have avoided or downplayed. Scholars have not sufficiently taken these issues into account in their efforts to produce a master narrative of the development of a Franciscan school of thought.[147]

This search for a master narrative is probably premature, or perhaps completely ill advised. Franciscan theologians of the later Middle Ages argued profoundly different positions. This was even true among those thinkers in the fourteenth and fifteenth centuries who identified themselves as disciples of Scotus. Roest wrote that they could enlist identical teachings in defense of directly opposing positions.[148] According to Roest, the writings of Scotus were undoubtedly influential, but they did not give rise to a coherent body of teachings presented in the schools.[149] It is more accurate to see the teachings of Scotus as a source of inspiration or a common starting point for theological reflection for late medieval Franciscan thinkers.[150]

Juan de Segovia was apparently among those who found inspiration, but not a defined path, in the works of leading Franciscan thinkers. As we have noted above, he used but departed significantly from Scotus's treatment of the Trinity.[151] And Ockham's *Dialogus inter magistrum et discipulum de imperatorum et pontificum potestate* challenged papal power. Segovia borrowed from it to argue for papal supremacy over all other powers. Whatever affinity he felt toward Franciscan thinkers, he did not follow them slavishly. Anyone hoping to locate him within a Franciscan "school of thought" must account for the indications, which Roest presents, that such a thing may not have existed until the sixteenth or seventeenth century.[152] It is more likely that Juan simply lived and studied in an age when Franciscan thinkers were respected and prominent, so much so that Heiko Oberman wrote that the entire later Middle Ages could be called the "Franciscan Middle Ages."[153] It is not surprising that Juan's writings betray a familiarity with these writers.

A second characteristic that scholars have noted in Segovia's works is a consistent reliance upon scripture.[154] Perhaps this is not all that noteworthy, since scripture served as the context for all study of theology in the Middle Ages and indeed pervaded discourse and popular culture far beyond the confines of theology lecture halls. As Lesley Smith has argued, "Medieval people had a biblical imagination, in which scriptural images and phrases were likely to rise and break the surface of the consciousness before any more systematic thought."[155] Yet in the considerable amount of systematic thought that Juan de Segovia committed to writing, he cited scripture and employed scriptural metaphors with a frequency that has impressed scholars as noteworthy even for that era. Juan apparently had a more highly developed biblical imagination than most.

When scholars comment on Segovia's emphasis on scriptural authority, they usually observe this in his works from the Basel period of his life.[156] This is understandable, since he is best known as a champion of the conciliarist cause. This focus on his later works, however, begs the question of whether Juan's affinity for scripture developed during his formative years in Salamanca or in Basel as a result of exchanges with other scholars from across Europe.[157] Jesse Mann hinted at an evolution in Juan's view of the proper relationship between scripture and tradition. In his 1426 *repetitio*, Segovia followed Ockham closely in outlining categories of "Catholic truths." Like Ockham, he included extrascriptural truths, such as those derived from the teachings of general councils, chronicles, histories, and legends about the saints.[158] At least the evidence from this *repetitio* suggests that Segovia belonged to that category of scholars who considered the source of Christian teaching to be scripture in combination with other authorities. Others treated scripture as the sole legitimate source of Christian teaching. Mann noted that Juan seemed to have edged toward seeing scripture as the sole legitimate source in later works.[159] But how indicative of his early approach to scripture was that 1426 *repetitio*?

Further clues toward his attitude on scriptural authority come from his only other surviving work from the years in Salamanca. This is another *repetitio*, which he delivered in May of 1427, *De fide catholica*.[160] Unlike his address the year earlier, it is not possible to suggest any specific local circumstances that might have prompted the thoughts he expressed in *De fide catholica*. Segovia seemed to have in mind the general need to be able to present Christian teachings credibly to others, but if he was addressing a particular event or controversy of that year, it is unknown to us. Perhaps because of its more explicitly theological subject matter, this work has a very different tone than Segovia's address the preceding year. Whereas the earlier *repetitio* contained arguments from canon law and references to various works by Aristotle, the second work relies much more heavily on the Bible, though it is not devoid of extrabiblical influences. In it, for example, Juan enlisted the late medieval scholastic distinction between acquired and infused faith, and he used Aristotle's language of causes to explore what it meant to say that God alone "causes" infused faith.[161] But Aristotle provided him with a framework for discussion in that section, not with the meat of his argument. Most texts and authors cited came from the Bible. Apart from scripture, the author whom Juan cited most in this text was Augustine, often to corroborate a view found in scripture or to provide an illuminating commentary on a scriptural verse he was discussing. More so than with his *repetitio* the year before, the reader senses the author's gravitation toward scriptural texts in grappling with the issues before him.

Toward the beginning of *De fide catholica*, Juan cited a "moral and practical doctrine" of Peter Lombard that no one who believes in many gods will be saved, and no one will attain eternal life who did not believe in it and anticipate it while in the flesh. Juan was careful to note that scripture contained such a teaching. He said, "which part is elicited from the authority of the Apostle, which the Master adduced through his own confirmation."[162] The Master, for all his enduring authority in theological circles, was in the position of confirming what scripture had already taught. Similarly, most of the definitions of faith that Juan rehearsed for his listeners were from scripture. According to Hebrews 11, faith was "the substance of things hoped for, the conviction of things unseen."[163] He described faith as constancy and firm adhesion, as commended in that same chapter in Hebrews, where Paul praised the faithfulness of Abel, Enoch, Noah, Abraham, Isaac, Jacob, Joseph, Moses, and the Israelites besieging the walls of Jericho. He wrote that time precluded him from telling more of Gideon, Barak, Samson, Jephthah, David, Samuel, and the prophets, "who through faith conquered kingdoms, administered justice, obtained promises, shut the mouths of lions, quenched raging fire, escaped the edge of the sword, won strength out of weakness, became mighty in war, put foreign armies to flight" (Hebrews 11:33–34). Juan did not recount the substance of this chapter in his address, but he cited it in connection with examples of faithfulness. Presumably any number of patristic authorities or stories about the saints could have just as readily provided him with examples of faithful people. In fact, if he had referred to popular local saints, it might even have gained him a rhetorical advantage with his audience. His instincts were to turn to scripture instead.

It is also significant that, for Juan, the act or response of faith was precisely the assent to things revealed by God in scripture. He wrote that faith was "a gift of the Holy Spirit infused freely by God through which enlightening the human mind assents with firm adhesion to those things which are beyond its faculty, to the truths revealed by God in sacred scripture."[164] There is no mention anywhere in this text of truths expressed in creeds of the church, decrees of the general councils, papal proclamations, and other venues. Indeed, Segovia appears to have believed that Christians could find the entire content of their faith in the scriptures. He stated, "Now, therefore, if the things I have said having been readily heard by you, some one of you should declare that our faith, which has been contained in sacred scripture always, since the beginning of the world, and even more so following the lead of Christ, is confirmed by miracles that only God can perform, I will think that I have sufficiently proven the minor premise posited above, namely, that God revealed directly and through his messengers the faith that the Christian religion preaches."[165] "Our faith" had always been contained in scripture, and the burden of his argument was that what was found there was revealed by God.

Toward that end, Juan offered his audience what he called "twelve foundations on which the wall of the city was founded, namely, of the church militant of which Apocalypse 12 treats."[166] These are reasons why Christians could be confident that their faith, which was contained in scripture, was revealed. Actually, his list only contained eleven foundations, a fact he failed to recognize in his ensuing discussion of them because as he enumerated each one as he introduced it, he jumped from the seventh to the ninth. In any case, six of the eleven foundations directly affirmed the validity of scripture as revealed, or otherwise associated "the faith" with biblical claims. Of the remaining foundations, four concerned the testimony of nonbelievers, including the witness of the ancient writings of the gentiles (by which he meant classical authors) and contemporary Jews and Muslims. The remaining foundation was the care or attentiveness of those who heard the revelation (*diligencia recipiencium*). Juan did not develop this foundation as fully as most of the others, but he referred in this section to the fact that people in general have been persuaded by the message.

The first three of the eleven foundations Juan presented directly concerned the status of the Bible as revealed. The first foundation was prophecy (*prenunciati prophetica*), and Juan argued that the prophets' knowledge must have been from divine revelation, since the things they foretold happened as they had said, and the future is known only to God.[167] In explaining the second foundation, the concordance of the scriptures (*scripturarum concordacio*), Juan argued that the fact that the scriptures agreed even when two authors wrote about something concerning which they had no hard evidence was similar to two blind men correctly identifying an object's color. Only divine revelation could explain such an agreement.[168] The third foundation was the credibility or authority of the biblical authors (*auctoritas scribentium*). Juan stated bluntly that either the books of the Bible were written by those who are said in those books to have written them, or they were not, in which case they were written by liars.[169] But it seems unlikely that they would have written, "The Lord God says these things" if God had not said them to those writers.[170] If the writers were Christians, they would not have undertaken to write falsehood because their very writings condemn lying. If they were instead Jews, Saracens, or pagans, it was odd that they went to so much trouble to write and expound upon things that were contrary to their beliefs. Furthermore, it exceeded human skill to compose such a work, in which the entire Old Testament was fulfilled.[171] So the Bible was reliable, its writers inspired and credible.

Given that, it was no surprise that, as the ninth foundation (*racionalitas contentorum*) claimed, the contents of sacred scripture were sound. Juan asserted that no more solid advice could be found concerning how to act. The Bible enjoined believers to love God with their whole heart and to love their neighbors as themselves, and to do to others what they themselves wanted done to them.[172] The stability of the church (*ecclesie stabilitas*) in spite of persecutions by tyrants and the fallacies of heretics constituted the eleventh (really tenth) foundation. Here he cited the words of the Pharisee Gamaliel before the council of elders, urging his colleagues not to attempt to put down the Christian movement because if it was not of God it would end on its own, and, if it was, they would be opposing God. Furthermore, had Jesus not assured Peter that he would pray that the disciple's faith would not fail him? Jesus had also promised to be with his followers until the end of time.[173] The stability of the church through persecutions and the peril of heresies seems a subject that could have lent itself nicely to support from chronicles, histories, and respected writers from Christianity's turbulent early centuries. Yet Juan apparently considered scripture the more compelling corroboration of this penultimate foundation.

The final foundation was the clarity provided by miracles (*miraculorum claritas*). This foundation embraced an odd variety of miracles, one of which was simply that the claims of Christianity were so outlandish that it was a miracle that the religion spread at all. Here he made reference to Augustine's *City of God*, saying, "Three unbelievable things are put before our eyes here: First, that Christ, a mortal man, having died, rose and ascended into heaven. Second, it is unbelievable that the world believes such an incredible thing so firmly. Third, that men so unlearned as the apostles were so effectively able to make them believe such an incredible thing."[174] Other miracles that Juan mentioned in this section were more conventional: "men by nature unrefined, fishermen, suddenly were filled with knowledge and were speaking all languages; they gave sight to the blind, expelled demons, healed the sick not only by the placing of a hand, but by the transmission of spittle, and whoever the shadow of one of them would touch would be healed of whatever illness they were suffering, all of these things being described fully in the Acts of the Apostles."[175] For good measure, Segovia included several more examples of miracles recounted in scripture.

Jesse Mann was correct in stating that Juan's 1426 *repetitio* on papal authority "must certainly be considered an important source for Segovia's early views on the relationship between Scripture and Tradition."[176] As the preceding discussion has shown, Juan's 1427 *repetitio* on faith is equally important. A more extensive study could reveal that his view on the relative authority of scripture and tradition was not consistent from one year to the next, or at least that in each case he chose the style of arguing that he thought would best advance his cause. Nevertheless, the second work seems to have as one of its main goals the defense of scripture as a revealed and trustworthy expression of the Christian faith. Juan may have been closer to seeing scripture as the sole source of authority at this time in his life than his first *repetitio* suggests. If so, it is possible that this inclination was nourished by an early interest in polemic or in striving to persuade Jews and Muslims of the truths of Christianity. Christian-Jewish polemic turned on whose interpretation of scripture was legitimate, since the issue of whether the New Testament was foreshadowed in the Old was a question of exegesis.[177] Sidney Griffith has recently shown how dependent Christian-Muslim polemic was on arguments from scripture.[178] It is possible that Segovia gravitated toward an emphasis on scripture in his thinking because he was interested in making the case for Christianity, and that case hinged on the validity of revelation found in scripture.

The archive at the University of Salamanca contains a document that may shed light on the development of Segovia's thoughts on these issues. The document is not long, just a single side of a folio. The first line, which is underlined, seems intended as a title: *Viae ad convertendum infideles ac fideles in veritate fidei catholicae.*[179] In his *Obras de Juan de Segovia*, Benigno Hernández Montes noted only that this was a "brief autographic extract of unknown origin."[180] The page is difficult to read—Hernández Montes put "illegible" on the line for the explicit in his inventory—and it appears to contain notes and phrases rather than actual sentences. The notes repeatedly refer to works by Augustine. What is striking is that several of the items on this folio correspond with some of the "foundations" for the city walls enumerated in his 1427 *repetitio*. For example, the first item listed is *praenunctiatio prophetica*, and Augustine's *The City of God*, Book 12, Chapter 1, is cited. The second item is *concordantia scripturarum*. A few lines later appears *auctoritas scribentium*. *Diligent reccipientium* [sic] is next, and at the end of this point Segovia listed sources, one of which was *The City of God*, Book 11, Chapter 2, and Book 18, Chapter 38. A little later there is mention of the rationality (*rationabilitas*) of "the contents" (*contentorum*) and the irrationality of the errors of pagans. At about mid-page, the stability of the church (*ecclesiae stabilitas*) and Gamaliel are mentioned, followed by the clarity of miracles (*miraculorum claritas*), and the citation of *The City of God*, Book 22, Chapter 18. Not all of the "foundations" found in the *repetitio* are present here, but it is uncanny how many are. I believe this page could have been his notes for his speech, or perhaps a set of notes he was taking on the issue of how to persuade non-Christians of the truth of Christian revelation, and from which he drew when composing his address. The page is in a volume with several other works, including other pages containing extracts and notes. It is one of those Juan de Segovia stipulated should go to the University of Salamanca upon his death.[181]

As for Augustine's inspiration for those twelve foundations, there are indeed parallels to Juan's arguments in *The City of God*, although his citations of book and chapter prove not to match modern editions of the work. For example, in Book 18, Chapter 41, Augustine compared the teachings of the prophets with the teachings of the philosophers. He admitted that the philosophers promoted some worthy values, such as virtue, love of country, and faithfulness in friendship. But the prophets urged such things not through controversy and argument, as the philosophers had, but through the divine voice speaking through them. The fact that they were in agreement with each other without such unseemly discord convinced others that they spoke of "that which is not the mere cleverness of man, but the utterance of God."[182] In his address, Juan de Segovia made a similar point, explaining, "If two human intellects agree in a certain thing, it is certain that the knowledge does not come from themselves, but from their minds being illumined by a superior cause."[183] He elaborated that this is what occurred with the prophets, who predicted things their natural intellects could not have known, and even made these predictions in different times and places. The philosophers, on the other hand, contradicted each other.[184]

This is but one example of a discussion appearing in Segovia's work, and specifically in this section on the truth of the Christian religion as expressed in the Bible, that is quite similar to a passage from *The City of God*. Certainly the authority of scripture is one of the topics Augustine took up in this massive work, although he did not frame his thoughts in terms of twelve foundations of the walls of the city, which was the church militant, as Segovia did. Also, these reasons for the validity of scripture do not appear together in Augustine's work or in any readily identifiable list, even if there are scattered places where he wrote something one might suspect was the inspiration for one of Segovia's "foundations." It appears that Juan de Segovia, then a young professor at Salamanca, was studying a copy of *The City of God* precisely with the intent of culling from it anything he could find that argued for the authority of scriptures, and therefore for Christian revelation, which might persuade nonbelievers.

All these proofs of the authority of scripture, including the rationality of its contents and the truth of its prophecy, seem superfluous as something directed to a highly educated, Christian audience at the University of Salamanca. This would not be the case if he were expressly arguing that scripture was a more important source on Christian living than another source, such as canon law, for example. But he was arguing that scripture should be believed on basic Christian teachings about Christ and the history of God's actions in the world, hardly an assertion his audience would have regarded with suspicion. A clue to Juan's purpose in presenting these "foundations" might come from his remarks toward the end of his speech. There he wondered why God had allowed so many to perish, and added that only the Christian religion was revealed to be a way of salvation, and that it was rational and had a sure foundation, so that others could be convinced of it.[185] He also reminded his audiences that prelates and professed religious had a responsibility to nurture the faith of the simple Christian, and he added, "It is a most clear sign of negligence of their own salvation if any simple Christian should be ignorant of the article of the Trinity with which he daily considers himself signed."[186] It appears that, in the mid-1420s, Segovia was actively thinking about the need to promote the faith of Christians and bring non-Christians to this faith by means of persuasion. He was reciting these reasons for believing what scripture says not to convince his audience, but probably to give them "talking points" for discussions with nonbelievers and the uninformed baptized.

His instincts to reach for the Bible in arguing a variety of issues, which certainly marked his work at Basel, might have arisen out of that goal. Early on, he sensed that the way to persuade others of the validity of Christian teachings was to persuade them of the authenticity of the Bible's message. If the place of scripture in Juan de Segovia's thought is an area that invites further study, Juan is at least not unusual in this. Lesley Smith has noted that scholarship on universities has focused on theological treatises on the sacraments, *artes praedicandi*, and ecclesiological discussions. Nearly every aspect of medieval intellectual and university life has received more attention than the thinkers' use of scripture.[187]

It is possible that Juan's enthusiasm for the Bible and his interest in Franciscan authors had a common inspiration. The Franciscan Alvaro de Salamanca was a leading figure during his years in Salamanca, which were also years of active interest in scripture in Franciscan circles.[188] A document in the papal registers from 1419 mentions that Fray Alvaro had been the chair (*cátedra*) in biblical study there since 1411.[189] He was prominent enough to be appointed the dean of theology for life in a papal bull concerning the organization of theological studies at Salamanca.[190] He also argued for an increase in the salary of the chair in Bible studies, insisting that laborers in sacred theology, the vineyard of the Lord (or "princely vineyard": *vinea dominica*) and the queen of all the earthly sciences, should not live in degrading conditions.[91] If Alvaro de Salamanca was a leading figure among the theology faculty, and taught scripture when Juan was there, and in addition was an advocate for the dignity of the discipline of theology, he could have been highly influential in Juan's formation. It is even possible, as Benigno Hernández Montes speculated, that Segovia was Alvaro's substitute when the latter was at the Council of Constance and later in Rome on university business. We know that Juan acted as the chair in Bible sometime around then, and that Alvaro was away.[192] Did Alvaro influence Juan's biblical outlook? Was it under his influence that Juan became acquainted with Ockham and Scotus as well? Both are possible. Whatever Juan's reasons were for studying the Bible so closely, this biblical orientation characterized his thinking at the Council of Basel. Indeed, it was common among the Basel conciliarists, who enlisted the Bible to counter the arguments of the canon lawyers about authority in the church.[193]

—∾— Juan de Segovia left Salamanca in 1431 and, deeply involved in the Council of Basel, never returned. After more than two decades, his relations with former colleagues from his Salamanca days must have been strained, at best, and many of those he knew would have died or moved on. Nevertheless, his love for this place apparently endured time and separation. In 1457, near the end of his life, Juan had nothing but lavish praise for his alma mater. In the introductory section of his *Donatio*, which Benigno Hernández Montes called a "hymn to the excellencies of Salamanca," Juan wrote that in nowhere else in the Latin church did students have the opportunity to hear three lectures daily in theology. The university had twenty-five salaried professorships, in addition to sumptuous buildings and elegant classrooms. Members of the *studium* were so faithful to the apostolic constitutions by which they were governed that there was no need

for reform, as Juan reminded readers that he himself had argued before the Council of Basel. Salamanca's splendor led those in other nations to praise Spaniards and to promote the university's graduates to
prominent positions.[194]

Juan's energetic adulation for the university was a *captatio bene-*
volentiae intended to dispose his readers to accept the truth of his
subsequent assertions regarding himself and his relationship with the
university.[195] This was a delicate matter, since years earlier the university had formally denounced Juan and retracted his authority to represent Salamanca at the council. Upon learning of this reversal, Pope
Eugene IV expressed his pleasure at what he called the university's
"good disposition" shown in its decision to stand against those who
had "gone astray in the way of Satan." The Council of Basel, he declared, was an affront to God, a disgrace to the faith, a scandal for
Christians, and the ruin of souls by the sons of perdition. According
to Eugene IV, the university showed its prudence by disassociating itself from those who persisted in such waywardness.[196] It would have
taken all of Juan's considerable rhetorical skills to overcome the wariness with which the university community would have regarded any
communication from him after such an ignominious severance of his
ties with the *studium*. If, in the months before he died, Juan de Segovia
found himself recalling his years in Salamanca with pride and perhaps
some nostalgia, he had good reason. After all, he had spent twenty-
four years at the university. Those years were apparently good ones,
good enough to overcome any hostility or hurt he experienced following the university's later repudiation of him and his conciliarist
positions.

Chapter Two —⚏—

CONTACT, CONVERSATIONS, AND CONVERSION

Early Thought on Islam

How Likely Was It That Juan de Segovia Knew Muslims in His Youth?

In his old age, Juan de Segovia held a view of Muslims that was remarkably sympathetic and counted a prominent Muslim scholar, Yça Gidelli, among his correspondents. Although he wanted Muslims to be converted, he was adamant that Christians must achieve this goal through peaceful means. Even in the shock that followed the Ottomans' seizure of Constantinople in 1453, he argued vigorously against war. An obvious and important question is that of how much this stance originated during the early part of his life, when he had the opportunity to interact with Muslims regularly in Castile. It would bring considerable satisfaction to trace his fairly empathetic attitude toward them to specific and sustained contacts with Muslims in his youth, which would likely imply family connections. How satisfying it would be to learn that the leading conciliarist at Basel was the son of a family of converts from Islam, or even to show regular commercial ties between his extended family and a group of

Muslim merchants living in the Spanish kingdom. Alas, existing records do not permit such nicely drawn connections.

In fact, one suggestion of a connection between Juan's family and the Muslim community disappears upon closer examination. Cabanelas wrote that Yça told Juan that he agreed to travel to Aiton in part because of the scholar's regard for Juan's relatives.[1] However, the document cited by Cabanelas, a copy of Yça's letter to Juan, in fact does not support even such an ambiguous connection between the renowned Muslim scholar and Segovia's family network. Gidelli referred to "your noble virtues" in two places in his letter. Cabanelas apparently understood the second person plural pronouns to refer to a group's virtues. But since Yça used this construction throughout the letter, not once addressing the recipient in the singular, it appears that he was simply referring to Juan himself in these phrases.[2]

I begin this chapter with a discussion of Castile's Muslim population, first a brief look at their history in the kingdom and then at the conditions prevailing during the time of Juan de Segovia's youth and young adulthood. This history, along with Segovia's own reports of interactions with Muslims, suggest that contact with them would have been fairly commonplace, but that knowledge about the religious beliefs of the other faith was nonetheless not as widespread as such contact might lead us to believe. I also show that Segovia's interest in Islam and how to approach Muslims predated both the events of 1453 and his participation in the Council of Basel. Some have stated or implied that his interest in matters Islamic began at Basel through his contact with Nicholas of Cusa, who loaned him a copy of a translation of the Qur'ān along with some other works related to Islam,[3] but this is clearly not true. In his study of Segovia's approach to Islam, Darío Rodríguez Cabanelas focused exclusively on his later works. Although he discussed two pivotal encounters between Segovia and members of the Muslim community in 1431, he did not explore the two *repetitios* of 1426 and 1427, discussed in the last chapter. Although these works have received almost no attention from scholars, they provide important information about the trajectory of Segovia's thinking on these issues. In this chapter I show that Juan de Segovia had been actively thinking about the problems presented by non-Christians as early as the mid-1420s. Moreover, his thought about Muslims and also Jews was linked, early on, to his interest in church renewal and reform.

Though no specific information links Juan de Segovia to the kingdom's Muslim community, the history of this religious minority in Castile provides necessary background for understanding Juan's knowledge of this group. Nevertheless, the history of the Mudéjars (subject Muslims) of Old Castile in the period that interests us has not been written, only sketchily outlined. This has not been for lack of interest from historians, at least not in recent generations. The scarcity of documentation related to this community, disheartening even for those accustomed to working in a period not particularly rich in archival sources, has constrained them.[4] Though in practically any foray into the archives of a Castilian city a researcher will come across a number of Jews in the documents, Muslims appear much less frequently. The records contain fewer business transactions with Muslim participants, few lawsuits, and to my knowledge no wills produced by Muslims. This is largely because Mudéjars were more likely than their Christian and Jewish counterparts to live in rural areas and small towns, whereas most paperwork was generated in cities, and because often they were poor and hardly typical clients for the notaries.

Most Muslims living in Old Castile when this area was taken by Christian forces over the course of the tenth and eleventh centuries either migrated south or were gradually absorbed into the majority Christian population. With the exception of large concentrations in a few places, by the thirteenth century the majority of Castile's Muslims were captives or descendants of captives, and they practiced diverse occupations. As a conquered people and recent immigrants, they often settled in the outskirts of cities or in villages in the countryside, where they provided agricultural labor. Serafín de Tapia Sánchez speculated that over the course of the thirteenth century, Muslim artisans from Toledo might well have migrated to Segovia or Avila, which were then growing, in search of more opportunities to ply their trades.[5] In any case, financial records suggest that by 1293 the *morerías*, or Muslim districts, of Avila and Segovia held a respectable number of people. Both *morerías* were assigned a tax of 6,515 *maravedis* annually, while those of Palencia and Burgos owed 5,671 and 1,092, respectively.

A census conducted of Avila's inhabitants in 1303 revealed that, of those whose religious affiliation was indicated, 68 percent were Christian, 22 percent Jewish, and 10 percent Muslim. It is important to note that these lists contained the names of those living in houses belonging to the cathedral. The proportion of Muslims residing in less central areas probably would have been higher.[6]

The beginning of the fourteenth century brought growing disparities in the conditions of the various Mudéjar populations in Castile. Fairly consolidated and vibrant Muslim districts existed in cities where the socioeconomic circumstances led the local oligarchy to protect them, but the communities weakened and diminished in the absence of these incentives. Tapia Sánchez counted Avila, Arévalo, and possibly Segovia among the first group.[7] A labor shortage following the mid-century plagues led to a more benevolent attitude toward the Mudéjar presence. In 1369, for example, Enrique II instituted several measures that were favorable toward this minority. The king reinstated the office of the *alcalde mayor de los moros de Castilla*, a prestigious administrative and judicial position over all Muslims in the realm, and he lifted restrictions on land ownership for his Muslim subjects. It simply was more important to keep them in Castile than to exploit and accentuate religious differences.[8]

Historians generally consider the decades bridging the fourteenth and fifteenth centuries as a time during which conditions worsened for the kingdom's Muslim communities. The Cortes of 1385 and 1389 imposed new restrictions, and a new tax was levied on Muslims and Jews in 1388, adding to the higher taxes they already paid in comparison to Christians. Tapia Sánchez suggested that Juan I (1379–90) might have been inspired to raise Muslims' taxes by the fact that John of Gaunt, the duke of Lancaster who claimed the Castilian throne on the basis of marriage connections, was receiving assistance from the kingdom of Granada.[9] This does not explain the fact that the new taxes applied to Jews, too, and that the king was constantly endeavoring to extract more money from the cities as well.[10] It seems more likely that Juan I simply found himself acutely in need of money, from anywhere he could obtain it, for the war against Portugal and its English allies.

The minority of Juan II (1406–19), which roughly coincided with Juan de Segovia's youth, saw a renewal of war with Granada, which began in 1407 and lasted until 1411 or 1412. This was the immediate context for the restrictive measures promulgated jointly by Fernando de Antequera and Queen Catalina de Lancaster, coregents for Juan II. Their Ordenamiento of 1408 obligated Muslims, but not Jews, to wear distinctive dress.[11] Miguel-Ángel Ladero Quesada has noted that these wars marked a new turn in the kingdom's relations with Granada. The politically ambitious sought through these military campaigns to smooth the kingdom's internal divisions and to coax more money from the Cortes and the clergy.[12] The campaign to resume a crusading war in 1407 found a strong advocate in Fernando de Antequera, but opposition from Catalina, the mother of the future king Juan II. It is quite possible that Juan de Segovia knew of this disagreement between the two regents. In February of 1407, the two delivered opposing addresses before the Cortes gathered in Segovia.[13]

As this latest round of wars with Granada was ending, the influential Dominican Vincent Ferrer was traveling throughout Castile urging conversion to Christianity (particularly for Jews) and separation between Christians and members of other religious communities. Following in the footsteps of other mendicant preachers who preached against the Jews in the late fourteenth century, Ferrer preached throughout the kingdom in 1411 and visited the royal court at Ayllón. He had been a chaplain of Pope Benedict XIII in Avignon, who counted Catalina de Lancaster among his ardent supporters. This connection may have led to his invitation to the royal court. In any case, the message that he preached was that Jews and Muslims should be kept separate from Christians lest dealings with them harm the Christians, especially the newly baptized.[14] On January 2, 1412, Catalina promulgated a new and more restrictive set of rules governing virtually every aspect of interaction between Christians and Jews or Muslims. According to her 1412 decrees, members of the minority religions had to live in separate sections of the cities, and they were forbidden to be physicians or pharmacists or to attend social events with Christians. City officials throughout the kingdom implemented the royal decrees with varying degrees of energy and effectiveness.[15]

Ferrer attracted large crowds in both Castile and Aragon and was something of a public sensation. In 1411 he preached in Salamanca, where Segovia could certainly have heard him.[16] By his own admission, Juan de Segovia was an admirer, even referring to himself as a one-time "disciple" of the popular preacher in a letter he wrote in 1456 to a hermit who had asked him for spiritual advice. Along with his letter, he sent along a copy of the *Tractatus consolatorius in temptationibus circa fidem*, which he described as a work by Ferrer, although scholars are not certain of its authorship.[17] The inventory of his works compiled for his *Donatio* also included a copy of this work, in addition to a volume containing some sermons by Ferrer.[18] In his history of the Council of Basel, Segovia recounted that he himself had reminded the assembly, during a discussion on the princes' obligation to try and convert those in their realm, of the preaching of Ferrer and its success in Castile in 1412. Sigismund had asked the council to work for the "reduction" and conversion from error of those in his kingdom, and the council was debating proposals for how to address this. The *Historia* records part of the discussion:

> The bishop of Friuli, ambassador of King Ludvig of Sicily, rose and said that the council must attend to the fact that the princes might not consent to the clause stipulating that the Jews will retain upon baptism the goods that they previously owned; indeed his lord, the king of Sicily, whenever they converted, would keep the goods, and though he more often made a generous donation to them, so for that reason [the bishop] urged that there should be no mandate to that effect under the penalty of anathema contained in the decree, but still exhortations could be made. The legate responded to him that the kings are not, simply because they are kings, lords of the goods that their subjects possess, as if they could dispose of them at will, since, if the Jews did not have their property seized while they remained in Judaism, how much less [should this happen] once they were converted to Christ. And besides, in these matters, since they concerned the faith, the church should attend not to the convenience of the princes but to the increase of the faith, and since, if their goods were to be confiscated, it would clearly lead to a hesitation to take up

the faith, it was fitting that the church take precautions. But Master Juan de Segovia, prefacing with the fact that the aforementioned bishop's proposition involved Christian leaders, said that, based on what he knew about the king of Castile, the form of the decree should not be changed, for the reason mentioned. In [Castile], when Jews were converted to the faith, not only were their goods not taken away, but many of them were made rich by [the king's] largesse; and when Master Vincent of holy memory preached before the king around the year 1412, arguing on many grounds for the conversion of the Jews, so that they might be converted in greater numbers, [the king] granted to all who would be baptized exemption from all payment of royal debts for ten years, and this exemption of theirs was respected.[19]

I have not found any corroboration of this tax exemption for the recently converted in the wake of Vincent Ferrer's preaching. Nonetheless, the passage offers further confirmation that Ferrer's preaching had attracted Segovia's attention.

However, if the young Segovia took any ideas about converting non-Christians from the Dominican preacher, he did not accept them outright. For one thing, Ferrer's overriding focus was the conversion of Jews, who were forced to listen to his sermons. Although he spoke critically of the forced conversions that had swept Castile in 1391, during which many Jews were terrorized into accepting baptism, his preaching inflamed public sentiment against Jews and sparked violence against them. He also advocated excommunication for Christians who still associated with Jews.[20] As chapter 5 will discuss at more length, Juan de Segovia appears not to have had any interest in converting Jews, and he certainly had no reservations about contact with non-Christians, at least with Muslims. He even sought it out. Conversely, his contemporaries, including Ferrer, showed little interest in converting Muslims. It would be another century before there was any organized attempt to convert Muslims.[21]

Segovia left little indication of what he thought of Ferrer's preaching or of the violence against Jews that had occurred twenty years earlier in the 1391 pogroms. There is no mention of the violence attending

Ferrer's preaching, either. This could be because that aspect of the conversions and their aftermath was not immediately relevant to the discussion at Basel, or it could be that he chose not to see it. In any case, this brief reference to events in Castile two decades earlier leaves us longing for a fuller record of his thoughts about Ferrer's preaching and its effects.

Similarly, Juan de Segovia must have known of the disputations held at Tortosa in neighboring Aragon in 1413–14, which the *converso* Jerónimo de Santa Fe, who converted in the wake of Ferrer's preaching, convinced the pope to sponsor. Aragon's Jewish communities were required to send delegates to debate with Jerónimo. After these debates, many more Jews, more demoralized than inspired, were baptized.[22] In his letter to Jean Germain in the winter of 1455, Segovia reflected on how the truth of Christianity had been proven repeatedly over more than fourteen hundred years because it had been tested in many debates (he used the word *disputacionibus*), beginning with Stephen and Paul, then as Christianity spread to Asia and Rome, through the time of the martyrs and persecutions, and now in the universities through the "public disputations on the mystery of the Trinity, the Incarnation, the sacrament of the Eucharist, and other truths of the faith."[23] In this part of his letter, he appears to have been trying to assure Germain that it would be possible to prevail in similar discussions with Muslims. It is interesting, especially since the Tortosa disputations were followed by many baptisms, that he did not refer to these public debates with Jews in his argument.

The situation of Muslims in Castile during the late fourteenth and early fifteenth centuries was less volatile than that of Jews. Although religious minorities were often in a vulnerable position, Jews received the brunt of the conversion efforts and the violence. And in this period we find that—Ferrer's preaching about the need for separation between Christians and non-Christians, royal decrees, and the tax increases notwithstanding—most signs point to the Mudéjars' continued presence in the region and to their routine participation in its social and economic life.[24] In September of 1390, for example, Juan I gave Cuéllar, an important town within the territory of Segovia, the right to hold two annual fairs. Those conducting business at the fairs were to be allowed safe passage and were not to be taken prisoner on account of any debt that they owed to a town council or an individual. The king specified that this assurance applied to everyone: men and women, Christians, Jews, and Muslims.[25] In 1411 a synod in Burgos lamented that in spite of the fact that church leaders had repeatedly stipulated that Jews and Muslims should not live among Christians, this was still happening.[26] Christians appear to have violated more rules than just the one about living in proximity to Muslims and Jews. In 1438, Pope Eugene IV delegated to the archbishop of Toledo the responsibility for absolving Castilians from the sin of giving food, arms, or bandages to the Saracens. He conceded this power, normally reserved to the pope, at the request of Juan II. The king argued that, for his subjects, the journey to Rome was long and expensive, leaving many with no means to be absolved of this sin.[27] Documents indicate that in 1474 some Mudéjars still lived within Segovia's city walls.[28]

One testament to contact between religious communities, and even to a certain fluidity between them, is Clemente Sánchez's *Sacramental*, written between 1421 and 1423 to help educate priests about the proper celebration of the sacraments. In the course of a discussion on situations that dissolve the bonds of marriage, Sánchez elaborated in some detail on the specifics of how a marriage might be abrogated or invalid if the couple were of different faiths or one of them was a heretic. He mentioned that *palabras de futuro*, a public promise to marry, could be made with the stipulation that a party that was not Christian would become Christian before the marriage took place. If that happened and the couple married as two Christians, they would avoid a host of complications, but if things were not so simple, Sánchez stood ready with detailed guidance. Sánchez's advice is fascinating, not least because harsh penalties, including death, theoretically awaited those who engaged in sexual intercourse between Christians and non-Christians. As Teofilo Ruíz has noted in his recent and helpful study of late medieval Spain, relations between members of the three religions were richer and more complex than the religious and legal prohibitions would suggest.[29]

Indeed, the range of possible marital complications envisioned by Clemente Sánchez is dizzying. For instance, if a Jewish or Muslim man were to convert to Christianity while already in a marriage to a non-Christian, he must remain in the marriage if there were any hope that his wife would convert. He was not to take a vow of celibacy or marry another woman. But if her resolve was hardened against converting, he was not obligated to stay with her. If a Jewish or Muslim man was married, "as is their custom," to a relative such as a sister, stepmother, or wife of his uncle and he later converted, the two could not remain married even if both became Christians. However, if the marriage was between people related in the third or fourth degree, as was permitted in the church, the marriage would remain in force if both converted or if one did and there remained a hope that the other might. If a Jewish or Muslim man had more than one wife before converting, after conversion he should have as a wife only the first of those, provided she agreed to convert. If she did not, he was free to marry one (only one) of the others who would. If a Jewish or Muslim man left his wife, married another woman, and then converted to Christianity, he was to return to the first wife. Sánchez even specified that if husband and wife were both Christian and one of them later converted to Judaism or Islam, which must have been rare, the other one was not free to marry again, even if they had never consummated their marriage, but was to live a celibate life.[30]

Whether Sánchez produced these guidelines himself or merely recorded practices at the time, mixed marriages and conversions were apparently frequent enough, despite all the prohibitions, to have prompted careful thought by church authorities about how to handle them. Equally clear is that Clemente Sánchez, a Salamanca-trained legal scholar, judged that his fellow priests and prospective readers in Castile needed this information.

Further clues regarding the contact between Christians and Muslims comes from none other than Yça Gidelli, the renowned *alfaquí mayor* (premier religious and legal scholar) of the Muslims of Castile who collaborated with Juan to produce the trilingual Qur'ān. Documents provide several different titles associated with Gidelli, and the authority structure among the Mudéjars of Old Castile is not well understood. Nonetheless, it is clear that Gidelli was a scholar of the Qur'ān who also served, at least for a time, as a judge in Segovia's

Muslim community. Some of his writings suggest that he was a Sufi.[31] Gidelli himself, in a letter to Juan de Segovia regarding the arrangements for his collaboration, informed the Castilian priest that traveling to Aiton would be an obstacle, saying, "There is no one here to replace me, for I have an office."[32] In 1462, only a few years after his return from Aiton, he wrote his *Breviario Sunni* outlining the essential beliefs and practices of Islam in Spanish for the benefit of his fellow believers who, increasingly, knew no Arabic and therefore could not read the traditional sources for themselves.

The first chapter of the *Breviario* discussed the main commandments and duties. Among them Gidelli included, "Be obedient to your father and mother, even if they are unbelievers."[33] This shows a clear recognition that conversions were not uncommon and even a certain resignation before this reality. He also urged good Muslims, "Be true to your lord, even if he is not a Muslim, since he will be your heir in the absence of an heir."[34] It appears that Muslims were not all living in the designated districts of their cities, since he stipulates that no one should live so far from the Muslim district that he could not easily travel to and from his house to the mosque every hour of the prescribed prayers. Nevertheless, he recognized that individual circumstances demanded flexibility on this and added, "And in this matter each one can see what is important to him in order not to fall short in the things pertaining to the service of Allah."[35] It was forbidden to pray in the houses of Christians or Jews, which were considered unworthy for it, but he encouraged readers that when it was unavoidable, they should at least put on clean clothes beforehand.[36] As in so many other places in the *Breviario*, he counseled compromise and accommodation in matters not pertaining to core beliefs and practices. The work consistently reveals its author's efforts to define faithfulness to a religious law that had to be lived in constant interaction with others who did not subscribe to it.

In addition to suggesting plenty of routine interactions between Muslims and non-Muslims, Gidelli's text reveals that he had even absorbed some aspects of the Christian religious language. He introduced his second chapter, for example, by announcing that it would explain what faith is and in what way it was the "salvation of the soul."[37] If four sons testified against their father, their testimony was inadmissible and they incurred "mortal sin."[38] He even recommended the novena, nine days spent in prayer and fasting in the mosque, as a good practice for Muslims.[39] Gidelli included guidelines for how to fulfill the requisite parts of a novena, and this without any suggestion that this was not a traditional Islamic practice. Either it had not occurred to him that it was not, or he knew that but nevertheless chose not to discourage the practice among his coreligionists.

Certainly the picture is not entirely one of shrinking Muslim populations restless under oppressive Christian rule. A telling legal dispute occurred in 1491, when the Muslim district of Segovia protested the resolution reached by Ferdinand and Isabel concerning a jurisdictional dispute over the office of the *alcalde mayor de las aljamas de moros* of the kingdom, a sort of chief judge for this community. The monarchs confirmed Don Abrahen Xarafi as their appointee and prohibited the Mudéjars Maestre Farax Beydeçi and Don Farax de Belvís from claiming this title. Farax de Belvís was given the lesser position of *alcalde* of the Muslims of the Guadalajara, and his decisions were subject to appeal to Xarafi as the *alcalde mayor*. The Muslims of Segovia objected to these appointments, explaining to the monarchs that for several decades they had not been subject to any *alcalde mayor*. For all this time, they had brought their disputes before the city's ordinary judge. According to documents they filed with the royal court, the Muslim community had been exempted from obedience to any *alcalde mayor* by King Enrique IV (1454–74) during a time of great upheaval and factions within that community, which had resulted in some thirty deaths. Since then, they said, they had lived peacefully under the legal jurisdiction of the city's Christian judge, and they requested that the present monarchs respect the decision of their predecessor and continue this proven arrangement.[40] It appears that, at least for roughly the second half of the fifteenth century, this important Castilian *aljama* was not especially eager to achieve and protect juridical autonomy, which suggests minimal conflict between Segovia's Muslims and the city's Christian majority and its elites.

New research continues to shed light on the status of Castile's Mudéjar communities. Though it is true that documentation is not as plentiful as one would like, enough exists to have prompted a challenge to earlier assessments of this community as uniformly rural, impoverished, and marginalized. This may have been true of many of the kingdom's Muslims, but it is increasingly clear that there was, indeed, a Muslim elite. Chronicles and fiscal records suggest that the Muslim *aljamas* were flourishing in the fifteenth century.[41] Toledo's Xarafi family, for example, was part of the urban oligarchy of that city. Abrahen Xarafi, whom Ferdinand and Isabel named as *alcalde mayor* in the 1491 document discussed above, was both a leading religious scholar in the Muslim community and the personal physician of the powerful archbishop of Toledo Alfonso Carrillo.[42] The Belvís family was an enormously wealthy and influential merchant family in Aragon throughout the fourteenth and fifteenth centuries, several members of which held the position of *alcalde mayor* of Valencia. In the mid-fourteenth century, prominent members of this family were engaged in diplomatic negotiations between the Aragonese and Granadan royal courts. After a branch of the Belvís established itself in Castile, the family's fortune rose in part through its association with a network of supporters that included men of such rank as the master of Santiago Alvaro de Luna and Diego Hurtado de Mendoza (1365?–1404).[43]

As for the renowned and erudite Yça Gidelli, Juan de Segovia's collaborator, there is no evidence that he belonged to one of these select families, the most elite Mudéjar power bases in the kingdom. However, given his renown and his erudition, we can surmise that his family, too, was one of means. Since he was a *faqīh* in Segovia when Segovia's Muslim community was under the jurisdiction of Toledo's *alcalde de moros*, we should also assume that he enjoyed the favor of the al-Qaysī family, prominent spice merchants. Indeed, it seems likely that he was the *alcalde* named Yça who was the delegate for *alcalde* Mahomad al-Qaysī around 1418.[44] If Juan de Segovia's family was among the rising Castilian oligarchy, there could well have been an acquaintance between his family and Gidelli's.

The preceding discussion leaves us with a helpful perspective on the state of Castile's Muslim population. Adherents to Islam were few, but certainly present in a wide spectrum of rural and urban populations. They were often but not always poor, and sometimes wealthy and well connected. Despite restrictive measures imposed in the early fifteenth century, Muslims were becoming increasingly assimilated. Leaders were concerned that few knew enough Arabic to read about their tradition in that language. Given this social milieu, we can surmise that Juan de Segovia would have seen Muslims in the course of his travels, business, and errands. It would have been natural for a Christian growing up in Castile to have encountered Muslims and formed impressions of them. Of course, what those impressions were and how much thought one gave to those Mudéjars trading in the markets or working on construction crews varied widely. Fortunately, Juan's writings offer clues concerning his own thoughts about them.

Juan's Observations and Thoughts Concerning Muslims During His Years in Castile

A letter Juan de Segovia wrote to the French theologian Jean Germain in December 1455 contains some general impressions that Segovia had of the Mudéjar community.[45] Germain had written to Segovia criticizing his proposals for achieving peace with the Muslims. That letter no longer exists, but in it Germain apparently pointed out that despite the regular contact between Christians and Muslims in Spain, where Muslims even held public office and inhabited extensive regions, scarcely one of them converted to Christianity every one hundred years. In his response to Germain, Juan de Segovia argued that he had not lived in his native city for a hundred years, and he had seen many conversions, even though the city's Muslim population consisted of no more than fifty people. Furthermore, he did not know of any Muslims who held public office with authority over Christians. They were, however, skilled artisans and good servants, ever eager to please. Due to this willing disposition, Juan wrote, many liked the Muslims more than they liked the Jews.[46]

He was even less receptive to Germain's reminder that wars against Muslims had long been launched by great kings and emperors, including in Spain. "As for those things that have been done in Spain, your lordship is speaking with a Spaniard," he retorted. From the forty years he had spent in his native land, he continued, he knew about the wars against the Muslims undertaken there, including those waged in the past, since he had heard and read much about them. Nevertheless, he had long thought that Christians should pursue the conversion of the Muslims through peaceful means (*via pacis et doctrine*).[47] Germain could not hope to convince him otherwise.

Germain apparently also argued that Christians in Muslim lands were highly susceptible to conversion to Islam. This may have been a way to argue that Christians should not be eager to enter Muslim lands for the purpose of the theological exchanges that Segovia envisioned. In any case, the Castilian questioned Germain's concerns about Christians converting. He said that not one in ten Christians in Saracen lands converted, even when they were offered beautiful young girls, wealth, and the favor of the king of Granada as incentives. There probably were few Christians in Segovia's day who had taken up residence in Granada, and the weakened Nasrid rulers of that kingdom were not generally inclined to aggressive conversion efforts.[48] This incentive plan that Juan mentioned to Germain could not have been common. The reader can only wonder if his response is a reference to a theme from legends or poetry rather than daily reality.

There is nothing surprising in Juan's recollections recounted here. They confirm the general outline of the social situation in Castile as told above. But there is more, and it allows us to address more searching questions about his thought: How well did he know and understand Muslims' beliefs? How much interest did he have in Islam during his years at Salamanca? How did he apply his impressive theological formation to the questions the other religion posed for Christianity?

Some important clues emerge in the university addresses (*repetitios*) he delivered in 1426 and 1427. As indicated in the last chapter, these are the earliest extant records of his thought and the only works by Juan that survive from his years at Salamanca. These works have received almost no attention from scholars.[49] I am not aware of any who have examined them for information on his early approaches to Islam. The *repetitios* demonstrate that Juan had been thinking about Muslims for several years before the 1431 exchanges, and thus they add credibility to his later comment that he had been mulling over the question of Islam for many years. His interest originated long before the events of 1453 pressed the issue upon Western leaders, and well before Basel colleague Nicholas of Cusa loaned him a copy of the Qur'ān.[50] The two *repetitios* provide a fascinating glimpse of an intellectual grappling with questions presented to him by his Castilian milieu.

Juan's 1426 *repetitio* on papal authority, discussed in the previous chapter, contains little regarding Muslims or their beliefs, but it is nonetheless illuminating. Some passages reveal what we might call an attitude of inclusivity toward the Muslims, although the context in which this appears would strike most modern readers as more intrusive than inviting. This section occurs in the manuscript after a long defense of the plenitude of papal power in all affairs. Juan expanded this to insist that the pope even had power over the infidels and gentiles, a point he argued was proven by the verse in John 10 in which Jesus said, "I have other sheep that are not of this flock, and it is fitting for me to lead them." Thus the pope had the authority to punish violations of the natural law committed by anyone, even gentiles, pagans, or barbarians. Further scriptural confirmation came from Genesis 19, in which God punished the Sodomites for their sins against the law of nature. God could also punish all idolaters, since the law of nature led people to believe that God is one and to worship God alone (Romans 1). Juan argued that this applied to the infidels, who refused to admit Christian preachers into their lands even though every rational creature is made for the praise of God. Indeed, Psalm 116 urged, "Praise God, all you peoples," and, "Let every spirit praise the Lord." Therefore the refusal to allow preachers was grounds for the declaration of a just war against the infidels.[51] As an elderly man, Juan would retreat from this justification for war and state unequivocally that it had no place in the preaching of the gospel. It is noteworthy that, war talk and papal power issues aside, even here he counted Muslims as "rational creatures" destined to praise God, and he considered Jesus to have claimed them as part of his flock.

One wonders whether he realized the full implication of a comment he made later in his address. In a discussion of papal authority and how various individuals could be subject to another, he explained that there were two ways in which a person could be subject to someone else: due to the merit of humility or due to the debt of obligation.

In accordance with humility, he said, "Every soul should humble itself to every human creature in so far as in it shines the image of God."[52] He did not explicitly mention Muslims or other non-Christians here, but neither did he limit himself to the baptized as people in whom God's image shone. "Every human creature" (*omni humanae creaturae*) is somewhat emphatic and seems a deliberate word choice.

Muslims appear more explicitly about one folio later. In this part of his address, Juan was answering an objection he posed, that temporal power did not reside in the pope because Jesus himself never claimed an earthly throne, in spite of the fact that people urged him to. To answer this objection, Segovia presented four reasons why Jesus never claimed earthly power. The third was that if he had taken up his kingdom, the Christian faith would not have been freely and sincerely embraced by people, as indeed was the case with the law of Muhammad, which began by the sword and was still sustained by it.[53] Juan thought that Jesus would hardly have wanted such a fate to befall his message.

If Muslims appeared only intermittently in Juan's address in July 1426, this was not the case in the *repetitio* he delivered the following May, *De fide catholica*, discussed in the previous chapter. In planning his address, Juan chose a text from Book 3, Distinction 25, of the *Sentences* on which to expound. In this text, Juan explained, Peter Lombard strove to establish the sufficiency of universal faith regardless of a person's status or walk of life.[54] Not surprisingly, he spent a considerable amount of time reminding his listeners of the various ways Christian thinkers have defined and discussed faith. No one, he said, will attain eternal salvation who does not have faith, hope, and love in the present life. But hope is the certain expectation of eternal happiness.[55] Faith by its very nature exceeds the faculty of the human intellect.[56] Instead, the will, informed by reason, must direct the intellect to believe.[57] Borrowing the late medieval distinction between acquired and infused faith, he discussed the differences between the two and explained that only infused faith is truly faith.[58] This led him to the assertion that faith, which creates believers, is "a certain spiritual virtue or gift of the Holy Spirit, infused freely by God, by which illustration the human mind assents by firm adhesion to those things which are beyond its faculty, to truths revealed by God in sacred scripture."[59] According to Augustine, faith was "the illumination of the mind to the highest truth,"[60] and Paul described it in Hebrews 11 as "the substance of things hoped for, the conviction of things unseen."[61] It is, furthermore, "the foundation of the entire spiritual edifice, that is, of all the virtues ordained to the attaining of eternal happiness."[62] Faith is the first of all the virtues.[63]

In the course of discussing the complexities of faith, Juan included comments about both Jews and Muslims. Sometimes he used the other faith communities as handy examples, as when he explained that people sometimes come to believe something by hearing it from people they trust. For example, a Jewish boy or another non-Christian who is raised among Christians and taught about their faith will come to believe it.[64] Similarly, one believes what others say about his father, and many believe that the city of Jerusalem and the holy sepulchre exist even though they have never seen them.[65] The Jews also served as an example of acquired faith, since they believed in the authors of sacred scripture merely because their fathers did, and they were unmoved by miracles and persuasion to accept the Christian faith. They said that they wanted to die in the law of their fathers.[66] In this case, too, Segovia mentioned the Jews because they provided a helpful illustration for his discussion on the differences between acquired and infused faith, which he concluded one page later.

Later in his address, his references to Jews and Muslims were less incidental. He invited his fellow academics to notice how their own faith found support in Jews and Muslims. Juan presented his listeners with what he called "the twelve foundations on which the wall of the city was erected"[67]—twelve reasons why they could be sure that what Christianity proclaimed was, in fact, true. Actually, he apparently lost track as he wrote, and his address contains only eleven such reasons. In the last chapter, I discussed how these foundations illustrated his reliance on scripture. Our attention here will fall on what this part of his *repetitio* reveals about his thinking about Jews and Muslims.

The sixth foundation, for example, was the testimony of unbelievers. If someone were to ask a Jew which of the other two religions he considered more true, Juan explained, he would certainly respond that Christianity was, and that the other was meaningless and fabulous.

A Muslim would respond in the same way. According to Juan, this is why any non-Christian who was considering abandoning his religion or who was facing death would often convert to Christianity.[68] Although conversions to Islam from both Judaism and Christianity were not uncommon historically in Muslim lands, Segovia understandably seemed to have contemporary Christian Iberia in mind as he made these observations.

The seventh foundation was "divine inspiration," which might lead a modern reader to expect a discussion of scripture as revelation, or perhaps the saints' writings as inspired. Instead, Juan cited the example of the many Jews and others who had converted to Christianity because God had moved them to assent to this faith. If an unbeliever, with due reverence for God, strove to avoid evil works and prayed daily asking God to illumine his soul and show him which faith to follow, God would not delay in responding. Before long, Juan asserted, this earnest seeker would "sense in his heart that which he accepted with a free mind." Having inspired this acceptance, God would preserve him firmly in his new faith.[69] So the divine inspiration that Juan presented as the seventh foundation of the Christian faith was specifically the inspiration to become Christian. The fact that others converted to Christianity was a sign of its validity. One would not know, from reading Segovia's account of how these conversions came about, that Jews in his day had been subject to pressure to convert. A good number of the *conversos* in Castile during these years would have accepted baptism, or descended from those who had, in the wake of the pogroms of 1391. Segovia's address envisioned only free seekers of God, whose illumination enabled them to see the truth of their heart's growing inclinations toward Christianity.

The tenth of the twelve (actually eleven) reasons his Christian listeners could be sure that their faith was true was the irrationality of discordant beliefs and heresies. Segovia stated that followers of Muhammad gave free reign to their sexual appetites and anticipated an eternal happiness consisting of "carnal and fetid delights." Jews, for their part, taught that God weeps daily over the destruction of the Temple, and that his tears fill the sea.[70] According to Juan, the irrationality of such beliefs lent tacit support to the Christian faith. As noted in the last chapter, the irrationality of other beliefs is one of the items listed on the page that may contain his notes for this *repetitio*, in which he repeatedly cited Augustine's *City of God*. In those notes, pagans seem to have been the irrational ones he had in mind, and if he was taking notes from Augustine, that would be expected. If he derived part of his thinking on this issue from Augustine, Segovia's expansion on this theme to Jews and Muslims is an interesting example of a thinker processing what he was reading from Christian classics and applying it to his own context.

While Jews and Muslims often appear together in the *repetitio*, Juan reserved for Muslims harsh criticism that found no parallel in his comments on Jews. Near the end of his address, he dedicated two entire columns to ways in which Islam differed from Christianity. It is striking how consistently the characteristics of Islam he listed repeated the standard Western criticisms of this rival religion. He explained, for example, that unlike Christianity, which was contrary to the law of nature,[71] the law of Muhammad was inclined toward the gratification of sexual impulses.[72] Those who originally accepted this religion were "bestial men living in deserts, completely ignorant of divine teaching."[73] He noted that the sect originated and spread through violence, and that its teachings derived no support from reason, miracles, or credible authority, but instead relied upon the sword for their defense.[74] Furthermore, Muhammad prohibited his followers from reading sacred scripture "lest his sect be unmasked for its falsity."[75]

Curiously, Juan attributed the rise of Islam in part to the pride and avarice of the Romans, who suppressed the eastern peoples as they did others, and thus incited them to rebellion. According to Segovia's understanding in 1427, "And then, seeing the growing discord between the eastern peoples and the Romans, Muhammad arose, presenting himself as [one] sent by God for their liberation from the yoke of the Roman Empire."[76] Plenty of medieval writers had accounted for the rise and spread of Islam by other means, most of the time presenting the Roman Empire in a positive light. According to one view of events, shared by many Western writers, the invading Arabs were the new Persians, the traditional foes of the Byzantine Empire, the successor of the original Roman Empire.[77] Though Segovia's version of events differed from this common line, he was not the only one to connect the rise of Muhammad to oppression by the Romans. This understanding of the origins of Islam appears in the *Additions* to the Apocalypse commentary of Nicholas of Lyra by Pablo de Santa María, also known as Paul or Pablo of Burgos or of Cartagena (1351–1435). This influential edition of the commentary was written between 1429 and 1431, and it circulated widely.[78] The idea of Muhammad liberating easterners oppressed by Rome is also echoed in the work of another of Segovia's contemporaries in the *Invencionario* of Alfonso de Toledo, written around 1467.[79] Alfonso de Toledo could easily have read this in the work of Pablo de Santa María. Regardless of where all three of these writers learned this, it obviously reveals a faulty knowledge of history and of Muhammad's rise. This inaccuracy did not reappear in Juan de Segovia's later writings on Islam. The aged Segovia remained troubled by the violence and lasciviousness he associated with the spread of Islam, but by then he had abandoned this notion that it originated as a rebellion against Roman oppression.

The reader is left with the impression of an earnest and rigorous thinker who was struggling actively with issues that concerned him deeply: the nature of faith, how one can know that faith claims are true, and whether it was necessary for all peoples to come to Christianity. At several points in his *repetitio,* he seemed to be anticipating efforts to persuade nonbelievers.

He noted, for instance, that he had established that God had shown the way for salvation, but it remained to ask whether this faith was the only way to salvation. If this address was intended merely to praise the benefits of faith for a Christian audience, this would be an odd question to ask. He said, "I say 'only' because, since as commonly all sects agree in some way and differ in another, so nevertheless they differ because such diversity is with regard to one or more aspects."[80] Jews and Christians, he pointed out, share a belief in one God who is creator and ruler, and yet they differ concerning a redeemer because Christians believe the redeemer has already come, while Jews still await one.[81] Since two contraries cannot be true, he concluded that if the truth of Christianity could be shown, it must be admitted other faiths could not be true.[82]

Similarly, he observed that Jews and Muslims were just as firmly convinced of the truth of their faiths as Christians were of theirs, and he recognized the problem this posed for his argument. He knew that he could not use the fact that Christianity had endured so long and been embraced by so many as proof of its legitimacy. As he explained to his listeners, few Christians quibbled with the statement that the sect of the Jews was without reason (*ratione*), but Jews nevertheless held to that faith with stubborn affection (*pertinaci affectione*). He observed that the same was true of numerous heresies that had arisen since the time of Christ, and Muslims held to their faith just as firmly as the Christians did to theirs, and there certainly were a lot of Muslims. This prompted Juan to wonder how so many had come to accept Islam in the first place. It would seem that either they believed without the testimony of any miracles, which he considered doubtful, or they believed because of miracles.[83]

But if there were miracles associated with the origin of Islam, Juan would have had quite a difficult time arguing that this faith was not a way revealed by God. There would have been one more thing to add to the list of things that were true of all three of these faiths: endurance through time, lots of firmly convinced believers, and now miracles. Why, then, should only one faith be worthy of anyone's allegiance? In fact, it was precisely this question of the role of miracles and what caused Muslims to embrace their faith that led him into his discussion of the ways that Christianity and Islam differ, discussed above. He concluded that it was *not* that miracles provided confirmation of the teachings of Islam, but that people accepted these teachings because they promised a reward to those who followed their sexual instincts.[84] In emphasizing what he saw as the immorality of Islam's beginnings, he found the additional proof he needed that Christianity was, indeed, the true faith. Thus the denunciations of Islam that he included, reiterations of stock Western beliefs though they were, were hardly gratuitous, and they served a startling purpose in this *repetitio*. They were the means by which Juan extricated himself from a line of reasoning that would have left him no choice but to admit that every faith has some truth to it. By implication, Christians could not be sure theirs was any truer than the others.

The trajectory of his reasoning here—that all believers assert their faith to be the true one, so that it had to be proven that Christianity was the only way to God—might at first glance seem a rhetorical exercise or an idiosyncratic turn. Many modern students of this period might think it inconceivable that a Christian writer in late medieval Castile could entertain the notion that perhaps every religion has some truth. Yet Stuart Schwartz has admirably explored the presence of just such a belief among common people living in Iberia, not exactly during Juan de Segovia's time there, but not so much later.[85] Inquisition records from Soria and Osma from 1490–1502 contain stories of a farmer who asked, "How does anyone know which of the three laws God loves best?" and two peasant women who offered that a good Jew would be saved, just as a good Muslim, for "why else would God make them?"[86] Schwartz points out that such views emerge in the records from *conversos* and Old Christians alike. As he observes, studies on tolerance often focus on a particular thinker, invariably a member of the educated elite, but lack a consideration of the milieu that produced them.[87] Strains of tolerance existed "deep in Christian thought" or could arise from "a kind of simple common sense," and these contributions from the masses need to be incorporated into the history of toleration.[88] I am certain that if we knew more about the common people's ideas about other faiths, it would enrich any understanding of the sources and development of Juan de Segovia's thought. Unfortunately, the early fifteenth century lacks the rich Inquisition sources that Schwartz uses to such profit. Nonetheless, his study of religious tolerance articulated by common people beginning a few decades after Segovia's time in Castile at least cautions against dismissing Segovia's discussion about the claims of different faiths as idiosyncratic or a mere detour in his argument. This could have been an active issue in the wider society, and that context could have contributed to his curiosity about other faith traditions.

It is no accident that Juan focused on Islam in this part of his discussion. It was easier to account for why so many Jews clung tenaciously to another faith; they were simply stubborn in their loyalty to a law that had been rendered outdated by the coming of Christ. Also, there were fewer of them. Muslims posed a greater challenge and thus set a higher bar for someone striving to prove that Christianity was true.

Segovia's deft negotiation of his quandary about how members knew their faith was true did not prevent him from distancing himself from his own argument enough to question the assertions he was making. If Islam encouraged its adherents to yield freely to their sexual impulses, nevertheless a few individual Muslims could be found who had less intense natural desires and who, following the dictates of perfect virtue, abstained from such carnal pleasures. For that matter, in spite of Christianity's clear injunctions against such license, many Christians seemed to Juan to exhibit just as little restraint as Muslims did.[89] And what about the signs and wonders he offered as testimony that Christianity was divinely revealed? Was it not said that the Antichrist would perform signs and wonders, too? As an answer to this counterargument, Juan reminded his listeners that the possibility that the devil was behind the miracles had arisen in encounters narrated in scripture, and it had not rendered the message false.[90]

In case they had not noticed one of Juan's objectives in delivering this *repetitio*, listeners heard it succinctly stated near the end of his address. He asked why divine providence had allowed so many to perish, and, bowing to timeless scholarly convention, hastened to declare that issue beyond the scope of the present discussion. Instead, it sufficed to declare that only the faith that Christianity preached was revealed by God as the path to salvation, and furthermore to declare that this faith was reasonable (*racionabile*) and had a certain foundation, so that others might be convinced and thus attain that happiness for which human beings are destined. Only in this way would those sects that diverged from the right path be directed to it.[91] After all, this faith had been the universal path to salvation since the beginning, since by the providence of God the gentiles had been saved.[92] It appears that among Juan's main intentions in delivering this address was to invite listeners to make eternal happiness available to all people by making it possible for all to accept the Christian faith. Concretely, this meant presenting it persuasively as both believable and divinely revealed.

Moreover, Juan linked his charge to the academics present, many of whom no doubt were clergy, to the broader task of fostering faith in those already baptized. Near the end of his address, he asserted that ecclesiastical leaders had responsibility for deciding or reconciling ambiguities in the faith, and it was their task, as well, to see that the simple Christians believed. In support of this exhortation, he cited two scriptural passages, from Malachi 2 and 1 Peter 3. The first text reads, "For the lips of a priest should guard knowledge, and the people should seek instruction from his mouth" (Malachi 2:7). The second urged, "Always be ready to make your defense to anyone who demands from you an accounting for the hope that is in you" (1 Peter 3:15).[93] He continued, noting that it was a most clear sign of negligence (*manifestissimum signum negligencie*) and a neglect of a priest's own salvation when a simple Christian was ignorant of the doctrine of the Trinity, with which he signed himself every day. A Christian must also know about the birth, passion, resurrection, and ascension of Christ, which were part of the faith of the universal church.[94] Segovia shared this concern with the quality of pastoral ministry with, among others, the Dominican Gonzalo de Alba, who had held the chair of prime in theology at Salamanca and served as bishop of the city early during Segovia's time there, from 1408 to 1412. In 1410, Alba had called a synod to address the state of pastoral leadership in the diocese.[95] It is possible that this had nourished Segovia's own thinking on the need for improving clerical leadership and strengthening the faith of the average Christian.

In any case, as early as 1427, the goal of inviting Muslims to eternal happiness and the cause of making the church itself more faithful to what it preached coalesced in the thought of Juan de Segovia. As we shall see, the link between these two goals was even more developed in his writings on Islam twenty years later.

In the years between his address at Salamanca in 1427 and his departure from Rome and thence to Basel (1431 or 1432), he had further occasion to reflect upon the possibility that Muslims might be won over to Christianity. One such occasion was a conversation he had in 1430. Over two decades later, Segovia wrote about this conversation in a letter to the Burgundian theologian Jean Germain, explaining that in August and September of that year he was in Córdoba conducting some business on the pope's behalf. In the course of his mission for Martin V, he met a bishop who had previously ministered to the Christian merchants and soldiers in Tunisia. The man told Juan about a drought that had stricken the land. The Saracens performed ceremonies to pray for rain, but none came. The desperate king asked the Christians, too, to pray for rain. The bishop replied that he would carry a cross in procession through the city and into the countryside, where he would celebrate Mass. The king's delegates responded that they would rather be hungry than see the cross of Christ processed through their city. After a few more days of drought, however, the Christians received permission to have their procession. The bishop enjoined on the Christians a period of fasting, confession, restitution, and reconciliation, and then proceeded with the procession and Mass. Down came the rain.[96]

When there was talk of this before the king, the bishop explained to the king and his assembled subjects, who were wavering in their loyalties, why God had heard the Christians rather than the Saracens. He told them that the events had confirmed one of the clever Saracens, presumably the one who had had the good sense to ask the Christians for help, rather than the sect of Muhammad itself. The God who had provided for the Christians with regard to the temporal things of this world would hardly confer an eternal reward on the Saracens in the other world.[97] And since the Qur'ān promised eternal joy (*beatitudinem*) to the Saracens for their good works, for those who know the book of their laws, an aforementioned difficulty seemed less urgent.[98] This "difficulty" was the seventeenth difficulty or objection that Germain had raised, to which Juan was now responding. Specifically, Germain suspected that if Christians were to pursue dialogue and the path of teaching (*viam doctrine*) with the Muslims, this would only fan the Muslims' fury and cause more aggression because they would see how great were the Christian monarchies and how much the Christians surpassed them in art, doctrine, and war.[99] This objection evaporated, Juan thought, when the Saracens found themselves face to face with the undeniable fact of the Christians' virtue. He wrote, "If they regard themselves as very great and the Christians as very excellent, let them prepare themselves, that they might hear the word of the discussion of peace from both sides forever."[100] Segovia apparently reasoned that since the Muslims already associated God's favor with good works, they would recognize that the Christians enjoyed this favor and therefore listen to them.

Juan's line of reasoning in addressing Germain's seventeenth counterargument was somewhat circuitous, but this story about the dramatic end to the drought served as an example in which contact with Christians created a possibility that Muslims would take Christianity seriously. It did not increase their animosity, as Germain suspected might occur. Though Juan's response seems a reach, for our purposes it is enough to notice that his conversation with the bishop who had served in Tunisia was memorable enough for him to press it into service in his letter over twenty years later. What he heard about Muslims from the unnamed bishop was that they were disinclined to let the Christians process a cross through their city, but also that they could waver in their faith when presented with indications that Christians were righteous.

In addition to the account Juan heard from this bishop, he recalled having heard of a man living somewhere across the seas (*in partibus ultramarinis*) who converted from Christianity to Islam. The man later appealed to Benedict XIII (Avignon 1394–1417) to allow him to return to the church with an assurance that he would face no penance for his apostasy. According to Juan, the pope, "attending to the honor of the church," did not consent.[101] Juan recounted this case, too, in his 1455 letter to Jean Germain, noting that he had heard about it during his youth. In this letter, Juan's recollection appears in a section in which he disputed Germain's contention that if Christians and Muslims met to discuss their differences, Christians would convert. Juan's point was that cases of Christians converting to Islam were rare. This one was one of only three that he knew about. Historically speaking, of course, Germain's point was not far-fetched. Over the centuries, many Christians living in Islamic lands had converted.[102] If Segovia was aware of that, he found it best not to bring it up in his argument with his Burgundian colleague. Since we do not have Germain's original letter, only Segovia's response, we do not know if Germain had introduced the issue of large-scale conversions over the years or only the hypothetical danger that apostasy might occur if an encounter were to take place. If he did enlist the historical loss of Christian communities in large areas of the world in his objections to Segovia's earlier letter, Segovia now chose to frame the discussion in the context of recent, known conversions, and he felt confident that the risk was minimal.

It is curious that the examples Juan presented about contact between Christians and Muslims did not come from his native Castile. This might have been because he was focusing on opportunities for conversion or at least for Muslims to learn about Christianity. Although his comments about Muslims in his 1427 *repetitio* suggest some familiarity with them, routine contacts were apparently not conducive to discussions of faith. Indeed, one of Germain's arguments was that daily interactions between people of the two faiths in such places as sub-Saharan Africa, Tunis, or Spain did not result in many conversions, so Juan's hopes for such encounters were misplaced. Segovia's answer to this was that those contacts did not lend themselves to the instruction of Muslims in the Christian faith. He pointed out that those involved were normally lesser mercenaries and boatmen or customs officials (*portitoribus*), who knew too little about the law of Christ or Muhammad to instruct anyone else.[103] Juan de Segovia appears to have had a passing familiarity with Muslims during his time in Castile, but it was not so extensive that reports he heard about others' experiences in their lands were superfluous. Years later, he remembered the account from the bishop and the report about the man seeking readmission to the church from Benedict XIII. And he had formed the impression that there was not much opportunity for meaningful exchanges about issues of faith.

This brings us to two important encounters reported by Darío Cabanelas Rodríguez in his *Juan de Segovia y el problema islámico* (1952). From Juan's later writings, we know that on two occasions in 1431, one successfully and the other not, the Castilian scholar sought to discuss points of theology and religious practice with educated Muslims. The first occurred in July, when Juan had traveled to Córdoba to resolve a matter for the university at the royal court. That spring, King Juan II had undertaken an expedition against the kingdom of Granada, which had been embroiled in a civil war since a 1419 coup. The famous battle of La Higueruela began July 1, 1430, and Castile prevailed but was not in a position to continue the campaign, so the kingdom reached a peace agreement with one of the leading aspirants to the position of emir of Granada, Yūsuf IV ibn al-Mawl (Abenalmao in the Castilian chronicles). Under this treaty, Yūsuf and the military leaders who supported him entered a state of vassalage to the Castilian king.[104]

In the very month in which these events occurred, Yūsuf was in Córdoba in the entourage of Juan II and found himself considering an unusual request from Juan de Segovia. Segovia requested that Yūsuf send his guard to him so that the Salamancan scholar could have a discussion with a learned Muslim about his beliefs. When the king's new vassal, the grandson of an earlier emir, responded that no Muslim dared to have such a discussion in Christian lands, Segovia offered to hold it secretly in one of their respective lodgings or out in the countryside where no one could hear them. In the 1455 letter to Jean Germain in which Juan recounted the incident, he recalled that the aspirant to the throne of Granada was taken aback by this unexpected proposal and admitted candidly that although there were cantors among them, there was no one qualified to discuss their religious laws.[105]

Juan's second and more successful attempt to engage a knowledgeable Muslim in such a discussion occurred in October of the same year, 1431. This time Segovia journeyed with a relative to Medina del Campo to meet with a Granadan ambassador who had business with the Castilian king, who had left Córdoba earlier that fall. Juan de Segovia discussed this encounter at some length in the work *De mittendo gladio*, which he wrote for Cardinal Juan de Cervantes over the years 1453 to 1457.[106] The purpose of Segovia's meeting was to inquire about the welfare of some friends from Córdoba who had been taken captive in the palace compound of the Alhambra in Granada. Reassured that his friends were being treated well, Juan asked the ambassador why he so often swore by God, implying that this struck him as irreverent. According to Darío Cabanelas Rodríguez, this was almost certainly a reference to the use of the phrase "por Dios" ("by God"), the Castilian equivalent of an Arabic phrase frequently used in conversation. According to Juan's account of this meeting, his question prompted a lengthy discussion in which the Muslim railed against the Christians for their polytheism, among other things, and Juan attempted to explain the Christian doctrines of the Incarnation and the Trinity in a way that would make sense to his skeptical interlocutor. Juan later wrote that the ambassador finally exclaimed that there was no one among the Christians except for his present interlocutor who knew how to explain these things. Furthermore, after that initial encounter, the Granadan came to visit Juan many times to continue their conversation, on one occasion bringing along a Spanish legal scholar (*alfaquí*) who happened to be at the Castilian court.[107]

After Juan's thwarted attempt at such a discussion in July in Córdoba, one wonders whether the imprisoned friends were just a pretext for initiating a discussion that he must have known would not have been received well if he had proposed it outright. If he went to the lodgings of this ambassador perhaps in fact concerned about the captives in the Alhambra but also hopeful for a more involved conversation, asking first about the man's ready use of "por Dios" was an astute move. It was, in effect, a way of asking about Muslim customs that would not have seemed like a formal inquiry or a challenge to debate. Probably not knowing in advance the level of the ambassador's familiarity with Islamic law, Juan might even have posed such a question as a probe and an opening for the man to reveal his level of knowledge. Whether through dumb luck or through some delicate maneuverings on his part, Juan de Segovia finally had his theological discussion with a Muslim at least learned enough to familiarize him with the standard Muslim criticisms of Christianity and apparently to follow Juan's own attempts to explain the Christian Trinity. If Juan's account is true, their conversations subsequent to the initial one ranged over topics such as the Eucharist and the apocalyptic beliefs of the two religions. In any case, his account of these conversations fills almost two full folios of small script.

Even given Juan's propensity for long-windedness and the possibility of distortion in his later recollections, the detail he accorded to these meetings suggests that he attached considerable significance to them. He had probably thought of them often through the years. In fact, in the conclusion to his lengthy letter to Cusa, Juan explicitly attributed his awareness of how Muslims perceived Christianity to those discussions with the Granadan ambassador. He lamented, "Truly how many more things about the Christian religion are rendered falsely, most absurd things to which we are believed to be witnesses. . . . I became truly convinced of this in discussions with the aforementioned ambassador of the king of the Granada, in which he raised as a point of objection, quite improperly, that Christians ate their God and absolved sins committed against God."[108] After a few more sentences recalling highlights of the encounter twenty years earlier, Juan wrote by way of conclusion to this part of his letter, "And so I learned then that in this and in many other things, in how great an ignorance of the divine law the whole multitude of Saracens labored, and that by virtue of a defect of the declaration of the truths of the faith, they vigorously detested and looked down upon Christians."[109] All indications are that before these remarkable conversations with the ambassador from Granada, Juan was not aware of quite common Muslim charges against Christianity, such as that Christians worshipped more than one God. These discussions apparently constituted a watershed in his developing thought about Islam.

If his later account of these meetings leads one to suspect a previously limited familiarity with Muslim beliefs, other aspects of these stories nevertheless suggest a certain ease around Muslims themselves and a sincere curiosity about their religion. However little he knew about Islam, he apparently recognized that he did not know much, and he had somehow come to believe it worthwhile to learn more. He did not assume that there was not much to know, or that whatever popular notions were circulating among the Christians at the time constituted sufficient information. It appears that his desire to learn about their beliefs and practices was an earnest one. He clearly was not seeking a disputation or confrontation, and he even offered to have the July discussion in a remote area in private. In a quite matter-of-fact manner, he noted the reactions of his interlocutors, as when he recorded Yūsuf's surprise at his suggestion of a secret meeting and the unnamed ambassador's indignance at the suggestion that he had been swearing using God's name. He seems to have been fixing his attention on them in the same way one would on any other party in a conversation. There is no indication that he regarded them as exotic or as uncommon figures. This is what we would expect from someone who had probably encountered Muslims in the markets and public squares from his youth. Another indication that Juan was at ease in these conversations is that after their first meeting, the ambassador sought him out and returned repeatedly in order to continue their talks. Presumably, this would not have been the case if he had sensed hostility or discourtesy on Segovia's part, or if the ambassador had felt awkward in his presence.

The year in which these pivotal conversations took place offers another glimpse at Juan de Segovia's early approach to Islam and to the question of crusade. It was precisely in 1431 that the crusade, enthusiastically authorized and encouraged in the 1420s by Pope Martin V, was finally preached. Castile's internal tensions and conflicts with Aragon had delayed the implementation of these hopes. But the time was ripe when, in June of 1431, Pope Eugene IV granted full indulgences to those joining Castile's military efforts against Granada, indulgences equal to those bestowed on those who fought in the Holy Land. He charged Cardinal Alfonso Carrillo with the unenviable task of collecting an additional tax, amounting to one tenth of their income, on all Castilian clergy to support these campaigns.[110] If Carrillo embraced this task at all, it could not have been for long. The cardinal was one of the early arrivals at the Council of Basel (incorporating in February of 1433), where according to José Goñi Gaztambide, he immediately became involved in various measures against the pope and died in Basel in 1434. Somewhere along the way, whether in Castile or in Basel or maybe both, he had impressed Juan de Segovia, who included an obituary for Carrillo in his history of the council. It was the only such obituary to appear in this history.[111] But it is interesting that it was precisely in an atmosphere of the renewed crusading efforts of 1431 that Segovia embarked on these efforts to engage in dialogue with Muslims. Quite possibly his misgivings about crusading, expressed so vehemently in his later writings, were present already and prompted this alternative initiative in response to the crusading momentum in Castile.

—⁓— We are now in a position to return to the question posed at the beginning of this chapter: What did Juan's years in Castile contribute to his subsequent approach to Islam and its adherents? The evidence presented here suggests that he had been around Muslims before 1431, but that this contact had not been extensive. Whether through lack of opportunity or lack of prior interest, he had not discussed matters of belief with them before the encounter in October of that year. His narratives suggest that Muslims' longstanding and widely held objections to Christianity were not common knowledge for Castile's Christian population, or even for its theologians. Perhaps this lack of familiarity disposed Segovia to accept and perpetuate the standard Western notions that Muslims were especially lascivious and violent.

In any case, the 1427 *repetitio* shows that Juan did not need those stimulating conversations with the Granadan ambassador to turn his thoughts toward the conversion of Muslims. He urged his colleagues to present Christianity in a credible way so that others might be persuaded of its truth and thereby enjoy the eternal happiness for which they were destined. Decades later, after the fall of Constantinople and when Juan was writing extensively and exclusively on the question of Islam, this exhortation to his fellow Christians remained at the core of his thinking. The remarkable exchanges between Segovia and the ambassador merely provided him with a clearer idea of what needed to be clarified about Christianity in order for Muslims to believe. This, too, he took with him into his final years. The conversation with the bishop who had served in Tunis fueled his hope that contact between Christians and Muslims would encourage the latter to convert.

On the eve of his departure for Basel, some essential elements of Juan de Segovia's subsequent approach to Islam were in place. Conversion was the goal, and he was sure that an accurate understanding of Christian beliefs would achieve it. In his later works on the subject, he explicitly associated preaching Christianity with announcing peace.

This he drew from the Christian scriptures, which permeate his later writings more thoroughly than those of his youth, but also from what he heard and experienced at Basel regarding the reconciliation with the heretical Hussites in Bohemia. His years at the Council of Basel, which sought to implement broad structural reforms in the church, would help to sharpen his sense of church. His later views on Islam resulted from a convergence of his experience with Muslims in Castile, Hussites at Basel, and the church reform efforts to which he gave tireless attention.

Chapter Three

THE BASEL YEARS

Juan Alfonso de Segovia did not merely attend the Council of Basel: he was one of its most active members. Respected at Salamanca already, at Basel he earned an international reputation and became one of Europe's leading intellectuals. He served numerous times as envoy of the council to assemblies in France and the Empire, and he held a number of administrative roles, particularly after 1436.[1] He was also heavily involved with the more theoretical and scholarly aspects of the council's activity, producing forty-eight works during the council, not including letters, extracts he compiled from other works, and collaborative works for which he was a minor contributor.[2] In addition to the works he wrote on the various issues it considered, Segovia left posterity a history of the council, *Historia gestorum generalis synodi Basiliensis,* which his contemporaries and modern scholars have praised for its thoroughness and balance. It remains an important source on the council's activities.[3] He was probably the person best qualified to write such a history. An active member almost since the council's first sessions, he remained until the end, well after other senior members had withdrawn their support. Well acquainted with the council's objectives, he emerged, as Antony Black asserted, as "the chief theoretical exponent of Basle conciliarism."[4]

This chapter explores Segovia's work during the years in which his main labors were on behalf of the Council of Basel and its objectives. One goal is to underscore the continuity, in thought and in personal qualities, linking his years at Salamanca and the last years of his life, when he turned more earnestly to the Turkish question. As his 1426 intervention in the power plays at Salamanca had suggested, he was sympathetic to conciliar aims—at least broadly construed as subjecting those in the clerical hierarchy to decisions enacted by collective, representative bodies—before arriving at Basel. He was active in articulating the conciliar agenda early in his years there, indeed practically immediately after his arrival. His arguments from this period show, as many conciliarists' writings did, a reliance on the Bible as the primary inspiration for ideas about how Christians should live and govern their church. It would be the main source, as well, for his proposals on how Christians should counter the threat of the Turks. In both areas of his thought, he was persistent in calling for greater faithfulness to the teachings of the gospel and the practices of the early church. This tendency to look to the example of the early church, which may well have been strengthened during his years at Basel, is one he shared with other conciliarists.

As in Salamanca, he showed a willingness to speak truth to power, take up unpopular positions, and defy high-ranking church authorities, all the while apparently commanding the respect of colleagues with diverse positions on the issues. The habit of doing these things so regularly at Basel probably helped to make him less reluctant than most to take another unpopular stance later—against war as a response to the 1453 fall of Constantinople to the Turks. His work on behalf of the council and his correspondence lend support to a comment from one of his accomplished peers. In his first account of the proceedings at Basel, future pope Aeneas Sylvius Piccolomini described a particularly contentious debate, at which Segovia was granted a hearing "amid so many noises, and so stormy an outcry" because "the conciliarists heard him with eagerness as being one of themselves, and the others even unwillingly respected the man's virtue and great goodness."[5]

If his character and his political and theological orientation were remarkably consistent with his activity at Salamanca, Basel gave Juan de Segovia new frames of reference for thinking about Muslims. The Turks could not have seemed much of an immediate threat to a Castilian living in Salamanca. In fact, Segovia's years there included some in which it seemed to a relieved Europe that Turkish power was diminishing, especially when the Ottoman sultan Bayezid I (1389–1403) was defeated and captured by the Mongol leader Tamerlane in 1402, who proceeded to dismantle much of the Ottoman state. Still, while Segovia was still in Castile, the Turkish empire regained ascendancy, and Murad II (1421–51) was able to subject Constantinople to siege in 1422 and wage war with Venice for the rest of the decade. On the eve of the council, in 1430, Murad's forces captured Europe's second largest city, Thessalonica.[6] In Basel it would have been impossible not to hear of the worries of Christians, Segovia's fellow council members, from the Eastern Mediterranean. Council business sometimes concerned the advances of the Turks, as when it directed funds to help victims in Cyprus, authorized indulgences for those who contributed to the defense of Constantinople, or voted to reimburse the travel expenses of the Greek delegation planning to come to Basel to discuss reunification.[7] Also, during these years, Christian forces lost several significant battles to Ottoman forces, including the disastrous crusade at Varna in 1444, where Cardinal Giuliano Cesarini, whom Segovia deeply respected, died while in retreat.[8] Juan de Segovia was curious about Islam while he was in Salamanca, but in Basel the realities of the Turkish expansion surely added new complexities and a new urgency to these concerns.

Basel also absorbed the young theologian from Salamanca in the problem of the Hussites, a group of Czech religious reformers whose support in their native Bohemia encompassed peasants and nobles alike. The leaders of this complex movement, John Hus and Jerome of Prague, were condemned as heretics at Constance in 1416 and remanded to the temporal power, in their case Emperor Sigismund, for execution. Among the views that earned Hus censure were his insistence on the primacy of scriptural authority and his teaching that lay people should receive communion under both forms, bread and wine. At the time, only priests took the wine. Although it might seem that these were issues unlikely to galvanize a social revolution, they touched upon widespread existing frustration with both church and secular authorities. As a result, the teaching and the death of Hus fanned nationalist sentiment, and the Hussite movement became a revolution.[9] While he was still in Salamanca, Segovia had been tangentially involved in the efforts to quell the rebellion. He later wrote that in 1428 he had been assigned to collect a subsidy from Spanish kings and prelates to fund the wars against the Hussites. As he recalled, one of the prelates who resisted paying told him that "the way of war is not fitting for the reduction of heretics, and furthermore that the 'way of peace and teaching' was more fitting and any other method would have little effect."[10] One of the goals of the Council of Basel, one in which Segovia was personally involved, was to end the spread of this movement. The council's efforts with the Hussites would inspire him to promote a similar *via pacis et doctrine* with the Muslims.

It is possible, even likely, that Juan de Segovia was quite conversant with the reform agenda that Basel took up well before he arrived there. The origins of the Council of Basel lay in the Council of Constance (1414–18), which been convened by Pope John XXIII (Avignon), during Segovia's days as a student at Salamanca. This pope had succeeded Alexander V, who had been elected by the Council of Pisa (1409), which had met to resolve the schism produced when two different popes were elected in 1378. Pisa deposed Gregory XII and Benedict XIII, elected Alexander V, charged a future council with the task of reforming the church, and adjourned. Neither of the two previously sitting popes, however, accepted these results, and both had the support of some regions. Alexander V had the most support of the three, from France, England, Germany, and most of Italy. Nevertheless, the ironic result of the Council of Pisa was a church with not two popes but three. As the successor to the one elected by the council and as the pope whose legitimacy was recognized by the majority of Latin Christians, even though he was not well regarded personally, John XXIII summoned the Council of Constance. The council was to end the schism definitively and undertake the reform of the church. It bears noting that the pope agreed to this council under pressure from Sigismund, then king of Germany and Hungary, and while he was a beleaguered guest of the Medicis in Florence, where he had taker refuge from his enemies.[11] Nevertheless, the fact that he was the strongest claimant to the papacy when he called this council must be considered a significant factor in subsequent arguments about whether the council was legitimate.[12]

John XXIII no doubt hoped the assembly gathered at Constance would be more tractable than it was. One reason delegates proved to be difficult to manage was that *doctores* and princes (and their proxies) were allowed to vote, not just prelates. In March 1415, the pope deserted the council and fled the city, possibly expecting this move to put an end to the gathering. Instead, his departure enabled the undaunted council to secure the resignation of Gregory XII and the deposition of Benedict XIII more readily and to enact some reform measures involving fiscal corruption and appointments to church office. When the delegates elected Cardinal Oddo Colonna in November 1417, they ended the schism that had been in effect longer than many people could remember. Colonna took the name Martin V.[13] It was to Martin V's court that Juan traveled in the hope of attaining the benefices while he was at Salamanca, and it was Martin V who approved that university's 1422 Constitutions.[14] It was also Martin V who announced the Council of Basel.

Ending the schism was a significant accomplishment in itself. However, the reason that Constance was closely linked with Basel, and the reason why it is still a subject of some interest in our own era, was that it also issued two bold decrees, *Haec sancta* (1415) and *Frequens* (1417). *Haec sancta* declared that the synod had been "legitimately assembled in the Holy Spirit" and derived its authority directly from Christ, and that every believer was bound to obey it in matters of faith, including the pope. Anyone who refused to honor the decisions and ordinances of this council or any other "legitimately assembled" general council would be subject to appropriate penance and punishment. As we shall see, Juan de Segovia took this principle seriously, citing it in his opposition to papal measures against Basel. *Frequens* established that henceforth councils would meet at regular intervals, beginning with another council in five years, a second in seven, and thereafter every ten years. Each council would determine the location of the next one before closing.[15] Antony Black noted that this decree was the most significant measure ever taken to limit papal power. It would have made the church "a strictly constitutional monarchy."[16] This was not unlike the limits to the power of the *maestre-scuela* that Juan de Segovia and others sought to impose in the smaller arena of Salamanca's *studium* in the 1420s. It seems possible that the discussions and issues raised by the conciliar thinkers at Constance could have contributed to the solutions the scholars at Salamanca envisioned to the problem of a meddling and powerful prelate.

The Council of Basel was called, probably reluctantly, by Martin V in accord with *Frequens* in February 1431. The Council of Pavia-Siena (1423–24) had met in the meantime, also in accord with *Frequens*, and Martin V had worked effectively to undermine its work and ultimately to dissolve it.[17] Those who gathered at Basel faced an agenda of by then familiar conciliar concerns. Unlike at Constance, there was no schism to end, but there remained the goals of thoroughgoing church reform, reunion with the Greeks, "reduction" of the Hussites, the rooting out of heresy, and the desire to bring peace to a conflict-ridden Western Europe. Thomas Ferguson emphasizes that this agenda had been taken up at Pavia-Siena, where it was a reiteration of the concerns that had arisen during Constance. There is an obvious continuity of goals from Constance through Basel.[18]

The Council of Basel, sometimes called Basel-Lausanne because it transferred to Lausanne in 1448, and the conciliar era in general suffer from inadequate study, despite the voluminous bibliography that has accumulated. In a bibliographical survey on the conciliar era published in 2000, Nelson Minnich stated flatly, "The Council of Basel-Lausanne (1431–49) has not been well studied."[19] The only comprehensive study of it was published in 1874; Minnich attributed the inadequate study of this council in part to the fact that so many of its main sources have not been published.[20] One reason for the dearth of credible comprehensive treatments of this council is that the period became a prime battleground for ideological and confessional posturing by Protestant scholars pointing with satisfaction to precursors to the Reformation, forward-thinking men who were ahead of their time, and Catholic scholars who exalted in the supposed inevitable triumph of the papacy and truth over dark forces that threatened both. Thus in one of the most cited and widely available general studies of church history, one reads that Eugene IV confronted the men at Basel with "la vérité romaine."[21] Beltrán de Heredia wrote scathingly of the "schismatics of Basel" and commented that those who praised the personal qualities that Juan de Segovia displayed there do so "as if . . . to downplay the grave consequences that his obstinate attitude, along with the other promoters of the schism, brought upon the church."[22]

Another reason that Basel still lacks an adequate general history is the enormity of the task. This is not only because of the quantity of studies already published,[23] but because of the number of people involved, not only the incorporated members of the council, and the complex interplay of their motivations and concerns. This complicated assembly lasted almost two decades and involved every Western Christian ruler, university, and religious order, not to mention representatives from the Greek church and the Hussites. As Gerald Christianson remarked, "Comprehensive research on the Council of Basel (1431–49) may not appeal to the faint-hearted."[24] Those with expertise in the diplomatic machinations and sources focus their attention on the secular leaders' political goals and the churchmen's career aspirations, while theologians and political theorists devote their energies to the highly intellectual treatises produced at Basel. Many of these, including many by Juan de Segovia, remain unpublished, further complicating the study of the protagonists' thought and goals. These understandable, even necessary, emphases have distorted the picture of the aims of the conciliar movement. Heiko Oberman lamented, for example, that a preoccupation with the means by which the conciliarists pursued their agenda has led scholars to neglect the goals these late medieval leaders sought to attain. He asserted that the goals should not be understood as simply "anti-papal." From Pisa forward, Oberman insisted, the conciliarists strove for peace, the restoration of one undivided church, and reform inspired by the practices of the early church.[25]

Through 1436

As noted in the discussion of Segovia's 1426 *repetitio* at Salamanca in chapter 1 of this volume, scholars have puzzled over Segovia's apparent rapid transformation into a conciliarist, given the strongly pro-papal argument he made in that address. As I have argued, that 1426 *repetitio* should not be read as the pro-papal manifesto that it seems, on the surface, to be. The early history of the council, which created the circumstances in which Segovia joined its efforts, provides further reason to believe that he was no convert to conciliarism but rather a supporter of its reform goals upon his arrival.

Juan de Segovia was not present for the council's opening sessions in the summer of 1431. As we have seen, he left Salamanca for Rome in late 1431 or early 1432 with Pedro Martínez de Covarrubias.[26] The two went to solicit new benefices for themselves and to defend the university's 1422 Constitutions against the challenges from the powerful Lope Fernández de Mendoza, the archbishop of Santiago. Juan never returned to Castile. Beltrán de Heredia and those who cite him have stated that he must have received word while in Rome that the *studium* at Salamanca wished him to represent this body at Basel.[27] Another possibility is that there had been some discussion of such a plan before he left for Rome, or at least that people there had raised the issue of his using his travels to learn more about what was happening in Basel. The council had opened in July of 1431, although with low attendance, and delegates from the University of Paris had been present and prominent from the fall of 1431 on.[28] The academic community at Salamanca, with its significant connections to Paris, must have known about the Parisians' role there, and might have known ahead of time of that university's stance and its plans to participate even before its representatives departed. In any case, every major university was sending a delegation. With their own international profile to consider, the faculty at Salamanca could hardly have remained on the sidelines while such an important international gathering was under way.

When the council opened, it had papal support, but that soon eroded. Martin V died shortly after announcing the new council, and it now became the concern of the new pope, Gabriel Condulmer, who took the name Eugene IV. In its first session, the council cited *Frequens* and examined other decrees related to the procedures for councils. In the months that followed, Eugene IV became wary of the council and in November issued a bull dissolving it. Stieber noted that the pope was concerned about the council eroding the authority of his office in general, and more specifically that an enemy of his, who had contested his election, would use it as a court of appeal.[29]

This attempt at dissolution aroused widespread indignation, and not only among those participating directly in the council. One of the reasons the pope's actions resulted in such frustration was that the Hussites had recently won several important victories, threatening neighboring lands. Some perceived this move by Eugene IV as a sign of ineptitude in the face of this danger.[30] The bull can be seen, in retrospect, as the move that pitched council and pope against each other in a long struggle over authority in the church. In the same bull, the pope also called for a new council to meet a year and a half later in Bologna. The projected council was to examine the issue of reunion with the Greek church. Both the dissolution of Basel and the start of a new council at the pope's personal initiative would have rendered both *Frequens* and *Haec sancta* effectively null.

Thus the first real order of business of the Council of Basel was to assert its right to exist. A main protagonist in this endeavor was, somewhat ironically, Cardinal Giuliano Cesarini. Cesarini had been appointed by Martin V and confirmed by Eugene IV as the papal delegate to preside over the council. His role as papal appointee notwithstanding, Cesarini refused to accept the bull of dissolution and wrote the pope to tell him that. The council issued a public letter on January 21, 1432, informing all Christians that it would not accept dissolution, and that the need for reform was urgent and demanded its attention. It also reissued *Haec sancta* and *Frequens*. This was not the last time that papal appointee Cesarini would act in a way that was sympathetic to the council's aims even when the council was in disagreement with the pope. Perhaps because of his willingness to do this, he was deeply respected by many of his contemporaries, not least by Juan de Segovia.[31] As Uta Fromherz has noted, Cesarini was a central figure in Segovia's *Historia*, so much so that he functioned in this narrative as a sort of symbol for the council's goals.[32]

After much evasion, decrees attempting to nullify Basel's decisions, and mediation by Emperor Sigismund, Eugene revoked his bull of dissolution and solemnly recognized the Council of Basel as a legitimate general council from its inception. This bull of retraction (retracting the bull of dissolution) was dated December 15, 1433. The pope continued, at least officially, to acknowledge the legitimacy of the council until September 1437. Meanwhile, in those two early years during which he was actively trying to undermine it, the council had not waited for his support. Its membership had grown signifi-cantly,[33] and it had begun discussions with Hussite theologians and initiated contact with the Greek emperor regarding a meeting to dis-cuss reunion.[34]

Juan was incorporated at the Council of Basel on April 8, 1433, in his own right. Soon he became a member of the household (*familiar*) of Cardinal Cervantes, which would afford him the opportunity to meet the bishop of Prague, who agreed with the Hussite position that lay people should receive both the bread and the wine at commu-nion.[35] It was a point of pride for Segovia that upon his incorporation at Basel he was directed to a seat of honor, right next to the delegation from Paris.[36] Still, he waited until the arrival of a delegation from Cas-tilian king Juan II to incorporate formally as a representative of the university. This he did on August 27, 1434. Hernández Montes seems to have been correct in reasoning that the delay must have been a ges-ture of deference to the royal delegation or a matter of political astute-ness.[37] Certainly it is not the case, as some have claimed, that he actu-ally became part of that delegation from the king. He never referred to himself as representing the king, and the documents do not support such an assumption.[38] As for Juan's view of what he was doing when he incorporated, Hernández Montes is one of those who refer to his "evolution" toward a conciliarist position, as if he left Salamanca skep-tical about the council but changed his mind later.[39] This does not seem to take into account the context in which Basel was meeting at the time of his incorporation. Juan's incorporation into the council at that par-ticular time and his early activity there reveal someone who was al-ready sympathetic to the conciliar cause.

When Segovia arrived in Basel, the council was still in full-blown conflict with Eugene IV. Invoking *Haec sancta* and insisting that it was "legitimately assembled," it continued to meet, and it had re-affirmed *Frequens* twice since the pope's bull of dissolution in No-vember 1431. Less than two months before Juan's incorporation, its procurators had sent to a committee of judges a formal accusation that Eugene was in contempt. Membership was swelling in response to the council's appeals for support.[40] Juan could not have had any misconceptions about the direction in which Basel was headed. If he had been opposed or even simply ambivalent about its legitimacy or its aims, he might have refrained from going until the pope recognized the council. He certainly would not have been so active in the faith committee (*deputatio fidei*) that he was asked to write the report on the presidency debate. He received this charge in early March 1434, and the report was to circulate to the four committees of the council.[41] His *Tractatus super presidentia* was his first conciliar writing, and in it he summarized the committee's decision on whether the council should accept papal appointments to the presidency of the council. After an introduction to the issues and the state of the question, Juan briefly presented the arguments in favor of the papal position, then spent almost the whole document expounding on the arguments against it. He concluded with a reference to continued discussion and attempts to resolve the issue. The work was an expansion of a report he gave orally before the faith committee on March 3.[42] Thus eleven months after his arrival at the council, he was articulate in his support for the majority position and had impressed his colleagues as a strong advocate of Basel's stance. All of this took place during a time of open conflict between the council and the pope. Surely Juan de Segovia was already supportive of the council's aims when he arrived.

This conciliarist stance might have reflected the majority position at Salamanca, or at least the views of a significant number of scholars affiliated with that institution. Adeline Rucquoi has shown that discussions at Salamanca included substantial reflection on the nature of power, and that those with political inclinations similar to the majority at Basel were well represented there. She argued that there was a strong democratic or constitutional current in fifteenth-century Spain, and that it coexisted with the monarchist position.[43] It is possible that Salamanca, situated as it was in a kingdom that was normally allied with France through the Hundred Years War, became a preferred destination for some conciliarists who left Paris in 1383. In that year the French king, who backed Clement VII in the schism, had ordered the University of Paris to stop calling for a council. Many of Paris's

strongest advocates for a council found their way to other universities.[44] In any case, many academics across Europe who came of age
during Pisa and Constance probably were favorably disposed toward
conciliar thought as expressed in the works of Gerson and d'Ailly.[45]
Segovia, who owned one of Gerson's works and listed it among the
books in his *Donatio*, praised Gerson as an "illuminatissimus in theologia doctor" and "clarissimus doctor."[46]

The universities' positions on the conciliar question were not always driven by intellectual convictions. Concerning the German universities in the years 1438–49, the second phase of the church conflict, Stieber observed that the various universities' support for the
council depended on "the degree of their economic and political in-
dependence vis-à-vis their local territorial princes."[47] A similar dynamic could have operated in the case of Salamanca in the early stages
of the council as well. Castile's political situation was anything but
stable in those years, and the king was only one powerful party in the
kingdom. The university was becoming a force in its own right. Since
Martin V had revoked his approval of the 1422 Constitutions that had
granted the *studium* freedom from the control of Archbishop Mendoza, Salamanca might not have seen a reliable protector in the pope.
Perhaps this disposed some there to entertain thoughts about a different authority structure for the church. In fact, the governance system
envisioned in those Constitutions, for which Juan had worked to secure papal approval, resembled the limitations the conciliarists wanted
to place on papal authority. In any case, Juan de Segovia continued to
represent the University of Salamanca at Basel probably until sometime late in 1440.[48] By that time, he had been energetically working for
at least three years to see Eugene IV deposed. If the university was not
sympathetic to the Basel majority, it seems that it would have distanced
itself from Segovia sooner.

The Crown had its own policies. There has been some dispute
about the level of Juan II's support for Basel in its early years, including which delegation (or delegations) represented the king and when.
Luís Suárez Fernández wrote that there were two delegations sent by
the king in those years. According to him, the first was a provisional
delegation, which had been sent for the purpose of observing and re-

porting back to the king. Its members were Juan de Torquemada, Ibo Moro, Juan de Medina (cantor in Salamanca's cathedral), and Juan Alfonso de Segovia, and this group was generally sympathetic to the goals of the Basel majority. According to Suárez Fernández, this delegation was incorporated on November 4, 1433. However, Hernández Montes pointed out that Suárez had based this supposition on documentation cited by Luís Serrano. When he returned to the document in question, Hernández Montes found no mention that this group had any authorization from or association with Juan II, and that it was not Juan de Segovia who incorporated that day, but Juan de Medina as procurator for Segovia. It is even probable that this Juan Alfonso de Segovia was not the same one as the subject of this study, despite their identical full names.[49] This discovery by Hernández Montes resolved the inconsistency between the sequence of events reported by Suárez Fernández and the fact that Juan wrote that he delayed incorporating as a representative of the university until the arrival of the king's embassy in August 1434, nine months later than that supposed first royal delegation arrived. It appears that the delegation that arrived in November 1433 did not represent the king of Castile.

Juan II sent a delegation, but only after Eugene IV had issued the bull accepting the council on December 15, 1433.[50] This delegation received its authority to represent the king on April 13, 1434.[51] Another indication that there had not been an official delegation from Castile itself before this is that on June 19, 1434, a motion was presented in the council that *Frequens* be renewed and nothing of its content changed until the Castilian ambassadors had arrived.[52] The king had been considering a delegation, much to the pope's distress,[53] but he apparently did not actually commission one until after Eugene had recognized the council as legitimate. Once there, the king's representatives did not share Segovia's enthusiasm for the council's agenda. One of them, Alvaro de Isorna, wrote to Juan II in January 1436 that he did not find the atmosphere at Basel conducive to realizing reform.[54] Castile's delegation remained at Basel until 1439, but it was skeptical toward the council's aims and generally supported the papal cause. Following the council's deposition of Eugene IV, the king's representatives left Basel for Strasbourg to await further instructions. From there they responded to a letter from France's Charles VII demanding to know why they had remained after the French delegation had departed. They assured the French king that they had indeed been present for the recent events at Basel, but they had been trying unsuccessfully to persuade the majority not to proceed with the deposition.[55] It seems that Juan de Segovia's conciliar pursuits were probably endorsed by the university but ran counter to the hopes his king had for the council.[56]

For the first few years Segovia's activities were not especially antipapal. It is true that he immediately became active in the majority's efforts, as has already been noted, and his treatise on the right to decide who would hold the presidency of the council placed him among those arguing for conciliar autonomy. Especially since he joined the assembly and then wrote that treatise after Eugene had declared Basel dissolved, his support for the conciliarist stance seems beyond doubt. However, in these early years of the council, he was much more extensively involved in other issues than he was in the struggle with the pope. As an active member of the faith committee, even serving as president of it at least once, he took part in the discussions with both the Greeks and the Hussites. Among the writings that Hernández Montes attributed to this period are extracts from Richard Fitzralph's *Summa in quaestionibus armenorum*, a treatise on the procession of the Holy Spirit from the Father and the Son, a summary of arguments on why it was not divinely mandated that the people receive communion under both species (wine as well as bread), and a summary of arguments on whether it was permissible that they do so. In preparation for meetings with the Greeks, he also compiled a concordance of indeclinable words in the Bible (*Concordantiae dictionum indeclinabilium*), which made him a pioneer in biblical studies.[57] According to Antony Black, this was Juan's only work printed during the Renaissance.[58] No doubt it was during this time that he made the acquaintance of Nicholas of Cusa, whose first involvement in conciliar affairs was over the Hussite question.[59]

This experience of participating in the council's overtures to the Hussites left a deep impression on Segovia and contributed significantly to his later views on how Christians should approach Muslims to convert them. In several of his works on Islam, all written almost twenty years after Basel's negotiations with the Hussites, he pointed to the Hussite affair as a model for how to approach Muslims. In his *Historia*, he used language with reference to the Hussite question that bears striking similarities to the wording that he would later use in reference to the Muslims. For example, at the beginning of his history of the Council of Basel, as he established the context for the council, he described the spread of the Hussite movement then afflicting the church in a way that was similar to how Christian writers often told of the spread of Islam by violence and intimidation. According to this narrative, the Hussite heresy was an armed heresy that cut deep into Europe at the time of the conclusion of the Council of Constance, burning a growing number of unfortunate souls. It "greatly vexed the church through bitter persecution, not as much by spreading the teaching by word as by fire and sword," carrying the devastation to cities, towns, and entire regions that would not assent to its errors.[60]

A few pages later, he dedicated Book I, Chapter 4, to the "insults of the heretic Bohemians against the faith and the church" and the discussion of how to proceed.[61] After criticizing the clergy for being too fearful to approach the Bohemians, he mused, "If they had the right path and divine charity, they would take up the books of sacred scripture and come to them as the apostles did to the pagans, with the arms of the divine word, and this would be their desire. But if the bishops and priests, in a spirit of mildness, as the apostle says, should prove themselves just and them [the Bohemians] unjust, if they refuse to accept instruction, then [the clergy] could get kings, princes, lords, and imperial cities to help them."[62] Two chapters later, still on the Hussite issue, he discussed previous councils' efforts to combat other heresies, and he explained that they had "prided themselves in having girded themselves with the sword of the word of God, correctly understood," which had resulted in the severing of the head from the body of the heresies.[63] Later he would argue that Christians should again arm themselves with the sword of the Spirit, which was the word of God, and imitate the apostles in spreading that word to the Muslims.

A particularly compelling testament to the parallels that Segovia drew between the Hussite danger and that of Islam comes from his own pen in the form of marginal notes he wrote in a copy of his

Historia that he owned. This volume, which is currently housed in the Escorial, has extensive marginalia in Segovia's hand.[64] In his discussion of the sixteenth session, in January 1432, he explained that letters were dispatched to the king of Poland and the duke of Lithuania advising these leaders of the council's interest in their lot, because it was feared that the heresy would spread. The marginal note he added reads, "And similarly the Turks [moving] towards the most terrible desolation of all of Christendom."[65]

Later, as he wrote about what Christians should do to counter that Turkish threat, he thought the experience with the Hussites offered a useful model to follow. In his *Liber de magna auctoritate episcoporum in concilio generali*, a work on ecclesiology dedicated to Juan Cervantes, which Hernández Montes dated to the early 1450s,[66] Segovia recalled that for the past three hundred years there had been numerous attempts by Christians to liberate the Holy Land by force, both by land and by sea, but these had little to show for them.[67] He offered a suggestion:

> Because the way of war must be judged extremely difficult, maybe it is not pointless or ill advised to try another means of achieving their reduction. For indeed, not always by the sword, but by many other means the enemy has been defeated, and that victory is all the greater: to strive for the salvation of their souls. Certainly, we have seen in our days, that against the Hussites and other heretics of the kingdom of Bohemia, devastating whole regions by fire and sword, an army of many and the greatest of the faithful was not strong enough. But when they acquiesced to the exhortation of the church, that the differences might be examined through public deliberation, it must be noted that they retreated from this [heresy], whereas previously they were continually bringing persecution against their neighbors on account of their errors.[68]

This was not the only time he suggested that Christians might try an approach with the Muslims that had worked with the Bohemians.

One reason the Hussites provided an especially important precedent for Segovia's later thought is that crusades had, in fact, been launched against them to no avail. It was none other than Cardinal

Cesarini who led the charge against them and then decided on another path instead. In 1431, as papal legate and before arriving at Basel,
he had led troops into Bohemia, hoping to crush the Hussite rebellion. This invasion headed by Cesarini was the last in a series of attempts by Sigismund to retake Bohemia. These efforts occurred over
the course of the 1420s under different auspices, and they left from
different surrounding regions, but all enjoyed papal support as crusades. Cesarini's invasion in 1431 ended in a humiliating defeat. His
troops did not even encounter the enemy forces but fled as soon as
they heard the Hussite battle song "You Warriors of God" and the
dreaded war wagons of Prokop the Great's army.[69]

Segovia would later state that he had heard about the whole affair,
which occurred almost two years before he arrived at Basel, from Cesarini himself. His letter in 1455 to the Burgundian theologian Jean
Germain recounts the incident as he had heard it:

> But I know that I heard from the most reverend lord Giuliano,
> president of the council, that while the army had been gathered,
> Giuliano, equipped for battle himself, wishing to enter or [already]
> having entered the kingdom of Bohemia, sent a letter to Prokop,
> the leader of the Taborites, exhorting him to the things of peace. And
> [Prokop] responded, "You come to me with the sword unsheathed
> and you ask me for peace," whereupon, considering it with a more
> careful mind, Guiliano, having been transformed, his spirit having
> been changed, as he put it, recognized that there was another, more
> appropriate method to be tried for the reduction of the Bohemians
> than to use the rod for their extermination. And so he did, addressing
> to them a synodal letter in all humility and Christian charity, as was
> well known then and is known today to those who know what hap-
> pened. It accomplished much more toward their conversion than the
> many very strong armies of Christians who invaded that kingdom
> and returned in disgraceful flight and with very high casualties.[70]

There is no reason to doubt his assertion that he heard about these
events directly from Cesarini. The cardinal's shift from leading the
charge in a crusade to promoting dialogue with the Bohemians at Basel
had impressed Segovia deeply, and he enlisted this example repeatedly

in his arguments that a similar change of heart on the part of Christian leaders might lead to success with the Muslims as well.

Cesarini's strategy with the Bohemians may have given Segovia more than simply a ready example of the failure of crusading. The Hussites had declared that they would be judged only by divine law (*lex divina*) or scripture, and not by human laws and definitely not by armies.[71] As we shall see in chapter 5, one of Segovia's main goals was to persuade Muslims by making their own "law," the Qur'ān, which he often referred to as *lex eorum* or *lex Mahumeti*, the basis for discussion. Of course he could have come to this method by other means, but it is quite possible that the Hussites' insistence on scripture as the basis for negotiations strengthened his belief that discussions with the Turks, too, should take the Qur'ān as their starting point.

Moreover, in 1432 Cesarini wrote a remarkable letter to Pope Eugene IV defending his newfound commitment to dialogue and negotiation with the Hussites. His task was similar to that which Segovia took up concerning the Muslims later: to prove that dialogue was appropriate and legitimate. To make his case, he enlisted precedents from the Bible, canon law, and history. Segovia included this letter in his *History* of Basel, like he did with so many other letters and council decrees.[72] He also mentioned the letter by Cesarini in his own letter to Jean Germain, saying that "the great Julianus," as president of the council, had sent a letter to the pope informing him of "how fitting and meritorious and useful, even necessary, it was to work toward the reduction of the Bohemians by means of peace and teaching."[73] Gerald Christianson noted that "more than once" Cesarini's letters to the pope included the argument that "when arms have contended so often in vain, another way should be tried."[74] As we have seen, Segovia went to Basel already interested in dialogue with Muslims, so his association with Cesarini and the cardinal's overtures to the Hussites was not his first exposure to the notion of holding peaceful discussions with those with different religious views. Nevertheless, it seems likely that his participation in these momentous negotiations, along with his respect for Cesarini, helped to convince him of the value of this approach.

In the end, the invitation to the Hussites to come to Basel and discuss their differences yielded exactly the results that Cesarini had hoped to see. The matter was entrusted to the faith committee, on which Segovia served, and the committee's work produced a compromise between the council and the moderate Hussites. Known as the Compacts of Prague or Basel, the agreement allowed the Hussite church to offer the cup to the laity during the Eucharist, in addition to some other concessions. Segovia described the events in his history of the council:

> It was also the council's keen wish to bring about the desired peace and, while preserving the faith and honour of the Church, it meant to leave no stone unturned. From that day the cardinals, and others meeting with them, worked out whether it was legitimate, respectable or expedient for the Church to concede to the Bohemians the sacrament of communion under both kinds, while the rest of the Christian people communicated under one kind only. . . . And when the deputies, after long and also searching discussions, had agreed that the freedom to be different should be conceded, it was decided that the question should not be settled in a general meeting because, in the prevailing circumstances, it was too risky for the council's decision to be published before it became known in the kingdom of Bohemia.[75]

Negotiations on the Compacts concluded in November 1433, but ratification from Bohemia and Moravia did not come until 1436, and the council ratified the Compacts in January of 1437.[76]

Juan de Segovia was active on the faith committee throughout this period, and this negotiated resolution to this longstanding crisis probably brought him rich satisfaction. In his *History*, he recorded not just the agreements and their ratification, but the celebrations in Basel when the news reached the council:

> While celebrating the divine mysteries on the feast of St. James, the holy synod received the letter from the delegates it had sent to Bohemia concerning the final agreement and peace obtained with the Bohemians; whereupon after Mass the hymn *Te deum laudamus* was joyfully sung with voices and organs. Such was the nature of the dispatch from Jihlava, dated the fifth, that its effect was that the

holy synod exulted and rejoiced, raising up thanks to the most high, because behold the long-awaited day had come, in which they would reap the fruits of their labors and return with full sheaves to the threshing floor of the Lord.[77]

The council's jubilation was not misplaced. Indeed, church historian Hubert Jedin remarked, "This settlement of the Bohemian affair was a great success for the Council. If there could have been an accommodation at Constance in regard to the chalice, Christendom would probably have been spared much anguish."[78]

The fact that the pope had objected to the presence of the Hussites in Basel and condemned the council for negotiating with them surely only added to the triumph felt by the assembly at Basel. In fact, Cesarini's fascinating letter to the pope defending the decision to invite the Hussites to dialogue was written in response to the bull *Quoniam alto*. In this bull, a revised version of which was issued late in 1431, the pope had condemned the council for summoning the Hussites and used this as a pretext for declaring the council terminated.[79] The gathering at Basel must have considered it an auspicious sign about the future of the council that the council continued to meet despite the pope's reaction, was taken seriously by the Hussites, and finally brought an end to the Hussite rebellion. Indeed, when the agreement was reached between the council and the Hussites, neither the council nor the pope was oblivious to the impact of the resolution of this conflict on the council's prestige and legitimacy. Segovia bluntly stated as much when he explained why it was judged risky for the council's decision to be widely known before it was announced in Bohemia: "The pope's envoys, waiting in Constance, could be counted on to be obstructive, on account of any such dealing with the Bohemians serving always to strengthen the position of the council."[80]

1437 to 1449

Following the Compacts, Juan de Segovia was probably encouraged by this success with the Hussites and hopeful about the prospects of reunion with the Greeks. If he shared the council's thoughts on the benefits and urgency of such a reunion, he might even have thought that once this was achieved, the conversion of the Muslims would follow. In a document the council issued in 1434 *ad perpetuam rei memoriam*, which Segovia included in his *Historia*, the council expressed its joy at certain developments in the negotiations with the Greeks and its hope that Christians would devote energy to this important endeavor. The assembly noted, "Hence we are confident that yet another advantage would be added to Christendom [*rei publice christiane*] through the grace of God, that from this union, once it is accomplished it is hoped that many will be converted from the abominable sect of Muhammad to the Catholic faith."[81] Whether Segovia shared that confidence or not, we know from a vote that he cast in 1437 that the issue of reunion with the Greeks was important to him. He must have been disappointed when negotiations with the Greeks presented more difficulties, which were not helped by a dispute over where these meetings should take place. The question of a suitable meeting place became the pivot around which a new confrontation between pope and council developed. The evolving conflict presented Segovia with a dilemma, and the decision he made set the course for his involvement in the council's efforts for its duration.

The issue of where to hold talks with the Greeks was no mere logistical detail. Eugene insisted on an Italian city, claiming that this would make it easier both for him and for a Greek delegation to attend. The pope's earlier attempt to dissolve Basel and hold his own council in Bologna had, not unreasonably, led council members to suspect that his real motive was to undermine their authority. Late in 1436, they rejected a number of Italian cities as potential sites and proposed instead Basel, Avignon, or a city in Savoy, to which the council would then transfer. Byzantine leaders insisted on holding a council of reunion in an Italian city with easy access, refusing to travel all the way to Basel, Avignon, or Savoy. Eugene once again openly challenged the council's authority by declaring it transferred to Ferrara, a city in the Papal States.[82] This suited the Greeks well, and they accepted the invitation to attend, but most of those at Basel were unwilling to meet in a city under papal authority or permit the appearance that the council was convened or headed by the pope. As Kenneth Setton put it, "The Greeks found the Council more difficult to deal with and less reliable than the pope, who was unreliable only when he dealt with the conciliarists."[83] Setton also explained that the Greeks were dismayed by the council's stubbornness in dealing with the pope. Byzantine patriarchs and emperors had always conducted their relations with the West through the pope. To them, it would be inconceivable to have a reunion meeting that the pope refused to attend and, in fact, considered invalid.[84]

In May 1437, the Council of Basel held a vote that was a turning point for Segovia personally as well as for the council. In the vote that May, the majority again refused to transfer the council to Italy and again invited the Greeks to Basel, Avignon, or a city in Savoy. However, a minority voted to accept the pope's plan to transfer to Italy and mentioned specifically either Florence or Udine.[85] This was a crucial vote because, after it, Eugene refused to deal with the council. In the September 1437 bull he issued dissolving the Council of Basel and translating it to Ferrara, he explained, "The synod of Basle does not remove the scandal of division but, alas, those who are making themselves the leaders and princes of the innovations there rather increase it further. . . . As a result of them neither we nor our representatives are free to propose or deal with business in that council safely, now that it has been brought under the more or less tyrannical control of our detractors."[86] His decision to proceed with the Ferrara meeting prompted the council to initiate proceedings against him. Stieber wrote that the transfer to Ferrara was, in retrospect, the event that ultimately lead to Basel's defeat in its challenge to papal power.[87] This turning point had much to do with the Turks, whose advances made the Greeks, who were hoping for Western support against the Turks, impatient with the council's delays in agreeing on a suitable meeting place. For pope and council, what was at stake was the prestige associated with ending a schism that had started in 1054. Ferrara signaled the victory of the pope on this important issue.[88]

It also brought the anguished departure of Cesarini, who chose to join the ranks of the papal party and travel to Ferrara. Cesarini had become disillusioned about various developments in the council's actions; his departure was not based solely on disagreement about the location for a meeting with the Greeks.[89] Uta Fromherz wrote that Segovia was more impacted by Cesarini's departure than any other of the cardinal's Basel colleagues. Although in the *Historia* Cesarini now figured as the enemy of the council, Segovia nevertheless portrayed the torment of this man he had so long admired. He also said that, just as the biblical Tamar had arrived in her father-in-law's presence with valuable objects, which testified against him, Cesarini too possessed such items, in the form of letters, speeches, and disputations, which the cardinal had left with Segovia.[90]

In this crucial vote, Segovia must have experienced his own inner torment. He voted with the minority, putting his support behind the pope's plans for a meeting. This was uncharacteristic, a fact noted by Piccolomini in his history of the council. It may have been the reason that a year later the new council president, Cardinal Aleman, called a special assembly to receive Juan's oath of allegiance to the council before Segovia and the Dominican John of Ragusa left to represent Basel at the diet in Nuremberg.[91] The most likely explanation for Juan's vote with the minority is that he genuinely wanted that council of union to take place and took seriously the Greeks' desire to have it in Italy. Whatever indignation he might have felt at the pope's obvious and ongoing efforts to control the council, he apparently thought the goal of reunion was more important than resisting those designs.

If anyone had been unsure of Segovia's commitment to the council following his vote, his next decision would have helped to clarify his position. Although he voted against the majority and continued to back the minority position on this issue, he remained at Basel and never left it for Ferrara. Thus even though he favored having a council of union in Italy, when faced with the choice between an action that would undermine the council's legitimacy and one that would uphold it, he chose to support the council. This decision would alter the focus of his energies and effectively determine his work for years. As Antony Black stated, "Whatever importance he may have attached to reunion with the Greeks, for the next fifteen years his whole energy was devoted to the pope-council controversy."[92] This must have represented not only a shift in intellectual focus, but a personal turning point, as well. A letter from Segovia to the University of Salamanca, now missing, reportedly notified colleagues there that he was renouncing the chair of prime in theology, held for him due to his absence on official business, and that he had no intention to return and resume these duties. Benigno Hernández Montes wrote that this letter probably dated to 1437, since his decision to remain in Basel would have made his association with the university untenable. Salamanca distanced itself from the assembly at Basel upon receiving word from Eugene IV that he had moved the council to Ferrara.[93] Segovia's new endeavors in the pope-council controversy led him to reflect further on the nature of the church, reflections that seem to have influenced his arguments about how the church should behave in the face of the Turkish expansions as well.

Segovia's colleague Nicholas of Cusa left the council in 1437 over this controversy and became a leading champion of the papacy. He earned the nickname "Hercules of the Eugenians" for his efforts.[94] A few years later, he had bitter words for those who remained at Basel after the pope had declared the council to be moved to Ferrara. He reported, "But those who remained at Basel, rushing ever downward into the abyss of the wicked, envying the good of unity, hastened to the horror of schism by their own will, contradicting all the nations and prelates, as well as the protests offered to their face by the envoys of kings and princes."[95] Whatever tensions there were between Juan and Nicholas during these tense months at Basel, they did not preclude cooperative intellectual exchanges on other issues. Juan later recalled that 1437 was the year that Nicholas of Cusa loaned him a copy of the Qur'ān.[96]

In the end, the papal council formally opened in Ferrara in January 1438. About a year later, it was moved to Florence, and in the summer of 1439 a decree of union with the Greek church was signed in that city. This decree, which would have been momentous if circumstances were different, in fact was all but meaningless. Upon returning home, the Greek delegates were soundly criticized for having signed it, and that church refused to accept the decree. Outside a small circle of Italian, pro-papal clerics, the decree found no more eager reception in the Western church.[97]

While the assembly at Ferrara-Florence was meeting, the Council of Basel hardly sat idle. Disturbed by the widening rift between Eugene and the council, secular leaders tried to mediate a reconciliation. Some proposals involved a new meeting with the Greeks, which this time would be attended by both Eugene and the council.[98] Such a meeting never transpired, and council and pope never arrived even at a pretense of cooperation. This latest attempt by Eugene to reassert papal authority over the council's proceedings was the last straw. This time the Council of Basel initiated formal procedures against him, which culminated in his deposition in June 1439, about a month before the decree of union was signed in Florence.[99]

Apparently confident that European leaders would accept its authority the council proceeded to elect a new pope, and Juan de Segovia was actively involved in this matter. He was one of three men who, in a process inspired by university electoral procedures, nominated and selected the twelve who would elect the next pope. In his *Historia*, he related, "Upon the unanimous deliberation of all of the sacred delegation, Thomas the abbot of Scotland, Juan de Segovia, and Thomas de Corcellis were nominated and elected as electors of the pontiff, and the authority was given to them, if they wished, to select one, two, or three others to join them."[100] If Piccolomini's account of these proceedings is reliable here, this activity made Juan the target of anger and bitterness from peers. In a letter to Francesco Pizzolpasso from Basel, Piccolomini wrote, "So that you may know what they decided, I am sending your paternity, in the enclosed list, the names of all the electors designated by them [the three], from which you easily can form an opinion of what will ensue. I want your paternity to know, however, that all things were done decently, purely, sacredly. Whomever they elect will be designated by God. Yet, many were deceived in this nomination, who I think were well known to your paternity. . . . Many were excluded who remained white and pale with rage at the nominations of the others, bitterly cursing the names of the three."[101]

In November 1439, a few months after the council's deposition of Eugene, the twelve electors chose Duke Amadeus VIII of Savoy. Juan de Segovia, who received some votes himself in the electoral proceedings, may have been one of those the council asked to make the journey to the duke's chateau in Ripaille, on the southern shore of Lake Geneva, to invite him to accept the office.[102] The duke agreed to come out of a quasi-retirement in a monastery to serve. He turned his duchy over to his son and was installed as pope in Basel in 1440, taking the name Felix V.[103] In describing these events, Nicholas of Cusa called those involved "these wretches," Amedeists, and a "conventicle of wicked schismatics."[104] Not surprisingly, Segovia's account was more sanguine. In his *Historia*, he recorded that the announcement of the election of Amadeus was made after lunch, and that Cardinal Arelatensis declared from a window, "I announce to you a great joy." He told the assembly that the election had happened "to the glory of God, the benefit of the church, the consolation of the council and of the city of Basel," in which the council had operated with such liberty. The *Te deum* was sung and bells rang out throughout the city.[105] Felix V made Juan de Segovia a cardinal in the same year that he accepted the papal office.[106]

For the remainder of the council, Juan was occupied with numerous responsibilities and diplomatic missions on behalf of the council, and the council's primary business was the defense of its deposition of Eugene and election of Felix. While the council sought the support of secular rulers for these steps, Eugene courted these same rulers' loyalties by promising various liberties and financial rewards.[107] Segovia served as Basel's envoy to the imperial diet at Nuremberg in the fall of 1438, to the congress at Mainz the following spring, to the meeting of the German electors and the ecclesiastical synod in Mainz that fall (1439), to the congress at Mainz in the spring of 1441, and to the imperial diet at Frankfurt (summer 1442). In 1443 and 1444 he returned to the diet at Nuremberg, and his last diplomatic mission was to Geneva in 1447. Though the exact circumstances of these meetings varied, his mission in general was to defend the council's actions regarding Eugene (whom he called by his given name, Gabriel, after the 1439 deposition) and to persuade various secular leaders to abandon their policies of neutrality and give their full support to Basel.[108] In a sympathetic account of events at Basel, Aeneas Sylvius Piccolomini described Juan de Segovia as "very distinguished in theology" and, describing the debate at one of these occasions, related that he "replied with reverence and modesty as befitted so great a prelate" to the propapal arguments of canon lawyer Nicolò de' Tudeschi (also known as Panormitanus).[109]

Juan's various responsibilities occasioned the composition of several treatises in which he argued the conciliar cause. Most of these were in preparation for an address he was to deliver before one of the governing bodies mentioned above, or they were written after an address to provide an account of what he had said. In his *Historia gestorum synodi Basiliensis*, Juan included highlights and excerpts from his own interventions and others' at the council itself.[110] In his summaries and treatises, he often repeated an argument he had made earlier, sometimes referring to the earlier works and sometimes not. Noting this tendency, Jesse Mann wrote, "Rather than see this practice as a sign of the lack of originality, it seems more accurate to say that once possessed by an argument's force, or better by its truth, Segovia was simply wont to employ it repeatedly."[111] There is nothing surprising in the repetition of themes and arguments in his conciliar texts, since his goal of persuading Germany's secular leaders to accept Basel's authority remained essentially the same through this period.

One of Segovia's most important works during this time was his *Explanatio de tribus veritatibus fidei*, which will serve here to illustrate his main arguments. This work was edited for the first time by Jesse Mann, whose 1993 dissertation consisted of the edited text and an accompanying study. The *Explanatio* originated as an address Juan gave to the provincial synod at Mainz in August 1439, but its significance extends beyond that assembly.[112] It was a major source for his March 1441 address to the German diet, also at Mainz, to which the kings of France and England had been invited and had sent representatives.[113] In that address, Segovia rose to answer the arguments of Nicholas of Cusa, who had formerly been active as a conciliarist at Basel. Cusa had since switched his allegiance to Eugene, and he argued that March that popes had authority over general councils and that the unity of the church could only be achieved if everyone submitted to Eugene's authority.[114] Stieber called Juan's response to these arguments "one of the most astounding tours de force among the disputations of the church conflict."[115] He spoke in the morning from seven till eleven, took a break for lunch and to rest his voice, and resumed for another three and a half hours in the afternoon.[116] This speech was among the major ones during the council.[117] Hence the *Explanatio* must be regarded as a significant work, the one in which, as Mann put it, arguments that "constitute part of Juan de Segovia's major contribution to theology and ecclesiology" first appeared.[118]

At the beginning of the *Explanatio*, Juan stated clearly why he was writing the work: "that all Christians might clearly see how reasonably the holy council judged him [Eugene IV] a heretic, and how necessary it is for the preservation of the Christian religion that the council's sentence be accepted and that all shun Gabriel as a heretic."[119] He began with a discussion of the great harm posed by a heretical pope, a danger much greater than other heretics posed because of the pope's stature and ability to corrupt and manipulate others.[120] He argued that resistance to such a pope was a moral duty for secular rulers.[121] Furthermore, there were three truths that all believers were bound to accept. The first was that a general council "legitimately assembled" (again the language from *Haec sancta*) received its authority directly from Christ, rather than through the pope as a sort of middleman. Secondly, all the faithful, including the pope, had an obligation to obey such a council in matters of faith, the extirpation of heresy, and church reform. Thirdly, Juan argued, the assertion that a council is superior to a pope and that the pope cannot dissolve it is a "truth of the Catholic faith," and anyone who "pertinaciously" denied the first two truths must be considered a heretic.[122] According to him, Gabriel (Eugene) clearly had done just that.

It was important for his argument that Gabriel had been "pertinacious" in his denial of the first truths. Persistence in error after learning of it was an integral part of the definition of heresy as it was widely disseminated and accepted by medieval canonists and theologians.[123] It was not necessary that the council establish that the pope was a heretic in order to depose him. In fact, the actual sentence of deposition charged him mainly with maladministration of his office. However, the added accusation of heresy strengthened the argument that secular rulers had a moral obligation to support the council.[124] Because a heretical pope posed an extreme danger, threatening the very salvation of those led astray, nonresistance to him would be, as Mann described it, "quite literally damnable."[125] Thus Segovia's argument before numerous assemblies was that "not political gain nor abstract notions such as constitutionalism, but heaven was at stake."[126]

The *Explanatio* provides a helpful look at how Juan de Segovia argued. As we noted, his tendency to cite the Bible and to employ biblical images has not gone unnoticed by scholars.[127] In this work, and presumably in the other writings and speeches modeled on it, Juan anchored his claim for the authority of general councils in scripture. He wrote that scripture was the foundation of all "Catholic truths," and accordingly the truth of the authority (*potestate*) of a general council was grounded in scripture, since Jesus had told the disciples, "Wherever two or three are gathered in my name, I am there among them" (Mt. 18:20).[128] In other words, the council was legitimate, regardless of the pope's disapproval, because Jesus was present there because he had said he would be. Juan also enlisted Jesus's words in Matthew 18:18, "Truly I tell you, whatever you bind on earth will be bound in heaven, and whatever you loose on earth will be loosed in heaven," and John 20:23, "If you forgive the sins of any, they are forgiven them; if you retain the sins of any, they are retained."[129] Of course, these lines from scripture had long been standard fare in arguments supporting supreme power for the papacy. Segovia's use of them rested, as Antony Black has noted, on his observation that in these passages Jesus was referring to a group, not an individual, as the recipient of the authority conferred.[130] The Gospel of Luke provided the committed conciliarist with "Whoever listens to you listens to me, and whoever rejects you rejects me" (Luke 10:16).[131] What Segovia clearly wanted readers to realize was that Christ had not only promised to be present in an assembly such as a council, but that he had invested the gathering with great authority and even equated its words with his own. Juan continued by pointing out that the council's authority was also rooted in the many sections in the Acts of the Apostles where this book tells of a council being held, especially chapters 1, 6, 15, 20, and 21.[132]

There was only one course of action possible for faithful Christians: support the council. Since a heretical pope led souls astray, effectively refusing to listen to Christ's own words, it was incumbent upon others to resist him. Citing James 5:19–20, Juan argued that those who stood against such a pope would be saving those imperiled souls.[133] Paul had opposed Peter, the supreme pontiff, to his face.[134] Peter, for his part, had written that the adversary, the devil, prowls around like a lion searching for prey. Juan likened a heretical pope to the prowling lion.[135] He also recalled Paul's Letter to Titus, where he wrote, "After a first and second admonition, have nothing more to do with anyone who causes divisions, since you know that such a person is perverted and sinful, being self-condemned" (Titus 3:10–11).[136] James provided Juan with the helpful advice, "Anyone, then, who knows the right thing to do and fails to do it commits sin" (James 4:17).[137] The Salamancan master thus argued that good Christians had not only a right to resist an errant pope such as Eugene/Gabriel, but a moral duty to do so.

The *Explanatio* contains references to *Haec sancta*, canon law, decrees and treatises issued at Basel, papal documents, and works by authors such as Ockham, Augustine, and Gerson.[138] Among all of these, however, scripture retained for Juan a certain pride of place. As in the examples provided above, he seemed to regard its message as binding and irrefutable, and the precedents it contained as compelling instruction on how Christians should act. Jesse Mann's study of the *Explanatio* led him to agree with Antony Black's observations on the primacy of theology, or the study of scripture, in Juan's ecclesiology.[139] This is perhaps not surprising for a professor of theology, and specifically of the Bible, at Salamanca. We shall see later how this privileging of scripture also directed his reflections on the proper response to Islam.

Far from being an idiosyncratic tendency, the emphasis that Segovia placed on the authority of scripture appears to have been typical of the conciliarists. Although Brian Tierney was right to highlight in his groundbreaking 1968 study that conciliar thinking had legitimate roots in canon law,[140] Antony Black is among those who have noted that theologians tended to be conciliarists, while canon lawyers were more likely to be proponents of a papal monarchy.[141] This seems generally true, with the usual cautions about overgeneralizing and accounting for the need of many participants at Basel to argue on the side of the bishop or monarch they represented.[142] In a study of Jean Gerson's conciliarist thought, John Ryan observed that those who study the conciliar period have not always given due attention to this concern for scripture.[143]

If the conciliarists saw the crisis over governance in the church as a question of whose reading of scripture was more defensible, their opponents decidedly did not. A useful illustration of the contrast between Segovia's heavy reliance on scripture and the canonists' more ready recourse to church authority appears in the address that Nicholas of Cusa made before the Diet of Frankfurt in 1442. Cusanus was urging the assembly to abandon neutrality, accept the authority of the pope, and reject the council. He stated, "That it is necessary, however, for the salvation of souls, the unity of the Church and the preservation of the honor of this illustrious nation to make such a declaration without delay is obvious from the fact that obedience to the Apostolic See and the Roman pontiff is necessary for salvation." In support of this "fact" he cited Gratian's *Si qui presbiteri*, the *Decretals* of Gregory IX, and Boniface VIII's decree *Unam sanctam*.[144] Since obedience to the pope was necessary for one to be in union with the church, he argued, "Those at Basel, making Duke Amadeus their head, schismatically separated themselves from the universal Church spread throughout the world and from our princes." The editorial notes provided by Thomas Izbicki, the translator of this work, highlight how often Cusa cited Gratian repeatedly as he continued the oration: "'One Church,' therefore, has only 'one' shepherd (the gloss on [Gratian] C. 7 q. i c. *Non autem*); and the Church is 'a flock' united 'to its shepherd' (ibid., c. *Scire debes*). Therefore they cannot be either the Church or a council ([Gratian], C. 24 q. I c. *Didicumus* [c. 31] and C. 24 c. 3 c. *Clericus* [c. 35] and c. *Cum quibus* [c. 36])."[145] These lines are typical of the arguments Nicholas of Cusa presented to his audience throughout this long address. The positive law of the institutional church provided the support that the pope's supporters marshaled against the conciliarists' arguments from natural law and divine law as it was communicated in scripture.[146]

The concilarists' reliance on the Bible was not merely a turn toward ready sources that would support their views. Some have situated Jean Gerson, whose writings were cited and praised by Segovia, and conciliarists in general within the tradition of medieval apostolic protest movements. For these thinkers, the goal was to return the church to its roots, to the practices of the church when the apostles were living and teaching.[147] Gordon Leff went as far as to suggest, "The ideal of the apostolic church was . . . the great new ecclesiological fact of the later Middle Ages."[148] The apostolic church was precisely the "church of scripture,"[149] and the Bible gained a new importance as a "vehicle of criticism"[150] of the current state of church affairs. It served this purpose, Leff argued, for thinkers such as Dante, Marsilius of Padua, William of Ockham, Dietrich of Niem, Wyclif, and Hus, and for groups such as the spiritual Franciscans, the Waldensians, and the Lollards.[151] He summarized, "Among all these groups the notion of an original church helped to furnish an historical justification for opposing the existing church in the name of loyalty to Christ."[152]

As Scott Hendrix has noted, the quest for the true church, the *vera ecclesia* or *ecclesia primitiva*, was hardly new to the later Middle Ages. What this period added was a more multifaceted impulse to the quest, resulting in "a much more complex ecclesiological landscape than had hitherto existed."[153] The new intensity and sophistication of the late medieval thinkers' invocation of the *ecclesia primitiva* was the product of a crisis of confidence in the papal order, fueled by the Waldensians, the spiritual Franciscans, and finally by the Great Schism (1378–1417).[154] The emphasis on biblical authority was now being used not only as a critique of prelates' individual qualities but also as a challenge to the institutional structure itself. Once again, but now with renewed force, "the past was being called in to redress the present."[155]

This link between the study of scripture and church renewal or reform did not end with the close of Basel and the fading of the great hopes of the conciliarists. It would find expression decades later in the labors of humanist scholars like Castile's Cardinal Francisco Ximénez de Cisneros, who coordinated the Complutensian polyglot Bible, the printing of which was completed in 1517.[156] Around the same time, Erasmus explicitly stated, in the dedication to Pope Leo X that appears in his Greek New Testament, that his intention was to advance the reform of Christendom by nurturing all Christians' knowledge of evangelical and apostolic teaching, which would best be accomplished by returning to the source, the original Greek.[157]

Juan de Segovia did not use the phrase *ecclesia primitiva* or *vera ecclesia*. Nonetheless, his writings are infused with the desire, shared with other late medieval thinkers, to bring the contemporary church into conformity with the teachings of the Gospels and with the practice of the early church. While certainly not averse to citing ecclesiastical decrees, Aristotle, or patristic writers, he normally anchored his arguments in scripture and quoted it extensively. During the council, he insisted that the course of action he proposed must be adopted, since it reflected what Christ and the apostles had taught. He made the same argument regarding his proposals for a new way of relating to the Islamic world, the focus of the next chapter.

Ultimately, the pope's methods proved more effective than council members' academic-style orations before various governing bodies, appealing to principle and abstract arguments. Secular leaders gradually withdrew support from the council and cast their lots with the pope instead. The council that Eugene IV convened in Ferrara in 1438 was later transferred to Florence and then Rome, where it concluded in 1445. Pope Eugene IV died in 1447, but he never succeeded in dissolving the Council of Basel. That council continued to meet, discuss needed reforms, and try to secure support for its goals. In June 1448, the Council of Basel transfered to Lausanne, where some months later Felix V abdicated, and the members voted to recognize Nicholas V, who had succeeded Eugene IV two years earlier. Later that month, in April 1449, the Council of Basel-Lausanne voted to adjourn, but not without first negotiating with Nicholas V the end of all censures against those who had participated.[158]

Segovia's impressive history of the council does not contain an account of its conclusion. He stopped work on this project when he reached the spring of 1444 in his narrative. Benigno Hernández Montes believed that Segovia worked most intensively on the *Historia* in the years 1450 to 1453 and abandoned it when he received news of the fall of Constantinople in 1453.[159] Uta Fromherz, who pieced together scattered references by Segovia to the conclusion of the council, wrote that he understood the peaceful conclusion of the council in 1449 neither as a submission to the pope nor as a compromise on the part of the council, but as a unification achieved through the union of justice and peace, which was a gift by God to the church.[160]

In the 1450s, Segovia's writings focused on church matters and the question of Islam, often woven together in curious ways. In the early part of this decade, for example, as he was writing the *Historia*, he was also working on the *Liber de magna auctoritate episcoporum in concilio generali*. This was a lengthy work on ecclesiology, but in one striking passage, he found it helpful to refer to Muslims as a counterexample in the course of his arguments about the nature of the church. The church, he explained, was one body under one head. If it had one head but two bodies, or one body and two heads, it would be monstrous.[161] The one head was none other than Jesus, as Paul attested often,[162] and as conciliarists at Basel had often argued; the head was not the pope as the successor of Peter. This question of the proper relationship of bodies and heads when it came to the church had drawn attention from others as well. After his switch of allegiance to the pope, Piccolomini referred to "the multitude" at Basel as a "multi-headed monster."[163] In his oration at the Diet of Frankfurt, Nicholas of Cusa stated that a council presuming to judge the "prince and head of the church" would be "acephalous."[164] The variation on this theme of heads and bodies that Segovia provided was a reflection on how Christians differed from Muslims in this respect. He explained in the *Liber de magna auctoritate* that Muslims differed from Christians because they did not have one head, since they placed Muhammad above Christ.[165] This is an interesting reference, since this work had nothing to do with anti-Islamic polemic, so there was no obvious reason for him to bring Muslims into the discussion. It is especially intriguing if Segovia was suggesting a parallel between Muslims, commonly considered the enemies of the Christian world, and those who exalted the pope as head of the church, ignoring Christ as the church's true head.[166]

What is clear is that Segovia's approach to Muslims in his later works, when he turned to this issue in earnest, was influenced by his thoughts on the church and by his experiences at Basel, especially the negotiations with the Hussites. The reference to Muslims not having the proper head points to the mingling of his thoughts on church matters and Islam. The years at Basel, which after all consumed most of his adult life, contributed to his uncommon views on how Christians should respond to the Ottoman threat no less than his pivotal experiences speaking with actual Muslims in Castile in his younger years. The next two chapters examine his energetic response to the fall of Constantinople to the Turks in 1453 and to the Christian drumbeat for war in the aftermath of this event.

Chapter Four —∿∿—

CONVERTING FELLOW CHRISTIANS

T he next two chapters examine Juan de Segovia's main preoccupation after Basel, in the final years of his life. During this time, he concerned himself with polemic on two fronts. One line of argument was directed against European Christians who were calling for crusade against the Turks, who succeeded in taking Contantinople in 1453. A second was against Islam, as he longed to convert Muslims to Christianity. Together these comprised his mature approach to the question of Islam, and more specifically to the ascendant Ottoman Empire. I begin with his argument against war because I believe his work is more properly understood as an anticrusading discourse than an argument against a rival faith. Although he might have argued that these were inseparable in his thought, examining each in turn allows us to appreciate more fully how distant he was from both peers and predecessors in the solutions he advanced.

Just how different his arguments were from those of others is a matter of some discussion. Norman Daniel wrote that the "inherited burden" of the long Western polemic against Islam weighed even on him, and credited him only with giving "old arguments a new twist and some allure."[1] More recently, John V. Tolan gave Segovia more credit by naming him as the best known exception to the general rule that "little truly new was written about Islam between 1300 and the Enlightenment."[2] Due to the scope and purpose of those two studies, Segovia's argument against crusade received little attention. To be sure, Cabanelas chose this as the centerpiece of his study of Segovia's perspectives on Islam, even referring to Segovia's proposals as his "pacifist method."[3] Nevertheless, Cabanelas offered little to place Juan de Segovia in the context of his times or within the trajectory of Christian thinking on this subject.

The goal of this chapter is to examine Segovia's arguments against crusade, giving due attention to this aspect of his thought while also viewing his approach against the backdrop of other discussions at the time. Although he was not the first to call for a peaceful approach to Islam, I submit that the vigor and consistency of his positions in this area, particularly in the atmosphere of fear and vulnerability following the events of 1453, give him a place of distinction within the Christian tradition. A few earlier thinkers may have argued for peace, but they also supported crusades. Segovia did not. In his own time, the overwhelming public fear made it virtually impossible to spurn plans for military action against the Turks. He knew his ideas would not be popular, and his steadfast assertion of them revealed, as his activities at Basel had, a person unswayed by what was popular and what would gain him acclaim. The strong biblical orientation to his thought was another characteristic to reappear in these later works. If anything, his inclination to reach for scriptural support intensified as he searched for firm footing in this post-1453 discourse.

Within the swelling tide of intellectuals writing on the Turkish problem, Segovia stood outside the mainstream. As Nancy Bisaha has shown, Italian humanists, at least, responded to the fall of Constantinople in two ways. Some attempted to summon the crusading zeal of the Middle Ages, which they regarded with admiration, while others enlisted secular, classical motifs, portraying the Turks as the new barbarians. After 1453, the second approach gained momentum.[4] As Bisaha notes, it is questionable whether Juan de Segovia was, indeed, a humanist.[5] It may be that Italian intellectuals' responses to 1453 were not the same as those of their counterparts in other regions.

Still, their discussion would surely have been an important one in Europe's efforts to grapple with this threat. Although Segovia was a personal acquaintance of many of these humanists, Italian and otherwise, from his Basel days, he steered clear of their interpretation of these events. He shared with the more traditionally inclined humanists the view that the problem with the Turks was a religious one, never once referring to them as barbarians, but he rejected the crusade as the appropriate religious response and offered a different solution no less based on religious ideals. His primary aim was to convert fellow Christians to what he saw as greater faithfulness to the gospel, which would be manifested by seeking peace rather than war.

It was a project he had to accomplish from relative seclusion rather than the stimulating social currents of Basel in which he had operated a few years earlier. Unlike many of his contemporaries and colleagues at Basel, Juan de Segovia was not confirmed as a cardinal by Nicholas V after the council adjourned. Instead, he succeeded his friend from Basel Louis de La Palud as bishop of St. Jean Maurienne, in the territory of Savoy, on October 13, 1451, only to turn this office over to Guillaume d'Estouteville in January of the following year in exchange for the title of archbishop of Caesarea and two hundred florins a year, to come from the episcopal revenues of Maurienne.[6] According to one history of this diocese, Juan was a compromise candidate, appointed after the cathedral chapter and the pope selected different men for the office.[7] If this is correct, it suggests at least that a local church unwilling to acquiesce to a decision by the pope nevertheless found Juan de Segovia acceptable. His record at Basel and in the service of their popular late duke might well have contributed to the Savoyards' willingness to have him as their bishop. In any case, Juan de Segovia spent the last few years of his life in the priory of Aiton, not far from St. Jean Maurienne. It was during his years in Aiton that he produced most of his writings on Islam and on how Christian Europe should respond to the Turks' advances. It was to Aiton that he welcomed Yça Gidelli, the Castilian Muslim leader who would provide him with what he hoped was a better translation of the Qur'ān.

Juan de Segovia probably expected, and Nicholas V probably hoped, that Segovia's retirement to the mountaintop priory would signal the end of his active participation in the great discussions of the time. It is somewhat ironic that he launched into such an intense discussion, with some of Europe's leading thinkers on perhaps the period's most pressing events, from such a location. The village of Aiton sits in the French Alps near the intersection of the Arc and Isére rivers, about two hundred and fifty kilometers from Basel. The priory was founded in the eleventh century and was originally home to Augustinian monks. However, by the time Juan established residence there, it had long been a Benedictine house dependent on the monastery of Saint Michael la Chiusa in the Piedmont. The 1451 bull of Nicholas V, which arranged for Juan de Segovia to live there, noted that there were only two monks in residence at the time.[8] Aiton seemed to him, a well-traveled churchman, to be frustratingly remote. He lamented his poor access to books, saying that he could not easily visit libraries because the priory was too far from any cities and towns. For this reason, he hired several scribes, who lived at the priory with him. Their work enabled him to increase his personal library.[9] Aeneas Sylvius Piccolomini corroborated Juan's opinion that his new home was off the beaten track, reporting that after Basel Juan "secluded" himself in some very high mountains, "content in his little monastery."[10]

Settled into life at his priory, Juan de Segovia learned of the fall of Constantinople from a visitor who was a canon of the cathedral of Seville. The man, whose name Segovia did not record, was a *familiar* of Cardinal Juan de Cervantes, as Segovia himself had once been.[11] This visitor was passing through and stayed only briefly. Aiton would have been on the way to many places, even though Juan's complaints about not being within easy distance of any libraries were true. In some ways Aiton was far from remote. The valley of the Arc River was the major thoroughfare for land travel between Italy and the regions around Chambery, Lyon, Annecy, and Geneva. This route facilitated transport so much, in fact, that armies had found it a convenient invasion route for centuries, as the numerous fortresses on the mountains on either side of the valley attest. From his quiet priory on the mountaintop, Juan could have gazed down at the valley and watched a stream of traffic that must have been fairly steady. Nevertheless, most of those travelers through the Arc valley had no reason to make the trek up the mountain to the priory. Juan might well have felt both quite close and yet far away from the considerably beaten track within sight of his new home. He was probably grateful for this visit from a fellow Castilian who no doubt brought news of friends and acquaintances from Castile and from the Basel years.

He may have been grateful, too, to be remembered and acknowledged, and to hear that Cervantes wished him well. In his 1443 petition to the pope to have Juan de Segovia removed from his *familiares*, Cardinal Cervantes had called Segovia a schismatic and asserted that he had been seduced by a diabolic spirit.[12] One wonders if the visiting associate of Seville's archbishop gleaned anything during his brief stay about how highly esteemed this diabolically inspired schismatic was in his new surroundings, where he enjoyed a reputation as a saintly and virtuous man.

One indication of this is a letter from Juan to one Guillielmus de Orliaco in October of 1456 held in the library at the University of Salamanca. Probably connected to the Dominican house in Annecy, Orliaco was a hermit or was about to begin life as a hermit, and he had written to Segovia to ask his advice on some spiritual matters.[13] In addition, Juan de Segovia apparently held his own in a dispute with local canon Pierre Girollet, who had been appointed by the cathedral chapter at St. Jean Maurienne to transport the body of Louis de La Palud, the city's recently deceased bishop, to the cathedral. Segovia was one of four executors of Palud's will, and he fought this move on the grounds that it was contrary to Palud's expressed wishes to be buried in the chapel at Varembon between his mother and father. He prevailed against the canon and the cathedral chapter.[14] After Segovia's own death, the locals kept the candles lit at his tomb at least till the late sixteenth century,[15] and chronicles reported that the site was associated with miracles.[16] If Juan's favorable reputation earned him the respect and affection of the locals, this might have been an especially impressive accomplishment at that time. Chambery's archive contains several papal bulls from the 1440s and 1450s directed against those who were vandalizing and robbing churches and committing violence against the local clergy.[17]

If Segovia had been troubled by these acts of violence against churches and clergy, the canon's visit turned his thoughts sharply beyond local tensions to violence in a wider arena. He did not record exactly what this canon from Seville related to him about the loss of Constantinople, referring to the event only as the "lamentable ruin of the city of Constantinople" (*flebilem ruinam Constantinopolitane civitatis*)[18] or the "lamentable plundering [or pillaging] of Constantinople" (*flebilem direptionem constantinopolitanam*).[19] Especially for one given to lengthy speeches and letters, these references to the fate of Constantinople are surprisingly brief. Many of his contemporaries were more dramatic. Cosimo de Medici, for example, characterized the event as the most tragic that history had seen for centuries.[20] Piccolomini wrote to Pope Nicholas V on July 12 of 1453, "But what is this execrable news which is borne to us concerning Constantinople? My hand trembles, even as I write; my soul is horrified, yet neither is it able to restrain its indignation, nor express its misery. Alas, wretched Christianity!"[21]

The brevity of his references to this stunning news is not an indication that Segovia was unaffected by it. On the contrary, it changed the direction of his work for the rest of his life, which lasted five more years. The problem of Christian-Muslim relations, a longstanding interest, became his top priority. Segovia wrote that he had long ago concluded that the *via pacis et doctrine* was the right course of action, but the news of the fate of Constantinople and the plans for a crusade finally galvanized him to develop these ideas further and make them more widely known.[22] Leaving several writing projects unfinished, including his history of the Council of Basel, he dedicated himself exclusively to the issue of Christian-Muslim relations for the remainder of his life. Never one for brevity, Juan's writings on the subject are voluminous. He was remarkably prolific at an advanced age.

The Interlocutors

Segovia diffused his ideas through letters that grew into lengthy treatises and shorter works that he also sent along to his correspondents as supplements. The main purpose of each letter, with the exception of his correspondence with a Castilian Muslim scholar, was to decry the folly of approaching the new challenges to Christian Europe by means of war. He was seeking a way to air these views and find an outlet for their expression in influential circles. At least four of his six contacts were colleagues from Basel. The first one to whom he turned was Cervantes, whose associate had delivered the news concerning Constantinople and whose southern Spanish diocese bordered the Muslim kingdom of Granada. It was for Cervantes that he wrote his *De gladio divini Spiritus in corda mittendo sarracenorum* and the *Liber de praeclara noticia*. The thesis of both was that the only proper means for Christians to pursue the conversion of Muslims was the path of peace and doctrine or teaching. In *De gladio*, he stressed the irrationality of Islam, and in the *Liber de praeclara noticia* he argued for the coherence of Christianity. We know from Juan's comments in other letters that these two works were interrupted by other correspondence and tasks, and that he worked on the two off and on from 1453 to 1457.[23]

It is interesting that his first inclination was to write to Cervantes, given the estrangement between them two years earlier, although it was also to Cervantes that Juan had addressed his *De magna auctoritate episcoporum in concilio generali* a few years earlier.[24] Perhaps Juan harbored no hard feelings from their break, or he sensed that past hurts could now be put aside and that Cervantes would welcome his work.[25] Segovia might have received news from the visiting canon that made him want to persuade Cervantes that crusading was not the right response. Quite possibly he learned from the visiting canon of Cervantes' own efforts to assemble a crusading force to invade the Muslim lands bordering his diocese of Seville. In 1449, Pope Nicholas V granted a petition that Cervantes made, in which the archbishop asked for clarity on the matter of whether people taking certain actions against the Saracens qualified for the indulgence associated with crusading, since some of the faithful in his region held back from participating due to their fears that such attacks might be considered irregular or unlawful. The pope ruled, "We [therefore] concede and entrust to your judgement, by apostolic authority and the present letters, that you and other suitable priests, whom you temporarily deputise for the purpose, may grant the same plenary remission, that is of all their sins, to all the faithful who dispatch substitutes with you at their costs and expenses, to engage with and attack the Saracens, as well as to anybody who takes part with you in the conflict against the Saracens, inside or outside their own lordships, provided that they are truly penitent and confessed." He added that Cervantes also had the authority to grant permission to priests, mendicants, and members of other religious orders to "freely and lawfully attack and assault the Saracens, laying hands on them violently, and disabling, wounding and killing them, without any irregularity or disqualification."[26] If Segovia knew of these endeavors of his former colleague at Basel, it may explain the fervor with which he undertook his arguments to Cervantes.

Segovia's letter was no tentative feeler to see if the archbishop was interested in hearing his ideas. He composed two volumes, at least one of which was quite long, apparently fully expecting that Cervantes would read them. Perhaps the canon who had relayed the news of the Turks' victory also gave Juan reason to believe that the cardinal still held him in high enough regard to be open to hearing about Segovia's proposals. It is even possible that Juan's optimism about this new work being received was due to some news from the canon about the cardinal's thoughts on *De magna auctoritate*. Unfortunately, Cervantes died in November 1453 and never saw the works Juan continued to write for him.

The second person to whom Juan wrote of his ideas was Nicholas of Cusa. Cusa was another colleague from the council, and the two had shared an interest in Islam since their early years at Basel. Like Cervantes, Cusanus had abandoned the conciliarist cause and even participated in a debate against Juan de Segovia in Mainz in March 1441. However, in a letter dated December 2, 1454, Juan addressed him with great esteem, recalling their previous acquaintance. He explained, "Certainly I would be embarrassed, most reverend father, to drag my pen on for so long, were it not for my trust that your most venerable lordship wishes always to be involved in those things that are of the Father, as is fitting."[27] He praised the work of his former friend and ally, and later adversary: "Indeed word travels fast and your tireless work toward reform in the German lands is well known, just as it is known that your mind delights in great and difficult work, as is characteristic of perfect men. Surely the best quality of a generous soul is (this), that it is stirred toward what is honorable."[28] Significantly shorter than the two-volume treatise Segovia had sent to Cervantes, this letter to Nicholas of Cusa fills around twenty to thirty folios, depending on the script. Juan seemed to have regarded this work as a clear and perhaps definitive expression of his views on Islam and Christian-Muslim relations. He sent a copy of it to Jean Germain the following summer and another copy to an unknown friend in the spring of 1458.[29]

From Innsbruck, Cusa sent a reply bearing a date in late December 1454, less than a month after Juan had sent his letter. His genuine pleasure at hearing from Segovia and receiving his proposals was almost palpable. Cusa addressed him as a most special friend (*amice singularissime*), and he wrote, "I received your letter, which I have read and reread and which has been very gratifying to me, and many aspects of it have afforded me great pleasure. In particular, I saw that the bond of the old friendship between us is—I understood with much joy—not only intact, but even sealed with glue, the clearest sign of which was shown to me when you revealed highly sensitive matters first to me, so that I might say, in brief, that we are and we will always remain friends, as attested by our feelings and our deeds."[30] This response must have cheered its recipient and evoked memories of the friendship they enjoyed before the split at Basel, before Cusa had redirected his formidable intellectual capacities to a defense of the papacy.

It was not just friendship that was affirmed in the reply from Innsbruck. Nicholas of Cusa bears the distinction of having been the only correspondent from whom Segovia received a positive response to his proposals for peace. After responding to Segovia's expressed desire for news related to the Turks and the Europeans' response, he turned to his Castilian colleague's request for feedback on his ideas about entering a dialogue with Muslims. These comments he prefaced by saying, "Concerning the other two points, most reverend father, you are too learned and prudent to need instruction, but lest I seem not to want to comply as I am able, let me touch on some things that come to mind."[31] He came right to the point in stating his approval of Segovia's approach: "And it seems to me that we must deal with the infidels in exactly the way that I see to please your most reverend paternity, and I have written a little book about this, which I entitled *De pace fidei.*"[32] He even agreed with Segovia on the need to be governed by Christ's teaching, saying, "If we will have proceeded in accordance with the teaching of Christ, we will not err, but his Spirit will speak in us, which all the adversaries of Christ will be unable to resist; but, if we choose the aggression of invasion by the sword, we have to fear lest, fighting by the sword, we perish by the sword. Therefore only defense is without danger for the Christian."[33] In the broad strokes of their thinking, Juan de Segovia and Nicholas of Cusa had much in common. Not without reason, scholarship on Christian approaches to Islam has often discussed the two thinkers as a pair.[34] Beyond the general interest in dialogue and peaceful overtures, however, there were significant and interesting differences between their respective approaches to matters Islamic.

One clue that these thinkers' inclinations were not in complete alignment comes from the work that Cusa mentioned in his response to Segovia's letter, his *De pace fidei*. It is curious that he mentioned this work in the context of telling Segovia that his ideas for a dialogue with Muslims were exactly the right approach, suggesting that this same approach is what Cusa himself had presented in *De pace fidei*. Any readers expecting to see parallel proposals in Cusa's work would be puzzled. This work is indeed a dialogue, but a fictional one among seventeen different participants, each representing a major region or people in the world. The faith of Muslims appears in the work, but by no means as the only set of beliefs under discussion. Among the interlocutors are an Arab, a Turk, a Persian, and a Syrian, but also a German, a Jew, a Frenchman, a Spaniard, an Englishman, a Greek, and a Bohemian. Their dialogue is narrated as a vision received by one "caught up to a certain intellectual height."[35] The entire affair takes place at the heavenly court, with interventions by the Logos, Peter, and Paul. As we shall see below in more detail, this is nothing like the dialogue that Juan de Segovia envisioned, which he hoped would take place firmly on earth, between Christians and Muslims, with a small group of leaders in attendance.[36]

Cusa surely realized that his work was not what Segovia was planning; he probably judged it useful toward the same end because it presented ways that non-Christians might come to find such beliefs and practices as the Trinity, the Incarnation, and the Eucharist as less objectionable than they had previously thought. In his letter to Segovia he included some suggestions on how to present these teachings, so we know that he was thinking about how others might come to understand these doctrines.[37] Still, Cusa's inclination in the face of the Ottoman advances was to produce a literary work that translators have suggested "should probably be classified with the literature of utopia,"[38] while his Spanish colleague undertook a painstaking new translation of the Qur'ān and elicited support for a summit meeting to discuss differences.

Even though Cusa's dialogue strikes the modern reader as more fanciful, it was certainly bold. Its boldness points to another significant difference between the writings of the two men. The goal of Segovia's efforts was to achieve, by peaceful means, the conversion of Muslims to Christianity. In *De pace fidei*, Nicholas of Cusa went well beyond this aim and called for one universal religion, with a common recognition that all worshipped the same God through a diversity of rites and practices. As recent translators of *De pace fidei* have noted, Cusa's work may be the first in Christian writing "to come to grips with the problem of world religions using an approach along lines other than conversion or mission."[39] Early in the work, the Word of God explains that "the Lord, King of heaven and earth" has heard the cries of those who have died or suffered oppression because of differences over religion. He announces, "And since all those who either cause this persecution or suffer it are led only by the belief that in this way it is expedient to be saved and pleasing to their Creator, therefore, the Lord has had mercy on his people and has decided that by the common consent of all men all diversity of religions be brought peacefully to one religion to remain inviolable from now on."[40]

The Word explains further that the King has entrusted to those assembled the responsibility of carrying this out and has assigned "ministering angelic spirits" to them as assistants to guide them.[41] The conversation among the participants is amicable throughout, and at the end they study their books about "the observances of the ancients" together. The narrator relates, "After these were examined it was discovered that all the diversity consisted in rites rather than in the worship of one God; from all the writings collected into one it was found that all from the beginning always presupposed and worshiped the one God in all practice of worship, although people in their simplicity, seduced by the adverse power of the Prince of Darkness, often did not consider what they were doing."[42] In the last lines of the book, the King of Kings enjoins everyone to "lead the nations to the unity of true worship" and to "come together in Jerusalem as to a common center and accept one faith in the name of all and thereupon establish an everlasting peace so that in peace the Creator of all, blessed forever, will be praised."[43]

Ambitious as he was about producing a new and improved translation of the Qur'ān and persuading Muslims to convert, Juan de Segovia did not dream of the achievement of a single world religion, and this concept would have been completely alien to him. As the next chapter will explore in more detail, he certainly did not consider the differences between Christianity and Islam to be mere differences in worship. Cusa's startling suggestion that the different religions in the world were really one is not something that Juan de Segovia would have embraced.

A few years after writing *De pace fidei*, Nicholas of Cusa completed another work, this one specifically on the Qur'ān. The goal of his *Cribratio Alkorani* (*A Scrutiny of the Qur'ān*) is clearly evident early in the work, where he explained, "I applied my mind to disclosing, even from the Koran, that the Gospel is true. And in order that this |disclosure| may readily be made, I will here set forth in a few words my overall conception."[44] This work also reveals a search for common ground, this time specifically between Christianity and Islam, but its tone is less genial. This is an extended scholarly argument that the gospel is true, and that this truth appears in the Qur'ān, despite Muslims' blindess to it. Gone is the amiability of the envisioned dialogue in heaven and the promising agreement it produced. Jasper Hopkins has noted, as others have, the undeniably polemical tone in this work, stating that it engages in "open invective" and even repeats some of the "denigrating attacks" on Islam already energetically presented by predecessors in the Christian polemical tradition.[45] This spirit is most evident in his charges against the Prophet. One example appears in Book II, where Cusanus, addressing Muhammad, wrote, "But how is it that you presume to speak with regard to other matters, since |to do so| is neither imposed upon you, nor granted to you, by God? Moreover, if you speak, why shall I believe you if |in speaking| you are not obeying God? Assuredly, you are without excuse— unless, as you are accustomed |to do|, you attribute variation to the immutable God, so that you escape |the charge against you| by thus blaspheming."[46] In Book III, he accused Muhammad of promulgating his new religion purely in order to gain power: "But you have seemed to me, O Muhammad, to have sought—under the pretext of religion—the power of dominating. . . . Does anyone fail to understand that the goal of your religion—that your zeal and the rite |prescribed| by your law—tends only toward your dominating? For does anyone make satisfaction to God and you by means of tribute? Your intent was none other than to become great by means of God and religion."[47] These charges would have offended any Muslim confronted with them and hardly advanced the goal of persuasion.

Nevertheless, it is possible to exaggerate the shift in tone from *De pace fidei* to the *Cribratio Alkorani*, as if the two works present a completely different line of thinking, one conciliatory and one adversarial. This view ignores the difference in genre between the two. The *Cribratio* is an extended argument about the proper way to understand a text, the Qur'ān. Derisive and offensive remarks such as the examples presented above are remarkably infrequent. Certainly this argument against Islam contains considerably less invective and more restraint than its author's arguments against the supporters of Basel found in his oration at the Diet of Frankfurt or his Dialogue against the Amedeists.[48] The tone Cusanus adopted in *Cribratio*, sometimes attributed to the influence of writers like John of Damascus, Peter the Venerable, and John of Torquemada,[49] may be less a testimony to enduring Western polemic against Islam than to conventions of argumentation, or even to his own style of arguing. In the end, both *De pace fidei* and the *Cribratio Alkorani* were forays into thinking about how others might view the central teachings of Christianity and how one might persuade them to accept these teachings. The latter is a serious and sustained consideration of what it might take to persuade

Muslims to convert, and it takes their reverence for the Qur'ān as its starting point. Although Juan de Segovia died three years before it was completed, this aspect of Cusa's approach would have resonated with his own.

Juan's third correspondent was another Basel colleague, Jean Germain, a theologian with close ties to the court of the duke of Burgundy. Juan initiated this correspondence after a visit in July 1455 from a Carmelite from Burgundy, who arrived in Aiton bearing greetings from Germain and news of two works by him on Islam. Probably excited to learn of this common interest, Juan hurried off a brief letter, essentially a cover letter, telling of his recent thinking on the subject and asking for Germain's advice and comments on his proposals. He attached a copy of his letter to Cusa, wrote that Cusa had already responded favorably, and asked Germain to keep these proposals in confidence for now. Juan told him that the bearer of this letter and the accompanying longer work, Sansón Telluti, would inform him of additional details verbally. The letter was dated July 31, 1455.[50] Along with a copy of his letter to Cusa, Segovia included two brief supplemental works. His *Allegationes libri Alchoran de peccatis primi parientis facientes mentionem* contains several passages from the Qur'ān regarding the sin of Adam.[51] The second short supplement among the materials Juan sent to Burgundy was entitled *Ex plurimis in ea contentis pauci errores legis Mahumeti excerpti de libro legis ipsius Alchoran nominato*, which began with the Qur'ān's description of paradise and proceeded to other "errors," especially the negation of the Christian doctrine of the Trinity.[52] Germain responded to these materials promptly in two letters, no longer extant, dated September 3 and 9, 1455.

Germain's reply was not what Juan had hoped. He disagreed vigorously with Segovia's ideas, and the latter composed a lengthy reply, answering Germain's objections with vigor of his own.[53] In his response, dated December 18, 1455, the Castilian recalled that twelve years earlier Germain had been in agreement with him that the *via pacis et doctrine* was the right course. In fact, Juan reminded him, he had even written back then to Nicholas V, the princes of Germany, and the kings of France, England, and Aragon urging them to pursue such a path.[54] The Castilian scholar probably read Germain's September letters with dismay.

It is surprising that Segovia remembered Germain as having supporting a *via pacis* twelve years earlier. This is not how historians remember him. Furthermore, if Segovia was surprised by Germain's response, this raises questions about how current Segovia's knowledge was of affairs beyond Aiton. Germain had long been involved in efforts to rally Christians to a crusade that would take back lands that were formerly in Christian hands. These began at least as early as 1437, when he argued at court for crusade in a homily given at the festivities for the Feast of Saint Andrew, the patron saint of Burgundy. There he reminded the court of the conquests of Godfrey of Bouillon and of Philip of Alsace, the count of Flanders who participated in the siege of Acre. He urged them to follow in their predecessors' footsteps. When he rose to deliver this homily, he spoke as one in a position of authority in such matters. In 1430, Philip the Good had named Germain chancellor of the newly formed Order of the Golden Fleece, an order comprised of the king, the chancellor, and selected knights, which had the purpose of exalting and furthering the "true faith" and the church. Jean Germain's finest hour may have been a homily he delivered at a chapter of this order meeting in Mons in 1451, just a few years before Segovia's initial correpondence with him. During this homily, which was delivered in French, he decried the horrible devastation that had befallen the church militant, the desecration of Christian holy places, the attacks on Cyprus and Rhodes, and the Turkish advances in the Balkans. Recalling once again the feats of Godfrey of Bouillon and the great kings of France, and also the wars in Hungary, he called on his listeners to assemble an army and respond to these attacks.[55] If Segovia knew about such addresses by Germain, he should not have been surprised to read Germain's response to his letter about seeking peace with Muslims.

Philip the Good was not exactly a difficult audience for a speaker promoting a crusade. Philip was the European leader who, apart from the Iberians, spent the most money and effort on fighting Muslims. His father had been captured at Nicopolis, and Philip had been persuaded by a Byzantine embassy to join a crusade in 1442. A Burgundian fleet fought at Rhodes, helping the Hospitallers to end the siege on the island, and sailed to aid Constantinople in 1444, but not before spending some time raiding the North African coast. Philip was married to

Isabel of Portugal, a strong proponent of crusading, whom Germain served as confessor. The duke was an active patron of works on Islam, crusades, and chivalry.[56]

Germain's 1451 homily, which did not articulate a precise goal the crusaders should accomplish, did not provoke the immediate response he desired, but the duke subsequently sent delegations to the kings of France, England, Naples, Hungary, and Poland, as well as the pope and the emperor, in which he communicated the message from Germain's sermon.[57] Germain himself traveled to France in 1452 to elicit the support of Charles VII for this crusade, which Robert Schwoebel noted might have saved Constantinople. Then the bishop of Chalon-sur-Saône, Germain wrote for this mission his *Le Discours du voyage d'oultremer au très victorieux roi Charles VII*, in which he described the rise of Islam, its present state, and the past triumphs of French kings who had opposed its adherents in battle. As if it were not enough humiliation that the Holy Land lay in enemy hands, he wrote, the Turks were planning to destroy Christianity in Greece. In this work, Germain warned that the Turks had relentlessly assaulted Hungary for two decades, and if they were not stopped, Constantinople itself would be theirs.[58] Part of his argument was that never, since the time of Godfrey, had conditions been so promising for success of a crusade in the East. He referred to the Council of Florence and the new union of the Latin and Greek churches, saying, "This had not been done for 500 years, since before Godfrey of Bouillon's conquests, for even at that time the Greeks and Latins were in schism and division, to Christendom's great harm. By contrast, their firm union will be of great assistance to its revival." After citing various regions ready to supply troops as soon as the West committed, Germain insisted, "It is helpful that the Christian people is more ready than it has been for a long time to do something good and fruitful on behalf of the faith."[59]

Not all of these embassies made a good impression, and this may have been the reason that Germain fell from favor sometime before early in 1454. Segovia may not have known of this change in his colleague's standing. He seemed to be writing to men he considered likely to be influential, and he might not have taken the trouble to write to Germain if the Burgundian no longer held the position of influence he had previously enjoyed. Polish chronicler John Dlugosz described the ill-fated embassy to his country as verbose, arrogant, and lacking in sense. Without placing Germain himself in this delegation, Jacques Pavio: called this delegation a "smarting diplomatic failure," which explains Germain's fall from grace.[60] In any case, 1453 provided the precise aim for a crusade that the duke needed. It also provided a new argument for the legitimacy of his own leadership of the crusading enterprise. In 1204, Baldwin of Flanders-Hainault, who was from lands that by the mid-1400s were under Burgundian rule, had been designated the Latin emperor of Constantinople. As duke of Burgundy, Philip could assert historical rights to Constantinople. This crusade had its origins in the efforts of the Order of the Golden Fleece and of Jean Germain as chancellor, despite his recent fall from favor.[61]

Germain had spent much of his adult life urging leaders to undertake a crusade. In Burgundy nostalgia for an old-fashioned crusade was strong, inspired no less by the memory of Godfrey of Bouillon and Baldwin of Flanders-Hainault. It is hard to understand why Juan de Segovia was so eager for Germain's comments on his proposals, or so frustrated at Germain's response. If he had known of his Burgundian colleague's activities, he should have seen it coming. Expected or not, Germain's letter prompted an energetic reply from Segovia. His December reply contained a refutation of the calculations based on scripture that predicted the victory of Philip the Good over Islam (which apparently Germain had presented to him in his own letter), nine arguments against Germain, and twenty-eight point-by-point rebuttals to Germain's objections. Much to his frustration, Juan never received a reply to this second letter.[62] Cabanelas suggested that the Burgundian had realized the superiority of Segovia's reasoning and dared not respond.[63] Another possibility is that Germain realized that the two men's ideas were too far apart for productive discussion, or that Juan was not a sympathetic reader who would affirm his own stance. Perhaps Germain preferred to dedicate his time to swaying the undecided toward launching a crusade, or perhaps he simply retreated from such exchanges, demoralized by his new status as a discredited adviser. He might simply not have felt up to the daunting task of making it through the ninety-five folios of Juan's response.

In addition to his correspondence with the Castilian Muslim Yça Gidelli, which the next chapter will discuss in more detail, Juan's writings from these years include three brief letters. The first was a letter that in the *Donatio* bears the title *Epistola Johannis ad Wilielmum de Orliaco, hermitani in Sabaudia, de quatuor Hostibus hominis et de consideracione dierum VII hebdomade habenda circa uitam Christi,* but the work itself does not contain a salutation naming the recipient, addressing him simply as *mi frater amantissime.*[64] Jesse Mann has offered a compelling argument that this man was probably Guillaume d'Orlyé, a hermit from a noble Savoyard family who was attached to the Dominican house at Annecy (in Savoy). One nineteenth-century source relates that in his youth, Guillaume d'Orlyé was part of the court of Amadeus VIII, the duke of Savoy, whom the Council of Basel would later elect as Pope Felix V.[65] This letter was unlike the others from this time in Segovia's life because it was a letter (really a short treatise) on the eremitic life, written in response to a request from its recipient asking for advice on this topic. This was not about the topic of Islam or the appropriate Christian response to the Turkish threat. This letter was dated October 13, 1456, and remains unpublished.

Segovia's letter of April 18, 1458, to an unknown friend has already been mentioned.[66] After citing various examples from scripture of people seeking another's advice, he reiterated the importance of consultation, especially when one was proposing a course of action that involved the whole church.[67] He told the recipient, whom he addressed as *mi dilectissime frater,* that the ideas he now presented were also in his earlier *De magna auctoritate episcoporum in concilio generali,* but that he had decided to expand on them following the devastating destruction of Constantinople and Nicholas V's efforts to launch a crusade.[68] Segovia's letter to this beloved *frater* acknowledged the recipient's profound knowledge of scripture and cited this as a reason for wanting his counsel. Juan wrote, "With great desire, I have longed for your counsel concerning the substance of the writings and the way in which it is to be made public; and truly to work in a way worthy of that help from you, who from early on, from the flower of youth, always have had time for the sacred scriptures and for consultations of them not through weak efforts, but through great efforts."[69] In this letter, which occupies about five pages in modern print, Segovia recounted his previous correspondence with others on the matter and reiterated that his goal was to show that the *via pacis et doctrine* was preferable to fire and sword as a way to put an end to the sect of the Saracens.[70] He also told the recipient about his translation project and about Gidelli's stay in Aiton; this news consumes about a fifth of the letter.[71] No details about his proposed *via pacis et doctrine* are offered, and no new themes are introduced in this letter. If there was ever a response, it has not come to light. We can only wonder if the unnamed *mi dilectissime frater* of this letter was also Guillaume d'Orlyé, addressed as *mi frater amantissime* in the letter from two years earlier. If so, the counsel he requested might not have been the only reason to write to him. This letter would be one more that Segovia wrote to men with connections. As he reached the end of his life, surely knowing that he would not be around to promote his plans, he turned toward others who might. If the date of the letter is accurate, he died a month later.[72]

Segovia's final letter was to another colleague from Basel, Aeneas Sylvius Piccolomini, who was then cardinal of Siena but who would be elected pope three months later. This letter was even shorter. He mentioned having heard from Piccolomini encouraging him to publish his work on the translation and refutation of the Qur'ān.[73] However, he wrote, he was in his final days and could not write more, although he was sending works concerning his proposal which had been exchanged with two "great men," Cusa and Germain.[74] Although there is no evidence that Segovia had remained in direct contact with Piccolomini in the later years of Basel or after it, the two had exchanged letters before,[75] and Piccolomini had sometimes asked other recipients of his letters to commend him to Segovia. In a 1444 letter to papal secretary Giovanni Peregallo, for example, he called Segovia "a good man and truly most beloved" and asked Peregallo to tell Segovia and some others that if he had not written to them for some time, it was due to his office.[76]

It is interesting that in his correspondence with Nicholas of Cusa over three years earlier, Cusa had encouraged Segovia to make his ideas widely known, and specifically to send his work to the pope, telling him that he had heard the pope speak highly of him.[77] Juan de Segovia had asked Cusa whether it was advisable that he disseminate his thoughts more publicly.[78] As far as we know, Segovia never did write to Nicholas V (1447–55), who was pope at that time, or to Calixtus III (1455–58), so this letter to Pius II (1458–64) appears to have been his first communication of these thoughts to a pope, or someone about to be pope. It may be that Cusa encouraged him to send along not his proposals for dialogue per se, but the translation of the Qur'ān that he intended to make. In the lines immediately preceding his encouragement to send his labors to the pope and assuring him of the pope's esteem for him, Cusa encouraged him to finish the work and to send it first to the pope and then to him and to others, saying, "It will be indeed one of the most valued treasures of the church."[79] This hope suggests that what he thought Segovia should send to the pope was not a copy of the letter he himself had received, which already formulated a proposal for negotiations with the Muslims, but rather the translation of the Qur'ān that Segovia planned to complete. Indeed, immediately before this, Cusa referred to another writer who had worked on a small text (*opus parvum*) against the errors of Muhammad, but he added, "It is no comparison to that glorious volume of your compilations."[80]

If Segovia was intending all along to send the pope the completion of his translation of the Qur'ān, this might explain the delay of over three years after his correspondence with Cusa before he wrote to any popes. As we will see in the next chapter, that project encountered delays even after the bulk of the work was completed. Segovia may have wished to send a definitive, completed version, which may well not have been ready. Or he may have hesitated after Nicholas V called a crusade. Piccolomini was no more likely to be receptive to his ideas about seeking peace with Muslims. In the fall of 1454, when Segovia was working on his proposals, which he would send to Nicholas of Cusa that December, Piccolomini delivered an enthusiastic speech at the Diet of Frankfurt urging those assembled to rouse themselves for a crusade.[81] If Segovia was receiving reasonably regular news from outside Aiton, he might have known about this oration.

Certainly Segovia's letter to Piccolomini differs from his communication with Cusa and Germain, and not only in length. In it, he cited the Gospel command to "go into the whole world and teach all peoples,"[82] and he referred to the parable in the Gospel of Luke about a king who sues for peace because he lacks the forces to counter his enemy, arguing that this passage further recommended that the church seek peace.[83] These themes were frequent enough in his letters to Cusa and Germain, but in this last letter, as in his letter the previous month, perhaps because his own strength was waning, he offered much less by way of specific advice on how to accomplish these goals. The plan he laid out elsewhere, which is discussed in more detail below, here was suggested but not explained. He mentioned his translation of the Qur'ān prominently, in the first few lines of his letter.[84] He seemed generally intent on urging the soon-to-be-pope to spread the Christian faith, but, unlike in his letters to Cusa and Germain, he refrained from directly condemning crusading as a solution or criticizing the church's recourse to war.

Despite his prior esteem for Segovia as a person, as reflected in the references to him that appear in Piccolomini's earlier letters, there is no evidence that the Italian prelate seriously considered Segovia's approach to the Turkish problem. In fact, in his *Commentarii rerum memorabilium que temporibus suis contingerunt*, full of colorful autobiographical anecdotes, Piccolomini briefly discussed Segovia's efforts toward peace with the Muslim world. His depiction reveals that he was hardly impressed by his colleague's recent work. He said that after Juan had some masters of the Islamic law come to him in his remote monastery, he translated into "our language" the book they call the Qur'ān, in which are contained "not so much the mysteries as the delusions of the pseudo-prophet Muhammad." Piccolomini's closing comment in his brief paragraph about Juan was that he "unraveled [the Qur'ān's] stupidities with reasons and arguments as well founded as they were realistic."[85]

As pope, Piccolomini certainly worked vigorously toward precisely the crusading activity that Segovia decried. In fact, he owed his meteoric rise up the church hierarchy to his eloquent calls for crusade. Judging from his own accounts of these speeches, he took pride in them. In his *Commentaries*, in which he wrote of himself in the third person, his pleasure at his own performance before a Diet at Regensburg is palpable:

> But when the Diet formally convened and Aeneas made his speech— wonderful to relate—the old enthusiasm for a crusade suddenly revived in every heart. His oration lasted nearly two hours; but the audience was so utterly absorbed that no one even cleared his throat or took his eyes off the speaker's face. No one thought the speech too long, and all were sorry to hear it end.[86]

Piccolomini's orations and letters in support of a crusade so impressed Pope Calixtus III (1455–58) that the pope named him a cardinal in 1456, only twelve years after Piccolomini was ordained.[87] One of his first moves when he became pope in 1458 was to convene a congress of European leaders at Mantua, which began in the fall of 1459 with the purpose of laying plans for a crusade.[88] Over the course of his pontificate, his rhetoric in favor of a crusade shifted in ways that Nancy Bisaha has ably explored. In the end, this lifetime poet and bureaucrat went so far as to accompany the crusading army as far as Ancona, even though his frail health made this likely to be a final journey, which in fact it was. Bisaha has noted that Pius II's "conviction in the divine righteousness of crusade" increased during his pontificate.[89] As she has argued, his attempts to undertake a crusade were multifaceted and must be understood, at least in large part, as efforts to rally Christians to have trust in the power of their beliefs and to summon, after Basel, renewed respect for the papacy.[90]

Some have suspected that Pius II's famously enigmatic letter to the Ottoman sultan Mehmed II, written in 1461, reflected the influence of Segovia or especially Cusa in contemplating persuasion and dialogue as an approach to this leader.[91] Piccolomini's letter was more a literary exercise than an actual overture toward the sultan, and in that sense it had more in common with Nicholas of Cusa's *De pace fidei* than with any interfaith dialogue envisioned by Segovia. It may be possible that the pope got the idea for such a letter, as a rhetorical exercise, from musing about how a conversation with a Muslim leader might go, but certainly there is no trace of Segovia's ideas or approach in the letter. If Segovia had anything at all to do with Piccolomini's idea for a letter to the sultan, it could only have been a loose inspiration.

The strongest argument against any connection between Segovia's proposals and Piccolomini's letter is the tone of the letter, which is much more derisive and condescending than the *Cribratio Alkorani*. Despite its sometimes benevolent and magnanimous statements, the pope also filled his letter with insults and hostility. He wrote, for example, "You see how great a difference there is between your kind of happiness and ours. Ours correponds to the nobler part of man, his soul, while yours corresponds to the viler, the body. Ours is spiritual, yours carnal. Ours is bright and pure, yours obscure and soiled. We hold ours in common with angels and God Himself, you have yours in common with swine and other animals."[92] Later on the reader encounters these inviting lines: "If we had to mention all the errors of your religion, we would not have the time to write about them nor you to read them. Besides, you realize yourself, since you are intelligent, that many of these things are so stupid that there is no way to defend them."[93] As Nancy Bisaha has observed, such declarations leave no doubt concerning Pius's own convictions, but "they seem out of character for a former diplomat and high-ranking prelate who appreciated the subtleties of tactful persuasion."[94]

Pius's letter should not be seen as a genuine attempt at conversion of Muslims, and as such cannot be considered in the same category as Juan de Segovia's intended dialogues with them. The letter was written in 1461 and enjoyed a wide circulation throughout Europe following its initial printing in 1470. However, it was never translated into Turkish, and there is no record that the sultan ever received it. Pius never referred to the letter or to the goal of converting the Turks anywhere else in his voluminous writings. Furthermore, in the spring of 1462, at the same time he was revising the letter, he announced a crusade. He told his cardinals that his "old blood boiled with rage against the Turks" and that the Christian armies could "wipe out the Turkish race."[95] As Bisaha concluded, this letter should be understood as a humanist's rhetorical work and an assertion of Western superiority, one written for Western readers or for Pius's own reflection and not for any actual Muslims.[96]

In addition to these individual interlocutors, Segovia apparently had a wider audience in mind and tried to anticipate the objections these others might raise. One hint of this wider audience comes from his careful and sustained rejection of the argument that Christians should wait for God to convert Muslims by miracles or by the actions of angels. This was a strategy, like crusade, that he explicitly renounced. He thought it ludicrous that Christians willingly engaged with Muslims regarding a number of temporal matters, but left everything to God or angels when the matter at hand concerned important questions of faith and peace.[97] Juan developed his thoughts about the possible intervention by angels quite extensively, recounting for several folios different interventions of angels found in the Bible. All of this was to demonstrate that angels were not an ideal means of communicating, since they so overwhelmed a mere mortal that the one being visited could not well participate in the interaction. This is why whenever they appeared, the first thing they said was, "Do not fear."[98] For this reason, God has usually relied on humans to communicate messages to humans. Juan pointed out that this was true during the law of nature and the law of scripture, and it was true of Jesus himself.[99]

Surely none of his correspondents would have needed to be convinced that waiting for the angels to exert themselves was not a promising way to respond to Turkish conquests, so this is a puzzling element in his argument. It would be tempting to see his attention to angels as a rhetorical device meant to nudge readers out of passivity, but his discussions of scriptural examples of angels' actions are too developed to be considered simply a rhetorical device. The prospect of angelic intervention received sustained thought from him, and we know that in other works angels played a significant role in his cosmology.[100] David Keck has called attention to how prevalent angels were in the medieval view of the world and devotional practice. They appeared in popular stories, pilgrimages, writings on the sacraments, iconography, and even chronicles and cartularies.[101] Perhaps Segovia thought that many Christians hoped to be defended by the angels when they found themselves in danger, so he thought it best to address their likely resistance to action. He might also have had more specific associations with angels in mind. The wildly popular and widely translated *Legenda Aurea*, by Jacobus de Voragine (1230–98), recounts that John Chrysostom successfully defended Constantinople against the Arian and barbarian Gaimas with the help of a host of angels whose appearance frightened the invaders. The story of how St. Michael intervened to help Christians battle pagans at Monte Gargano was preserved by Jacobus and in liturgical treatises, where they discussed the feast day of St. Michael. In the eleventh century, Andreas of Fleury attributed the Christian victory over Muslims in Tora, Spain, to the timely appearance of Michael, Mary, and Peter, who each killed five thousand of the seventeen thousand enemies and made a Christian victory possible.[102] Even if Juan's illustrious colleagues and correspondents were not likely to look for angelic help in countering the Turkish threat, others might have been. Whatever his reasons for going to the trouble of discounting a hope in angelic assistance, Segovia appears to have taken this aspect of Christian thinking seriously and to have anticipated a wider audience than Cusa, Germain, Cervantes, and Piccolomini.

A different audience is suggested in another possible solution that Segovia rejected: sending preachers. Admittedly, this one strikes modern readers as less surprising than waiting for angels. But none of his interlocutors was likely to suggest the sending of preachers as a solution, and indeed neither of the two who replied at length supported such a plan. In the wake of 1453's shocking events, not many people in the general public would have embraced this solution, either. The most likely people to suggest this might have been mendicant leaders, some of whom could have nursed a nostalgia for the days of their orders' thirteenth-century missions. Juan's argument against this method was based on the fact that Christians typically were not allowed to preach in Muslim lands, a point also made by Thomas Aquinas, although Segovia did not cite the earlier thinker.[103] Juan reasoned that disguising the preachers as merchants would not work, either, since a fire cannot be hidden for long, and once they were exposed, the local authorities would prevent them from preaching.[104] Segovia dismissed this method on practical grounds; he did not share Germain's apparent belief that Muslims simply were not receptive to hearing the preached word of God. To Germain's objection that even Dominic's efforts had been in vain, Juan implied that that was because Dominic had not been well informed about the teachings of Islam.[105] The fact that Segovia also pointedly argued that this strategy would not be effective suggests that he expected his work to be read by some who might propose it.

If Segovia intended his works for wider circulation, he had plenty of company. His was an era in which letter writing flourished and new literary forms evolved, including the treatise and the open letter. Public intellectuals in northern Europe and the Mediterranean alike employed the letter to make their thoughts known on a variety of issues. Often their letters served as a means of self-fashioning or creating a public persona.[106] In the lengthy letter-treatises he wrote from Aiton, Segovia was nearing the end of his life and hardly needed to fashion a persona. If he had any inclination to reconcile with those still angered by his loyalty to Basel, he surely would not have helped his cause by promulgating his unconventional views. But if he had wanted to influence public discussion and contribute his perspectives, writing letters to powerful correspondents was an appropriate strategy, probably the only one available to him. It is interesting that he chose, in his *De mittendo gladio*, an organizational style that Daniel Hobbins has attributed to Jean Gerson. Many of Gerson's writings, like Segovia's *De mittendo*, are organized into not chapters or articles, but "considerations," which allowed a more flowing and reflective writing style that he thought was more accessible to readers than extended dialectical reasoning. For Hobbins, this was part of Gerson's reflection about writing and its role in influencing a wider public.[107]

Juan's later works on Islam, then, were all produced between 1453 and May 1458. Though some of these are longer than others, offering more scriptural support or examples from history, the argument he made in each of these works is consistent. Perhaps because he had spent decades reflecting on the matter by that time, his thought on Christian-Muslim relations did not change discernibly over these five final years of his life. His main ideas were present in their most succinct form in the letter he sent to Nicholas of Cusa on December 2, 1454.

Since Juan sent copies of this text to others, too, he apparently considered it an important presentation of his ideas. In the following discussion, I have taken Juan's lead and treated it as a base text, while including references to his other writings where appropriate. As he stated unambiguously to Cusanus, his former colleague, the "beginning, middle, and end" of his work was that "the way of peace be preferred to the way of war for the conversion of the Saracens."[108] He added, moreover, that this matter touched upon "the heart of the Catholic faith."[109] His insistent repetition of these themes commends them to our consideration.

The Case for Peace

One reason Segovia rejected war was that, historically, this practice did not have much to show for it. In asserting the futility of crusading, he departed sharply from the prevailing attitudes of the time and inverted historical figures others used to support the crusading ideal. Norman Housley has written of the enthusiasm that crusading enjoyed in the later Middle Ages, when it captured the imagination of the nobility as the quintessential chivalric activity. A desire to emulate valiant predecessors who had fought Muslims, such as Charlemagne and Godfrey of Bouillon, tantalized many, and prophecies of a last emperor merged with predictions of a second Charlemagne who would arise and defeat the Muslim armies once and for all. The First Crusade retained a special place in the fantasies about past glories on behalf of God, which explains why William Caxton's decision to publish an English translation of *Godfrey de Bouillon or the Siege and Conquest of Jerusalem* in 1481 showed astute business acumen.[110] When Juan de Segovia surveyed history for its lessons, he saw a different history. When he reflected on the course of history, he saw great numbers of unbelievers converted by the efforts of the apostles and by later messengers such as Ladislao, whose death converted Poland. Hungary and England embraced Christianity in similar circumstances, and the preaching of Boniface converted most of Germany.[111] In contrast, he observed that armies were not so successful in effecting conversions because the newfound faith of the conquered was not voluntary and sincere.[112] After recounting numerous Christian crusading victories by such luminaries as Godfrey of Bouillon and Conrad III of Germany, Juan wrote that experience showed that crusading armies could not maintain possession of the lands they had conquered from the Saracens.[113] He also cited the Spanish experience as evidence of the futility of war for converting Muslims, saying, "The Spaniards, moreover, have a perfect example of this through the experience of the frequent wars waged by them, proving that the Saracens would rather be killed than be converted to the faith through fear of the sword, but now, with so many wars having been waged, ample knowledge concerning these things is provided."[114] Segovia's interpretation of all of this crusading activity, glorified in contemporary discourse and arts, as ultimately useless was iconoclastic and would have been jarring to most readers.

This may have been the reason that he also included, in all the longer works he wrote on the question of Islam, an account of Basel's success with the Hussites. In this story, which always featured Cesarini prominently, crusading was useless, but a promising alternative emerged. In one example, Segovia reminded Cardinal Cervantes of the conversion his fellow cardinal had experienced two decades earlier:

> Indeed when, in the time of the council of Constance, following the condemnation of the errors of John Voutzleph and John Hus, and the burning of John Hus and Jerome of Prague, almost the whole kingdom of Bohemia had withdrawn from the unity of the church, and also from the obedience to the Roman Empire and their natural king, Sigismund. According to those men who saw with their eyes and ears or who read the annals, many very powerful hosts of armed men, a hundred thousand, but sometimes a hundred-fifty thousand horses [102r], and a good part of the faithful as well, were poised to enter their kingdom in order to reduce the Bohemians back to the unity of the faith and of obedience or to exterminate them. But they were attended by none or scarcely any of the fruit that was hoped for, but eventually retreated in disgraceful flight, as a wicked man would flee, with no one in pursuit. And such a great fear of these

Bohemians had seized their neighbors that an overwhelming temptation impelled a great number [of neighbors] to arrange a peace agreement with them, and accept their Articles, just as [the Bohemians] themselves were coming to understand [the Articles] as erroneous. But a legate of the apostolic see who had previously preached the cross against them and, with a mighty army assembled, had entered their kingdom—clearly understanding that the way of war, so frequently ordered, accomplishes nothing—directed his feet on the way of peace, since, by the intervention of his amiable treatment, these very Bohemians, sitting in the shadow of death, were enlightened in their darkness. And he thought this the best and only solution.[115]

By reminding his readers, all of them former colleagues from Basel, of this success with the Hussites, Segovia was making his unconventional ideas less shocking. He probably hoped that his references to this earlier rejection of crusading, particularly by a papal legate and cardinal so well respected, would make his proposals more palatable. He hoped to persuade others that the armies were ineffective against the Hussites; they would enjoy no more success against the Turks.

Even more important than his citation of the armies' inability to neutralize threats to Christian Europe, however, was his recourse to Christian teaching. For Segovia, this matter lay at the "heart of the Catholic faith" because of the church's obligation to honor the words of Christ about his goals and the use of force. His *via pacis et doctrine*, as he often called it, marks him as atypical in a tradition where, as Norman Daniel has explained, "There was little recognition that Christians were inconsistent to advocate the use of force against Islam, while condemning Islam for its theoretical approval of the use of force."[116] Juan did, indeed, recognize this contradiction in the Christian approach and offered arguments explaining to his correspondents how Europe might conform more closely to Christian doctrine.

After all, Christ had urged his followers to preach, and according to Segovia's reading of the Bible, preaching meant specifically preaching peace. As Juan reminded his various correspondents repeatedly, Christ's instructions to announce the kingdom of God to all peoples were coupled with the command that they should announce peace to any house they entered.[117] Christ's peace began a new era in human history. The law of nature, of which Cain and Abel were prime representatives, was characterized by malice. The law of Moses, the law of "an eye for an eye," taught retaliation, although Juan noted that even that law stipulated that one should first offer peace.[118] The law of grace initiated by Christ had peace at its core, since announcing the new kingdom entailed announcing peace. And since he came to send peace to the whole world, it was only fitting that the church procure it for unbelievers.[119]

Part of seeking peace was finding love for enemies. In his letter to Juan de Cervantes, Segovia noted that the apostle Paul had told the Romans not to return evil with evil, but to fan the fire of love in enemies through showing them good works.[120] Furthermore, Christ had taught the disciples to love their enemies, do good to those who hated them, and pray for those who persecuted them. Juan also reminded Cervantes of Christ's comment that God makes the sun rise over the good and the bad.[121]

Moreover, Segovia wanted Christians to be guided by God's plan to bring all humanity together. He cited Paul's ideal that there would be no more divisions such as Gentile or Jew, servant or free[122] because Christ and the disciples labored to form one people where before there had been many.[123] Juan reminded Germain that Christ came not to redeem only some people but to redeem all.[124] Echoing a theme he explored decades before, in his 1427 *repetitio* at Salamanca, he insisted that the Saracens were rational people capable of enjoying eternal happiness. Therefore it was proper for Christians not to want them to suffer in hell, but to save them through their good teaching.[125]

Another way in which Juan de Segovia thought that the "way of peace" pertained to the heart of the Christian faith was that, in pursuing such a path, Christians would be placing due trust in the power of the word of God. Even in his years at Salamanca, Juan articulated the great value he placed in scripture. In his 1426 *repetitio*, he insisted that this text was sufficient for all teaching and arguing.[126] We have seen how heavily he relied on it in arguing before secular and church leaders in France and the Holy Roman Empire during the Council of Basel.

In 1455 he argued to Germain that the word of God was efficacious and penetrating (*efficax et penetrabilior*).[127] If the church were to strive for peace, Christians could trust what the Bible told them about God's promise to complete the work he had begun, which included sending "that peace which surpasses all understanding."[128] After all, God had promised to be with them to the end of time.[129] By pursuing peace with their Muslim enemies in the way Juan suggested, Christians would be fully and radically trusting in God's promises as relayed in scripture. This is yet one more reason why Juan argued that this matter was at the heart of the Christian faith. The peaceful evangelization of Muslims was a duty binding on all Christians, like supporting a general council. For him, both were a matter of being faithful to God's word and to the example set by the early church.

Just as in his earlier writings, one of the things that is most striking about Segovia's prose in these works is how much of it was scriptural. It is not that he punctuated comments with references to scripture; he filled page after page with sentences constructed from biblical lines, often juxtaposing ideas and images in startling or curious ways. He seems even to have revelled in the melding of metaphors, fusing one image into another easily and unselfconsciously.

A good example of this proclivity occurs in his letter to Cervantes, *De gladio divini Spiritus in corda mittendo Sarracenorum*, currently housed in Seville's Biblioteca Colombina.[130] We have already seen how he equated peace with the word of God. Peace was also the buried treasure of the Gospels, so precious that the procurement of it merited, as in the parable, the farmer's selling all that he had in order to buy the field in which it was buried.[131] It was also, ironically, a sword, specifically the sword that Christ sent to earth.[132] The word of God was the sword of the Spirit, which was part of the arms that belong to the Christian militia, along with the breastplate of justice and other such armaments.[133] This sword was also the fire of divine love,[134] and the peace was the food that Christ told the disciples he was about to eat.[135] In Juan's mental universe, the peace that he equated with the word of God blurred into a sword, fire, food, and a buried treasure. Each image represented in some way Christ's mission in the world or his plan for the church.

Juan's constant citation of scripture in such a way makes it impossible to attribute his calls for peace, vague though they were, to any specific medieval thinker, although his recourse to scripture in this way suggests yet another way that his experience at Basel contributed to how he approached the proper Christian response to Islam. For him, the word of God was Christianity's "being and conserving," and it was fitting that the Christian religion take up its origin in this word and by it subdue the nations.[136] Antony Black has shown that this emphasis on "principles of being and conserving" was developed at Basel in the disputes over church governance. At the Council of Constance, conciliarists such as Pierre d'Ailly and Jean Gerson argued that the church, like all creatures of God, contained an inalienable strength and power to maintain its existence and to rule itself. This position enabled its proponents to argue that the church could act to preserve and govern itself, even without the pope and indeed in defiance of a pope. The power was intrinsic to the church as a whole and did not rest in any one individual.[137] In his *Tractatus super presidentia*, Segovia adopted this line of reasoning in writing, "Just as God has given to every creature . . . its own special innate and intrinsic energy (*propriam virtutem innatam et intrinsecam*), by which to preserve itself in its own being and to resist destruction by its adversaries—so too he has given to the Church, which he wished to last until the end of time, energy and power by which to preserve and govern itself in its own being. . . . The principles of existence and preservation are inherent in every object."[138] In insisting that the church must conduct itself in its interactions with Muslims according to the word of God, by which it was formed and which preserved it still, Segovia was applying a central idea in conciliar ecclesiology to the Turkish problem.

To Juan, a church that strove to respond to the word of God, and specifically to God's charge to offer peace, was a church that was the complete opposite of Islam's community of believers.[139] Juan was surely not the first Christian thinker to conceive of the church's identity as the exact opposite of Islam's. For a European who viewed Islam as inherently violent, this comparison would have been practically inevitable. What is striking about Juan's use of this comparison is his indefatigable insistence that this meant that the church should not resort to violence and his confident reliance on scripture to support his conviction.

There is another possible inspiration for Segovia's *via pacis*, one that marks still another connection between his approach to the Turkish question and the disputes about church governance in which he participated. In 1394, during the schism, the University of Paris proposed three methods for resolving the schism: the *via cessionis*, the *via compromissi*, and the *via concilii*.[140] Pedro de Luna, the Aragonese legate of Clement VII (Avignon) to Iberia who later became Pope Benedict XIII (also Avignon), espoused an approach that he called the *via iustitiae*. According to this method, the rival popes would meet in a neutral location, accompanied by their respective consultants and experts, in order to debate their positions and determine which of them had the stronger claim to the papacy. Once Luna became pope, Vincent Ferrer was among those who tried to convince him to adopt the *via cessionis*. When he would not, Ferrer argued for the subtraction of obedience from Benedict XIII. A sermon by Ferrer on this theme in Perpiñan in January 1416 convinced Fernando I of Aragon to withdraw obedience, and the kings of Castile and Navarre soon followed.[141] As we saw in chapter 1, as a student in Salamanca, Segovia would have heard of the various proposals of the University of Paris for ending the schism, and he may well also have learned of Pedro de Luna's proposed meeting of the rival popes. His library contained a work that he called Sentencia Parisiensis, which Benigno Hernández Montes suggested may have been the resolution passed in Paris in 1394 articulating the three *vias*.[142] Segovia could have come into adulthood having heard much about diverse *vias* for peacefully solving problems and later employed a parallel terminology for his own proposals.

Seeing the Call for Peace in Context

Juan de Segovia's polemic against crusading defies any attempts to categorize his thought. To be sure, some of his views recall those presented by other thinkers on this subject, both in his own time and earlier. But they diverge in important respects from those they echo, and they stand in marked contrast to most approaches to the Muslim world that leading Christians articulated.

For example, in noting that crusades had not produced any great results, Juan was not alone. Others had made this observation, especially following the disastrous Second Crusade.[143] But, for the most part, those making this criticism against the crusades were not opposed to crusading on principle. Sometimes they thought the failure pointed to flaws in the execution or in the virtue of those involved. Sometimes they simply reasoned that if God endorsed the crusades, they would have succeeded. Ramón Llull (ca. 1233–ca. 1315), who in some places opposed crusading and in others supported it, expressed such a concern when he wrote, "So many knights and noble princes had gone to the land beyond the sea, O Lord, to conquer it, and if this manner would have pleased You, surely they would have wrested it from the Saracens who hold it against our will." To Llull, at least this time, the failure of the crusades suggested that God was hoping that Christians would instead adopt a peaceful approach to converting the Saracens, namely, the approach that Jesus himself had adopted. He wrote, "This indicates, O Lord, to the holy monks that You hope every day that they do out of love for You what You did out of love for them; and they can be sure and certain that should they throw themselves into martyrdom out of love for You, You shall hear them out in all they want to accomplish in this world in order to give praise to You."[144] Later in this same work, his *Llibre de contemplació en Déu*, Llull argued that Christians should force Muslim and Jewish captives to listen to teachings about Christianity. Even in someone like Llull, more inclined to peaceful approaches than most, the emphasis on nonviolent means was not consistent. In Juan de Segovia, it was a constant refrain.

Llull was not the only medieval thinker to argue that Christians should attempt to convert Muslims. Peter the Venerable is often credited with a fairly respectful attitude toward Islam and a desire for peaceful relations.[145] Saint Francis traveled to Egypt to convert the sultan, and Jacques of Vitry, bishop of Acre in the Crusader states (r. 1216–28), argued vigorously that local clergy should be converting the local Muslims. The Dominican William of Tripoli, also in Acre, hoped for peaceful conversions. As Nancy Bisaha has noted, however, none of these proponents of peaceful methods rejected crusading. In fact, Peter the Venerable vigorously supported the Second Crusade and wrote works in favor of crusading.[146] Thirteenth-century Franciscans and Dominicans engaged in missions to convert Muslims peacefully and also preached crusades to their Christian audiences. Benjamin Kedar noted that this simultaneous embrace by the mendicants of both crusade and mission prompted no criticism within the orders or by outsiders.[147] Elizabeth Siberry explained that most agreed that Muslims should not be forced to convert, but that force and conquest had a place in creating the conditions under which they might freely choose to accept Christianity.[148]

One medieval thinker whose views could have contributed to Juan de Segovia's on the issue of the proper Christian stance toward the Muslim world was Roger Bacon (ca. 1214/1220–92). In the 1260s, by then a Franciscan, Bacon argued that the crusades actually impeded the conversion of Muslims.[149] Like Juan de Segovia, Bacon urged his fellow Christians to take the early church, which converted others by preaching alone, as their model. Following the defeat of Louis IX (r. 1226–70), he offered in his *Opus maius* a passage with a striking similarity to arguments articulated by Segovia three centuries later:

> If the Christians are victorious, no one stays behind to defend the conquests. Nor are unbelievers converted in this way, but killed and sent to hell. Those who survive the wars together with their children are more and more embittered against the Christian faith because of these wars and are indefinitely alienated from Christ and inflamed to do all the harm possible to Christians.[150]

Segovia never expressed all of these ideas in one place, but he certainly shared these concerns. Repeatedly he recounted Christian military advances that were followed by the loss of the conquered land or the need to continually send more men in order to keep the land gained.[151] In his letter to Cervantes, he explained that the Saracens were "rational creatures capable of eternal happiness" (*rationales sint creature beatitudinis eterne capaces*), and as such, "Surely that purpose, it seems, more closely fits a work accomplished by Christians, not that the living descend into hell, but that their souls be saved by the taking up of the sound doctrine."[152] To Cusa he expressed his concern that if Christians waged war against Muslims, this would create an impediment to their conversion because they would come to hate Christ, in whose name the Christians fought.[153] Segovia's own thinking may have led him to these positions. He never cited Roger Bacon, at least that I have seen, and apparently did not simply extract text from Bacon. Nonetheless, the parallels in their thinking on this point are undeniable, even if Segovia did not share Bacon's related interest in astrology or developing a science of religion.[154]

There are other ideas they did not share, as well. As Benjamin Kedar has explained, it is not accurate to consider Bacon a committed opponent of the crusade because Bacon argued that the obstinate who would not be persuaded by preaching should be opposed not only with an army but also with *opera sapientie*, works of wisdom or science. By this he meant a curious combination of technological and psychological warfare involving mirrors. He encouraged the use of optics to arrange mirrors so that they would start fires in the enemy camp and terrify the enemy by making the Christian army look bigger than it was. Kedar noted that the advocacy of such advances in warfare "is not the hallmark of the pacifist."[155]

Certainly even Segovia shared with other thinkers language and imagery that seem, on the surface, contradictory to his vision. Given his insistence that the purpose of his writing was to promote the "way of peace," it is startling that Juan de Segovia used such strong military imagery in the title of his lengthy treatise written to Juan de Cervantes: *De mittendo gladio divini Spiritus in corda sarracenorum (On Driving the Sword of the Divine Spirit into the Hearts of the Saracens)*. In choosing such language, he took his place in a long tradition. Peter the Venerable, often remembered as the "apostle of nonviolence," nonetheless referred to the translations he sponsored as a "Christian armory" against Islam.[156] The Dominican Ramón Martí composed his *Pugio fidei (Dagger of Faith)* in 1278. Martí's dagger was not to be plunged into the hearts of the enemies, though. It was intended to cut "the bread of the divine word" for the Jews. Jean Germain took the military analogies even further and described the apostles as knights, their missions as conquests.[157] Segovia's Castilian contemporary Alonso de Espina included in the first part of his *Fortalitium fidei* (*Fortress of Faith*) a lengthy discussion of the armor that Christians needed in order to fight their many enemies. This armor included various virtues, the example of the saints, the shield of faith, the galley of hope. As for the preachers, their armor was the word of God.[158] Segovia similarly explained that the word of God was the sword of the Spirit, which was one of the armaments in the Christian militia, along with the breastplate of justice and other implements.[159]

Ana Echevarría rightly noted that for Iberian writers the long war against the Saracens ensured that all chivalric ideals would be linked to the fight against the Muslims. This imagery was common in the literature of the fifteenth century and certainly not a special characteristic of religious polemic.[160] However, in the circles of those writing about other religions, it was typically used by writers who were also associated with crusading. Germain and Espina both advocated a renewed crusade.[161] Peter the Venerable requested a refutation of Islam from none other than Bernard of Clairvaux.[162] Martí, who preached in North Africa, enjoyed the support of two crusading kings.[163] The Franciscans and the Dominicans both commissioned missionaries and preached crusades.[164] Despite the Franciscans' cherished models of Francis and the early martyrs, Pope Eugene IV turned to them in 1443 to ask their help in preaching a crusade,[165] which turned out to be the unsuccessful campaign at Varna.

Unlike these individuals, Juan de Segovia was against, on principle, the use of force to spread Christianity. When he used military imagery, he may well have been reaching reflexively for a familiar motif or recalling the often combative terminology used to refer to academic debates. But another possibility is that he used this imagery deliberately in order to turn it on its head. This language of force and swords was not reserved to his discussion of Muslims. In his *Historia*, he highlighted the success that councils had achieved historically, including in the case of the Hussites, in "severing the head of heresies from the body," noting that this occurred through "the sword of the divine word rightly understood."[166]

Perhaps he hoped the use of familiar martial imagery would make his ideas more palatable to skeptical audiences. Certainly he knew that what he proposed was highly unusual in his time. In December 1455 he wrote to Germain that he had not told anyone outside the Aiton priory of his proposals, except for his secretary and one other person.[167] He pleaded with both Germain and Cusa not to let anyone else know of his ideas until the time was right.[168] He might have faced opposition to his ideas close to home. Guillaume d'Estouteville, who had replaced him as bishop of nearby St. Jean Maurienne in 1452, was among those the pope commissioned to promote a crusade and solicit funds for it.[169]

Indeed, the times were not hospitable to suggestions that the best course of action to pursue concerning the Muslims was a policy of peaceful conversion. The threat from Islam was not a philosophical one for academics to confront, or a fanciful one already resolved in legends and epic poems. It consisted of devastating and concrete victories by the Ottomans against European armies and cities. The Turks had been celebrating victory after victory, if not without some setbacks, since the accession of Murad II as sultan in 1421.[170] Emissaries from the Council of Basel wrote urgent letters suggesting that the Turks were becoming stronger and urging both defensive measures in Eastern Europe and a prompt union with the Greeks.[171] Well before Murad II or the Council of Basel, humanists had been concerned about the Turkish threat and had written various texts exhorting leaders to embark on crusades. According to Robert Black, the exhortation to crusade was a common rhetorical exercise, and there is even contemporary evidence that teachers assigned it to students. The cause of crusade was taken up in dialogues, funeral orations, and narrative poetry. Humanist authors intensified their rhetorical campaign after 1453.[172]

If Segovia remained sufficiently informed of major political events and debates while in Aiton, there may have been another forum that provided an important context for his later writings. Johannes Helmrath has described a new genre of oration that emerged in the German imperial assemblies in the 1450s, led by none other than Aeneas Sylvius Piccolomini, one of Segovia's Basel colleagues and the recipient of his last letter. These orations are called *Türkenrede* (oration against the Turks) or *Türkenkriegsrede* (oration for a war against the Turks). The goal was to convince German princes of the necessity and feasibility of a war against the Turks, by employing reason and appealing to emotion.[173] This type of oration was so prominent at the *Reichstage* in Regensburg and Frankfurt in 1454 and Wiener Neustadt in 1455 that these three assemblies became known as the "Turkish *Reichstage*." The orations were disseminated throughout Europe and took their place among the writings of many other humanist writers on the theme, but Helmrath notes that the only assemblies at which they were a regular feature were the German ones. Although these *Türkenkriegsrede* were an example of classical deliberative rhetoric, the deliberation was not about whether to launch a military campaign, but when and how to do it, and especially under whose sponsorship. For example, attending as bishop of Siena and representative of the emperor, Piccolomini had a sustained debate with Giovanni da Castiglione (d. 1460), who was the bishop of Pavia and a papal legate. Each argued for the sponsorship of the respective leaders they were representing. According to Helmrath, the power of the persuasive efforts under way created a climate in which it was virtually impossible for anyone to "declare himself opposed to the protection of Christendom."[174]

If Juan de Segovia knew of the oratorical fireworks going on in the *Reichstage*, where he himself had spoken in the 1440s as an emissary from Basel, then he had even more reason for his caution about how widely he shared his ideas. He also may have envisioned his letter-treatises as a contribution to the deliberations about launching crusading expeditions. They could have been an anti-*Türkenkriegsrede*. Even if he knew little about this developing oratory, the genre surely offers a lens into the contemporary discussion of the issue among his peers and former colleagues, and underscores the extraordinary divergence his thought represented in an international forum.

It is worth wondering why the spring of 1453 came as such a shock at all, given Europe's longstanding anxiety about the Turks' advances and the danger to Constantinople. The fall of Constantinople had been feared for decades, and there had been ominous losses already at Kosovo in 1389, Nicopolis in 1396, and Varna in 1444. A contemporary biographer of the French knight Geoffrey Boucicaut, a participant at Nicopolis, later described how the news of the defeat at Varna was received:

When these reports were made known and published, nobody could describe the great grief which they caused in France, both on the part of the duke of Burgundy, who doubted that he would be able to get his son back for money, and [thought] that he would be put to death, and on that of the fathers, mothers, wives, and male and female relatives of the other lords, knights and squires who were dead. A great mourning began throughout the kingdom of France by those whom it concerned; and, more personally, everybody lamented the noble knights who had fallen there, who represented the flowers of France.[175]

Yet as Nancy Bisaha suggests, Constantinople was different because of the number of civilians killed and captured this time, and because of the importance of this city as a political and cultural capital of the Roman Empire. Even if that empire by this time amounted to little more than the urban nucleus and its environs, the city retained a powerful symbolic value. As a result, even though it had long been feared, the loss of Constantinople was psychologically devastating for Europeans.[176]

Well beyond the halls of the *Reichstage* debates, stories of atrocities committed by the Turks during the conquest of this city circulated widely, and hearers often feared they would be next. One of the first extant eyewitness accounts came from Giacomo Tetaldi, a Florentine merchant who had fought to defend the city, had escaped from it, and then had been rescued in the harbor by one of several galleys that transported survivors to safety.[177] He arrived in Venice on July 5. His account describes a terrifying, huge cannon, a "bronze fire bombard," which surpassed all other artillery used in the assault. This instrument he described as "made in one piece, without any segments, which fired (it is hard to believe!) stone projectiles of eleven palms and three digits in overall circumference."[178] According to Tetaldi, the Turks were ruthless in their treatment of Christians they faced in battle: "They executed their prisoners in a horrible manner, to instill terror among the other Christians. They butchered them cruelly and savagely, as they slashed them, with their entrails exposed, as if they were fish or sheep, which they shamelessly displayed to the Christians."[179] Once inside the city, he reports, the Turks slaughtered all whom they found. Either Tedaldi himself or a contemporary editor added a discussion of the significance of the event, in which Mehmed is described as more infamous than Nero in the spilling of Christian blood.[180] By one account, the sultan ordered the captured nobles to assemble before him and then, "First he had the wives and sons executed before their parents and spouses and then the men themselves after they had witnessed the previous executions; then he commanded that they be dismembered; for women, virgins, and nuns he commanded the most inhuman treatment, such as you would not use even to cattle. He sold many young boys, girls, and townspeople and within a few days he emptied the entire city of almost all its inhabitants."[181] The details differed from one contemporary account to another, but typical elements included ruthless and indiscriminate bloodshed, the desecration of holy sites, plunderings, and captivity for survivors. Such reports fanned the fears of leaders and commoners alike and did much to perpetuate and further establish the Turks' reputation as savage, bloodthirsty, and excessively cruel.[182]

Added to the horror were the repeated predictions of an impending similar fate for still more cities. Never mentioning this possibility or addressing this as a concern of his readers, Juan de Segovia seems to have been oblivious to this prospect. Others were not. The grandmaster of Rhodes, Jean de Lastic, for example, wrote that the Grand Turk's insatiable thirst for human blood had resulted in the submission of Pera, Chios, and Mitylene already, and Serbia, Trebizond, and Kaffa had been reduced to tribute. Convinced, not unreasonably, that Rhodes would itself soon be a target of Turkish advances, Lastic pleaded for aid.[183] The Latin version of Tetaldi's account reported regarding the "prince of the Turks" that "he loves triumphs of all sorts, and that he wants to create a world empire that will surpass those of Alexander the Great, of Julius [Caesar], of Augustus, or of any other powerful emperors throughout the world."[184] Ominous warnings also came from the Greek prelate Isidore, the metropolitan of Kiev, who had traveled to the West in 1434 as a member of the Greek delegation to Basel.[185] Wounded during the siege, he had escaped and headed for Rome, predicting along the way that Italy itself was at risk and urging

Italians to join forces against the common menace. He told worried hearers that Mehmed II planned to gain a foothold in either Calabria or Venice and occupy all of Italy within two years.[186] Jean Germain apparently was among those who harbored such fears for Italy. One of his objections to Juan's proposals for achieving peace with Muslims was that there was no time for those endeavors to work. Within three years, he predicted, the Turks would have conquered many more lands, including Italy.[187] Juan de Segovia's calls for peace and the rejection of violence are all the more remarkable when considered in the light of such pervasive alarm and fear.

Another context that underscores the gulf between Segovia's proposals and the dominant views of his contemporaries was the Council of Basel. With its interest in relations with the Greeks, the council was often a conduit for information about affairs in the eastern Mediterranean, and this information came with warnings. For example, John of Ragusa wrote from Constantinople, where he was the council's ambassador, in November 1436. He told of horrors suffered by the Hungarians at the hands of the Turks and said that if the Western leaders understood what had been happening, they would immediately abandon all their internal wars and launch a crusade. People even feared that Constantinople itself would be attacked, he wrote. Especially given the impending threat from the Turks, union between the Western and Eastern churches was all the more urgent. The emperor had asked Ragusa to invite the council to consider how absurd it was that such divisions were due to differences over a preposition ("through" the Son in the creed, referring to the procession of the Holy Spirit in the Trinity). According to the emperor, the infidels marveled that so many wise and learned men could not agree on such a thing, and they considered it a judgment from God.[188] But when the council discussed what to do about Muslims, it seems that no one suggested trying to make peace with them. As in the *Reichstage*, the only question was how best to unite the Christian world against them.

Nonetheless, the Council of Basel served, ironically and unwittingly, to advance Juan de Segovia's goal of halting the rush to war. An effective crusade required a pope strong enough to persuade or pressure enough rulers into participating. The years of the Great Schism

(1378–1417), followed by the councils of Constance (1414–18), Pavia-Siena (1423–24), and Basel (1431–48) with their efforts to restrict the power of the papacy, had taken their toll on the influence a pope could wield over other rulers. The conciliarists' fiscal reforms had undoubtedly been one factor in the dramatic fall in the revenues of the holy see. Kenneth Setton wrote that it was this reduction in income that rendered Martin V (1417–31) virtually powerless in the efforts to contain the Turks.[189] Norman Housley has highlighted the inherent link between preaching crusade and fund-raising, noting that resistance to tax levies for crusading was fierce from the laity, the clergy, and royal courts.[190] Wariness regarding papal power was one of the reasons that European leaders rejected successive popes' calls for a crusade. When Eugene IV proclaimed a crusade against the Turks in the Balkans on New Year's Day of 1443, he hoped to enlist the participation of Poland as well as Hungary. However, the influential Zbigniew Oleśnicki, bishop of Crakow and chancellor of the kingdom, opposed the papal crusade. A firm supporter of the Council of Basel, and in fact one of those whom Felix V had made a cardinal in 1440, Oleśnicki could hardly regard as legitimate a crusade launched by a man he considered a deposed schismatic. He also knew that the pope had instructed his delegate to persuade the Polish king Wladyslaw III to pressure the Polish clergy to withdraw their support for Basel. Due to Oleśnicki's refusal to support Eugene's crusade, as well as the refusal by the majority of other Polish notables, crusading forces departed in 1443 and 1444 almost entirely with Hungarian troops. The Christian forces were defeated at Varna in November 1444.[191]

Even after the fall of Constantinople, when we might expect that renewed calls for a crusade would find a more attentive reception, lingering loyalty some had toward the council's aims contributed to the popes' failure to initiate a crusade. The Carthusian prior Vinzenz of Aggsbach even wrote to the Benedictine prior at Melk that the church had always been afflicted by troubles from emperors, pagans, heretics, and simoniacs, and that, compared to all of those, the Turks were a minor threat. All they asked was subjection and the payment of taxes, so Vinzenz declared that a recent call to war against the Turks could not be called a war for the faith. This former supporter of Basel even suggested that God might have allowed the Turks to take Constantinople in order to punish the Greeks for failing to honor the agreement they had reached with Basel, and proceeding instead to negotiations with Eugene IV at Ferrara and Florence.[192] In Germany, resentment toward papal taxation policies, which had led Basel to enact serious reforms of the papal finances, plagued the popes' efforts to raise funds for crusades well after the council was over. German princes decided to maintain control over local resources, thus undermining papal centrality in a way that was consistent with the conciliarist aims and detrimental to any attempt at a crusade.[193] The crusading ideal was inextricably linked to a strong papacy. When Pius II spoke of his longing for a crusade, he lamented:

> We are seeking to effect this; we are searching out ways; none practicable presents itself. If we think of convening a council, Mantua teaches us that the idea is in vain. If we send envoys to ask aid of sovereigns, they are laughed at. If we impose tithes on the clergy, they appeal to a future council. If we issue indulgences and encourage the contribution of money by spiritual gifts, we are accused of avarice. People think our sole object is to amass gold. No one believes what we say. Like insolvent tradesmen we are without credit.[194]

The conciliar movement frustrated crusading efforts precisely because it eroded the pope's authority.

Juan never argued against crusading on the basis that launching one would enhance the prestige of the papacy, possibly because he knew well that the pope had enough supporters to have made that an obstacle to the diffusion of his pleas. The council was not opposed to a military solution to the Turkish threat. Still, there is a paradoxical convergence in the results they obtained, although with divergent goals.

Less convergence appears between Juan de Segovia's anticrusading arguments and the dominant strains of fifteenth-century humanists' thinking on Islam, which offer another background against which to consider his writings. Nancy Bisaha has shown that two currents coexisted in the thought of fifteenth-century Italian humanists. Some still echoed the crusading ideal of the Middle Ages. One example is

Poggio Bracciolini (1380–1459), a leading humanist who served as papal secretary and chancellor of Florence. His funeral oration for Cesarini portrayed him as having died in a holy war, in defense of the faithful, as a martyr giving testimony of his faith.[195] Others, among them Leonardo Bruni (1370–1444), reached back to classical motifs and described the Turks as the new barbarians, similar to the Goths who destroyed Rome. Aeneas Sylvius Piccolomini compared the Turks to the Goths, but added that the Turks were even more destructive because at least the Goths spared the churches.[196] This mingling of medieval and classical images was typical of humanists' voluminous writings on the Turks before 1453. According to Bisaha, after 1453 the language crystallized, and writers increasingly referred to the struggle against the Turks as one of civilization versus barbarism.[197] This discourse was not necessarily any more favorable toward the Turks, but it was definitely a secular discourse, and this was a significant contribution Renaissance thinkers made to European thinking about not just the Turks, but other Muslims, and perhaps about other peoples as well.[198]

Juan de Segovia is a curious figure within this period of transition. Most of his writings on Islam originated after 1453. Nothing in his works referred to the Turks or Muslims as barbarians threatening civilization. Juan knew plenty of Europe's leading thinkers, and he had long been interested in questions related to Islam and probably engaged in conversations with plenty of others around these issues. Even if his own intellectual training and orientation made him less of a humanist thinker than many of his peers, he must have been well aware of his colleagues' growing inclination to enlist such classical motifs to explore the dilemma of their times. The fact that this new, more secular language does not appear in his writings may well reflect a conscious rejection of such images, especially since by using them he could have appealed to the sensibilities of readers of his day. Perhaps he rejected such recourse to language about uncivilized barbarians because, although his acquaintances included humanists from around Europe, they had also, decades before, included Muslims. Certainly, Juan's two conversations with Muslims in Castile in 1431 had produced lasting memories, to which he returned as he wrote in the aftermath of the fall of Constantinople.

Segovia's approach had at least one feature in common with those humanists who nursed a nostalgia for the medieval crusading ideal. Like them, he saw the problem of Ottoman expansion as fundamentally a religious issue, one that he thought required a response that was rooted in religious belief. In this sense, Juan de Segovia's mature thought on Islam and what Europe should do about it was deeply traditional. Nonetheless, unlike the more traditionally oriented humanists, Segovia rejected crusading as a proper solution for the problem. The next chapter will explore in more detail both his understanding of Muslims' beliefs and practices and the strategy he proposed for responding to Turkish power.

Chapter Five —⚋⚋—

CONVERTING MUSLIMS

J uan de Segovia was not content merely to reject war and other solutions to the Turkish problem. He offered a solution of his own, which involved persuading Muslims of the wrongness of their beliefs and telling them the truth about Christianity. This second front of polemic is the subject of this chapter. Any contemporaries who had hoped for a quick solution would have been frustrated by his long-range approach to their problem. He proposed ongoing talks between European notables and Muslim leaders, and he embarked on a quest for a better translation of the Qur'ān, which led him to a remarkable collaboration with Castilian Muslim scholar Yça Gidelli. Segovia wrote no major anti-Islamic works; his arguments against Islam appear instead in the course of his recommendations to others on how to conduct the peaceful discussions with Muslims that he envisioned.

I argue that, even as he recycled such well-worn themes of Western polemic as the alleged lascivious and violent nature of Islam, Segovia differed from others engaged in this polemic in significant ways. As he wrote from Aiton, he was responding less to earlier writers' thoughts than to his memory of conversations with real Muslims back home in 1431, to which he made repeated reference. By his own account, those interlocutors provided him with his main incentive for wanting to convert Muslims, an incentive that may have been unique in Western thought on the issue. Moreover, the success that Cesarini had when he turned away from crusading and embraced dialogue with the Hussites provided the aging Segovia with the inspiration that dialogue could work, even with an armed and dangerous enemy. For him this desire to convert Muslims was not linked, as it often was, to an effort to convert Jews, nor to any apocalyptic or millenarian hopes. What he seemed to envision was an inclusive, expanded Christian society that would include these former Muslims. Sure of the ultimate success of his method, he was prepared to wait.

Convening Meetings

The approach for which he is known first became widely known to modern readers with the publication of Cabanelas Rodríguez's *Juan de Segovia y el problema islámico* in 1952. Cabanelas presented Juan's plan as a fully developed method with three distinct phases: (1) establish and maintain peace with Muslim peoples; (2) intensify, within this context of peace, relations between Christians and Muslims, preferably on a cultural level; (3) slowly initiate peaceful discussions of the principal doctrines that separated the two faiths, emphasizing the points of agreement.[1] Richard Southern discussed Segovia's approach in the context of contemporaries Nicholas of Cusa, Aeneas Sylvius, and Jean Germain in a lecture at Harvard in 1961 in which he called this generation "a moment of vision" in the evolution of medieval views of Islam. Southern explained that Juan thought that his proposals offered advantages beyond the actual conversion of Muslims.[2] Actually, as James Biechler has noted, Segovia did not present any systematic method, and nowhere in his writings did he fully and coherently develop his alternative approach. It comes into focus only by assembling various elements of it that he scattered through several post-1453 works.[3]

The most concrete element of Juan's proposals was that Christian leaders should send a delegation to meet with Muslim leaders. He did not specify any particular Christian leaders or kingdoms that should involve themselves in this enterprise, nor any particular Muslim ruler or region. However, given the geopolitical situation of the time, presumably he would have had the Ottoman sultan in mind, if not for the first such delegation, then at least for subsequent ones that could follow upon visits to regional leaders. He was more explicit about the Christian delegation, emphasizing that it should consist of only a small number of people, and they should be of high social rank. According to Juan, their status was more important than how learned they were.[4]

The reasons he gave for assembling a group with these characteristics are interesting. He reasoned that a small group had the possibility of catching the Saracens off guard. They would not suspect that Christians would send such a vulnerable group into their midst. Probably it was this element of surprise that he hoped to maintain in also specifying that the group should keep a low profile and proceed without fanfare. After all, the delegation would need to reach the court of the ruler; the whole plan would fail if it were blocked or detained before getting there. It was important that the delegates be of an exalted status because this would ensure that they would be received.[5] A further advantage of proceeding in this way was that the church would be imitating the actions of Christ, who came to preach peace (*evangelizare pacem*) to those far off and nearby.[6] Juan cited the Gospel parable in which the man instructed his servant to go out and search the roads and fences to compel people to attend his wedding feast so that the home might be filled.[7]

Richard Southern referred to the meeting that Segovia proposed between Christians and Muslims as a *contraferentia*, implying that Segovia employed this term for the dialogues he was advocating.[8] It would be misleading, however, to suggest that Segovia attached this term to his plans consistently, or even often. Most of the time, he referred to his approach to the Muslims simply as the *via pacis* or *via pacis et doctrine*. James Biechler wrote that the term *contraferentia* appears only once, in Juan's letter to Piccolomini.[9] I have seen the term in scattered other places, as well, and the context of these other times is yet another suggestion of a link between his experience at the council and his later thought on Islam. In his letter to Jean Germain, for

example, he used *contraferentia* to refer to past conversations between the Latins and the Greeks and to lament that this strategy was
not more frequently employed: "If, however, there was occasionally
a meeting [*contraferencia*], certainly that was, at most, between the
Latins and the Greeks."[10] In his history of the Council of Basel, the
word appears in a section about the deposition of Eugene IV, where
he pointed out that active participation of a council in determining a
pope had precedent: "When the contenders for the papacy, those
called Benedict XIII and Gregory XII, had been definitively deposed
at the Council of Pisa, the cardinals entered a conclave for the election
of the next shepherd on the tenth day thereafter. At the holy synod
of Constance, however, the beginning of the conclave suffered delay,
although not as great a delay as at Basel, on account of the great meetings [*contraferencias magnas*] at that time regarding the question of
whether the election was to be conducted by the cardinals or through
the cardinals together with others appointed by the council."[11] *Contraferentia* is an unusual term and not at all an obvious choice for
someone writing about assemblies, meetings, debates, or dialogues.
The fact that Segovia used it to refer to discussions at the council,
meetings between leaders of the Western and Eastern churches, and
dialogues between Christians and Muslims suggests that he saw similarities across these diverse encounters.

This brings us to the question of what exactly this intrepid group
of European notables was supposed to do upon meeting the Muslim
rulers. As noted earlier, Darío Cabanelas Rodríguez discerned three
successive phases to the encounter Juan proposed, beginning with establishing peace and proceeding gradually to the peaceful discussion
of doctrine.[12] However, it proves impossible to find such a clear-cut
sequence in Juan's writings. Cabanelas may have thought that Juan
had a sequence in mind because of the fact that early in his discussion
of the group's mission he used phrases like "invite them to peace" and
"talk of peace." But Segovia's concept of "peace" is both too diffuse
and too nuanced to support the conclusion that he was presenting
these overtures of military and diplomatic peace as a first step in an
ordered process.

Peace for him was simultaneously the actual cessation of armed
conflict, which kings and princes would have to embrace and offer to

Muslims,[13] and the gospel itself. He noted that the Muslims' own law enjoined them to seek peace,[14] and the peace the Qur'ān was referring to obviously would have been of the political and military variety. However, in his discussions of the delegation's mission, Juan generally emphasized the spiritual form. Not only would the group's efforts parallel those of Christ's own preaching, as noted above,[15] but it was fitting for the cardinals to pursue this peace because they were the successors of the apostles, to whom Christ had left his peace.[16] When the Saracens agreed to join a discussion of peace, they would come to know the love that Christians had for them, which certainly seems a result more closely associated with hearing the gospel than with practical negotiations for a truce. Juan also linked "hearing of peace" to "hearing the word of God" when he stated, as he did not often do, that if the Christians sincerely offered peace to the Muslims and the latter refused to hear of it, then war would be justified because they were "unwilling to hear the word of God."[17] On the other hand, he thought this was unlikely because once the Saracens understood that all the Christian kings and princes, as well as the pope and priests, were united in offering them peace, they would find the offer irresistible.[18] The fact that he thought the participation of kings and princes was a useful incentive shows that the peace he had in mind was not only the peace afforded by the word of God. The two forms of peace were inseparable in his thinking.

Once these discussions of peace were under way, Juan predicted, all sorts of good things would happen. The Saracens would know the love Christians had for them. Newly aware of this benevolence, they would be moved to regret their wars against Christians. If they willingly confessed the causes of these wars, they could make satisfaction. If they hesitated to do that, Christians could at least point out the many reasons for having peace and love between Christians and themselves. It would be especially compelling when they heard the arguments for divine unity explained in a serious way because, he thought, when they realized that Christians did not, after all, worship more than one God, they would surely have to take a fresh look at their law. Thus Christianity would be freed from the infamy that afflicted it.[19] The morale of the Saracen armies would weaken because the justifications for war against the Christians would unravel when they saw their own learned men either agreeing with the Christians or at least differing among themselves regarding their differences.[20] In short, the benefits of Juan's proposed high-level dialogues simply knew no bounds.

Moreover, as optimistic as he was about the likely results of this delegation, Segovia was prepared to be patient. It is even possible that he envisioned this mission to be a recurring or even annual one. In his letter to Cusa, he referred to it as a "legacionem solempnem ad pertractandum de mediis pacis."[21] *Solempnem* may be a corruption of *sollemnis (-e)*, meaning yearly or recurring, although it could also be a variant of *solemnis (-e)*, which meant simply solemn or religious. Although this word is not enough to conclude that his plan was for recurring discussions, this reading would be consistent with his response to Germain's objection that an approach based on peaceful dialogue would take too long to work. The prospect that it might take a long time for these efforts to bear fruit appeared not to bother him. In December 1455, he argued to Germain that Christ had preached for three years, but that even then it took another three hundred years before his teaching found ready acceptance. He reasoned, "If now for four hundred years, or rather eight hundred, the way of war has been followed, it is fitting to resume anew that way Christ wished to be followed until the end of the world, since the three-year-old 'way of teaching' must not be interrupted."[22] Given Segovia's confidence in God's promises in scripture, it is likely that he simply considered it impossible that any course of action that was modeled after the example of Christ and the apostles, and in accord with God's charge to Christians, could fail. For him, success might take a while, but it was sure.

In proposing a delegation to speak with Muslim leaders and seek to persuade them of the truth of Christianity, Segovia might have been inspired by the accounts of Franciscan missionaries. Although the hagiography on Francis was inconsistent, some of it praising him as an ardent crusader,[23] much focused on his visit to the sultan of Egypt, during which he reportedly almost achieved success in converting this leader.[24] Jacques de Vitry, whose own assessment of the Franciscan missions was ambivalent, nonetheless described Francis's mission favorably in his *Historia occidentalis*. He helped to spread the report that Francis's very presence was enough to change the demeanor of the sultan and to dispose him to listen to Francis's presentation about Chrisitianity for days. Jacques de Vitry told readers that Muslims readily listened to the word of God—until the speakers began to insult the Prophet.[25] In addition to the endeavors of Francis, in the mid-thirteenth century several Franciscan missionaries journeyed to the Mongols with the goal of preaching Christianity and talking peace. Some hagiographies praised Franciscan friars who intentionally sought martyrdom in Muslim lands.[26]

It is clear that Segovia knew of these precedents and had them in mind as he wrote to his former colleagues about his hopes. He directly referred to the missions of John of Plano Carpini, Benedict the Pole, and William of Rubruck. In his letter to Cusa, he complained about the slant he found in the historical accounts. He pointed out that Pope Innocent IV had sent these men on a mission of peace, and it irked him that what was remembered and emphasized by history was this same pope's crusading efforts. He even mentioned that this delegation to pursue peace was sent precisely following great slaughters of Christians in Hungary, Poland, and Moravia. He explained, "The delegation, moreover, was content with the papal letters because it pleased the pope, who was lord and father of Christians, that all Christians be as friends, and to have peace with the Tartars. And, desiring that they be great in heaven, he warned that they should accept the faith of Christ, and otherwise they could not be saved." According to Segovia, the pope informed these people through his legates that "God was gravely offended" by the murders of Christians they had perpetrated and they should "do penance." Despite this overture of peace he attributed to Innocent IV, he complained about the account of these events, saying, "It does not refer to the offer of peace, which was subsequently maintained, but rather that a war was undertaken by this same Innocent IV."[27]

Segovia's frustration at the memory of Innocent IV's actions reveals an innovative interpretation of that pope's legacy. Remembering Innocent IV as someone who supported crusading was not, in fact, a distortion of the facts, as Segovia asserted. Innocent argued that unbelievers should not be forcibly converted, but that warfare intended to pave the way for the arrival of missionaries was permissible if authorized by the pope. As Benjamin Kedar has shown, the connection this pope formulated between warfare and preaching became influential in subsequent thought on justifications for war.[28] It appears that Segovia was aware of the efforts of the Franciscans who preached to the Muslims, and also of those who sought martyrdom in the process, and he rejected their approach as ineffective. To Cervantes, he wrote, "Experience has often shown that whenever some extraordinary individuals, led by zeal for the faith, go forth to preach the truth to the Saracens, they [the Muslims] do not want to listen to them. Sometimes, indeed, they do not kill them, as was the case with Saint Francis. If, indeed, [the missionaries] are killed, it is not because of that that many of [the Saracens] are converted to the faith, as it was in the time of the martyrs, but rather by having an audience, which would seem to recommend the other means [than martyrdom]."[29] In other words, the witness of martyrdom was not what converted people. Instead, it was the actual hearing of the teachings of Christianity, through the audience granted the preachers, that brought about conversions.

His own experience, and not just those of adventuresome Franciscans, could also have led him to propose this approach. It is interesting that he used the term *contraferencia* in his letter to Germain to refer to conversations between the Latins and the Greeks,[30] and that the only place he used this word in connection with his proposed delegation to Muslims was in his letter to Piccolomini, a colleague from Basel who, he had reason to suspect, would not be receptive to overtures of peace with Muslims.[31] His vision of how the discussions might go might have been influenced by the discussions at the Council of Basel over differences with the Greeks or the Hussites, and perhaps he wished to suggest a similarity to his colleague from the Basel years. Another passage in which he suggested a similarity between the Bohemian situation and that of the Muslims was toward the end of his letter to Germain, where he described Sigismund's efforts to make peace with the Hussites and even pointed out that peace was achieved before the errors were relinquished. But at least the arms were put down, and their armies were no longer a threat. He suggested that a similar result might be achieved with the Saracens, saying, "Whether [or not] the name of the heresy has been destroyed, it is certain that a multitude of Catholics no longer speak of it, as they used to, nor need the church occupy itself in its eradication as before. Would that someday there might begin a similar overture of peace with the community of Saracens, so that whatever is not repugnant to the divine law having been conceded to them, even if it is by positive law, they will choose to accept the peace and unity of the church."[32] His use of the term *universitas* here is curious. Although this term could be used to indicate any collective group, Segovia did not usually employ the term, and this is the only place I have seen where he used it to refer to the Muslims. Here he seems to have been making a connection with a brief discussion on the previous folio about the universities being the place where public disputations on matters related to faith were conducted. In this discussion, he pointedly used the word *universitas* and not only *studium*. It is clear that, as he articulated and developed his ideas about this delegation, he thought of parallels to other groups with whom the Western church had engaged in discussions of peace and faith.

Another clue to his understanding of what these meetings could be comes from references he made to how the credibility of religious beliefs was established. He seemed to associate this process with disputation. For example, he wrote to Germain that the Saracens laugh at Christian texts, as if they were not to be taken seriously, but that they were wrong, since the texts had been tested (as "gold that is tested by fire") by disputation first with Jews (through the work of Paul and Stephen), but also with Greeks, and later such discussions took place in universities.[33] If Juan de Segovia thought of these longed-for discussions with Muslims as yet another instance of delegations and discussions such as those held with contemporary Greeks, Hussites, Jews, and Greeks of the early Christian world, and university personnel, then he was considering Muslims in the same category as these other interlocutors. They were simply another people in his worldview, not marked by any special depravity or malevolence.

Although he did not offer any detailed "talking points" nor a suggested order for the issues the Christian notables should broach once they had been received by the Muslim leader, Segovia's writings permit us to envision what he thought should be on the agenda. One of his priorities was to put an end to what he considered the defamation of Christians and their beliefs. He was deeply troubled that Muslims thought Christians worshipped three Gods, and that Christians did far too little to disabuse them of this notion. He lamented, "For some time, they have erred, thinking that the Christians are worshippers of a God of parts and of 'associates.' But yet if Christians keep silent regarding this, they will be able to infer, with audacious constancy, that Christians are those unbelievers reputed in their law to be worshippers of a God of parts and associates."[34]

Part of convincing Muslims that Christians were not, in fact, worshipping three Gods was explaining the doctrine of the Trinity to them in a way that would put such allegations to rest. Segovia's longer letters on how to approach Muslims contain lengthy sections comprised of intricate explorations of the theology of the Trinity. He apparently considered this information necessary background for those who might be involved in the discussions, not because Muslims would come to believe the teachings of Christianity because of these dizzying arguments, but because such a grounding would enable a Christian participant in this encounter to show how conceiving of God as a Trinity did not preclude monotheism. This alone would be a great breakthrough, since Muslims would have to doubt their longstanding dismissal of Christians and "worshippers of a God of parts and associates." In the treatise that he sent to Cervantes, Segovia recounted his conversation with the Muslim in Medina del Campo in October 1431. After long discussion about the Christian belief in a triune God, the man finally exclaimed, "By God, there is no one among the Christians who knows how to explain these things but you!" According to his own account, Segovia told the man, "Do not believe that the Christian religion so lacks literate men, since even today in this town, there are twenty people who can explain these things."[35] With the exception of his short letters to Piccolomini and to the unnamed *frater*, all of his works on the question of Islam in the 1450s recount this encounter in Castile in 1431. Segovia was impressed with the impact that his explanations of the Trinity had on this man and convinced that having a coherent way to reconcile a triune God with monotheism was essential, should his dream of this summit meeting come to fruition.

Nicholas of Cusa agreed with him on this point. In his reply to the letter from Segovia, he said, "It is to be hoped that all the Turks come to faith in the most holy Trinity, for the reasons mentioned in the writing of your more reverend paternity, reasons which, among others, I heard from you in Basel when you praised Richard of St. Victor to me. And many more can be formulated which demonstrate sufficiently that faith in the Trinity leads to supreme knowledge of the one God."[36] In addition, he said that in his experience, both with Jews and with Turks, it was not so difficult for them to accept the Trinity as a "unity of substance," but it was more difficult for them to believe in the union of the divine and human natures found in Christ.[37] He told his former colleague, "This part will be, as it has always been, very difficult, and I do not see it solved in the writings which you have now sent to me."[38]

Juan de Segovia certainly believed that if Christians succeeded in convincing Muslims that they were not polytheists after all, this would be one of the principal benefits of the "way of peace" that he proposed, since it would remove a major reason that the Saracens waged war on Christians. He explained to Cusanus, "And this is one of the greatest goods that the discussion of peace could not only bring about, but even complete at its very beginning: publicly stating on the part of the Christian religion this truth of law and fact that God is one, exactly one, and that all Christians believe this with the utmost firmness. And so there is no reason for war against these people, as if they were worshippers of many gods."[39] This was all because their law, the Qur'ān, "enjoins them to wage battles and wars with discretion, saying that it is useful and just, even in months of liberty and rest, to fight against those who do not call God one, as they allege of all Christians, who are called unbelievers throughout their law."[40] The unqualified affirmation of monotheism on the part of their Christian visitors would also bring an end to another accusation Muslims levied against Christians. "From this, indeed," Segovia continued, "another infamy, no small one, can be abolished: that Christians worship their presumptuous and unworthy priests, as their law says, as if they were God."[41] In this, too, Muslims would learn that what they have heard from their law about Christians was false. He reiterated, "If such people are not [to be found] among the Christians, the Saracens themselves consequently can understand that those upon whom their law places this accusation are other than the Christians."[42]

This list of benefits that would come from converting Muslims is interesting for several reasons. One is that these items were not common features of Western thought on polemic and conversion. Unlike the inspiration Juan de Segovia likely drew from reports of Franciscan missions of peace, for example, this element in his thought appears inspired by his personal experience. Those two conversations with real Muslims that he had in Córdoba and Medina del Campo in 1431 had left a lasting impression. As we saw in chapter 2 of this volume, the meetings with the ambassador from Granada were especially illuminating, as he admitted to Cusa, saying, "Truly how many more things about the Christian religion are rendered falsely, most absurd things to which we are believed to be witnesses. . . . I became truly convinced of this in discussions with the aforementioned ambassador of the king of the Granada, in which he raised as a point of objection, quite improperly, that Christians ate their God and absolved sins committed against God."[43] Those meetings left him convinced that it was simply a matter of lack of accurate knowledge; the Christian faith had not been adequately communicated. As he remembered these talks two decades later, he reported, "And so I learned then that in this and in many other things, in how great an ignorance of the divine law the whole multitude of Saracens labored, and that by virtue of a defect of the declaration of the truths of the faith, they vigorously detested and looked down upon Christians."[44] The idea that a major advantage of having discussions with Muslims would be that they would be disabused of their inaccurate notions of Christianity and thus delivered of the Qur'ānic command to fight them as unbelievers was original, and the direct result of some memorable conversations in Castile. Not surprisingly, it is a theme that he seems to have found particularly compelling after the summer of 1453 and the fall of Constantinople, when it became more urgent to undermine the Muslims' motivations for war.

Convinced as he was that the Turks waged war on Christians because they thought the Christians were polytheists and worshipped priests and ate their God, he seems never to have considered more mundane motivations for war. It apparently did not occur to him that the Ottomans, like their Christian counterparts, might fix their sights on land revenues or control of lucrative trade routes. It may appear from this that he considered them exotic and "other," not exhibiting the interests and behaviors common to all societies and kingdoms. But the fact that he drew parallels to the Greeks and the Hussites as he reflected on the "Muslim question" complicates this picture, since, not unreasonably, he saw the West's conflicts with these others, too, as religious disputes. If there was a secular turn occurring among humanist writers in the aftermath of 1453, as Nancy Bisaha has deftly argued,[45] then Juan de Segovia did not participate in it. He was not drawn to the view of Muslims as barbarians who were enemies to culture and civilization. For him they were a religious people waging war for religious reasons. Hence the best way to mitigate the threat was to challenge the aggressors' religious belief system.

The Qur'ān in Juan de Segovia's Work and Thought

Because many of the falsehoods that Segovia thought animated the Muslims' attacks on Christian lands were not merely popular misconceptions about Christianity but actual teachings in the Qur'ān, it would have been unthinkable for him to correct the Muslims' misunderstandings regarding Christianity without showing that their sacred text itself was not accurate. When they learned that Muhammad had asserted such great falsehoods, Juan reasoned, they could not possibly regard the Prophet highly.[46] Their conversion would be the natural consequence of Christians challenging the slander against their own religion, and it was the only way to end that slander permanently. This explains the importance of the Qur'ān in his approach to this problem.

Although his most intense encounter with the Qur'ān occurred while in Aiton, he had been trying to secure a good translation much earlier, even before his 1431 discussions with Muslims in Castile. In his Preface to the trilingual Qur'ān, he recalled that in 1429, when he was in Rome, the patriarch of Constantinople had asked him to find a copy. Since he could not find a copy in Italy, he requested that one be sent from Spain. The experience taught him something he said he had not known before: that very few Christians and few libraries had a copy. In 1437, he said, he found a copy, a chained one, in Germany, and had it copied. But afterward, he saw that this copy deviated significantly from the contents of the Arabic text. It is not clear how he would have known that, since he did not know Arabic. Perhaps it conflicted with things he had heard from his Muslim interlocutors in Spain, or maybe he recognized that some of what he was reading could not have been in the Qur'ān, and this caused him to lose confidence in the translation. He was alarmed at the depiction of Muslims that he found there, saying that it portrayed them as "far from being men of reason, almost bestial, and childish."[47] In his letter to Cusa, he referred to a translation that he had used with Cusa's permission (*vestra concessione*), which he said he had read and "lifted out" the errors.[48] There was still another attempt to secure a faithful translation. He traveled to the Dominican library in Basel to look at a copy he had previously seen there, but found that that translation was the same as one he already owned.[49] Toward the end of his life, when he was writing his *Donatio*, he possessed three Latin translations of the Qur'ān.[50]

Still, he was determined to obtain a more faithful translation, and his efforts toward that goal were more persistent than most. They even included writing back to Spain to find a Muslim scholar who could come and help him produce a better translation. Remarkably, this effort finally succeeded. Segovia must have been overjoyed when, in December 1455, just a couple weeks before he finished his reply to Germain, the renowned Castilian Muslim scholar Yça Gidelli arrived at his little priory in the Alps.[51] His exuberance is palpable in his account of this development:

> When subsequently a royal order had been given to one of the senior *fuqahā'* of the Kingdom of Castile this man answered that he could not come, because he was not competent, and because it would not yet be possible [for him to collaborate]. Then it pleased God to

fulfil my wish, a wish which complied with the glory of His name. My family and friends guaranteed the inviolability of his [Yça's] person and the salary that he had asked for his efforts. Then, on the 5th of December 1455, he arrived at the place where I live, in the priory of Aiton, in the diocese of St. Jean de Maurienne, a man who was of great renown among the Saracens of Castile, Yca [sic] Gidelli, *faqīh* of Segovia, accompanied by someone belonging to his sect.[52]

Gidelli had originally declined to make this trip. Then he had written in April 1454 to say that, upon further consideration, he had decided to come after all.[53] Given all his difficulties in securing a good translation, Segovia probably tried to restrain himself from getting his hopes up that Gidelli would actually arrive. He could only have been delighted at the uncommon skill and knowledge that Yça brought to the task.

In his study of Yça's environment and works, Gerard Wiegers noted that Gidelli was the *faqīh* of Segovia for some time. Although much less is known about the structure of the Muslim community in Castile than that in Aragon, this title seems to have designated a profession, rather than merely a student of *fiqh*, or the law. This person was normally learned in Arabic and was entrusted with various tasks for the Muslim community. Gidelli, whom Wiegers suggests may have been a Sufi as well, also served as an *imām* (prayer leader) and *qādi* (judge) of the *aljama*, the Muslim community, in Segovia.[54] So Gidelli was not merely a Muslim, but a scholar and leader in that community. Segovia must have been thrilled to have him as his guest, and very interested in the information he could provide.

Accustomed to life in the sizable city of Segovia, one of the regular residences of the royal court, Yça Gidelli would spend four months as a guest in Segovia's small and isolated Benedictine priory atop a mountain. Possibly the experience of winter in the Alps was one of the factors motivating him to finish his work quickly and return home. Juan wrote that his long-awaited guest worked twelve hours a day except on the birthday of the Prophet. He drank no wine, and after learning that a purée of peas he had eaten for dinner had contained some, he limited himself to a diet of bread the next evening as a penance.[55] Yça produced a translation of the Qur'ān from Arabic to Castilian, and Juan later added a Latin translation to this work. This trilingual Qur'ān is now lost, but the preface is extant and is a remarkable account of Juan's efforts to secure a better translation and of his impressions of Arabic grammar and the Qur'ān gleaned in the course of working with Gidelli.[56] The *faqīh* wanted to return to Spain with the translation that he had done, so another copyist was hired in order to ensure that both scholars could retain a copy.[57]

When the translation from Arabic to Spanish was completed, Segovia pleaded with his collaborator to stay longer and teach him more Arabic and more about the meaning of the verses in the Qur'ān.[58] Gidelli insisted on returning to Spain. He had married recently, he said, and wished to return to his wife, but he promised Juan that he would try to convince his unmarried brother to come in his place.[59] There is no way to know how much energy he put into convincing his brother to make the journey. His brother did not go, much to the dismay of Segovia, who interpreted this as a failure of nerve, even though the duke of Savoy had guaranteed the man safe conduct.[60] Ana Echevarría has noted that the 1450s saw tumult within the *al-jama* of Segovia and disturbances in the relationship between this community and other powers such as the city and the Crown. As she suggests, these could have been the reason that Yça's brother, as a member of a prestigious family in the *aljama*, was not able to go to Aiton at this time. In fact, life for this family became so difficult that they had to take refuge in the kingdom of Granada and did not return until 1480.[61]

In any case, Juan de Segovia was left without anyone competent in Arabic to assist him with the translation to Latin. He wrote to the minister general of the Franciscans to ask him to send one of their members who knew both Arabic and Latin well, promising to pay him handsomely. After learning that such a friar was then living in Rome, he sent the man a passage from the Qur'ān to test his abilities. Cabanelas related that Juan must have been satisfied with the result, but that the two could not reach an agreement on the payment arrangements. He based this on his reading of a phrase in Juan's preface to the trilingual Qur'ān (*ut expensis parcerem*). My own reading of this text leads me to believe instead that the man's response was not adequate, and that Juan considered himself to have saved money by having sent that test first.[62] Next he wrote to a man who was living closer to home, in Savoy, who had been the secretary to the king of Cyprus and his ambassador to Mecca. This man sent a reply explaining that he would not be able to help because, just as among Christians there was a vernacular language and Latin, which few could read, few among Saracens could read Arabic.[63] After these two unsuccessful attempts to find someone else to assist him, Segovia was left to complete the Latin translation with no one there to consult when he was unsure about a passage.

Gidelli's departure from the priory was not, however, the end of his contact with Juan de Segovia. Yça wrote at least one letter to Juan after he had returned to Castile. We know about this letter because Juan later related to his unnamed "most beloved *frater*" that the *faqīh* had composed a list of twelve doubts (*dubia*) concerning the teachings of Christianity, doubts he said were held by all Muslims. Juan wrote that he had explicitly encouraged his counterpart to compile this list and send it to him, and when it arrived it came with a demand from its writer that Segovia offer a satisfactory reply. This is probably the letter mentioned in Juan's *Donatio*, in which he said that the *faqīh* "thought himself to be saying lofty things concerning the unity of God and the ultimate end [of humanity]."[64] Yça never received his reply, not because Juan neglected to write him, but because before his response was finished he began to suffer from an illness that afflicted his bones and later, he wrote, his liver. He was no longer able to write as he wished. Yça probably never knew that his fellow Castilian had, in fact, interrupted another work to answer him, citing as his motivation the Gospel teaching, "Give to anyone who begs from you" (Luke 6:30).[65] In fact, as Benigno Hernández Montes argued, Segovia wrote two works to send to the Muslim scholar, the letter and a work which in his *Donatio* bears the title *Elucidatorium precipue ueritatis catholice fidei: Jesum, Marie filium, esse uerum Dei filium Deumque uerum*. No longer extant, both the letter and this theological treatise were written in Castilian.[66]

Unfortunately, the trilingual edition of the Qur'ān that meant so much to Juan de Segovia has not survived.[67] However, the Preface to it has, and it provides an invaluable lens into a fifteenth-century intellectual's close encounter with Islam's sacred text. This Preface, along with Segovia's discussion of the Qur'ān in some of his other late works, reveals a complex engagement with this text and the faith community it nourished. On the one hand, he repeated well-worn themes from medieval Western polemic against Islam, such as that Muhammad was diabolically inspired and that uncontrolled lust was a major feature of the spread of Islam. But, as Thomas Burman has argued, he was also curious, as an intellectual, about what the Qur'ān said and how Muslims read it. In addition, he seems to have mulled over how Muslims would hear or view certain things that Christians said or did, almost attending to a psychology of persuasion, and he paused mid-thought occasionally to note some parallel between the Christian and Muslim experience. One has the feeling, while reading his works, that if Gidelli knew how Segovia described and saw his religion, he could not have worked and lived with him for so long. On the other hand, if Segovia really had such an interest in Muslims' reading of their sacred text and saw them with the absence of malice that is often apparent in his discussions, how could he have been so attracted to some of the harsh notions from centuries of polemic? There can be no doubt, though, that he was engaged, in much more than a superficial way, in thinking about this other religion and its holy book.[68]

Curiously, although he attributed the Muslims' keen interest in war to commandments in the Qur'ān, he also found in this text reason to believe they would be open to overtures of peace. Enlisting a quote from the Qur'ān urging believers to love peace, he told Nicholas of Cusa, "Since, therefore, their law commands that the Saracens love peace and welcome it, we must not fear a rejection, [or fear] that they might not wish to hear of those things pertaining to peace, having been called to it."[69] He even likened this to a hypothetical situation in which the Saracens approached the church to speak of peace, and wondered who among the Christians would ever reject such a gesture.[70] He admitted to Jean Germain that the Qur'ān discouraged Muslims from engaging in disputations with Christians, but he pointed out that it also urged them to trust God, obey his commands, and seek peace.[71] Certainly he used these passages from the Qur'ān to convince his Christian readers that a bid for peace would be received well.

He also may have been searching for passages from the Qur'ān itself that Christians could enlist when they approached Muslims.

Segovia appears, in his writings, to have been keenly interested in how Muslims themselves read and understood this book. He knew that Muhammad was, according to Islam, only the bearer (*lator*) of this law, and that Muslims considered the Qur'ān to be God's word and from heaven. He explained, "Not just in one place, but in many passages it is affirmed that the book, the Qur'ān, was sent from heaven."[72] He seemed fascinated with the idea that Muslims thought the Qur'ān could not be altered or put in a new form (*nova composicio*). He observed, "Furthermore, if it is assembled anew, unless all the books of their law throughout the world were to be burned, and that new edition were to be had everywhere, these very books would serve as witness that that new work would not be the law given by the angel Gabriel, as the Qur'ān says, to [God's] Prophet, Muhammad."[73] He continued, explaining that since Muslims viewed the Qur'ān as sent from heaven, they viewed it as audacious and rash to alter it, and this included translations.[74] This is followed by a striking thought—that if all the books containing the Qur'ān that existed among the Saracens were destroyed, there would remain those owned by Christians.[75] It is tempting to wonder if such knowledge about how Muslims viewed translations, and these speculations about the value of having copies among the Christians, were prompted by his correspondence with Gidelli in which he would have been trying to convince this scholar to engage in this translation endeavor with him.

The protests of Muslims notwithstanding, Segovia could not see how the whole Qur'ān could be said to be revealed from heaven. He reasoned, "Since the whole doctrine of this sect can be reduced, as it were, to these two things, that God is one and that Muhammad is his Prophet and messenger and legate, as if it holds whatever things are written in that most vain law as from the mouth of God, from this very thing they confess that the words of their law are not the words of God, but that their law was instead composed by their wise men [*sapientibus*] by means of questioning and learned discourse."[76] As he thought about how this might have occurred, he thought of pedagogical models, such as a dialogue or a teacher questioning a student, or the question and response method one finds in the works of the scholastics.[77] He thought this explained why, since the wise men among them in modern times were not the original authors, they struggled to understand this text.[78]

Juan de Segovia's own struggle to understand the text led him to a fascination with Arabic and how the Qur'ān is written. As Thomas Burman has observed, Segovia specifically requested that Gidelli was to help him to make a translation of the Qur'ān "without glosses, limitations, expositions, or insertions in the text."[79] In the Preface to the trilingual Qur'ān, Juan wrote that he had begun to be able to sound out the syllables in Arabic, and he explained that Arabic has twenty-nine letters, but vowels are indicated by small marks above a line of writing. In manuscripts of the Qur'ān, he learned, vowel markings appear in blue, red, green, or yellow ink. He even noticed, from his own examination of Arabic copies of the Qur'ān, that some of them had more such vowel markings than the one his guest was making. He also discussed Arabic noun cases and verb conjugations. As for the content of the Qur'ān, he told readers that the suras appeared in descending order of length, "with the exception of the first which is quite short and is reputed to be the substantial statement of all the others." Paragraph divisions within the suras, he noticed, varied among manuscripts.[80] He was clearly absorbed in the philological and textual intricacies of the Qur'ān.

It would be misguided to suppose from this that he read the Qur'ān sympathetically. To be sure, his encounter with this text stimulated his intellectual curiosity, but it did not dampen his polemical intentions. Neither did it dislodge from his thinking several judgments against the Qur'ān that he shared with longstanding Western polemic. For example, he wrote that the Qur'ān was "a most cursed law" (*maledictissima lex*)[81] and "a most damned law lacking all reason" (*illius dampnatissime legis omni profecto carentis racione*).[82] This judgment was not withstanding his admission that the Qur'ān contained inspiring texts on moral virtues and possessed great eloquence and sweetness. These qualities, he lamented, only covered up the shame of the carnality found there.[83] Figuring prominently among his reasons for concluding that Islam's holy book was cursed was that the text promised a paradise of sexual pleasures, which was a common motif in the Christian polemic against Islam.[84] Even worse, the Qur'ān attributed false things to Christ, such as that he predicted the coming of Muhammad.[85] It distorted the gospel and slandered Christians.[86] The law revealed to Muhammad reduced people to an earlier law, the law of nature, thereby subverting and denying the later and more perfect laws of scripture and grace.[87]

Given the lies, slander, and obfuscation of divine revelation that Juan saw in the Qur'ān, it is not surprising that he decided that its inspiration had been demonic. He stated unequivocally, "It seems from the law that Beelzebub, prince of demons, father of lies, was the giver of the law itself."[88] Typically Juan referred to this inspiration behind the Qur'ān as "the spirit that inspired Muhammad" or "Muhammad's spirit." In one place, he referred to this spirit as "the guiding spirit, more like their subverter."[89] This spirit was also the "prince of this world," a term used by Jesus to refer to the devil.[90] This association between Muhammad's revelation and demonic activity was not uncommon. In the mid-twelfth century, Peter the Venerable described Muhammad as a diabolical prophet,[91] and Pedro Pascual (d. 1300) and Roger Bacon (d. ca. 1294) described the Prophet as possessed by a demon.[92]

Though it was hardly one of Juan's favorite themes, he was not averse to comparing Islam to the beast described in Revelation. According to this apocalyptic text, a beast would rise up from the earth and subdue many lands and peoples. It would reign for a thousand years, during which time anyone who refused to submit would be killed. Juan noted that he was not the first to recall this first-century text and consider it anew in the light of the menace of Islam's power. In 1456 he wrote that for eight hundred years this "beast" had grown stronger, taking over all the Christian lands except for parts of Gaul and Spain.[93] Juan's reference to this motif from the Western tradition on Islam appears in the Preface to his trilingual Qur'ān, where his language is markedly more strident than in his other works. Perhaps this was because, more than his letters to Cusa, Germain, and Piccolomini, he intended the Qur'ān to have a wide circulation, and this was his opportunity to impress upon his fellow Christians the urgency of the threat from Islam so that they might rally to the work of converting Muslims. He was not generally inclined toward a typological reading of scripture, and this is the only place I have seen where he appropriated this apocalyptic image to refer to Islam. Still, he invoked it here, thus associating himself in yet one more way with the West's vitriolic denunciations of Islam.

If there is one thinker to whom Juan de Segovia is routinely compared, it is Nicholas of Cusa.[94] Both of these thinkers, as scholars have noted, called for a nonviolent means of dealing with the threat from the Turks, and both were in favor of dialogue. Nonetheless, concerning the nature of the Qur'ān, the two held views that differed in important ways. Although Cusa was no lover of the Qur'ān, and thought it to, as Jasper Hopkins put it, "promulgate turpitude and to propound heresies, lies, and contradictions,"[95] he went to great lengths to argue that this sacred text was nonetheless substantially compatible with the Gospels and the Hebrew Bible. A good example of this was his discussion in the *Cribratio* of the Qur'ān assertion that it was not Christ who died on the cross, but someone who looked like him and was mistakenly crucified. Cusanus explained:

> Therefore, it is certain that if without an explication of the mysteries |of Christ's death| the Koran had openly affirmed to the Arabs that Christ was crucified, it would not |thereby| have been magnifying Christ in their minds. Therefore, |the Koran,| on a devout interpretation |thereof,| aimed to hide from the Arabs |Christ's| lowly death and to affirm that He was still living and would come |again|. Now, |the Koran| would not have been able to teach of Christ's resurrection from the dead through His power to lay down His life and to take it up again (as He avows in the Gospel) unless it had showed Christ to be not only a man but also God—|a view| which it supposed to be at odds with |the doctrine of| God's oneness, which it was preaching. Moreover, it was not consistent with the Koran's faith to maintain that Christ had already risen from the dead—as will be explained in a moment. So perhaps these are the reasons that |the Koran| spoke in the way it did. Nevertheless, |the Koran| makes |these statements| in such way that the wise can infer that the Gospel is altogether true, as will be evident.[96]

According to Cusa, God willed that even with the Qur'ān's errors and blasphemies, "there also be inserted things in which the splendor of the Gospel was so contained as hidden that it would manifest itself to the wise if it were sought for with diligent effort."[97] This kind of edifying interpretation, in which the gospel was obscured but discernible to the especially savvy reader, is what is known as Cusa's method of *pia interpretatio*.[98]

In addition to God's light infusing even this corrupt and blasphemous text, unbeknownst even to its author, Nicholas of Cusa thought that Muhammad himself deliberately chose to present things in a way that was sometimes distorted but that ultimately affirmed broader truths. This is how he interpreted the Qur'ān's sensual depiction of paradise, for example. According to his analysis, Muhammad used these sensual pleasures in order to move the uneducated Arabs to desire the joy of this future life. If he had not done this, they would not have understood and been stirred toward what God promised. But, he wrote, "This good is none other than God." Muhammad appears here as a skilled teacher, choosing apt examples to advance his pedagogical aims, aims that Cusa considered ultimately consistent with the gospel.[99]

Muhammad got no such credit from Juan de Segovia. Juan even echoed the interpretation of paradise that Cusa articulated, that Muhammad presented it as a sensory paradise so it would appeal to uneducated Arabs, but he included no exculpatory spin.[100] He certainly harbored no vision of Muhammad as a talented teacher who knew how to reach his unsophisticated followers. If anything, he typically portrayed Muhammad as something of a con artist. He admitted that the Qur'ān contains profound statements about moral virtues and that it has a certain eloquence and beauty to it. However, in almost an exact reversal of Cusa's view that its corruption obscured the divine light present in it, the Spaniard thought the text's profundity and eloquence covered the shameful carnality found there.[101] In his long letter to Jean Germain, he noted that the Qur'ān refers to Christ as the word of God and that Christian teachers (*doctoribus christianis*) should find this a useful foothold for their conversations with Muslims.[102] Cusanus might have seen this as evidence of God revealing truth even in the Qur'ān, but Segovia merely noted it as a practical matter for the discussions he envisioned and moved on.

He even asserted that one reason Muhammad's sect was still growing was that people erroneously thought the Qur'ān was not contrary to the gospel, whereas Muslims in fact hated the gospel.[103] Far from believing that God's hand was at work in the Qur'ān, Juan invariably emphasized that the spirit that inspired Muhammad was a deceiver. He called this spirit a *pseudo magister*,[104] a most impudent spirit[105] whom he often identified with Beelzebub, the prince of demons.[106] If Nicholas of Cusa was inclined toward an "exegetical exuberance" concerning the Qur'ān, as Jasper Hopkins wrote,[107] Segovia's approach was less given to interpretive gymnastics. For him, the Qur'ān simply was contrary to the gospel, and Christian leaders needed to take its inimical nature seriously.

Accounting for the Attraction of the Rival Faith

As he reflected on how best to work toward the conversion of Muslims, Segovia returned often to the question of how so many people had been attracted to this faith through the centuries. This was relevant to how Christians should go about pointing out the folly of their beliefs and their book. His dilemma was not unlike that highlighted by John V. Tolan, who framed his *Saracens: Islam in the Medieval European Imagination* around the "predicament" of thirteenth-century Dominican missionary Riccoldo da Montecroce, who wondered how to explain the fact that God allowed such prosperity and military success to the Saracens at the expense of the Christians.[108] Unlike some Christian writers who addressed this dilemma presented by the ascendancy and attraction of Islam, Segovia did not interpret Muslim advances as the judgment of God for Christians' sins, nor did he offer prophecies of Christian victories not far off. But he did repeat some of the themes that were standard fare in Western writing long before 1453.

When Christian responses first arose in the eighth century, they were prompted by the spread of Islam, then a new faith, into the Byzantine Empire. Early authors like John of Damascus portrayed Islam as a new heresy, and their defense against it mirrored existing arguments against various heresies that had arisen within Christianity.

Western European intellectuals' first attempts to grapple with Islam began in the twelfth century, when thinkers such Peter the Venerable of Cluny and Petrus Alfonsi echoed this view of Islam as a heresy.[109] As writers struggled to account for the attraction of Islam, they came to portray Muhammad as a master of the dark arts, a trickster inspired by Satan. According to this version of events, Muhammad did not perform miracles but deceived his followers into thinking that he had. Reports of polygamy and sexual promiscuity among Muslims, augmented by the promise of a paradise of sexual delights in the next life, only added to these perceptions. Also, some chroniclers of the crusades, among them Guibert of Nogent, portrayed heresy as an affliction associated with the Orientals. For Guibert, the Greeks were "clever, flighty intellectuals whose brilliant circumlocutions carry them off into heresy, constrasted implicitly to the stodgy, earthbound, authority-respecting Latins."[110] Heresies tended to spring up in the East, and Muhammad was simply the most recent and most ominous of the heresiarchs the East had produced.[111] Peter the Venerable's presentation of Islam as conceived by the devil in ancient times, to be further promulgated by Arius and then Muhammad, was typical of medieval Christian writers' polemical efforts. Peter believed that the devil's plan, in which Muhammad played a pivotal role, would come to full fruition with the arrival of the Antichrist.[112]

For the most part, Segovia did not gravitate toward the image of Muslims as heretics. At the beginning of his Preface to the Qur'ān, he referred to them as "those who err in the true faith, erroneous ones, heretics and indeed perfect heretics, above all those who have been so until now."[113] However, the tenor of that work was, as previously noted, more vigorous and aggressive than most of his works. Certainly he saw Muslims as people who had been led astray, but typically he did not explicitly refer to them as heretics, despite the parallels he sometimes drew between their situation and that of the Hussites. Instead, he attributed the spread of Islam to violence and to sexual appetites out of control. The latter, he believed, was still a significant attraction to this faith.

In his letter to Cusa dated December 2, 1454, for example, he wrote that the Saracens had been able to reoccupy lands the Christians had gained because their law encouraged them to fight and because many women had been sent to them so that their numbers would increase.[114] He told Cervantes that the Qur'ān contained twelve legitimate causes for war against Christians, whom it called unbelievers.[115] He called violence and seduction the "two arms" by which Islam grew in strength and number.[116] He wrote that, a century after the sect's founding, it had grown so quickly that a hundred thousand crossed into Spain, and Peter of Cluny commented that it covered half the earth.[117] This was because the Saracens had multiple wives.[118] Also, they were encouraged to procreate often. Segovia was disgusted, for example, by the Qur'ānic advice, "Women are to you as a field of tillage. So, as you will, come to your fertile field."[119] This verse summoned indignation and considerable attention from European commentators.[120] According to Segovia, Christians knew from daily experience that the "sect" was sustained through prolific offspring and continuous wars.[121] Already in his 1427 *repetitio* at Salamanca, he had warned his audience that Muhammad's sect "loosens the brakes on carnal concupiscence to many vices and after death places its happiness in carnal and fetid delights."[122] He was sure that the promise of eternal sexual gratification was at least partly responsible for the spread of Islam. He reasoned that if such an attractive goal were presented to an uneducated Arabic public, the listeners would surely strive to attain it.[123] Juan's preoccupation with the nature of the paradise that Islam promised placed him in the company of Christian writers in many periods. Norman Daniel explained, "Because Christian thought is so wholly bound up in the concept of eternal life, the irrationality of Islam *propter finem quem promittit* has seemed to Christians so clear a mark of its invalidity."[124]

This recourse to a supposed prodigious sexual appetite is perhaps not so surprising given that the Christian thinkers like Segovia were struggling to explain, after all, the rapid spread of a people. But recent scholarship on gender has indicated some intriguing complexity surrounding such language, which suggests that further research on gender and religious polemic might be fruitful. For example, Louise Mirrer has shown that medieval Spain's epic poems and frontier ballads, which date to the fourteenth and fifteenth centuries, present aggression and sexual assertiveness as admirable, manly qualities, but deny these qualities to the Muslim men portrayed in these stories.

Unlike their robustly masculine Christian counterparts, Muslim men often appear as friendly, polite, and conciliatory. In short, their behavior and speech were precisely those associated with feminine qualities, and indeed urged on women in medieval courtesy books.[125] Moreover, although sexual assertion and dominance were "manly" attributes, lust was condemned and was considered a special affliction of women, since it was associated with weakness. Medieval and early modern norms held that when excessive passion occurred in men, it was alarming precisely because it made them effeminate.[126] But Christian writers, including Juan de Segovia, decried Muslims as lascivious, normally a weak and feminine quality, and yet credited them with military might. Given the Ottoman successes during this time, it is not surprising that Segovia and others saw at least these particular Muslims as powerful warriors, but the pairing of this with an ongoing portrayal of them as lascivious raises interesting questions for the study of these themes in polemical discourse.

In Spain, the image of sexual desires out of control may even have had political connotations that influenced Juan de Segovia's thinking. Recently, Barbara Weissberger has explored the power of the legend of Rodrigo and the fall of Visigothic Spain to the Muslim invaders. According to this legend, the downfall of the troubled Visigothic kingdom occurred as a revenge for King Rodrigo's rape of Cava (or Alacava in some accounts), the daughter of Count Julián, who governed the North African province of Ceuta. Angry at the dishonor perpetrated against his daughter, Count Julián urged his Muslim allies to cross the strait and invade the peninsula. The story of the rape and the revenge is the central plot in the *Crónica del Rey don Rodrigo* or *Crónica sarracina*, written by Pedro del Corral around 1430. This version was a strong influence on the ballads surrounding Rodrigo, which circulated beginning in the second half of the century. Weissberger has demonstrated that this illicit sexual union and the destruction it brought served as a paradigm for the dangers of transgressive sexuality when applied to the body politic as well. In the fifteenth-century propaganda for the Trastámara dynasty, this violated, virginal young woman was conflated with the body of Hispania, which needed "restoring" or "recovering." In promoting the legitimacy of

Isabel's reign, chroniclers described Enrique IV, her predecessor, as prone to various sexual transgressions. Isabel was then the monarch who would restore the broken body of Spain. Diego de Valera and other chroniclers subtly compared Isabel to the Virgin Mary, making her a woman who would undo the fall brought about by a woman, since some accounts blamed Cava for her own rape.[127]

Once again, there is an interesting paradox in how sexual lasciviousness and conquest were presented in the texts. According to these fifteenth-century accounts of the Muslim invasion of the peninsula, lust or at least sexual transgression by Christians brought ruin upon the Visigothic kingdom. King Enrique's own excessive sexual desires, according to these writers, weakened the kingdom and brought disgrace to him. If inordinate sexual desire was associated with loss or even feminine weakness, how is it that Muslims demonstrating excessive sexual appetites gained kingdoms, even whole empires, through their lust? It is possible that language of sexual desire and lust operated differently in different types of discourse, or even that writers, had they been pressed on this question, would have pointed out that sexual excess was detrimental to Christians because it invoked the punishment of the Christian God, but the Muslim God was not angered by such matters. If lust made a people, and especially leaders, effeminate and weak, Christian polemicists may have been subtly, even unknowingly, suggesting that it was a matter of time before the Muslims' behavior caught up with them, that the seeds of eventual Christian triumph were sown in the very expansion of Muslim rule. But clearly this language of sexual depravity, as used in standard Christian polemic against Islam, begs further study in the light of these observations about the way this language functioned in diverse contemporary texts.[128]

Related to the theme of violence and lasciviousness was Segovia's concern to show that Islam arose through "corporeal generation."[129] This he explained by noting that Muslims practiced circumcision, and it was that practice that constituted their community. He knew that the Qur'ān did not enjoin this on believers, and also that Muslims considered the custom to have originated through the example of their "first father," Ishmael.[130] The fact that they traced their beginning to

Ishmael, who was not an heir to God's covenant, explained to him why they did not respect the sacred texts. Moreover, since they did not take their origin from the word of life, they accorded little importance to the divine word that God spoke to Abraham. He articulated this in his letter to Nicholas of Cusa:

> For the Jews, especially, make use of the fact that the statute, pact, and agreement offered by God was to the descendants of the seed of Isaac and not of that of Ishmael. From this, it is made clear why the Saracens do not venerate sacred writings, which in this and in many other matters gives explicit testimony against their law. Thus they do not take their origin from the word of life. And so they give little heed to this divine word that God spoke to Abraham, but pride themselves in having their law; indeed they pride themselves on that by which they took their origin—in corporeal generation and in the clash of swords.[131]

Segovia placed great emphasis on the origins of the other faith.

The "corporeal origins" of the faith revealed to Muhammad marked it for a specific treatment within Juan's worldview. As we have seen, a central organizing structure of his thought was the notion of the "principles of being and conserving," a term that Jean Gerson had used at Constance in his writings on the church.[132] Juan de Segovia used the term *principia essendi et conservandi* fairly often and invariably assumed that his readers were familiar with it. The idea was that something's origin determined its nature, and that the thing would fare best when it was true to its nature (its "principles of being") because it was by these very principles that it would also be "conserved." He argued, "It is fitting that the Christian religion take up its origin from the word of the living God and that it continue by this same means and by it subdue the nations of the world by such arms as it had received."[133] The sect of Muhammad did not share these principles of being. In Segovia's mental framework, given Islam's violent and carnal origins, it could not help but continue on a course marked by these traits, and one needed to look no further for an explanation of its continued existence. The religion was preserved by the very principles that initiated it. As we have seen, these "principles of being and conserving" also indicated to Juan the correct path for the church to follow in its relations with the Muslim world. He insisted that the church must be faithful to the teaching upon which it was founded.

Having an origin not rooted in divine inspiration and action brought certain consequences. One was that Muhammad was unable to perform any miracles. Western writers were often quick to note this and to use it as an argument that Muhammad could not have been a real prophet.[134] Segovia, on the other hand, wrote, "But the law of Muhammad takes pride in that it is not ambiguous, but that it says through constant assertion that its bearer did not come with miracles."[135] Not all Christian thinkers knew that Muslims were aware of the fact that their Prophet never claimed any miracles and were untroubled by it. Segovia did know this, and knew as well that they held the Qur'ān itself to be a miracle.[136] Accordingly, he did not waste much ink reiterating the absence of miracles and instead directed his efforts toward discrediting the Qur'ān as a revealed text and promoting his idea for a peace delegation.

Both of these initiatives imply a Muslim audience that was rational and capable of being persuaded. This was not a view that all Christian thinkers espoused, but it is one that Juan de Segovia shared with intellectuals such as Nicholas of Cusa, Ramón Llull (ca. 1232–1316), and even Peter the Venerable in the mid-twelfth century. The latter praised the rationality of his Arab audience, calling his intended readers "not only rational by nature, but logical in temperament and training"[137] and "learned in worldly knowledge."[138] Tolan noted that this recognition of the Muslims as rational was even more remarkable because elsewhere Peter described the Jews, by contrast, as "beasts without reason" because they failed to accept the truth of Christianity.[139] Thirteenth-century Riccoldo da Montecroce was less optimistic about the success of rational dialogue and advocated force when it did not succeed. He portrayed the Saracens as "violent and irrational zealots who are impervious to reason."[140] His work was one of the most influential anti-Islamic works from the fourteenth to the sixteenth centuries.[141]

Riccoldo's was a view that Segovia, Cusa, and Llull rejected. For both Cusa and Segovia, getting Muslims to accept the Trinity was merely a matter of explaining it in a credible way. Segovia dedicated some forty folios of his letter to Germain to spelling out how the Christian doctrine of the Trinity made sense, so that it might be persuasively presented to potential converts from Islam. Cusa was convinced that the truth was one and could be grasped by any free intellect.[142] As we have seen, Segovia insisted that Muslims were rational beings who were tragically ill-informed about the central Christian teachings. Once someone had taken the trouble to clarify things, he thought, they would easily see their errors.[143] Similarly, both Segovia and Llull believed that Muslims could be converted by reason, and both appreciated the centrality of the Qur'ān in any discussion with Muslims. Both thought a spiritual crusade preferable to a military one, and both cited as support for this stance the example of the apostles having spread Christianity through peaceful means.[144] Especially after the failure of the thirteenth-century missions, Western intellectuals who thought Muslims were rational were increasingly a minority.[145] In this, Segovia was outside the mainstream, even though he had company.

As the preceding discussion suggests, Juan de Segovia's perspectives on Muslims and their faith contained much from the traditional European stock of images.[146] Though scholars as accomplished as Cabanelas, Izbicki, and Biechler have emphasized the ways in which Segovia stepped outside the tradition,[147] it is indisputable that he was beholden to that tradition in significant ways. He did not begin his search for information on Islam in 1431 with a blank slate, and any familiarity with actual Muslims that he acquired in Castile or Aiton did not significantly shake him from his confident assertion of some longstanding "truths" regarding them. Nevertheless, it is not readily apparent how he was exposed to this long tradition of European polemics. It was not exclusively through personal contacts and books acquired at Basel, since so much of it already appeared in his 1427 *repetitio*. Hernández Montes wrote that Juan took the contents of his *Errores sarracenorum et albigensium*, a one-page sheet of notes, from Nicolaus Eymerichus's (d. 1399) *Directorium inquisitorum*, but Jesse Mann's closer study of both texts revealed that this is not accurate. There is little correspondence between the "errors" compiled there by Juan and the earlier Dominican's work, so the source of this compilation remains a mystery.[148]

Neither Juan's citations nor the inventory to his library are much help in tracing the origins of his thought. Certainly he knew of Peter the Venerable and Raymond Llull,[149] but his discussions about Muslims' beliefs and Qur'ānic teachings are conspicuously and curiously devoid of any citation of precursors' writings. This contrasts with his discussions on scripture, the church, papal policy, or historical events such as the crusades. In those sections, he often cited an authoritative source by author and title. Why was this not the case with his treatment of Muslims' beliefs and practices?

One possible reason is that he did not trust those sources. Indeed, in the Preface to his trilingual Qur'ān, he complained that despite the great quantity of treatises that Christian writers had produced against Islam, scarcely any of them was accurate in its portrayal of that religion's teachings. Often they asserted outlandish things as beliefs common to Muslims, he wrote.[150] He wrote to Jean Germain that in 1437 he had written to Castile for a translation of the Qur'ān into Spanish, and it arrived full of invective and inaccuracies.[151] This was probably Pedro Pascual's translation, since it corresponds to a comment that Juan made in his Preface about a version by the bishop of Jaén that he had requested, a version that imputed many things to Islam not found in the Qur'ān.[152] If Segovia had his doubts about the credibility of existing works on Islam, he might have been reticent about drawing from them heavily and not especially eager to acknowledge any debt to them.

Polemic and Conversion

Juan de Segovia's thoughts on Islam and his desire to see Muslims converted make him an interesting case in the tradition of Christian polemic against Islam. As Lucy Pick has noted, scholars have studied religious polemic as disruptive of routine social interactions among people of different faiths, and as a sign of opposition to this coexistence. Traditionally, students of this tradition have seen conversion as a main goal of the polemic.[153] And yet, in her examination of the thirteenth-century contributions to this tradition, Pick observes that polemic against unbelievers often served instead to help Christians (and the others, particularly Jews) to define their identity and reinforce community boundaries.[154] Certainly Peter the Venerable, a leading figure in Western polemical tradition, made a telling comment roughly a century earlier. He explained that his *Contra sectam siue Saracenorum* (1155–56) would help Christian readers, even if it were never translated into Arabic for his intended Muslim audience, because it would fortify the faith of any Christians who might be tempted to view Islam with respect or admiration. In a letter to Bernard of Clairvaux intended to convince him of the value of his translation efforts, Peter admitted, "Although I think this might not be of much use to the lost ones [the Muslims], nevertheless it would be proper to have a really suitable reply as a Christian armory." He continued, "If thereby those in error cannot be converted, at least a learned man, or a teacher, if he has zeal for justice, should look after and provide for the weak ones in the Church, who are inclined to be tempted to evil or to be obscurely shaken by slight causes, and not to neglect them."[155] As Tolan noted, the most likely Christians to benefit from this were the intellectuals who were studying and translating Arabic philosophical and scientific texts. So even Peter's seminal polemical work could be seen as a defense of Christianity more than a genuine attempt to convert Muslims.[156] This could well have been true of later polemicists' work as well. Nancy Bisaha has argued that Pius II's letter to the sultan, written in 1461, is best understood not as a genuine attempt to convert the Ottoman leader, but as an assertion of "Western and Christian superiority."[157]

Juan de Segovia seems to have been genuinely interested in conversion and not merely the fortification of Christians' confidence or pride. The conversations he envisioned were to take place in Muslim lands, so there would have been no large audience of Europeans whose faith would be bolstered by watching Christian teaching affirmed. In this respect, at least, any comparison to academic disputations collapses. In fact, he apparently did not conceive of these meetings as public at all; they were rather like summit meetings between leaders.

According to his account, he proposed to the reluctant Granadan in 1431 that the two of them meet out in the countryside, away from the crowds.

If he were not concerned about conversion, and merely wanted to posture, it is hard to account for the passages in his works which reveal a certain astuteness about the psychology of persuasion. In the Preface to his trilingual Qur'ān, for example, he lamented that Christians attribute such outlandish things to Islam that the Muslims are insulted and driven away. Complaining about the lack of adequate translations of the Qur'ān, Segovia noted that a translation he had examined "deviated from the contents of the Arabic text in many places" and that he realized that hardly any Christian thinker "aimed to refute their sect" through reference to accurate information about it. He explained to those he hoped would use his new Qur'ān why this was so troubling:

> But very often [Christians] recite gross (errors) exceedingly distant from things of rational men, even bestial and silly things which they think is their law. And things that the Saracens themselves consider an insult. Then they recoil on account of this from inclining their ears to sound doctrine. Indeed, nothing is a greater obstacle to the reduction of heretics than to impute false testimony to them concerning their teachings, since this creates an occasion such that in no way would they accept the doctrine of the Catholic teachers, whom [the Saracens] see as referring to their own teachings as different from what they are.[158]

Elsewhere he argued that it was only natural that the Saracens would hate Christ if the soldiers who were killing them did so in Christ's name. He reasoned, "Because indeed it hinders and poses an impediment to their conversion if, [learning] from the lesson of wars against them, there rises up in the Saracens a hatred for Christians, and incomparably more so against Christ, since they think, as in fact truth holds, that all Christians fight for his honor, having him as their leader and protector. They can not ignore it, seeing all the fighters marked with the sign of Christ."[159]

Segovia seemed to devote great attention to reflection about how people are persuaded. He asserted that people can only come to knowledge of God by trusting what another person says, and God willed it this way. Since faith requires a fledgling believer to trust another, the person preaching needs to be credible and the one hearing about the faith must know that the other desires his good. He spent some time on this point in his letter to Cusa:

> Besides, if Christ appeared for forty days after his resurrection to his disciples, speaking of the reign of God, the Gospels maintain that, while he came, he taught in mortal flesh. And indeed, because without trust, men can not come together because it is necessary that they believe each other and also, concerning hidden things that cannot be shown through reason or sight, God wills that mortal men believe each other in those things which pertain to the understanding of God and the salvation of their soul, just as they do in those things that are judged to pertain to the health of the body or the use of matter; and as they do this, they adhere not to a base faith, but a great faith. Moreover, how much more weighty, indeed, since they sometimes easily believe those persuading them toward those things that [lead to] the damnation of the soul or to evil. . . . From this it can be perceived if, as long as they will see them with such a disposition, they believe the Christian teachers (*doctoribus*) who are preaching about the truth of the Catholic faith. The law of nature dictates that a man not trust his enemy. Also, divine law testifies that he is understood when he speaks with his lips, and when he sets traps in the heart, do not believe him when he speaks gently because there are seven evils in his heart. [See Sirach 12:16.] And again in another place, it says "Do not believe your enemy because he raises up arms through his wickedness. And if he should leave having been humilitated and bent over, keep your soul away and guard yourself from him." [See Sirach 12:11.] Therefore the law of nature holds and affirms what the divine word says, that an enemy is not believed, but rather a friend, so, that the Saracens may believe the Christians to be procuring the health of their souls, it is fitting that they see that the Christians are attending to the teaching concerning love of

enemies and doing good to those they hate, since those who conquer evil through good heap coals of fire over their [enemies'] heads.
For in fact the command to love is of such great importance that
according to the teaching of the philosopher and of sacred scripture, to love is to choose the good of another rather than oneself,
since they, those conquering evil with good, heap coals over the
heads of those [others]. To be sure, the command "love" is of utmost importance.[160]

This was a pragmatic argument on Segovia's part, that one wishing
to be trusted and credible cannot be an enemy. The fact that he concerned himself with these observations about the disposition and psychology of the listeners marks his approach as different from that of
some Christian thinkers, from Peter the Venerable in the twelfth century to Piccolomini in Segovia's own time, whose arguments against
Islam were mostly for the benefit of other Christians.

This concern to be seen by Muslims as trustworthy and genuine
appears to have been operative in his direct encounters with them
as well. Despite the denunciations of the Qur'ān or Islam in which
he sometimes engaged, when he was actually in the company of a real
Muslim he seems to have been reasonably courteous. Otherwise, once
again, it is hard to explain why his Muslim interlocutor in Medina de
Campo engaged with him in discussion about matters of faith, apparently on repeated occasions. If Segovia had been derisive or rude to
him, would he not have declined any discussions after the first? One
would also be hard pressed to explain Segovia's clear elation at the arrival of Gidelli to Aiton, especially since, as Leyla Rouhi has pointed
out, Gidelli's correspondence about the terms of their arrangement
had a tone that was "respectful and friendly but by no means subservient."[161] In fact, Gidelli balked at the pay he had been offered, writing
to Segovia, "How then could it be, my lord, that, after this task is . . .
completed truly and faithfully as the words demand, after calculating
the length of time to do this, it should not work out to be more than
it would cost to engage a gravedigger?"[162] The two eventually reached
an agreement on a suitable payment. The source of these funds invites some speculation. According to a local history of the diocese of

Maurienne, Segovia's friend from Basel Louis de La Palud (d. 1451) was generous in his donations to various church institutions in the diocese of St. Jean Maurienne, and one of his bequests was to the priory at Aiton.[163] It is certainly possible that his bequest helped fund Segovia's work and perhaps this payment to Gidelli. If so, it would be one more connection between Segovia's conciliar activities and his writings on Islam.

Regardless of his funding source, if Segovia had expected deference from a Muslim or felt entitled to treat a Muslim badly, would he so readily and enthusiastically have welcomed this one to Aiton, even exalting in the skill the man brought to his task? Also, when Juan described his guest's response to the alcohol in the peas, his tone was respectful, not sneering or dismissive.[164] If Gidelli had found Segovia offensive, or even just annoying, he probably would have headed back down to the valley from the priory at Aiton and left for Castile, happy not to have any further engagement with him. But the *faqīh* wrote to him from Castile, sending along twelve objections to Christianity, and he demanded a response. The picture of Juan de Segovia that emerges is of a man engaged in genuine, seemingly respectful dialogue with Muslims, and none of this pursued in front of an audience. There is no reason to question the sincerity of his desire to learn about Islam and ultimately to convert Muslims to Christianity.

Another way in which Segovia differed sharply from most others writing polemic was his minimal interest in Jews. Typically writers countered both these perceived threats to the well-being of Christendom in their arguments. In fact, one of the most influential polemical works on Islam was Petrus Alfonsi's *Dialogues Against the Jews*, which was composed in 1110 and contained one anti-Islamic chapter. It enjoyed a broad readership among monastics interested in exegesis, Judaism, or Islam. There are sixty-three extant copies, not including manuscripts containing adaptations or solely the anti-Islamic chapter. As John V. Tolan has written, dozens of later writers learned about the teachings of Islam through this work. Petrus portrayed both the Talmud and the Qur'ān as "illegitimate pseudorevelations" that could be countered through arguments based on scripture and reason.[165] Juan de Segovia's contemporaries, too, usually linked Islam and Judaism in their works. Alonso de Espina, for example, linked both faiths to demonic forces when he wrote that two races, Jews and demons, had descended from Adam, through two different wives. Espina explained that the Qur'ān had come from the devil, and Muhammad's ancestors were idolaters and hence bore the banners of the devil. The two strains of demonic agency in the world merged when a Jewish astronomer foretold the birth of Muhammad.[166] One of Espina's favorite topics was circumcision, a practice that allowed him to link the two religions in his own day. Like most polemicists, he directed his aim at both rival faiths.[167]

Because this approach was customary, it is significant that Juan de Segovia did not use it. Jews are occasionally mentioned in his works, including in his 1427 *repetitio* at Salamanca. However, these mentions are casual, such as when he responded to Jean Germain's alarm at rumors that Muslims were in positions of authority in Castile by denying this and adding that they were often in subservient positions, and people preferred them to the Jews because they were more obsequious.[168] In that same letter to Germain, he noted that the law of Christ differed from the law of Moses in that "Christ was the redeemer not of these ones or those, but for all."[169] There simply is no polemic against Jews in these references. His letter to Nicholas of Cusa even contains a statement that suggests that converting Jews was not a goal at all. Reflecting on Christ's charge to his disciples to preach the gospel to all nations, he commented that "today" all "nations" referred "not so much to Christians or Jews, but rather to Muslims and Tartars."[170]

This leaves Jews in an interesting position in his worldview. Although he did not think it was important that Christians exert themselves to convert Jews, it it not clear why the prospect of Jews perishing through not accepting Christ would be any less alarming than the perishing of all those lost Muslims. To Germain, he lamented that for eight hundred years Muslims had lived and died without knowing about Christ and unsaved, noting that this was a great tragedy.[171] Did he think it more acceptable for Jews to perish, or was there some other place for them in God's plan? Certainly Augustine had articulated a view of the Jews that served, for centuries, to discourage efforts to convert or harass them. He saw them as beneficial to Christian society because their existence and continued practice of their faith served as a testimony to the law of Moses, which was God's law.[172] It is possible that Juan de Segovia was influenced by this long tradition in Christian thought, but if he was, he provided no indication of it. He never gave any reason why Jews should not be converted, and he never referred to any works by Augustine on this subject. I suspect that the explanation for his unusual lack of interest in converting Jews is that, as we have seen, conversion was a strategy to end the Muslims' slander against Christianity and their wars against Christians, which he attributed to the teachings of Islam. Jews, on the other hand, posed no such menace.

It is also possible that Juan de Segovia did not think it urgent to find ways to convert Jews because so many Jews already had been converting. Fear of persecution led many Jews to the baptismal font in the wake of the 1391 persecutions. Although Jews had been excluded from many professions and positions of authority, this had been based on religion, not race. Their embrace of Christianity, whether willing or under duress, made the *conversos* (converts from Judaism and their descendants) eligible now for many public offices. As a result, during the decades that Segovia spent in Castile, the urban oligarchies in many cities were dominated by prominent *converso* families, provoking a backlash of hostility from the traditional urban elites. Segovia and Burgos were two of the cities where their presence was strongest.[173] As someone whose circles included the royal court and several of the kingdom's leading figures, Juan de Segovia probably knew many *conversos*. He may have come to know some Jews and *conversos* in Salamanca as well. Records from the cathedral chapter meetings contain references to numerous Jews and *conversos* in this town, and they were living in the center of the city, in houses neighboring those of university and cathedral personnel. Some were involved in the book trade, such as Reina (no last name given), who is described as a *judía* and *librera* (bookseller) in the late fourteenth century and Alfonso Rodríguez, a *converso* and *pergaminero* (parchment maker) in 1414.[174] Presumably university and cathedral personnel would have been their main customers. Some names appear without any reference to the person's status as Jewish or *converso*, but the names make one suspect Jewish roots, as in the case of *libreros* Abraham (who is listed as a former occupant of some houses in 1417) and Jacob (1404) or the *plateros* (silversmiths) Yuçe Cohen (a former occupant of some houses in 1414) and Samuel Cohen (1415).[175]

At least one *converso*, Alonso de Cartagena, was a colleague at Basel. So perhaps one reason he was not as eager to convert Jews as he was to convert Muslims was that he thought the tide was already turning for the Jews and their conversion was already under way. However, I suspect that the most important reason for this departure from his contemporaries is that he was not so concerned with eliminating religious difference as a goal in itself, but only when the tenets of the other religion, at least as he understood them, encouraged attacks on Christian lands.

Another important difference between Segovia and many other thinkers who wrote about Islam (and Judaism) is that the events of his day, alarming though they were, did not send him scurrying to treatises on the apocalypse or to the book of Revelation to decipher them. His perspective on history was too sober for that, and his reading of scripture did not support it. Medieval commentaries on Revelation commonly associated Muhammad with the beast of the apocalypse, which would be defeated when Christ returned. Alonso de Espina calculated the arrival of the end times from the death of Muhammad, and Juan de Torquemada followed Jacques of Vitry's *History of the Eastern Church* in offering an elaborate account of the signs that Muhammad was, indeed, this beast. In the great drama of history, Muslims were cast in the role of persecutors of Christians and precursors of the Antichrist. Although the seven heads of the beast were not always associated with the same historical figures in the commentaries, Nero, Arius, the Saracens, and the Turks figured prominently in many lists, along with the Antichrist. According to Ana Echevarría, almost every medieval author saw Islam as an instrument of divine punishment.[176] Juan de Segovia did not refer to Islam in this way, and the only place I have seen him employ the "beast of the apocalypse" language is his Preface to the trilingual Qur'ān, as mentioned above. This may have more to do with his methods of reading the Bible than with his opinions of Islam per se. He rejected as mere human invention others' attempts to make predictions about the end of the world based on calculations from various events related to the beast. In the book of Revelation, he sought not coded predictions but paradigms for human behavior.[177]

In addition, nowhere in his writings do we see any indication of a millenarian or apocalyptic expectation that when Muslims or other peoples were finally converted, Christ would return and a new world begin. Franciscan missions, in particular, often were animated by this hope.[178] According to John Leddy Phelan, this sense of their mission also drove the Franciscans' work in the New World in the sixteenth century.[179] With its deep roots in medieval cosmology and biblical exegesis, it was certainly a significant motivation for Christopher Columbus a few decades after Segovia died. As Delno West has observed, Columbus saw himself as chosen by God for the evangelization of newly discovered lands, an accomplishment "that was to be only a prelude to the military recapture of Jerusalem by the Spanish, when the Holy Temple would be rebuilt in the last days, enabling the assemblage of Christians from a converted world."[180] All the central texts from which Columbus drew existed in Juan's day, and indeed several influential Spanish thinkers flirted with Joachimism in the late fourteenth and early fifteenth centuries.[181] Yet Juan's writings contain no such apocalyptic conception of conversion, neither for Muslims nor for Jews, and no eagerness to hasten conversion in anticipation of some great event. Segovia simply did not engage in this type of exegesis. In fact, he insisted to Jean Germain that since peace was, in principle, a better means of converting Muslims than war, it was not appropriate to set a deadline by which this goal must be accomplished before resorting to war. He argued, "If the way of peace and teaching is better suited than the way of war for the conversion of the Saracens to the sacraments of the Catholic faith, it does not fix a deadline before which that effort must be started or finished, since, as divine wisdom says, 'Let him who believes not hurry or be rushed; I will weigh justice and injustice in proportion.'"[182]

Thus even though he sometimes borrowed language from a long tradition of polemic against Muslims, he may have been unique in his reasons for wanting to convert them. Conversion was necessary to end their wars and their insulting assessment of Christianity, which remained deeply troubling to him. His closing reflections in his letter to Nicholas of Cusa make clear the inspiration for his approach:

> Indeed, a spirit of anxiety greatly filled my heart, seeing that an innumerable multitude of men perish under the error of their heresy, so destructive, and furthermore how much the Christian religion suffers unless it shows them, directly to their face, that the things their law imputes to the Lord, our Savior Jesus Christ, and to his priests, and generally to all Christians, are false, [among them] that [the Christians] worship a God of parts and his associates. And if these things are contained in their law, truly how many other things are said of the Christian religion, judging us to believe the most absurd things, and by these things these very ones congratulating themselves that they are not of a society holding these things as [part of its] faith. Having learned from experience, I observed this in discussions held with the above-mentioned ambassador of the king of Granada, with him putting forth most improperly that Christians ate their God and absolved sins committed against God.[183]

When he waded into the stream of Western polemic, it was no mere rhetorical exercise for him, and he was not, in fact, responding to earlier writers' thoughts as much as he was to his formative memory of a conversation in Castile.

One reason he gave for striving to convert Muslims was that this would enable them to enjoy the eternal happiness for which all human beings are created. This concern appears both in his earliest extant writings and in those he composed in the 1450s. In 1427 he told his audience that this happiness was the ultimate end or destiny for human nature, and the Christian faith was the only way that led to it.[184] In 1455 he seemed genuinely saddened by the thought of Muslims spending their whole lives without hearing of God's love: "What, then, of the pitiable Saracens who have not heard for their whole lives? And . . . for eight hundred years hardly ever or never was the smallest charity preached or declared to them, that God so loved the world that he gave his only son for their salvation."[185]

A third reason that Juan de Segovia thought Christians should exert themselves to bring the Muslims to Christianity was that, in doing so, they would be cooperating with the will of God. They would fulfil Jesus's command to preach the gospel to all peoples: "Thus he gave an eternal command to preach the gospel to them when he said, 'Go, teach all nations; behold I am with you always until the end of time.' . . . If, therefore, the church is obligated to preach the word of God to the nations, may every effort be made so that a hearing is granted."[186] In doing so, Juan reminded his reader, they would be "doing the will of their father, who did not desire the death of sinners, but that [the sinner] convert and live."[187] Furthermore, he told Germain, "To be sure, the Christian law in this way differs from any other sect due to the fact that in it there is no acceptance of divisions among people, whereby in the Apostle's testimony, there is no male or female, Gentile and Jew, circumcised and uncircumcised, barbarian and Scythian, servant and free . . . when Christ was the redeemer not of these or of those, but of all."[188] In attending to the Muslims, Christians would be faithful to Jesus's command and help to work toward God's plan for the world.

The desire to convert one's enemies shows an ability to conceive of them as something other than perennial enemies. As we have seen, Segovia was encouraged in this by the success that the Council of Basel had in its negotiation with the Hussites in Bohemia, with whom peace was achieved after a period of armed revolt. Since he envisioned a different relationship between Europeans and their neighbors to the south and east, he apparently did not consider those neighbors constitutionally inferior or savage. His inclination to convert Muslims, offensive as that might sound to medieval or even modern Muslims, nevertheless aimed at the establishment of meaningful connections between Muslims and Christians and ultimately at the Muslims' inclusion in the Christian community. Juan's appropriation of the apostolic tradition as an example to follow extended to Paul's preaching in Athens, recounted in the Acts of the Apostles. There Paul converted many who had previously accepted no biblical authority and who did not even believe in the one God. Muslims, by contrast, already firmly believed in one God and accepted much of scriptural revelation.[189]

Segovia's native Castile might have provided him with a vision of what his world might look like once those multitudes of Muslims were converted and God's plan to "gather all people into one" was accomplished. Several fifteenth-century writers in Juan's native land wrote impassioned letters and treatises defending the *conversos* from persecution and calling for their full social integration. In the late fourteenth and early fifteenth centuries, there was a sharp increase in the number of *conversos* across Iberia, mainly in the cities, and the resulting social tensions heightened as the fifteenth century progressed. This increase in the *converso* population occurred in the aftermath of a wave of massacres carried in 1391 by popular mobs against the Jewish quarters in Seville, Valencia, Barcelona, Burgos, Segovia, Cuenca, and other cities. Twenty years later, Vincent Ferrer's preaching brought both baptisms and new legislation against Jews, adding again to the number of *conversos*. "Old Christians" questioned the sincerity of their new coreligionists' faith and resented them for holding prominent positions in urban and royal power circles. The resentful sought ways to limit the *conversos*' full participation in Spanish society, frequently by restricting their access to public office.[190]

Spain's "new Christians," as they were called, were not without strong and articulate advocates. Among them were men such as Lope de Barrientos, Alonso de Cartagena (a *converso* himself), and Juan de Torquemada, the uncle of the future inquisitor of the same name. Cartagena's *Defensorium unitatis christianae*, for example, was, as its title suggests, an argument against discrimination against the *conversos* on the grounds that divisions among the people of God were an attack on the body of Christ. Cartagena likened those who introduced such divisions to heretics, specifically mentioning the Hussites. The third of his four theses sounds like a position Juan de Segovia would have endorsed heartily: "That Israelites and Gentiles alike, having entered the Catholic faith through the door of holy baptism, do not remain two peoples or two nations divided, but rather from the two, one new people is created."[191] Torquemada, for his part, argued that all Christians, after all, were descendants of converts, and it was not right to regard people with suspicion because of the sins of their fathers. Instead, converts were members of the "Christian brotherhood," in which was found the peace that was to be enjoyed by all Christians.[192] An anonymous sermon, delivered before Juan II in the mid-fifteenth century, also defended the *conversos* against their detractors, and called upon the king to intervene to stop the persecution. The sermon was on Ephesians 4:3: "making every effort to maintain the unity of the Spirit in the bond of peace." In explaining the nature of the church and its unity, the speaker enlisted one of Juan de Segovia's favorite passages, in which the apostle Paul argued that there was now no Jew or Gentile, servant and free, because all were one in Christ.[193] The unknown deliverer of this sermon urged the king to take action against the malefactors who were rupturing the peace by not respecting this fundamental unity.[194]

The general spirit of Juan de Segovia's proposals concerning Christian-Muslim relations was intriguingly close to that of these defenders of the *conversos*. There is no evidence of a direct link between Juan's works and the arguments offered by these Castilian thinkers on behalf of Spain's *conversos*. Certainly Torquemada and Cartagena had represented Juan II at Basel, where presumably they would have known Segovia, if they were not already acquainted before then.[195] Lope de Barrientos taught theology at Salamanca while Juan was there.[196] Still, in the early 1450s, when these former colleagues' works on the *conversos* were written, Basel had already ended, and it does not seem likely that Segovia was in close contact with their authors. Furthermore, he had not been in Castile for twenty years. Even if he had had occasion to discuss the plight of the *conversos* with his fellow Castilians during the council,[197] it is difficult to imagine that this issue weighed heavily on his mind all that time. Nonetheless, there is an affinity between his desire to convert Muslims and bring them within the Christian society and his fellow Castilians' arguments for the integration and acceptance of their new coreligionists.

Interesting parallels between Segovia's vision and arguments made by others appear both beyond Castile and beyond Segovia's lifetime. Erasmus, for example, made many of the same arguments that Segovia did against crusading, and he enlisted many of the same scriptural texts to support his positions. Norman Housley even noted that when Erasmus proposed that the solution to Turkish aggression was conversion, he was "following in the footsteps" of predecessors including Juan de Segovia.[198] In 1515, Erasmus wrote bluntly to Pope Leo X about the pope's plans for a crusade, saying, "To fight the Turks we get no instructions from Christ and no encouragement from the apostles." A few years later, in 1523, he wrote, "The sum and substance of our religion is peace and concord."[199] Juan de Segovia might have been especially gratified to hear the Dutch reformer take up an argument that he himself had made several decades earlier: "If a handful of disciples were able to place the entire world under Christ's yoke, armed with nothing but their trust in God and the sword of the [Holy] Spirit, surely we can manage the same with Christ's assistance?"[200] The similarities between the two men's thinking are undeniable, even though there are no indications that Erasmus even knew of Juan de Segovia, much less had read any of his works. What they had in common, at least on this issue, is that both drew their inspiration from gospel teachings and the example of the early church.

Not everything about their approach to Turkish matters was similar. Unlike Juan de Segovia, Erasmus was openly skeptical about the use of crusading to legitimize conflicts between Christian powers, to increase taxes, or to promote fraudulent indulgences.[201] In his writings, at least, Segovia never attributed the desire for crusading to these motives. Also, Erasmus was among those thinkers who associated the recent Turkish advances with punishment for Christians' sins, along with other afflictions of the era like syphilis and inflation. Sometimes he was even quite specific in identifying something as a divine punishment for wrongdoing. For example, he thought the Christian defeat at Varna in 1444 was God's punishment of Wladislaw of Poland because the king had broken an oath not to attack the Turks.[202] Juan de Segovia never adopted this line of thinking. He never intepreted events as punishment for sins.

If he were inclined toward such an interpretation, the defeat at Varna might have been more likely than most events to draw such an analysis from him. It could have been tempting, for someone given to such lines of thinking, to consider Varna a sign of God's displeasure with Segovia's mentor and friend from Basel, Giuliano Cesarini, who died while leading the crusading army against the Turks. The cardinal's body was never recovered.[203] Cesarini had abandoned Basel and, Segovia might have thought, abandoned also his earlier realization, during the Hussite crisis, that crusading did not work and that dialogue had more success. If he had been inclined to make comparisons between the earlier Hussite rebellion and the ascendant Turkish empire, Cesarini probably thought that the Turks were less amenable to discussion or maybe that the potential for danger at their hands was greater than it had been for the Hussites. Whatever he thought of his former colleague's manner of death, Segovia must have thought about the cardinal often in his later years. He continued to reflect on the cardinal's battlefield realization that another, more peaceful method might be better. As an elderly man, he drew from his reading of scripture, his memories of conversations with Muslims in Castile, and triumphs celebrated at the heart of the movement for church reform as he formulated a response to the fall of Constantinople.

Juan de Segovia lived during a time in which leading European thinkers articulated a vision of the Islamic world that would endure into our own times. Nancy Bisaha has written that the Renaissance humanists left behind a complex legacy "with which we continue to wrestle but cannot afford to ignore."[204] The humanist legacy she studied encouraged a relativism that allowed some to admire the Turks and call for greater understanding, but by far the dominant part of this legacy was that it generated a rhetoric about barbaric, backward Turks.[205] It is debatable whether Juan de Segovia should be numbered among humanists. Certainly his intense interest in securing an accurate translation of the Qur'ān, as well as his enjoyment of the linguistic aspects of this project, associate him at least with that characteristic of humanists' interests.[206] Other features of his writing, notably his writing style and his sources, mark him more firmly as a medieval thinker. In any case, he ranks among the most important writers of the fifteenth century on the dilemma that the Islamic Turks presented to Christian Europe. He is all the more interesting because his views were forged from the experience of talking with actual

Muslims in Castile and the experience of Basel in negotiating with the Hussites. Few European intellectuals to write on this question had the benefit of personal encounters with Muslims, and fewer still developed ideas gained from such encounters within the crucible of a church council. Further study of Juan de Segovia offers much to scholars in diverse fields of interests in the late medieval and early modern periods.

EPILOGUE

It is humbling to observe that Juan de Segovia, who was one of Europe's finest intellects and who had personally known and addressed popes, kings, and emperors, had so little impact after death on the goals most important to him.

Sometime before 1658, someone commissioned a proper tomb to house Segovia's remains. A description of it from that year offered that in the sculpture of the reclining man, the deceased wore a cardinal's cap under a bishop's mitre. In what may have been an effort by the artist or patron to defend Segovia's worthiness for such honors, and perhaps the duke's right to bestow them, an angel positioned behind his head supported the mitre with both hands. The anonymous writer said that he was not able to learn who had ordered the tomb built. He reported that the man whose remains it housed was reputed a saint by the parishioners, one of whom told him that he never slept except under the saint's vine branches (*par les paroissiens dont l'un me dit qu'il ne couchait que sur des sarments*). This 1658 description made no mention of an inscription concerning Juan de Segovia having been exiled to Aiton by the persecution he suffered at the hands of the Roman cardinals, which a visitor several decades earlier had noted. The report made by ecclesiastical visitor Antonius Cortailius in 1592, which recorded this commentary, mentioned a tomb with many candles, but it did not mention this seemingly skillfully sculpted tomb. It seems possible that this was the same tomb that Cortailius saw and that the sculpture itself was added sometime between 1592 and 1658. In any case, it was no longer to be found in 1890, when an anonymous scholar recorded having seen this description in an archive, but said that he could find no sign of the tomb itself.[1]

The tomb was not mentioned in a history of the diocese of Maurienne written in 1680 by a local canon. Chapter 15 is a history of the bishops of Maurienne, an office Juan held for about a year. In contrast to the sections devoted to Louis de La Palud and Guillaume de Estouteville, Juan's predecessor and successor respectively, the section on Juan de Segovia is nothing but a three-line entry, which mentions that he had been appointed to the see of Maurienne by Nicholas V, but not that Felix V had made him a cardinal. One wonders whether the author had seen the tomb sculpture with the cardinal's cap in the village church in Aiton.[2] Although the author of this history offered no hint of continuing local devotion to him, another author writing over a century later included this information. He also mentioned Felix V and noted that Juan was greatly revered.[3]

The chronicles of Savoy, published in the nineteenth century, perpetuated Segovia's reputation as a posthumous miracle worker. He appears there, along with colleague Louis Aleman, at the end of the section dedicated to Amadeus VIII, the powerful first duke of Savoy who was elected pope (Felix V) by the delegates at Basel after they had declared Eugene IV deposed. After recording the most sorrowful death and burial of Amadeus, the chronicler commented that "to this day" miracles occurred at the duke's tomb. He added that miracles also graced the tombs of two cardinals who had been faithful to Amadeus during his pontificate and afterwards, namely, Louis Aleman and Juan de Segovia.[4]

Segovia's peers in Europe's most exalted circles certainly did not treasure his memory. If his plans for peaceful dialogue with Muslims had any influence on others' thinking, the most likely place to find it would be in Nicholas of Cusa, whose *Cribratio* had the same broad goals as Segovia's efforts: to persuade Muslims that the Qur'ān was unreliable and that Christian teaching was credible. Still, there is no reason to think that Cusa derived the ideas developed in the *Cribratio* from things he heard from his Castilian colleague. As we have seen, his own ideas were similar enough to Segovia's even before he knew of the other's work on these matters. All of the other Christian thinkers that Juan de Segovia tried to enlist as supporters preceded him in death (Cardinal Cervantes) or rejected his line of reasoning (Jean Germain and Pius II). His Muslim visitor from Castile, Yça Gidelli, at least engaged with him in an ongoing discussion about matters of faith. Gidelli would certainly not have seen himself as a likely candidate for conversion, but I suspect that Segovia was optimistic about the prospects, since the Castilian Muslim did, after all, write to him once he had returned home. This conversation, at least, was not a dead end.

If he could have looked into the future, even the eternally optimistic Juan de Segovia would have been discouraged. Every single endeavor that was important to him—conciliarism, a diplomatic approach to the Muslim world, and the donation of his impressive personal library after his death—was thwarted not long after his death.

Moreover, every one of those projects was impeded in one way or another by Pius II, with whom Segovia had once enjoyed an amicable relationship. We have already seen, in chapter 4, that Pius II was committed to crusading. This was not the only way in which his decisions as pope worked against the hopes of his colleague from Basel. Even though Piccolomini had once served at Basel as a dedicated conciliarist, he was among many prelates who later turned away from their conciliarist activities and scorned their earlier positions. In 1447, he wrote the first of several letters disavowing his earlier ideals. Writing to Jordan Mallant, rector at the University of Cologne, he said that he had heard that the previous evening Mallant had been at a banquet held by the bishop of Cologne, at which the many civil and canon lawyers "discussed ecclesiastical affairs amid wine and entrees." Among the issues discussed by the dinner guests was his own "switching from one party to another," which he wanted in this letter to explain.[5] In the course of his explanation, he offered, "God's grace has shown upon me, which has opened my mist-covered eyes and illuminated me with the rays of his splendor, since I sinned out of ignorance. I erred, I admit, after the manner of Basel and walked in its crimes. Nor was I like one of the lesser players but did combat in the front ranks, exalted in spirit, proud in mind, full of wind. I spoke foolishly; I wrote more foolishly."[6] Over the next several years, his transfer of allegiance to Rome and the papacy became more firmly established.[7]

As a pope, he was in a position to take more vigorous action on behalf of the power of the papacy, contributing further to the gradual weakening of the conciliar movement. In the late 1450s, Pius II found himself involved in a dispute over the succession to the position of archbishop of Mainz. After he demanded a large payment to the curia from Diether von Isenberg, the victor in this dispute, the man appealed the pope's decisions to a future council.[8] This situation prompted Pius II to issue the first condemnation of such an appeal in the history of the church. The bull, *Execrabilis* (1459), condemned all appeals to future councils. For good measure, he even elaborated that it was forbidden henceforth to appeal not only his own judgments and commands but also those of his successors, and not only to make such an appeal but also to accept it as valid—as he put it, "to adhere to such an appeal." He called down upon any person defying this ban "the wrath of almighty God and of the blessed apostles Peter and Paul."[9] Admittedly, contemporaries greeted this document not with submission to it as the final word, but with demands that the pope explain how this bull could come from someone who had previously been so committed to the conciliar cause.[10] Still, in the long run it contributed to the erosion of support for the conciliar ideal.

Back in Castile, wars against Muslims continued. No one tried teaching them about Christianity instead. The fifteenth century saw a number of crusading initiatives, which culminated in the conquest of Muslim Granada in the final decade of this century. Just as the Council of Basel was dissolving, Pope Nicholas V issued a new crusading bull (May 30, 1449) to support the campaign against Granada. Instability in the kingdom prevented vigorous implementation of this bull, but early in the reign of Enrique IV (1454–74), the *converso* royal treasurer Diego Arias Dávila urged the new king to undertake a crusade against Granada. Pope Calixtus III (1455–58), the Valencian Alfonso Borja (Borgia), granted a new crusading bull, which even granted indulgences to those already dead.[11] Enrique IV has been branded, beginning with political opponents in his own time, as personally and militarily inept.[12] Ana Echevarría Arsuaga has argued that this image is inaccurate and called for further study of the defamed king's military endeavors.[13]

Crusading efforts certainly surged during the reign of Isabel and Ferdinand. During Isabel's reign in Castile (the two ruled their respective kingdoms separately), royal delegates engaged in repeated negotiations with the pope about how much of the money collected in Iberia under papal bulls could be used for the war against Granada and how much needed to be diverted to funding the defense of Europe against the Ottomans. John Edwards wrote that in Castile somehow the papal collectors never succeeded in getting their hands on the money earmarked for the Ottoman front.[14] When Granada finally surrendered in 1492, just over three decades after Juan de Segovia died, it marked both the end of a Muslim political presence in Iberia that had begun in the eighth century and the triumph of the crusading ideal Segovia had decried.

If things had gone according to his plans, subsequent generations of scholars at Salamanca might have embraced another approach to the Muslim world through their study of books that Segovia wanted them to have. Lamenting the tendency of books to "fly off like birds on a mountain from one tree to another" when they were owned by private individuals,[15] he donated the greater part of his impressive library, consisting of over a hundred works, to his alma mater.[16] All but three volumes from his collection were to go to Salamanca's *studium*, unless the university lacked a suitable place for them, in which case they were to be housed in the library of Salamanca's cathedral.[17] A donation of this size would have been a significant addition to the university's library. The oldest extant university document mentioning the number of books in the library dates to 1471, and this document attests that there were then 201 books. Comparisons to contemporary libraries are illustrative; in 1443 the Vatican Library held 350 volumes (although it increased to 1160 by 1455), and in 1456 the library of the Medicis held 158.[18] To keep his books from flying off, Segovia stipulated that they could only be unchained and used off the premises when someone intended to make a parchment copy of a book that was currently in paper and left a deposit.[19]

Moreover, he did not hesitate to put some controversial works in the hands of the *studium*'s students and faculty. Segovia defended the reading of heretical authors, saying that their books enabled others to better refute their assertions.[20] The university was to receive no fewer than four copies of the Qur'ān, one apologetic work in favor of Islam, other works by visionaries banned by church authorities, and many books in defense of conciliarism and against Pope Eugene IV. Hernández Montes called attention to the intellectual openness implied by Segovia's decision to make such works readily available. He remarked that theology students at Catholic institutions in the early twentieth century would have encountered difficulties obtaining such works.[21] We know that some of these works were, indeed, consulted. Extant university documents record five times that the university granted someone permission to remove a book under the terms that Segovia specified for this. In the fifteenth century, the archbishop of Santiago, Alfonso de Fonseca, borrowed a copy of the Qur'ān, and the bishop of Salamanca, Gonzalo de Vivero, borrowed three other books that Hernández Montes believed pertained to Segovia's collection. Finally, in 1565 a Master Francisco Sancho borrowed a book listed as "Ioannes Segoviensis: Contra legem Maumeti" because the Inquisition had requested it.[22]

However, most of the volumes Segovia intended to put at the disposal of scholars at Salamanca never made it there, for reasons likely connected, once again, to Pius II. Books mentioned in the fifteenth-century records of the *claustro* and listed in the earliest extant inventory of the library's holdings (in 1611) permitted Hernández Montes to identify thirty-five volumes from Segovia's donation that either certainly or probably were in the university's possession.[23] Although it is natural to suspect causes such as fire for the loss of books, in this case there is another likely explanation. In a bull issued in February 1459, Pius II claimed papal prerogative and directed that "some" (*nonnullos*) books from Juan de Segovia's *Donatio* be delivered to him, and that perpetual silence be imposed on the University of Salamanca concerning the matter.[24] The bull specified that one Fernando Dunes, a member of the pope's household (*familiares*), was entrusted with the transfer of the books. Indeed, in Rome's Archivio di Stato there is even a document recording the payment of fourteen gold florins to Fernando de Virues, who is identified as a relative (*nepos*) of Juan de Segovia, for expenses incurred in his travels to Geneva, not far from Aiton, to transport some books for the pope. I am inclined to agree with Hernández Montes that Fernando Dunes and Fernando de Virues were likely the same person.[25] Some of the volumes from the *Donatio* have turned up in libraries like the Escorial, but there is no trace of most of them, although since Fernando de Virues was paid, we should suppose that at least some were delivered to the pope as ordered. Searches in the Vatican Library have yielded no clues.[26] Only fifteen volumes from the *Donatio* are currently housed in the Biblioteca General Histórica at the University of Salamanca; these are the same volumes that were present in an inventory conducted in 1854–55.[27]

—⚋— As far as I have been able to determine, with the exception of the Inquisition's request for the book about Islam in 1565, Castile's intellectuals had no interest in Juan's career and thought until well into the seventeenth century. The interest, when it occurred, had nothing to do with Segovia's writings on Christian-Muslim relations or his conciliar writings. It was occasioned by the discovery of a treatise by Juan defending the immaculate conception of Mary, a topic debated at the Council of Basel. This work was unearthed in the library of the cathedral of Seville. Don Pedro de Castro, archbishop of Seville, described it as composed "by hand in an old script."[28] He wrote to the king in August of 1618, advising him that he had shown it to many theologians, and he thought it would advance the greatness of the church in Seville and of Spain in general if it were published.[29] The work was published, after some delay, with an explanatory preface by the Jesuit Juan de Pineda (d. 1636) on Juan's life and works.[30]

Pineda's narrative is interesting for what it reveals about his sources of information and for its delicate handling of Juan's participation at Basel. The Jesuit priest drew heavily from Piccolomini's *De Europa* and his histories of the council. He included the pope's praise for Juan's character and learning, and added as further proof of his great prudence, probity, and skill the fact that Juan was one of the three men chosen by the council representatives to elect a new pope.[31] However, this fact and Juan's active participation in Basel in general presented Pineda with a dilemma: how to praise the Castilian theologian's erudition and character and yet still account for his energetic activity in a council, not to mention a papal election, considered illegitimate in Pineda's day. He explained that Segovia's zeal and ardor had led him to embrace Basel, and he reminded his readers that everyone errs sometimes, and that even credible and illustrious men have sometimes supported illegitimate councils. He also noted that Piccolomini wrote a letter to Juan describing the coronation festivities of Felix V, and he concluded that Juan must not have attended. In fact, Pineda wrote, after the thirty-seventh session, in which Felix V was elected, Juan was not mentioned at all in Piccolomini's history of the council. This led Pineda to suspect that Segovia had misgivings about the council and withdrew from its endeavors.[32] Finally, Pineda suggested two reasons why Juan was not confirmed when the council had ended and Nicholas V confirmed most of the cardinals Felix had appointed. One was that the new pope was honoring an earlier agreement between Eugene IV and King Alfonso of Naples about the appointments to these offices. The second was that Nicholas was acceding to Juan's natural modesty, the same modesty that led him to spontaneously renounce all public honors and move to a remote monastery in the mountains. Pineda offered that it was perhaps fitting not to make Juan a cardinal, lest a cardinal's pressing duties deprive others of his counsel and prayer.[33] He confessed that Juan's family background and the circumstances and place of his death were unknown to him.[34]

Much more was unknown, including the existence of Pineda's text, to Don Antonio Calderones, when he wrote to someone in Toledo in 1653 requesting that he search that cathedral's records for information on Juan. Once again, what prompted this interest in the Castilian theologian who had then been dead for two centuries was the news that Calderones had received about the finding of the manuscript in Seville's cathedral library. He advised that the author was one "Joan de Segovia, maestro de Salamanca," who was mentioned in the records from the Council of Basel and whom some sources considered the archdean of Villaviciosa in Oviedo. Like Pineda, he noted that the manuscript in Seville bore a line identifying its author as a canon in the cathedral in Toledo. There is nothing in Calderones's letter of Juan's problematic activities at Basel and no awareness of any other works that he wrote.[35]

Juan de Segovia was too interesting a thinker to consign to the ranks of the barely known. In recent years, he has fared better, attracting the attention of scholars working on Basel, Castile's intellectual circles in the fifteenth century, and late medieval Europeans' views on Islam. But much more remains to be discovered about his work and thought. Antony Black noted that on such issues as the nature of rulership, secular monarchy, and the interaction between "civil society" and the "state of nature," Segovia anticipated much later thinkers. Black's study of Juan's contributions demonstrated that "the continuity between late-medieval and early-modern political thought is so apparent as to render the customary dividing-line ('Renaissance', 'Reformation', c. 1500) in important respects meaningless."[36] I suspect that further study will reveal that Segovia blurs the dividing lines in other areas as well, and this book will have fulfilled its purpose if it inspires more scholars to explore his work. Since Segovia's work has received relatively little attention, considerably less than the work of Nicholas of Cusa or Aeneas Sylvius Piccolomini, new discoveries await intrepid scholars in practically any area of his thought. Those with the requisite background, for example, in Trinitarian theology will probably find interesting ways in which he articulated this body of teaching as he thought about how Muslims would hear it. He makes a fascinating case in how thinkers in his era read the Bible, or read anything, for that matter.

The most pressing need is for editions of Juan de Segovia's works, most of which remain unpublished. In addition to the editions listed in the bibliography, I have begun work on an edition of his *repetitios* from 1426 and 1427, and Jesse Mann has been preparing one of his letter to Guillaume d'Orlyé. In 2012, Ulli Roth's edition of *De gladio* was published. Hopefully, more such endeavors will follow, including a more readily available text of Segovia's *Historia* than the one contained in the *Monumenta Conciliorum Generalium*. He deserves to be better known outside small academic circles and the village of Aiton. Juan Alfonso de Segovia was one of Europe's foremost thinkers in his era. It is time he took his place among his peers and received attention worthy of his bold and provocative ideas.

Excerpt from Juan de Segovia,
Repetitio de fide catholica

Córdoba, Biblioteca de la Catedral, MS 128, fols. 192r A–192v A

Respondetur in multis esse difficile invalere argumentum
asimili de secta machometi et de religione christi. Primum
manifestum est legem machometi non esse contrariam legi
nature que habet inclinare ad carnales delectationes ymo in
5   hoc laxat frena carnalis concupiscencie dum multa precipit,
consulit, aut impunita permittit que carnalibus desideriis
conforma sunt. Similiter et felicitatem quam promittit in
delectationibus carnalibus consistere dicit. Et quia propter
nimis intensam inclinationem nature vix pauci reperiuntur
10 qui perfecte secundum racionem virtutis a carnalibus
delectationibus abstineant. Ymo licet in religione christiana
quamcumque pro huiusmodi abstinencia premia eterna que
tante sunt dignitatis ut nec occulis viderit nec auris audierit
nec ascenderit in cor hominis promittuntur et contrarium
15 facientibus eterni supplicii cominetur pena. De hoc etiam sunt
nimium multiplicate prohibitiones et contrarium facientes in
hoc mundo gravi per iurisdictionem ecclesiasticam
temporalem torquntur supplicio et adhuc tamen
christianorum multi has sequuntur delectationes carnales.

It is responded that it is difficult to prove by argument that the sect of Muḥammad and the Christian religion are similar. First, it is clear that the law of Muhammad is not contrary to the law of nature, which is inclined toward carnal delights; rather it loosens the reins of carnal concupiscence because it teaches, counsels, or permits with impunity many things that are aligned with carnal desires. Moreover, it says that the happiness that it promises consists in carnal pleasures. Due to nature's very strong inclination, no one or hardly anyone is found who abstains from carnal pleasures to the extent demanded by perfect virtue.[1] Nay, even though in the Christian religion eternal rewards are promised for abstinence of this type—[rewards] that are so worthy that neither eye has seen nor has ear heard nor has it arisen in the heart of man—and for those who do the contrary, a penalty of eternal punishment is threatened, and [even though] prohibitions also are multiplied and [even though] those who do the contrary are punished in this world with severe punishments through the church's temporal jurisdiction, many Christians still pursue these carnal pleasures.

1. The *quia* in this sentence makes no sense and in the interest of clarity has not been reflected here.

20   Non igitur miraculis opus erat ad confirmandam illam
doctrinam que carnales sequentibus delectationes promium
promittit quas multi etiam cominato supplicio student
summopere adimplere. Non sic autem de religione christiana
que in multis, ut declaratum est, est legi nature contraria.

25   Similiter non talia tradidit documenta que incredibilia
apparent sed que mediocri pollens sciencia et ingenio
comprehendere posset nec primo sapientissimos et omni
polentes virtute ad eam sunt conversi, sed homines bestiales in
desertis morantes, omnis doctrine divine prorsus ignari, per

30   quorum multitudinem alios armorum violencia in suam
legem. Et quemadmodum inicium [192 B] habuit per
violenciam armorum ita precepit ut cum ultimo positi examini
de veritate legis impeterentur non racionibus miraculis vel
auctoritate sed gladio legem defenderent pro quo ut in

35   multitudine vincere possint permisit ad libitum multitudinem
uxorum accipere et filios procreare. Fuit etiam causa tam
facilis conversionis ad sectam illam etenim quia romani
propter nimiam eorum superbiam et avariciam sicut fuit
semper eorum condicio orientales populos sicut subditas sibi

40   alias naciones graviter depriment exactionibus et tributis
tempore erachi imperatoris, scilicet anno vi sui imperii
dedignatibus orientis gentibus vectigalia et tributa reddere
romanis ceperunt pro viribus rebellare et tunc machometus,
videns inter orientales et romanos ortam discoriam, surrexit

45   fingens se a deo missum pro liberatione eorum a iugo romani
imperii. Illi igitur cupientes se eripere a tiranica opressione
romanorum, videntes quod libertatem eis promitteret,
adheserunt ei ut ipsos eriperet maxime quia, ut dictum est,
promittebat felicitatem sequentibus carnalem concupicenciam

Therefore no miracles were needed to confirm that doctrine that promises a reward to those who pursue the carnal pleasures that many strive to the utmost to achieve even when punishment is threatened. Not so for the Christian religion, which, as has been said, is contrary to the law of nature in many things. Similarly, [Islam] has not passed down such teachings as might appear impossible to believe, but instead the sort that a person of moderate knowledge and intelligence can understand. At first it was not the wise and those rich in every virtue who were converted to the sect, but bestial men living in deserts, completely ignorant of all divine teaching—and by means of a multitude of such men, [early Muslims converted] others to their law by the violence of arms. And just as it had its origin [192r B] through the violence of arms, so it also has commanded [followers] that, when they are put to the ultimate test and attacked regarding the truth of [their] law, they should defend it not by arguments, miracles, or authority, but by the sword. For this reason, so that they might be able to conquer through their numbers, it permits them to take as many wives as they please and have many children. And this is why it grew, having multiplied in such a brief time, and why it persists today. This is why it said that it was sent out through the power of arms, just as thieves and tyrants are sent out. Indeed, another reason conversions to the sect happened so easily was that the Romans, due to their customary excessive pride and avarice, heavily oppressed the eastern peoples, just as they did with other conquered nations, with high taxes and tributes in the time of the emperor Heraclius. Specifically, in the sixth year of his rule, the eastern peoples, scorned and forced to pay taxes and tribute to the Romans, began to rebel by force, and then Muhammad, seeing discord breaking out between the easterners and the Romans, rose up, presenting himself as sent from God for their liberation from the yoke of the Roman Empire. Therefore, wishing to free themselves from the tyrannical oppression of the Romans, and seeing that he was promising them freedom, they adhered to him in order that he free them, especially because, as it has been stated, he promised happiness to [his] followers, [namely] the carnal concupiscence

50   quam fides christi vetabat. Et ut cetera pretermittam satis
      patet manifestum istud argumentum asimili non valere. Et
      quidem discurrenti per singula xii fundamenta superius posita
      patet quod nullum ipsorum in se contineat secta machometi.
      Non enim antiquitus sancti et prophete predixerunt talem
55   prophetam in mundum venire debere. Et quod pro obtinenda
      eterna salute omnes deberent eum sequi sicut de christo in
      multis locis legis et prophetarum et dictis gentilium, ymo ipse
      machometus in lege sua fabulosa narratione depravat omnia
      documenta novi et veteris testamenti et astuto consilio libros
60   [192v A] novi et veteris testamenti suis sequencibus non
      reliquit legendos ne per eos de falsitate sua secta
      redargueretur. Et hodie ex sua apparet obstinatione quod
      sectam illam magis pertinaci affectione quam racione tenent.
      Siquidem audire nolunt qualecumque verbum eis proponatur
65   timentes inde posse accedere ad confuctationem sue secte
      quam facile ipsi cognoscunt posse redargui. Non decet
      superius xii^m fundamenta posita singilatim comemorari.
      Et enim cuilibet circumspecto statim apparet in maximo et
      principali difficilitudine que est ad legem christi ex secta
70   machometi precipue si quis attendat ad contenta in lege illa
      quorum plurima sine aliqua racione conflicta alia vero
      reperiuntur manifeste contraria racioni.

that the faith of Christ prohibited. So, that I might pass over the rest, it is clear enough that this argument from similarity[2] is not valid. And, running through each one of the twelve foundations presented above,[3] it is clear that the sect of Muhammad contains not one of these [foundations] within it. For the saints and prophets of antiquity did not predict that such a prophet must come into the world, or that in order to obtain eternal salvation all must follow him—as many places in the law and the prophets and the writings of the Gentiles say of Christ— but rather this Muhammad in his law distorts by fabulous narration all documents of the Old Testament and New Testament, and, planning astutely, he did not leave the books [192v A] of the Old Testament and New Testament to be read by his followers, lest his sect be unmasked for its falsity through them.[4] And today it appears from that sect's endurance that they hold to it more through pertinacious affection than through reason, as they are unwilling to hear any [challenging] word whatsoever proposed to them, fearing that it might lead to the refutation of their sect, which they themselves recognize can be easily disproved. It is not proper that the aforementioned twelve foundations be recounted individually. For indeed it is immediately apparent to any prudent person the great and fundamental difficulty that the law of Christ poses for the sect of Muhammad, especially if one pays attention to the things contained in that law, very many of which are found to be thrown together without any reason, while others are found to be manifestly opposed to reason.

    2. That is, the argument that Christianity and Islam are similar.

    3. In other words, the twelve foundations of faith Segovia had previously presented. See the discussion on pp. 78–80 and 86–87 of this volume.

    4. That is, the books of the Old and New Testaments.

Excerpt from Juan de Segovia, *De mittendo gladio divini Spiritus in corda sarracenorum*

Seville, Biblioteca Colombina MS 7-6-14, fols. 19v–21r

De mense quippe Octobris Anno domini M°cccc°xxxi°
dum essem in opido Medina del Campo Salamanticensis
diocesis, Serenissimo Rege Castelle et sua Curia ibidem
existente, colaciones habui multas cum primo ex duobus
5 Ambaxiatoribus Regis Granate ibidem constitutis conscio
plene yspani ydeomatis, quarum prima ut de sublimiori
sacramento, ita fuit tempore diuturnior. Uno etenim die
assumpto iurisperito Sororio meo Dydaco ffernandi de
Ubeda civitate Regno Granate confini adii Sarracenorum
10 ipsorum hospitium ei quod morabar vicinum. Cum autem
Sarracenus ipse locutione preveniens velut congratulans de
visitacione, adventus causam interrogasset, dixissemque ut
scirem de aliquibus amicis meis Cordubensis proxime apud
eos bello detentis specialiter de Iurato Magdalene, ille

In the month of October in the year of the Lord 1431, while I was in the town of Medina del Campo in the diocese of Salamanca, where the most serene king of Castile and his curia were staying, I had many meetings with the first of two ambassadors of the king of Granada. The ambassador had settled himself in that place as well and was fully proficient in the Spanish language. The first of these meetings, since it was about the most holy sacrament, was quite long. One day, indeed, taking with me my cousin, the legal expert Diego Fernández from the city of Úbeda, which borders on the kingdom of Granada, I came to an inn belonging to the Saracens themselves, which was near to where I was staying. But the Saracen, speaking first, as if rejoicing at the visit, asked the reason for my visit, and I said that I hoped to learn of some of my friends from Córdoba who had just recently been detained among them through war, especially of the jurist from Magdalena.[2]

2. There are several locations with this name in Spain, including one in the north-eastern part of the peninsula, near Huesca, and another called Huertas de Magdalena in Extremadura. It is not clear where this man was from.

15   respondit bene eum tractari nominato apud quem
      detinebatur captivus. Inter verba autem hec aliaque urbanitas
      quia frequenter iurabit per deum, interrogavi utrum
      segundum legem suam licitum esset tam sepe et absque
      necessitate per deum iurare, si quidem per nomen dei iurare
20   esset deum adducere in testem, persone vero magne
      auctoritatis quamvis rarissime et pro maxima causa ac in
      necessitate non tamen sepe. Et pro causis minimis vellent in
      testimonium adduci. Item quia primo sistente mandato legis
      Moysi ut quis non haberet plures deos statim, in secundo
25   tamquam grave nimium crimen esset prohibebatur ne quis
      assumeret nomen dei invanum. Tunc ille stomacho plenus
      irrupit dicens, Quomodo igitur vos christiani plures habetis
      et adoratis deos, unum in celo alium in terra, unum
      creatorem, alium hominem filium Marie, unum patrem alium
30   filium, unum inmortalem alium mortuum, crucifixum, atque
      sepultum. Et dicitis quod deus pater eum tradidit ut pro
      salute vestra moreretur. Est tamen ita quod pater habens
      filium si sciat eum carceri traditum, rogat quo potest iudicem,
      munera mittit, et osculatur manus eius ut liberet eum. Cum
35   hec aliaque propositi huius ex habundancia cordis ut
      loquendi modus ostendebat dixisset, illi respondi duo
      quantum percipiebam absurda ei viderentur credi per
      christianos: quod deus filium haberet et ille mortuus esset
      pro salute humani generis, de quo istorum vellet ut primo
40   loqueremur. Illo autem subito respondente quod de primo,
      dixi optare me ut noticiam haberet de philosophia Aristotilis
      presertim quantum ad libros de anima. Sed dato ita non esse
      sperarem, dei auxiliante gratia, tam palpabilibus me
      locuturum exemplis ut priusquam e domo illa exirem clara
45   perciperet racione deum habere filium nec ex tempore sed ab
      eterno ut sicut deus eternus est sic quoque filius eius.
      Cumque ad hec audienda permaxime attentum se obtulerit
      quod et complevit auditu sistente, sermonem effudi illi,
      exponens trinitatis mysterium, de personarum pluralitate

He responded that my friend was being treated well, and he named the one by whom he was being held captive. But since in the course of this and the rest of our polite conversation he frequently swore by God, I asked him whether, according to his law, it was permitted to swear by God so often and needlessly, since to swear by the name of God is to enlist God as a witness, but persons of great authority, even though they be willing to be brought to testify on rare occasions, in important cases, and when there is need, [do not willingly testify] frequently and in minor cases. And furthermore, while the first commandment of the law of Moses firmly states that one must not have multiple gods, in the second to take the name of the Lord in vain was prohibited as though it were a grave offense. Then the man, full of anger, interrupted, saying, "How then do you Christians have and worship many gods, one in heaven and another on earth, one creator, another a man and the son of Mary, one a father and the other son, one immortal and another dead, crucified, and even buried? And you say that God the father gave him up to die for your salvation, although it is actually the case that a father, having a son, if he knows that he has been put in prison, begs the judge as he is able, and sends money, and kisses his hands so that he may free him." When he had said these words and others on this subject from the abundance of his heart, as his manner of speaking showed, I responded to him that, as far as I could tell, two things believed by Christians seemed absurd to him: that God had a son and that he had died for the salvation of the human race. [So I asked] which of these he wished us to discuss first. And when he immediately responded that we should discuss the first, I said that I wished he were acquainted with the philosophy of Aristotle, especially with the books on the soul.[3] But, given that that was not the case, I [told him that I] hoped, with the help of God's grace, to speak with such clear examples that before I left that house he would understand through clear reasoning that God had a son—and not in time, but from eternity, so that just as God is eternal, so also is his son. And when he offered himself, highly attentive, to hearing these things (which [action] he also completed with constant attention), I poured out a sermon, expounding the mystery of the Trinity, conveying the plurality of persons

---

3. Presumably Aristotle's *De Anima.*

50   unitateque essentie earum multipharia raciocinatione
     insinuans. Non propterea quia plures essent persone dii
     essent plures. Sed quomodo singula earum deus, ita omnes
     deus tantum unus. Et sicut necesse erat deum esse, ita eadem
     necessitate deus esset plures persone, ut sicut impossibile est
55   deum non esse, ita foret impossibile deum unicam solum esse
     personam. Sed quanta necessitate deus erat unus, tanta erat
     persone tres. Sic tamen ut nullatenus [20r] intelligi posset
     plures in deo quam tres esse personas, nec tribus pauciores
     quarum singula eciam si omnipotens esset non posset aliam
60   seu alias quam tres iste essent personam seu personas
     producere. Nec simul omnes tres. Exposita quoque fuit racio
     nominationis earum ut prima sic pater esset quod nullathenus
     dici posset filius. Et secunda ita filius quod nullatenus pater.
     Similiter de spiritu sancto quod nec pater poterat esse nec
65   filius. Item nec pater aut filius potera esse spiritus sanctus.
     At quoniam sicut exposicio hec de rebus magnis, ita plurimo
     fuit opus sermone, ne hoc loco interrupta videatur prosecutio
     consideracionum ad questionem propositam expectantium,
     illa que explanata Sarraceno ipsi de misterio trinitatis tunc
70   fuere, et alia quedam de incarnationis sacramento inseruntur
     circa medium tractatuli huius, relata pro nunc questione
     eventuque predicte exposicionis. Et quidem liberiori audacia,
     cum replicandi facultatem deesse illi viderem, Sarraceno ipsi
     dictum per me fuit, quoniam tam evidentissima prout
75   audierat constaret racione deum habere filium, quod reputare
     non deberet absurdum si christiani confitebantur in deo esse
     patrem et filium ac eciam et spiritum sanctum qui nullatenus
     dii tres, sed erant unus tantum deus, christianis cunctis
     permaxime abhorrentibus nec dum credere sed audire
80   pluralitatem deorum. Cumque in eiusmodi raciocinatione
     multum transierat temporis valedicto Sarracenis ipsis
     recessum est, non visitata amplius illorum habitacione. Sed
     ille doctior ac ydeomatis yspani plene conscius frequenter
     visitavit domum loquentis, utrarumque multis legum

and unity of their essence by means of many arguments. A plurality of persons does not necessitate a plurality of Gods. But just as each of them is God, so also all [of them together] are only one God. And just as it is necessary for God to be, so by that same necessity God is a plurality of person; thus, just as it is impossible for God not to be, so also is it impossible for God to be only one person. But it is just as necessary that God be three persons as that he be one God, but in such a way that it cannot by any means [20r] be understood that there are more than three persons in God, nor less than three, of which a single one, even though it be omnipotent, cannot produce another person or other persons than these three. And indeed it is the same with all three together. And also the reason for their names was explained—that the first is Father because in no way can it be called Son, and the second is Son because in no way can it be called Father. Similarly with the Holy Spirit, since it could not be the Father nor the Son. Likewise neither the Father nor the Son could be the Holy Spirit. But even though this exposition was about important matters, much speech would be required [to give a full account of the conversation], so lest the pursuit of considerations relevant to the proposed question seem to be interrupted here, those things regarding the mystery of the Trinity that were explained to this very Saracen on that occasion, as well as certain other things about the mystery of the Incarnation, are inserted near the middle of this little tract. But for the present I relate [the Saracen's] question and the outcome of my aforementioned exposition. And indeed, with rather free boldness, as I saw that he was unable to reply, I said to the Saracen (since it was established on such extremely clear reasoning, as he had heard, that God had a Son) that he should not consider it absurd if Christians believe there to be a Father and a Son in God, and even a Holy Spirit too, who are in no way three Gods, but instead are one God, all Christians being utterly horrified even to hear [spoken] of, let alone to believe in, a plurality of Gods. And when a long time had passed in this manner of discussion, we left, and having said goodbye to those Saracens, I did not visit their dwelling again. But that one who was more learned [than the rest] and fully fluent in Spanish frequently visited the home

85   interrogacionibus et responsionibus datis. Persenciens autem
auxilio opus esse die uno veneris adduxit secum Alfaquinum
quendam yspanum sapienciorem legis sue quem invenerat in
curia Regis. Hic argumento ex tempore facto quia religio
christiana antiquior esset lex quoque iudeorum, secta vero

90   sua nisi ab viii^c annis cepisset ideoque oportebat sarracenos
credere antiquioribus servis dei et amicis sine quibus
numquam fuit mundus ab inicio, respondit et si vocati
Sarraceni non semper fuissent, ipsi tamen erant illi qui
semper fuerunt credentes in deum. Ostenso autem minime

95   esse in deum credentes qui deo non crederent, hoc est
omnibus verbis eius revelatis amicis suis, quos prophetas
constituit, quia non crederent omnibus dictis Moysi, David,
Ysaie aliorumque prophetarum sicut in Alchorano, de hac
obiectione mencione facta non respondetur. Ita hic

100 superdictus[1] Alphaquinus non amplius comparuit
elocucionem de legum differencia continuaturus, fortasseque
erubuit dare responsionem libri sui: quod christiani
obicientes eis talia sunt insipientes, et propterea si Sarraceni
boni sunt nullathenus eos participes hec suorum tractatores

105 negociorum statuant; et quia cum Sarracenis christiani
peyores sint quosdam symias et porcos ac ydolatras
constituit deus; et quod christiani confitentur fidem suam sed
semper adventu atque discessu corda gestant incredula. Alio
Rursus loco respondet quod si solum deo placeret quod et

110 predecessores sui fecerunt usque dum malum gravissimum
eis incubuit. Et si quid constans atque scitum habent coram
veniat. Nec ulterius pro more suo rem incertam sequantur.
Heccine sunt responsa quinque contenta in libro Alchoran
excusante suos ne teneant fidem legemque predecessorum

1. The manuscript has *superductus* here.

of the speaker, with many questions and responses about both laws offered. Moreover, perceiving that he had need of assistance, one Friday he brought with him a faqīh, a certain Spaniard wise in their law whom he had found in the royal court. When an argument from time had been made, that the Christian religion is older, and so is the law of the Jews,[4] whereas his sect began only eight hundred years ago (so how could the Saracens consider themselves the older servants and friends of God, whom the world never lacked since the beginning?), this man responded that even if they had not always been called Saracens, nevertheless they themselves were those who had always been believers in God. I pointed out that those who do not believe God— that is, all of his words revealed to his friends, whom he established as the prophets—could hardly be believers in God, since they did not believe all the words of Moses, David, Isaiah, and of the other prophets, as is clear in the Qur'ān. When this objection was raised, there was no response. So this aforementioned faqīh did not appear ready to continue speaking on the difference of laws, perhaps because he was embarrassed to give the response of his book: [1] that the Christians who make such objections to them [Muslims] are fools, and because of this, if the Saracens are good, they should not make them [Christians] participants and dealers in their business; and [2] that, because Christians are worse than Saracens, God established them as apes and pigs and idolaters; and [3] that the Christians profess their faith but always, in [their] coming and [their] going, bear unbelieving hearts. Once again, in another place, it responds, [4] "If only he would please God, which his predecessors did until great evil befell them," and [5] "if they have anything reliable or known, let it come before me." And let them no longer follow an uncertain thing through their own custom. Are these not the five answers contained in the Qur'ān, whereby it excuses its people from holding the faith and law of their predecessors?

4. The manuscript is problematic here. It reads "Hic argumentationam . . .", but with a small superscripted "o" over the *argumentationam*, which may have been intended as a correction. Also, I have corrected the *facte* from the manuscript to *facto*. My thanks to Damon Smith for suggesting these solutions.

115   suorum. Post eiusmodi autem collacionem veritatis amore vel
       alio quovis respectu pluries me ipsum qui loquor adiit
       prefatus Ambaxiator qui uno die cum pro maxima [20v]
       absurditate obiceret quod christiani sacerdotes dicebant se
       absolvere a peccatis et tamen nullus posset peccata remittere
120   nisi deus solus, audita resolucione qua utitur communis scola
       theologorum, anmiratus verba hec dixit in effectu Et per
       deum nullus est inter christianos qui sciat hec declarare nisi
       vos solus. Cui Responsum est non credatis christianam
       religionem tam defectuosam in litteratis viris quia eciam
125   hodie in hoc opido sunt xx persone scientes ista declarare.
       Altero vero die interroganti utrum in Evangelio contineretur
       quod christus duas haberet mensas e celo. Et quando volebat
       posita aliqua earum convivabat omnes quos vellet usque ad
       saturitatem, absque deliberacione maiori Responsum fuit
130   quod non; recordacione autem facta ad statim illi dictum est
       qui hoc de christo dixerant poetice fuisse locutos mensam
       pro refectione sumentes. Namque in Evangelio legebatur
       quod semel de v panibus et duobus piscibus saturavit christus
       v milia hominum preter parvulos et mulieres, et iterum
135   quatuor milia de septem panibus. In Alchorano autem ut
       postea visum est de una mensa fit mentio. Dicit enim *sic deus*
       christum filium Marie affatus cui tribuit animam mundam
       atque benedictam qua iuvenes et infantulos afatus est et
       formis volatilium a se factis insufflans volatum prebuit, cecum
140   *natum ac leprosum curavit, mortuos resuscitavit. Quem item*
       librum et sapientiam nec non Evangelium et testamentum
       docuit, inquit, Te sic ad filios Israel cum virtutibus et meo
       velle venientem increduli magnum esse perhibent. Tu vero de
       bonis tibi matrique tue divinitus datis michi gratias redde.

And following this sort of discussion, the aforementioned ambassador, out of the love of truth or for some other reason, on several occasions came to see me (the one now speaking). One day [20v], when he cited it as great absurdity that Christians said that priests absolved them from sins and yet no one can forgive sins but God alone, having heard the explanation that is commonly used by theologians, he marvelled and said these words, in effect: "And by God, there is no one among the Christians who knows how to explain these things except for you! ' I responded, "Do not believe that the Christian religion is so lacking in scholarly men, since even today in this very town there are twenty people who know how to explain these things." The next day, he asked whether it is stated in the Gospel that Christ has two tables in heaven, and when he wished, one of them is set up and he offers a feast for all those whom he wishes [to invite], until all are satisfied. I responded without much deliberation, "No." But then I remembered and immediately said to him that those who had said this of Christ were speaking poetically, using the word "table" in place of "nourishment." For it was read in the Gospel that on one occasion Christ fed five thousand men, not including women and children, with five loaves of bread and two fish, and another four thousand with seven loaves of bread. But in the Qur'ān, as it later seemed, there is mention of a table. For it speaks thus: "God addressed Jesus, Son of Mary, to whom he gave a pure and blessed soul, by which he addressed children and infants, and blowing on the forms of birds made by himself, he gave them flight; he cured the one born blind and the leper; he resuscitated the dead."[5] He [God] also taught him [Jesus] a book and wisdom and also the Gospel and the Testament. He says, "The infidels say that you, who come thus to the sons of Israel with miraculous deeds and with my will, are great. But you, render thanks to me for the good things that have been given from

5. This roughly corresponds to Qur'ān 5:110.

145   *Deo item a viris vestibus albis indutis querente an in se*
      nunciumque suum crederent. Responderunt: Ita credimus, et
      tu testis es. Inde eisdem a ihesu Marie filio querentibus an
      deus super eos mensam celestem ponere potens esset. Ipse
      respondit Si creditis in deum ipsum timete. Illis autem
150   *dicentibus volumus inde comedere ad nostrorum cordium*
      confirmationem. Ut cum te verum dixisse sciamus, cum nostro
      testimonio confirmemus. Deum inde sic exorat, O deus nobis
      mensam celestem que sit nobis pascha omnibusque presentibus
      primis scilicet atque ceteris atque miraculum tribue. Quem
155   *deus exaudiens inquit illis eam prebebo. Sed quisquis eorum*
      deinceps incredulus factus fuerit, eum pre cunctis mundi
      gentibus, penis atque miseriis affligam. Hec Azoara xiii[a] ex
      incidenti hoc inserta loco quia materiam dedit prefato
      Sarraceno ut desuper interrogaret. Quod autem hic dicit de
160   viris indutis albis vestibus aliis eciam duobus conmemorat
      locis per illos intelligens christi sequentes doctrinam. Nec
      enim latebat Machumetum vel spiritum eius seu Auctorem
      quicumque ille sit libri Alchoran, que in Apocalypsi descripta
      sunt *de animabus occisorum propter verbum dei et propter*
165   *testimonium ihesu quod date sunt illis singule stole albe*
      quodque turba magna quam dinumerare nemo poterat stabat
      ante thronum in conspectu agni amicti stolis albis et palme in
      manibus eorum. Adhuc eciam quod *hii amicti stolis albis*
      venerunt de tribulatione magna et laverunt stolas suas et
170   *dealbaverunt eas in sanguine Agni.* Et quod hii cum
      mulieribus non coinquinati virgines existentes secuntur
      agnum quocumque ierit. Non latebat Rursus quod super
      equum album sedentem cuius nomen erat verbum exercitus,
      qui sunt in celo sequebantur in equis albis vestiti bissino albo
175   et mundo. Unde Machometus [21r] loquens de christo
      designat eum ex societate eum sequente virorum qui induti
      sunt vestibus albis. Hec autem de libro Apoc et de libro
      Alchoran quem adhuc non videram non fuerunt tunc
      exposita predicto Sarraceno.

God to you and to your mother." Also, when God asked men wearing white garments whether they believed in him and in his Messenger, they answered, "Thus we do believe, and you are [our] witness." Then when these same men asked Jesus the son of Mary whether God was able to put a heavenly table over them, Jesus answered, "If you believe in God, fear him." But when they said, "We wish to eat from it for the strengthening of our hearts, so that when we know that you have spoken the truth we may confirm it with our testimony," he prays to God thus: "O God, give to us a heavenly table to be a Passover for us (that is, first for all those present, and also for the rest) and a miracle." God heard him and said, "I shall give it to them. But whichever of them thereafter becomes an infidel, him I shall afflict with punishments and pains more than all the nations of the world." This 13th sura[6] is inserted here incidentally, because it furnished the material for the aforementioned Saracen to ask about. But what it says here about men dressed in white garments it also relates in two other places, understanding them as the followers of Christ's teaching. For Muhammad (or his spirit, or the author of the Qur'ān, whoever he is) was not unaware of the things which are described in the Apocalypse about the souls of those who were slain on account of the word of God and for the sake of their witness to Christ, that "white robes, one each, were given to them" and that "a great throng that no one could count stood before the throne in the sight of the lamb, all dressed in white robes, and there were palms in their hands" [Rev. 7:9], and in addition that "these men dressed in white robes came from great tribulation and washed their stoles and made them white in the blood of the Lamb" [Rev. 7 :14], and that "they, being virgins, not polluted by women, follow the lamb wherever he goes" [Rev. 14 :4]. Furthermore, he was not unaware that "the host who are in heaven, on white horses and wearing robes of silk white and clean, followed the one sitting upon a white horse, whose name was the Word" [see Rev. 19 :14]. Hence Muhammad, [21r] when speaking about Christ, marks him by the band of men following him, who are dressed in white robes. But on that occasion I did not explain these passages from Revelation and from the Qur'ān, the latter of which I had not yet seen, to the Saracen.

6. All of this, or some semblance thereof, appears in Sura 5 in modern editions of the Qur'ān.

180   *Insert.*

Sed et multe alie fuerunt collaciones utrimque. Exprobrationum
illius quibusdam iuxta opportunitatem responso aliis
quandoque eciam silentio preteritis. Si quidem aliquando velut
185   furiens obloquebatur Ex quo intelligi manifeste potuit quam
magno odio et despectu quodam Sarracenorum animi vehuntur
in christum, a nemine audientes illam nimiam caritatem qua
deus sic dilexit mundum ut filium suum unigenitum daret ut
omnis qui credit in eum non pereat sed habeat vitam eternam.
190   Similiter et illum inexplicabilem amorem quo filius ipse dedit
semetipsum pro nobis factus obediens usque ad mortem crucis
ut nos redimeret ab omni iniquitate et mundaret sibi populum
acceptabilem sectatorem bonorum operum. De originali peccato
eciam nullam vel minimam habent noticiam, absurdissimum
195   reputantes quod christiani dicunt se comedere deum suum.
Itaque maximus est in ipsis intelligentie defectus quantum ad
principalia sacramenta dei. Sicut autem perceptum est a multis
qui eorum noverunt condicionem si audientia obtineri posset,
magna spes foret permaxime ipsorum multitudinis convertende.

Insert.[7]

But there were also many other exchanges, wherein response was made to some of his accusations, as opportunity allowed, and others were sometimes passed over in silence, since sometimes he railed like a madman, whence it could be plainly perceived with what great hatred, and a certain contempt, the minds of Saracens attack Christ, not having heard from anyone of that great love with which God so loved the world that he gave his only-begotten Son so that everyone who believes in him may not perish but have eternal life [John 3:16]. Likewise also [they have not heard of] that inexplicable love with which that Son gave himself for us, having become obedient unto death on a cross [Phil 2:8], in order to redeem us from all iniquity and purify for himself an acceptable people, pursuers of good works [Titus 2:14]. The Saracens also have not even the slightest knowledge of original sin, and consider it most absurd that Christians say they eat their God. So there is a great lack of understanding among these people as it pertains to the principal sacraments of God, but, as has been perceived by many who know their condition, if it were possible to obtain a hearing [with them], there would be great hope of converting a vast number of them.

7. There is a fairly lengthy text intended for insertion here. It runs for nine lines in the top margin of the page, and then for twenty-eight short lines down the left margin. The script is very small, and some of the words are partially in the binding, so it is difficult to read. It appears to refer to passages in the Qur'ān about Jesus and Mary and the apostles. The regular text resumes with the next lines in this appendix.

Excerpt from Juan de Segovia, Letter to Nicholas of Cusa, December 2, 1454

Salamanca, Biblioteca Universitaria de Salamanca,
MS 19, fols. 179v–180v

Qualis vero aut quanta esset desuper huiusmodi pace ad
sarracenos mittenda legacio status cuius aut pre-eminencie de
personarum quoque numero aut modo meum dicere non est
re ipsa plenissimam factura noticiam rei considerata

5   magnitudine fine quoque necnon ad quos et a quibus
huiusmodi legacio procederet futura quippe tali ac tanta ut et
si perimi facile tamen contepni non posset, personis numero
adeo dignitateque resplendentibus qui et si non fungerentur
legacione merito audirentur. Sed et supra vires meas est vel

10 cogitare superficie tenus quam numerose et quam maxime
secuture sint utilitates si huiusmodi fiat legacio ad
sarracenorum communitatem parte christiane religionis. Illa
quippe una notissima est quod sic agendo ecclesia imitaretur
christi actiones qui evangelizare venit pacem hiis qui longe et

15 hiis qui prope Quodque eiusmodi facta diligencia omni ex
parte iustificatur bellum in sarracenos christianorum parte.

But it is not up to me to specify the character or the size of the delegation that should be sent to the Saracens regarding such a peace, [or] of
what status or preeminence [it should be], or [to say anything] about
the number of persons or the means, since [the matter itself] will provide that information most fully, when the greatness of the matter is
considered, as well as its purpose, and to whom and from whom such
a legation would go—for it would certainly be of such a character
and size that, even if it could easily be destroyed, it could not be dis-
dained, [since it would be] comprised of persons so impressive in their
number and dignity that they would be heard even if they were not
functioning as a delegation. But it is also beyond the power of my
imagination even to scratch the surface of how numerous and great
would be the benefits that would ensue if such an embassy were to be
sent to the Saracen community on behalf of the Christian religion. Of
course, one of the chief benefits is that, by proceeding in this way, the
church would be imitating the actions of Christ, who came to preach
peace to those both near and far; and [another benefit would be]
that with such diligence having been done by all parties, war against
the Saracens would be justified on the part of the Christians; and

Ultra illam que defensionis precipua sistente causa quia
audire nolunt verbum dei. Equidem precepit dominus servo
suo quod exiturus in vias et sepes compelleret intrare ut
20   domus eius impleretur facto primum mandato ut ituri ad
exitus viarum servi sui ad nupcias vocarent quoscumque
invenirent vocacione igitur previa per invitacionem ad ea
quae pacis inter christianos et sarracenos habende, omnino
iniustificatur tam eorum qui invitati ad pacem, suscipere
25   recusant quam etiam ipsi iuxta legem suam tenentur vocare.
Et si ipsi iniquam habentes legem, christiani amplius multa de
hoc tot tamque gravia divine legis habentes mandata. Ad huc
iustificaretur bellum contra eos. Multo amplius si de pace
audire nollent vel prestare securitatem ut de super ad eos
30   legati mittantur. Quod verisimile non est dum intelligent in
eam rem videlicet ut de pace tractetur consentire
christianorum reges et principes una cum papa et sacerdocio.
Quomodo hoc fiet intelligere potest qui legit audivit et vidit
quomodo passagia [180] ad bellum faciendum contra
35   sarracenos indicta sunt a diebus antiquis et nostris equa aut
fortiori multo ratione quod ad papam pertinet intendere ad
ea que pacis sunt Iherusalem, Auctore christo qui apostolis
eorumque successoribus pacem dedit suam pacemque
reliquit. Et quomodo in prefacione luterule[1] huius dictum
40   extitit Cardinales veri et manifesti sunt collegii apostolorum
successores. Si vero contingat divina operante clementia
consentire sarracenos ut pacis interveniat tractatus illa ad
dirigendos pedes eorum in viam pacis non mediocris utilitas
erit quoniam sarraceni persencient christiani populi in eos
45   eximiam caritatem, deductis in eorum conspectu que
multiphariam se offerunt rationibus quare eos diligunt
diligereque volunt. Unde, captata benivolencia et attencione,

---

1. Seemingly an irregular spelling of *litterulae*.

furthermore, there is the fact that there would be all the more cause for defense because they are unwilling to hear the word of God. And indeed the master instructed his servant to go out to the highways and the fences and compel [people] to come in, so that his house might be filled, having first made the command that his servants go out to the end of the roads and invite to the wedding feast whomever they found [Luke 14:23]. Therefore, since an initial invitation has been made, [inviting them] to [the discussion of] matters pertaining to bringing about peace between Christians and Saracens, it would be entirely unjustified of them [to decline], both insofar as they refuse peace when they are invited to it, and insofar as they themselves are bound by their own law to call for it. And if these people, even though they have a perverse law, [are unjust to refuse peace], all the more then [are] Christians [unjust to refuse peace] since they have so many and serious commands regarding this in their divine law. Furthermore, war would be justified against them, all the more so if they should refuse to hear of peace or provide for the security of those who are sent to them to speak of it. But that is not likely, provided that they understand that the kings and princes of the Christians, along with the pope and the clergy, are in agreement on this matter, namely, that peace be discussed. How this could happen can be understood by one who has read, heard, and seen how the campaigns [180] to wage war against the Saracens have been proclaimed in former times and in our own, with equal or much greater cause, because it belongs to the pope to see those things which concern the peace of Jerusalem, on the authority of Christ, who gave his peace to his apostles and to their successors and left peace [for them]. And as it has been stated in the preface to this little letter, the cardinals are the true and manifest successors of the college of the apostles. If, indeed, it should happen that, through the workings of divine clemency, the Saracens agree that a discussion of peace should occur, it will be of no small benefit for the directing of their steps toward the path of peace [Luke 1:79] because the Saracens will perceive the great love of the Christian people for them, and they will offer themselves in many places,[2] having deduced the reasons why [the Christians] love and want to love them. Whereupon, once their

---

2. Here he seems to mean surrender, although the verb could also mean that the Saracens present themselves in order to participate in a discussion of peace.

queri ab eis potest que sint parte eorum bellorum cause in
christianos quas si aperiant satisfieri poterit vel si aperire
50   nolint, notificari eis possunt quam plurime cause habende
pacis et dilectionis inter christianos et ipsos Illa presertim
quam conformitas est quantum ad divinum cultum,
christianis dumtaxat unum credentibus deum illumque solum
adorantibus quod sarraceni ipsi ita credere compellentur dum
55   audient rationes divine unitatis seriosius eis coram
exponendas quatenus evidentissime percipiant quam
longissime distat christianorum fidei nec solum credere sed
vel leviter plures estimare deos esse, scientes probare ad
oculum hoc esse maximum omnium impossibilium sicut
60   deum esse unum maximum est omnium necessitorum
quodque ita hoc clarissime sciunt esse verum deum esse
dumtaxat unum quod longgissime quin ymmo omnino distat
ab eorum fide credere aliquos esse dei socios atque participes
quam tale asserere divine repugnat unitati. Cumque ipsi hoc
65   intelligent etiam si christiani id aperte non dicerent
sarracenos ipsos necesse est de sua cogitare lege. Centum fere
passibus invehente contra ponentes deo participes aut socios
sive consortes quomodo tam diucius erraverant, existimantes
christianos adoratores esse participum dei et sociorum. Sed et
70   si hoc taceant christiani audacissima constancia, inferre
poterunt christianos nullatenus incredulos fore illos per suam
legem reputatos: adoratores participum dei et sociorum. Et
per hoc tota christianitas purgabit infamiam qua apud
sarracenos labefactatur quod omnes christiani sint plures
75   deos adorantes quoniam publico ac solempni testimonio
coram maioribus sarracenorum christiana religio affirmabit
nullum ex christianis talem esse notum saltem aliis. Si vero de
tali sciretur quod acerrima fieret punicio. Et hoc unum est ex
maximis bonis quod non solum efficere sed eciam perficere

benevolence and their attention have been captured, it can be asked of them what, on their part, are the reasons for war against the Christians: if they reveal them, satisfaction can be made, or if they do not wish to reveal them, there can be pointed out to them very many reasons for having peace and love between them and the Christians. Chief among them is that there is such great agreement concerning divine worship: Christians believe in one God and worship only him, [a fact] that the Saracens themselves will be compelled to believe when they listen to explanations for divine unity expounded before them with seriousness, so that they might come to see most clearly how far it is from the faith of Christians not only to believe, but even casually to suggest, that there are many gods, since they know how to prove to the eye[3] that this is the greatest of all impossibilities, just as it is the greatest of all necessities that God be one. And [the Saracens will also see] that [the Christians] know this clearly to be true: that God is one, and that it is very far—indeed, absolutely so—from their faith to believe that there are any associates and affiliates of God, and how offensive it is to divine unity to assert such a thing. And when these Saracens understand this, even if Christians do not state it explicitly, the Saracens will need to reconsider their own law, which in about a hundred places inveighs against those who put forward participants in or associates or consorts of God, [and they will have to consider] for so long they had erred, thinking of Christians as worshippers of parts and associates of God. And even if the Christians should keep silent about this with audacious consistency, [the Saracens] will be able to infer that they are in no way the unbelievers that their law alleges them to be: worshippers of parts and associates of God. And through this all Christendom will purge the infamy with which it is weakened among Saracens—that all the Christians are worshippers of multiple Gods—since the Christian religion will affirm, through public and solemn testimony in the presence of leaders of the Saracens, that no one from among the Christians believes such a thing, or at least [if someone does] it is not noted by others. Indeed, if it were known [that someone believed this], the punishment would be harsh. And this is one of the greatest goods that the discussion of peace could not only

---

3. In other words, make clear beyond a doubt. This appears to be an idiomatic expression.

80   posset in sui principio pacis tractatus veritatem hanc iuris et
      facti parte religionis christiane publice notificando deum esse
      tantum unum et ita plusquam firmissime omnis credere
      christianos. Itaque nulla belli est causa in ipsos tanquam
      plurium sint adoratores deorum Lex quippe eorum iniungit
85   eis accuracius facere lites et bella, dicens quod hoc etiam in
      mensibus libertatis et quietis est utile et iustum facere contra
      non Invocantes deum unum tantum quales reputant
      christianos omnes a lege ipsa per totum fere vocatos
      incredulos. Ex quo alia etiam non exilis infamia aboleri
90   posset quod christiani adorent sicut deum sacerdotes suos
      presumptuosos, ut lex eorum inquit, indignantes ve quod in
      promptu illis ostendere est quoniam percipient christianos
      credere unum tantum deum illumque adorare solum modo
      Qui si talia fieri scirent in tota christiana religione et de
95   adorantibus et de adoratis horrendum fieret iudicium. Unde
      et si tales non sunt apud [180v] christianos, intelligere igitur
      ipsi possunt alios esse quam christianos quibus lex sua hoc
      imponit. Quo vero ad infamiam bonorum sacerdotum quod
      cum lacrimis petunt associari sarracenis a principio tractatus
100   pacis non tam se offert locus dicendi magis autem quanto ex
      maioris necesitatis debito ut publicent non esse verum
      testimonium per quod putant habere robur omnem legem
      eorum, videlicet quod christus in evangelio dixit venturum
      esse Mahumetum tanquam nuncium gaudii expresso nomine
105   eius. Ac quod eius nomen in evangelio et in testamento
      continetur Istud iudeis illud vero christianis publice
      ostensuris ut de verbo ad verbum legatur novum
      testamentum quia in multo passu reperietur. De falsificatione
      autem ut quidam dicunt christianis imposita per eos
110   multiplicatissima et habundans deo auxiliante aderit
      satisfactio evangelium per christianos minime fuisse
      corruptum per ipsos iudeos quoque antiquum testamentum.
      Quod autem super huiusmodi tuenda christi Innocencia ut

bring about, but even complete at its very beginning: publicly stating on the part of the Christian religion this truth of law and fact that God is one, exactly one, and that all Christians believe this with the utmost firmness. And so there is no reason for war against these people, as if they were worshippers of many gods. For the Saracens' law enjoins them to wage battles and wars with discretion, saying that it is useful and just, even in months of liberty and rest, to fight against those who do not call God one, as they allege of all Christians, who are called unbelievers throughout their law. From this indeed another infamy, no small one, can be abolished: that Christians worship their presumptuous and unworthy priests, as [the Saracens'] law says, as if they were God. It is easy to show them this, since they [will by then] perceive that Christians believe God to be one and they worship only him alone. And if Christians were to learn that such things were being done,[4] there would be a frightful judgment of the worshippers and the worshipped throughout all of Christendom. And therefore if such people are not [to be found] among [180v] Christians, the Saracens themselves consequently can understand that those upon whom their law places this accusation are other than the Christians. However, there is not much opportunity right at the beginning of the discussion of peace to address that slander against good priests: that they beg tearfully to join the Saracens. But rather, what a duty of utmost importance it is that [the Christians] make public that the testimony—on the basis of which [the Saracens] believe their entire law to rest—is not true, namely, [the testimony] that Christ said in the Gospel that Muhammad, called there by name, was to come as a messenger of joy. And since, in order to show that his name is contained in the Gospel and the testament, [the Saracens] will show the latter to the Jews and the former to the Christians, [it will also be necessary] that the New Testament be read word for word, since [they suppose] it will be found in many a passage. But concerning the falsification that some say was imputed to the Christians by [the Saracens], with the help of God, manifold and abundant satisfaction will be made—[which will prove] that the Gospel was hardly corrupted by Christians, nor even the Old Testament by the Jews. But as far as protecting the innocence

---

4. That is, the worshipping of priests.

christum nunquam approbasse Mahumeti adventum
115 suamque legem sermones fiant dixi fore debitum necessitatis
maioris, propterea quod si episcopum oportet bonum habere
testimonium ab hiis qui foris sunt Christus vero pastor est et
episcopus animarum omnium christianorum decet utique hos
intendere ut falsum christo impositum testimonium
120 aboleatur. Episcopis quoque et sacerdotibus christianorum
sive boni aut mali sint utrisque turpissime diffamatis in
Mahumeti lege. Sed et christianos omnes reputatos
adoratores participum dei et sic plurium deorum Et que
ydolatria ignominiosior aut maior infamia esse potest. Unum
125 de me ipso dixero quod plurimum admiratus et quasi
stupidus factus fui quando intellexi in lege illa tot infamias
christo christianis omnibus sacerdotibus quoque eorum
impositas quod tam diu populus christianus sive presides et
doctores illius aliam non fecerunt diligenciam. Cum inter
130 alias hec minima tam non sit alienate mentis eorum a
professione christiani nominis, sua lege triplicem ydolatriam
imponente christianis et quia adoratores sociorum dei
suorumque sacerdotum et ymaginum. Magna profecto
sperari potest utilitas quoniam ipsi oculo ad oculum videbunt
135 legem eorum in hiis et aliis quam plurimis falsa continere,
etiam si propter non interrumpi tractatum pacis verbo id
ipsum eis non dicatur.

of Christ in this matter is concerned, I have already said that it would be a duty of greater urgency that speeches be made to the effect that Christ never asserted the coming of Muhammad and his law. For if it is necessary for a bishop to be well regarded by those who are outside [the Christian community] [1 Tim. 3:7], and Christ is indeed the shepherd and bishop of the souls of all Christians, then it is certainly fitting that these [bishops] see to it that the false testimony imputed to Christ is abolished, since the Christians' bishops and priests, whether they are good or bad, are both disgracefully shamed in the law of Muhammad. But [it is] also [fitting for] all Christians [to see to it that the false testimonies are abolished], since they are considered worshippers of sharers in God and therefore of many Gods. And what more ignominious idolatry or great infamy could there be? I will say one thing about myself: that I was utterly amazed and even stunned when I learned all the infamies imputed to Christ, all Christians, and also their priests, in that law, because for so long the Christian people, or their leaders and teachers, have not made any effort [to challenge the infamies]. Because, among other efforts that are made, there is not even the slightest effort of this kind, [the Saracens'] minds are driven away from the profession of the name of Christ, since their law imputes a triple idolatry to Christians that they are worshippers of associates of God, and of their own priests, and of images. Really the advantage [of addressing this misperception] can be expected to be tremendous because they themselves will see, eye to eye, that their law in these and so many other matters contains untruth, even if, so that the discussion of peace is not interrupted, that point is not made to them in so many words.

Notes ——∿——

Introduction

1. Document V in *Mémoires et Documents*, 2nd series, vol. 52 (1912), p. 188: "nec non Cardinalis in Ethonis duos, et abbas predicti in Fricteripe prioratibus hujusmodi unum monachos manute[ne]rent." See the discussion of the history of this establishment in Gros, *Histoire du diocèse de Maurienne*, chap. 13, "Jean de Segovie," esp. pp. 131–32.

2. *Acta Sanctorum*, vol. 27, June 25th.

3. The prologue is contained in BAV Vat. Lat. 2923, fols. 186–196. This version is published in Cabanelas Rodríguez, *Juan de Segovia y el problema islámico*, 279–302. A much later copy (eighteenth century?) is in Madrid's Biblioteca Nacional, MS 9250, fols. 107–121v. Some have argued that Toledo, Biblioteca Pública, MS 235, is a later copy of Yça Gidelli's Spanish translation of the Qur'ān. See the discussion in Wiegers, *Islamic Literature in Spanish and Aljamiado*, 110–14, and López-Morillas, "'Trilingual' Marginal Notes." On Segovia's study of the Qur'ān, see Burman, *Reading the Qur'ān in Latin Christendom*, 178–97.

4. The basics of Juan de Segovia's life are recounted succinctly in Cabanelas Rodríguez, *Juan de Segovia y el problema islámico*, chap. 1; Vázquez Janeiro, "Historia de la iglesia y las ciencias sagradas," esp. 258–59; A. Black, *Council and Commune*, 118–27; Beltrán de Heredia, *Cartulario de la Universidad de Salamanca*, 1:362–76; Melquíades Andrés, *Historia de la teología española*, 1:511–15.

5. Tolan, *Saracens*, xv–xvi.

6. See the discussion in Tolan, *Saracens*, xv–xviii, and Pick, *Conflict and Coexistence*, 2–3.

7. Tolan, *Saracens*, xviii–xix.

8. Tolan, *Saracens*, 276.

9. Bisaha, *Creating East and West*, 3–6.

10. See, for example, Tolan, *Saracens*, 276; N. Daniel, *Islam and the West*, 307; Southern, *Western Views of Islam*, 103; Bisaha, *Creating East and West*, 144–45. Also Biechler, "A New Face Toward Islam," and Izbicki, "The Possibility of Dialogue with Islam."

11. These events are narrated succinctly in Reilly, *The Medieval Spains*, chaps. 3 and 4.

12. A helpful review article on this question is Novikoff, "Between Tolerance and Intolerance in Medieval Spain."

13. Burns, *Muslims, Christians, and Jews*, 3–9.

14. Nirenberg, *Communities of Violence*. Another, more recent, work to question how important religious differences were is Catlos, *The Victors and the Vanquished*.

15. Pick, *Conflict and Coexistence*, 1.

16. For a discussion of the various approaches to the conciliar movement, see A. Black, "What Was Conciliarism?" A landmark work in showing that the movement had deep roots in tradition is Tierney, *Foundations of Conciliar Theory*.

17. A. Black, *Council and Commune*, 1–2.

18. I have also not included in this tally a sermon on the Epiphany (no. 44 in Hernández Montes, *Obras*); a collection of the decrees of Constance, which he made at Basel's request; or the glosses and notations in his and others' works, which Hernández Montes listed as a separate work (no. 81). See the list by theme in Hernández Montes, *Obras*, p. 269, which shows that the overwhelming majority of his works were related to intraecclesial matters (presidency of the council, authority in the church, etc.). Other topics he addressed as part of his participation in the council were the discussions with the Greeks and Hussites and the controversy surrounding the immaculate conception.

19. Segovia's *Concordantiae dictionum indeclinabilium Bibliae* is no. 16 in Hernández Montes, *Obras*, p. 280.

20. A. Black, *Council and Commune*, 2.

21. For a good overview of the literature on Cusa's shift in position, see the discussion by McDermott, "Nicholas of Cusa: Continuity and Conciliation." Unlike Cusa, who never explained his shift, Aeneas Sylvius Piccolomini did. See the discussion in the introduction to Izbicki, Christianson, and Krey, *Reject Aeneas, Accept Pius*; Christianson, "Aeneas Sylvius Piccolomini and the Historiography of the Council of Basel."

Chapter One. The Years at the University of Salamanca

1. Karras, *From Boys to Men*, 69–72. Also see García y García, "The Medieval Students at the University of Salamanca."

2. See the discussion in Wolf, "Juan de Segovia and Western Perspectives on Islam in the Fifteenth Century," 9–35.

3. See *Bulario* II, #776, 839, 841a, 861.

4. Cabanelas Rodríguez (*Juan de Segovia y el problema islámico*, 33) and A. Black (*Council and Commune*, 118) are among those who have used this surname for him. The González comes from an account of an inscription above the main entrance to the chapel of the Escuelas Mayores at the University of Salamanca. The inscription, which is known solely from Pedro Chacón's 1569 history of the university, bore the year 1433 and proclaimed that construction on the chapel was begun in 1415. It named faculty and administrators who played a role in construction efforts at the time, and one of the names was Juan González de Segovia, who was described as a "maestro en teología." It is, of course, impossible to know whether this was "our" Juan Alfonso de Segovia, erroneously listed, or whether it was a different person. In any case, none of the Vatican documentation in which Segovia was seeking benefices repeated this name, and it appears in no other references to him. See the discussions in Cabanelas Rodríguez, *Juan de Segovia y el problema islámico*, 33–34, and Carabias Torres, *Historia de la Universidad de Salamanca hecha por el maestro Pedro Chacón*, 11 and 94.

5. One of these is Hernández Montes, who compared it to Boniface VIII's *Unam Sanctam*. He noted that this was surprising given the subsequent evolution of Segovia into a conciliarist. See Hernández Montes, *Obras*, 271. Biechler also wrote that Segovia went to Basel as a supporter of papal authority and was "converted" to the conciliar cause. See his "A New Face Toward Islam," 188. In his *Council and Commune*, Antony Black noted (118) the interest in political theory that this work revealed, but wrote that connections between this work and Segovia's later thought ended there.

6. Beceiro Pita, "Educación y cultura en la nobleza," 579.

7. It was even run by one Fernando Alfonso (a relative?), who in 1338 successfully petitioned for a *canonicato* in Santander after teaching and directing Segovia's school for seven years. ASV Reg. Avin. 52, fols. 97v–98, in *Bulario* I, #33.

8. Barrio Gonzalo, "La iglesia de Segovia durante el pontificado de Arias Dávila (1461–1497)," 85.

9. Rucquoi, "Éducation et société," 17.

10. This year comes from his *Donatio*, written in 1457, in which he wrote that he had begun his studies at Salamanca fifty years earlier. Juan de Segovia, *Donatio*, 81.

11. González García, *Salamanca*, 59.

12. González García, *Salamanca*, 51.

13. González García, *Salamanca*, 67.

14. González García, *Salamanca*, 55.

15. González García, *Salamanca*, 76.

16. Nader, *Mendoza Family*, 142.

17. On the *studium*'s fate under the Avignon popes, see *Bulario* I, 50–57.

18. *Bulario* I, 52–53.

19. Hernández Montes, *Biblioteca*, 36.

20. Juan de Segovia, *Donatio*, 114.

21. *Bulario* I, 57.

22. Val Valdivieso, "Universidad y oligarquía," 135.

23. Avignon pope Benedict XIII (1394–1417), the Spaniard Pedro de Luna, was a strong supporter of the university and its personnel. For more on his importance in the institution's history, see Beltrán de Heredia, *Bulario* I, 63–83.

24. Val Valdivieso, "Universidad y oligarquía," 146.

25. Van Liere, "Humanism and Scholasticism in Sixteenth-Century Academe," 75. For more on this thinker, see Lawrence, "Humanism in the Iberian Peninsula"; Camillo, *El humanismo castellano del siglo XV*; Santiago Otero and Soto Rábanos, "Los saberes y su transmisión en la península ibérica," 246; Cantera Burgos, *Alvar García de Santa María y su familia de conversos*, esp. 416–64; Serrano, *Los conversos don Pablo de Santa María y don Alfonso de Cartagena*. The volume by Cantera Burgos is still the standard work on this family.

26. Santiago Otero and Soto Rábanos, "Los saberes y su transmisión en la península ibérica," 244.

27. On these various activities, see Martínez Casado, *Lope de Barrientos*, 17–23, 27–42, 71–79. There is much valuable information as well in Cuenca Muñoz, *El "Tractado de la Divinança" de Lope de Barrientos*. Four of his works are published in Alonso Getino, *Vida y obras de fray Lope de Barrientos*.

28. ASV Reg. Avin. 272, fol. 398, in *Bulario* I, #218.

29. See the detailed study of this event and this man's ascent in Nieto Soria, *Un crimen en la corte*.

30. ASV Reg. Avin. 339, fols. 677v–678, in *Bulario* II, #453.

31. There is no index to these. They are scattered throughout Beltrán de Heredia's *Bulario* volumes.

32. See Marcos Rodríguez, *Extractos de los libros de claustros*.

33. Juan de Segovia, *Donatio*, 82.

34. ASV Reg. Avin. 45, fol. 161, in *Bulario* I, #28.

35. *Bulario* II, #647, section 31: "unum de quatuor orbis generalibus studiis ex dispositione apostolica."

36. ASV Reg. Suppl. 235, fol. 221v, in *Bulario* II, #802.

37. *Bulario* I, p. 67.

38. Beltrán de Heredia, "El Convento de San Esteban," 105. Salamanca did not confer degrees in theology at the time he was studying.

39. *Bulario* I, p. 80.

40. *Cartulario* I, 250–85; Goñi Gaztambide, "Presencia de España en los concilios generales."

41. Cantelar Rodríguez, "Luces y sombras en un 'speculum' del siglo XV," 9, 17–18, 20–21. See also Soto Rábanos, "Consideraciones jurídico-morales." This work is entitled *Speculum peccatoris, confessoris et praedicatoris in materia restitutionis seu satisfactionis*. It is MS 37 in the Biblioteca de la Real Colegiata de San Isidoro de León. I am grateful to José María Soto Rábanos for informing me about it and for the references cited here.

42. Madrid, Real Academia de Historia, M-95, folios 173–177.

43. Santamaría Lancho, "El cabildo catedralicio de Segovia," 72–73.

44. This letter is #95 in Vaca and Bonilla, *Salamanca en la documentación medieval de la Casa de Alba*. On the duties and prestige of this office, see García y García, "Terminología universitaria de Salamanca," 164.

45. *Bulario* I, 50–57.

46. ASV Reg. Suppl. 104, fol. 285, in *Bulario* II, #515.

47. ASV Reg. Suppl. 106, fol. 178, in *Bulario* II, #534.

48. ASV Reg. Avin. 341, fol. 574, in *Bulario* II, #481.

49. See, for example, Williams, "Governance at the University of Salamanca, 1200–1500." Also see the discussion in Alonso Romero, *Universidad y sociedad corporativa*, chap. 2, which is entitled "El siglo de los papas."

50. Val Valdivieso, "Universidad y luchas urbanas," 216–17.

51. Nieto Soria, *Un crimen en la corte*, 190–94.

52. ASV Reg. Vat. 365, fol. 4, in *Bulario* II, pp. 363–64, #844.

53. The man had been imprisoned by Enrique III following an extensive investigation into the 1402 murder of Juan Serrano, a rival for ecclesiastical positions. The bishop had finally succeeded in poisoning Serrano upon the third attempt. Nieto Soria, *Un crimen en la corte,* offers an extensive and fascinating study of the voluminous documentation related to this event and to the bishop's subsequent career.

54. AGS Patronato Real 60-174, bull #1 of 5, dated September 3, 1423.

55. AGS Patronato Real 60-174, bull #4 of 5, dated November 28, 1426.

56. AGS Patronato Real 60-174, bull #5 of 5, dated August 21, 1430.

57. *Bulario*, II, provides ample documentation related to physical violence involving members of the *studium*.

58. Clemente Sánchez de Vercial, *Sacramental*, Escorial 75-VI-15. I am grateful to José María Soto Rábanos for telling me about this text and allowing me to use his photocopy of this incunable. For a discussion on Clemente

Sánchez's work and influence, see García y García, "Nuevas obras de Clemente Sánchez."

59. See, for example, A. Black, *Council and Commune*, 128–37. On his use of the Bible, see Wolf, "Precedents and Paradigms."

60. Southern, *Western Views of Islam*, 85–90; Fromherz, *Johannes von Segovia*, 59–64; Bonmann, "De testamento librorum Iohannis de Segovia."

61. Many of these documents concerning Juan de Segovia from the papal registers have been published in *Bulario* II.

62. On the importance of Franciscans' writings in Segovia's personal library, see Vázquez Janeiro, "En torno a la biblioteca de Juan de Segovia (+ 1458)." On Juan's indebtedness to William of Ockham, O. F. M. (d. 1350) and John Duns Scotus, O. F. M. (ca. 1265–1308), see these excellent studies by Mann: "Ockham Redivivus or Ockham Confutator?"; "William of Ockham, Juan de Segovia, and Heretical Pertinacity"; "Duns Scotus, Juan de Segovia, and Their Common Devil."

63. Sources for these years of Juan de Segovia's life include three works written by him: two annual addresses delivered in Salamanca in 1426 and 1427 and the document known as his *Donatio*, written in 1457, a year before his death, in which he described his books and stipulated where he wanted them to be kept after he died. The university in Salamanca was to receive the majority of the works in his possession, which numbered around one hundred. There is some disagreement about the precise number due to the way the works are grouped and categorized in this *Donatio*. Hernández Montes counted 108. See the discussion in his *Biblioteca*, 37–45. The library itself has since mostly disappeared, which has made it impossible to verify these counts from the physical works. Vatican registers offer additional information about Segovia's activities while at Salamanca. The reason that Vatican records, which now also contain the papal paperwork generated in Avignon by that papal curia, are helpful is that students and professors often received financial support from holding benefices and offices related to cathedrals, and these were conferred by the popes. Popes also settled disputes at the universities, excommunicated offenders, and levied fines, all of which generated a paper trail. General information on affairs at the university can also be gleaned from the constitutions, which were periodically changed or renewed, and from scattered references to the university in other archival or textual sources from the period. Unfortunately, the University of Salamanca's own archival documentation for this period is meager.

64. ASV Reg. Suppl. 275, fols. 272v–273, dated March 3, 1432; Reg. Suppl. 276, fol. 142, dated April 26, 1432; Reg. Suppl. 276, fols. 142v–143, also dated April 26, 1432. These are in *Bulario* II, #839, 841a, and 842, respectively. Article 31 of the constitutions approved by Martin V in 1422 (in *Bulario* II,

#647, p. 203) stipulates that no secular or nonmendicant cleric was to be admitted to bachelor studies in theology unless he was already *baccalariatus*, not a *magister*, in arts, and until he had completed an additional five years of study in the *Sentences*, during two of which he also attended lectures on the Bible. Whether this was a new policy at Salamanca or a reflection of an existing one, Juan definitely held the *magister* in arts, making it likely that his academic background fit the prevailing practice at Paris more closely than this course of study outlined in 1422, when he was already nearing completion of his training.

65. See, for example, the statistics provided in A. Black, *Council and Commune*, 32–33.

66. ASV Reg. Avin. 328, fols. 389v–391. The original of this document is also one of the few documents from this period still housed in the Archivo Universitario in Salamanca. It is published in *Bulario* II, #514. The sections summarized here are on pp. 80–81. See also the discussion by Beltrán de Heredia in *Cartulario* I, 232. Segovia would have begun theological study a little before 1416, and thus might have studied under the program in place in Paris instead. However, the Parisian program of study included a similar set of public discourses and exams. For more on the details of his likely course of study, see Wolf, "Juan de Segovia and Western Perspectives on Islam in the Fifteenth Century," 47–56.

67. Karras, *From Boys to Men*, 67.

68. Karras, *From Boys to Men*, 90–91.

69. This work is in Seville, Colombina, MS 7-6-14, folios 1r–110v.

70. Karras, *From Boys to Men*, 93–94.

71. *Cartulario* I, 226–31.

72. Courtenay, "The Institutionalization of Theology," 254.

73. ASV Reg. Avin. 328, fols. 389v–391. Also in Archivo Universitario de Salamanca, and published in *Bulario* II, #514. This section is on p. 80. The chair in the Bible had already existed for some time, but as a supplementary position. Unlike the other chairs, the master holding this position did not direct students teaching and studying under him. *Cartulario* I, 233.

74. In *Cartulario* I, 363, Beltrán de Heredia mentioned a document dated Jan. 26, 1418, in which Juan obtained *canonicatos in expectativa* (reserved in advance) in Segovia and Toledo, but he did not include it in his *Bulario*. In 1428, Juan had still not actually assumed these titles; he was still litigating for them. See #786 and 784, both from 1428, in *Bulario* II. On the offices in the other cities, see *Bulario* II, #836, 839, and 841a. Although the archdeans in the thirteenth century carried the authority of the bishop in their designated region, by the fifteenth, this title was almost solely an honorific one. Barrio Gonzalo, "La iglesia de Segovia durante el pontificado de Arias Dávila (1461–1497)," 85–86.

75. *Cartulario* I, 372.

76. See the lucid account of these years in Ruiz, *Spain's Centuries of Crisis, 1300–1474*, 87–90.

77. Courtenay, "The Institutionalization of Theology," 254.

78. ASV Reg. Lat. 317, fols. 302–303, in *Bulario* II, #846.

79. The best discussion of the evidence and its contradictions is that of Hernández Montes in his notes to the text of Juan's *Donatio*. See Hernández Montes, *Biblioteca*, 126–29.

80. *Cartulario* I, 249, and *Cartulario* II, 223–24.

81. Goñi Gaztambide, "Presencia de España en los concilios generales," 45–47.

82. ASV Reg. Avin. 349, fols. 346–347, in *Bulario* II, pp. 86–87, #522.

83. *Bulario* I, 162–63. Also see the discussion in Hernández Montes, *Biblioteca*, 126–29.

84. Goñi Gaztambide, "Presencia de España en los concilios generales," 60–61.

85. Avilés, "La teología española en el siglo XV," 504–9.

86. Juan de Segovia, *Tractatus de tribus veritatibus fidei*, BAV Cod. Pal. Lat. 601, fol. 95v, cited in Hernández Montes, *Biblioteca*, 223. For the dating and brief description of this work, see Hernández Montes, *Obras*, 293–94.

87. Avilés, "La teología española en el siglo XV," 504–6.

88. Avilés, "La teología española en el siglo XV," 506.

89. Avilés, "La teología española en el siglo XV," 509; also see Álvarez Palenzuela, *La situación europea*, 9–14.

90. Álvarez Palenzuela, *La situación europea*, 11.

91. Phillips, *Enrique IV and the Crisis of Fifteenth-Century Castile*, 32–37.

92. For a helpful discussion of the power struggles in these years, see Valdeón Baruque, "Las cortes de Castilla y las luchas del s. XV."

93. ASV Reg. Suppl. 169, fol. 138, in *Bulario* II, p. 238, #677.

94. Esperabé Arteaga, *Historia pragmática e interna de la Universidad de Salamanca*, 114–15. See the discussion of the tenure of Antonio Rodríguez de Segovia, whom Beltrán de Heredia identified with Antón Ruíz, as *maestrescuela* in Beltrán de Heredia, "La cancillería de la Universidad de Salamanca," 22–24.

95. I am grateful to the staff there for making me a copy, and to Dr. Klaus Reinhardt of the University of Trier, who generously provided me with an unpublished transcription. According to Hernández Montes, *Obras*, 272, two extracts of this work exist as well, in Rome's Bibl. Casanatense MS 1406, fols. 510b–514b, and Salamanca's Biblioteca Universitaria MS 18, fols. 90–94r.

96. Juan de Segovia, *Repetitio de superioritate*, fol. 132r.

97. Juan de Segovia, *Repetitio de superioritate*, fol. 144v.

98. Juan de Segovia, *Repetitio de superioritate*, fols. 144v–145r.

99. Juan de Segovia, *Repetitio de superioritate*, fol. 161r. For an excellent study of Juan de Segovia's use of Ockham's *Dialogus* throughout this work, see Mann, "Ockham Redivivus or Ockham Confutator?"

100. Hernández Montes, *Obras*, 271. Antony Black went so far as to credit Juan de Segovia with being the "chief exponent" of conciliar political theory. A. Black, *Council and Commune*, 1.

101. A. Black, *Council and Commune*, 118–19.

102. Vázquez Janeiro, "Historia de la iglesia y ciencias sagradas," 262.

103. Biechler, "A New Face Toward Islam," 188.

104. A. Black, "Political Languages in Later Medieval Europe," 313.

105. A. Black, "Political Languages in Later Medieval Europe," 313.

106. A. Black, "Political Languages in Later Medieval Europe," 314.

107. Juan de Segovia, *Repetitio de superioritate*, fol. 130: "De his igitur hodierno die in hac nostra scholastica inquisitione perscrutari licebit, necdum ex ratione praefata, quoniam sic ad supremos artifices agere spectat, sed quia fortassis tempore moderno ad haec in publicum ferenda compellit urgens necessitae."

108. See the discussion by Fromherz, *Johannes von Segovia*, 20; Cabanelas Rodríguez, *Juan de Segovia y el problema islámico*, 41; Hernández Montes, *Biblioteca*, 30.

109. *Bulario* I, 88–89.

110. *Bulario* I, 88–89. Text of the bull is in ASV Reg. Avin. 341, fol. 670, in *Bulario* II, #482.

111. ASV Reg. Avin. 341, fol. 670, in *Bulario* II, #482: "ponere et deponere administratorem salariorum quorumcumque legentium ac officiorum in dicto studio ex antiqua et approbata consuetudine."

112. ASV Reg. Avin. 341, fol. 670, in *Bulario* II, #482: "tamen venerabilis frater noster Lupus, archiepiscopus Compostellan., falso asserens ad ipsum positionem et depositionem administratoris praedicti pertinere, eosdem universitatem super hoc indebite molestare praesumit; quare dicti universitas ad sedem apostolicam appellarunt."

113. *Bulario* I, 89.

114. Beltrán de Heredia, "La cancillería de la Universidad de Salamanca," 17–18.

115. ASV Reg. Avin. 337, fols. 299–305, Article 32, in *Bulario* II, #444, p. 35: "nos, volentes dubium tollere supradictum, tenore praesentium declaramus nostrae intentionis tempore editionis dictarum constitutionum fuisse, et nunc esse, per dictam commissionem praefatae jurisdictioni dicti scholastici nullatenus derogare, sed executionem ipsius archiepiscopi ut praemittitur sibi

commissam in subsidium executionis jurisdictionis dicti scholastici accumulasse." Beltrán de Heredia also noted (*Bulario* I, p. 90) that Benedict XIII's constitutions repeatedly declared that the immediate jurisdiction over the university rested with the *maestrescuela* after the pope.

116. ASV Reg. Avin. 341, fol. 670, in *Bulario* II, #482. It is not clear what exactly the duties of the *administrator* were. I suspect they were more managerial, perhaps of a business nature, than those of the *maestrescuela* (*scholasticus* in the Vatican registers).

117. ASV Reg. Suppl. 121, fols. 39v–40, *Bulario* II, #577.

118. Alonso Romero, *Universidad y sociedad corporativa*, 57–60. The holder of this office at Salamanca enjoyed a wider range of powers than was typical in most universities. See the discussion in García y García, "Terminología universitaria de Salamanca," 164.

119. In addition to the text of these constitutions found in *Bulario* II, #647, pp. 177–211, these constitutions have been published in a facsimile edition, with an accompanying Spanish translation, in Valero García and Pérez Martín, *Constituciones de Martín V*.

120. "omnium et singulorum praesentium nostrorum constitutionum, ordinationum, statutorum et concessionum, necnon privilegiorum eidem universitati et singularibus personis ejusdem." This is in Articles 6 and 33; translated texts appear in Valero García and Pérez Martín, *Constituciones de Martín V*, 124–25 and 161–70. See also Alonso Romero, *Universidad y sociedad corporativa*, 70.

121. He did, however, retain the right to decide whether to admit a student to exams in cases where the *maestrescuela* was suspected of negligence or wrongdoing in certifying that a candidate fulfilled the prerequisites. Alonso Romero, *Universidad y sociedad corporativa*, 70.

122. *Bulario* II, #647, Article 33, p. 206: "apostolica auctoritate statuimus et ordinamus quod deinceps futuris perpetuis temporibus post praesentium nostrarum constituionum publicationem, per rectorem et scholasticum ac viginti alios de ipsa universitate diffinitores nuncupandos, qui annuatim, ut sequitur, videlicet per universitatem de nobilibus vel in dignitatibus constitutis, licentiatis, baccalariis et studentibus decem, quorum quilibet ad minus vicesimumquintum aetatis annum attingat, intra octavas resurrectionis dominicae; de regentibus vero cathedras salariatas per ipsosmet intra dictas octavas, alii decem nominentur et deputentur"; p. 209: "non obstantibus constitutionibus et ordinationibus apostolicis statutisque et consuetudinibus ecclesiae ac studii praedictorum contrariis, juramento, confirmatione apostolica vel quacumque firmitate alia roboratis, et aliis contrariis quibuscumque, decernentes ex nunc irritum et innane si secus super his a quoquam quavis auctoritate, scienter vel ignoranter, contigerit imposterum attemtari. per praedicta

tamen praefato archiepiscopo nullam potestatem seu jurisdictionem aut superioritatem supra scholasticum praedictum attribuere vel concedere volumus seu intendimus quoquo modo." See the Spanish translation in Valero García and Pérez Martín, *Constituciones de Martín V,* 162 and 166. Beltrán de Heredia wrote (*Cartulario* I, 206) that this body of "diffinitores" was a new institution in the history of academia, but it should be noted that this system mirrors the practice in Paris and at other universities that followed Parisian norms. Various general assemblies of faculty members made the key decisions. The rector was accountable to these bodies and was elected for limited terms and endowed with limited powers. See Rashdall, *The Universities of Europe,* vol. 1, esp. 321–34, 402–5.

123. For this reason, he rejected as tendentious Beltrán's conclusion that the university only charged these two with the task because they were on their way to Rome anyway to pursue matters related to their own appointments. Hernández Montes believed that it was the other way around: they took advantage of the trip to Rome on behalf of the university to pursue other matters while they were there.

124. For a discussion of Juan's positions at Salamanca and his travels undertaken while there, see Hernández Montes, *Biblioteca,* 126–29. For more details on Juan's stays in Rome, see Diener, "Zur Persönlichkeit des Johannes de Segovia."

125. Alonso Romero, *Universidad y sociedad corporativa,* 79.

126. ASV Reg. Suppl. 185, fol. 65, *Bulario* II, #708.

127. ASV Reg. Lat. 263, fols. 202v–203v, *Bulario* II, #726.

128. Juan de Segovia, *Repetitio de superioritate,* fol. 161r: "Ita ut de eo possit dici quod iuxta voluntatem suam facit tam in virtutibus coeli quam in habitatoribus terrae, et non est qui resistat manui eius nec dicere ei quisquam cur ita facis; sed sermo eius potestate plenus est et sub eo curvantur omnes rectores, qui comportant orbem, Job 9, Ecclesiastes 8 et Deut 4." This sentence contains exact wording from Daniel 4:32 as well.

129. Emphasis added. Juan de Segovia, *Repetitio de superioritate,* fols. 163–163v: "Extendit ergo se ad mandata disciplinae, de quibus constat quod solum eorum sunt quae sunt indifferentia [163v] ad salutem, et ad id et non alias quam ex praecepto superioris, obligamur. Quale fuit mandatum datum primo homini quod non comederet de ligno scientiae boni et mali, quod alias non erat malum nisi quia prohibitum. Ita summus Pontifex multa etiam in temporalibus praecipere potest, quae non sunt necessaria nec de se ordinata ad vitam aeternam; nec possumus ab eo petere rationem mandati, quia nemo ei dicere potest cur ita facis, Job 9."

130. Tierney, *Foundations of the Conciliar Theory,* 88.

131. *Cartulario* I, 363; Hernández Montes, *Biblioteca,* 32.

132. Juan de Segovia, *Repetitio de superioritate*, fols. 144–144v: "Et ex hoc dicuntur esse a Christo commissa Petro iura coelestis et terreni imperii, ita ut etiam in temporalibus plenum iudicium et liberam habeat administrationem. Cui enim conceditur principale, et accessorium; bona vero temporalia sunt accessoria spiritualium, Mt 6 quaerite primum regnum Dei et iustitiam eius, et haec omnia, scilicet, temporalia adicientur vobis. Unde et si potestas temporalis aliquid iubeat contrarium spirituali, oboediendum simpliciter spirituali supremae; nec ad hunc locum adaptatur illa communis distinctio quod saeculari in temporalibus et civilibus magis oboediendum est, ecclesiasticae vero in spiritualibus; hoc enim verum habet in inferioribus potestatibus ecclesiasticis, non autem in suprema, cui simpliciter in omnibus [144v] oboedientia exhibenda est, siquidem ipse summus Pontifex est universalis monarcha populi christiani et de iure totius mundi."

133. Juan de Segovia, *Donatio*, 81: "Et enim cum instancia quorumdam alie quedam constituciones subdelegata edite fuissent auctoritate, apostolicas ipsas non exigue mutilantes, permaxime autem in substanciali exempcione uidelicet a dyocesana et metropolitana jurisdiccione, anno XXXV° in publico me opponens consistorio et coram commisariis, uelut habundancius emulator dictarum apostolicarum constitucionum, quoniam exempcio ipsa Studii racione firmata plenaque foret justicia, copiosas, quibus aduersantes non respondere, feci allegaciones; priuatas uero collaciones seorsum persepe super competencia aliquarum ex ipsis constitucionum." See also the discussion by Hernández Montes on Juan's presence and mission at the papal court (in Florence then, not in Rome, as some have thought); *Biblioteca*, 139.

134. See the analyses of the political dynamics of this period by Valdeón Baruque, "Las cortes de Castilla y las luchas del s. XV," and Phillips, *Enrique IV and the Crisis of Fifteenth-Century Castile*, 21–29.

135. For a discussion of the aims of the conciliar movement, see A. Black, "What Was Conciliarism?"

136. *Cartulario* I, 223–25.

137. For a survey of the diversity in political opinions voiced at Salamanca, see, for example, Rucquoi, "Democratie ou monarchie," 237–55.

138. Haubst, "Johannes von Segovia im Gespräch mit Nikolaus von Kues und Jean Germain," 124, 128; Mann, "Duns Scotus, Juan de Segovia, and Their Common Devil," 135–37.

139. This letter survives in a single manuscript, Salamanca Biblioteca Universitaria MS 202, fols. 172r–184r. It has received little attention from scholars. For a persuasive discussion of the identity of the recipient, see Mann, "Juan de Segovia's 'Epistola ad Guillielmum de Orliaco.'"

140. Mann, "Duns Scotus, Juan de Segovia, and Their Common Devil," 145–48.

141. Without giving any reason, Hernández Montes included Mayronis's commentary on the *Sentences* among the works he believed Juan acquired while still in Salamanca. See Hernández Montes, *Biblioteca*, 53.

142. Hernández Montes, *Biblioteca*, 220.

143. Mann, "Ockham Redivivus or Ockham Confutator?"

144. Mann, "Ockham Redivivus or Ockham Confutator?" 186–87. For bibliography on this question, see his note 2.

145. Mann, "Ockham Redivivus or Ockham Confutator?" 194. For a helpful bibliography on this, see his note 41.

146. Mann, "William of Ockham, Juan de Segovia, and Heretical Pertinacity," esp. 80; Mann, "The Historian and the Truths," 182–93.

147. Roest, *A History of Franciscan Education*, 185–89.

148. Roest, *A History of Franciscan Education*, 192.

149. Roest, *A History of Franciscan Education*, 195.

150. Roest, *A History of Franciscan Education*, 193. Roest admits that there might have been a "Franciscan sensibility," characterized by a general sympathy for a more affective theology than the scholastic syntheses encouraged. Those with this sensibility would have found as much that was objectionable in Scotus as in Thomas. In any case, Roest argues, such an affective theology would not have flourished in the formal university setting and thus must be sought in the nonacademic environment of religious education rather than in the theological faculties at the leading schools. See pp. 195–96.

151. Haubst, "Johannes von Segovia im Grespräch mit Nikolaus von Kues und Jean Germain," 124, 128.

152. Roest, *A History of Franciscan Education*, 192.

153. Oberman, *The Dawn of the Reformation*, 2.

154. See, for example, Hernández Montes, *Biblioteca*, 60–62.

155. Smith, "The Use of Scripture in Teaching at the Medieval University," 230.

156. See, for example, A. Black, *Council and Commune*, 128–37.

157. The appeal to scriptural authority was a key element of the conciliarists' arguments. Leading conciliarists, including Juan de Segovia, strove to reduce the authority of canon law in favor of scripture. See A. Black, *Council and Commune*, 5, 11.

158. Juan de Segovia, *Repetitio de superioritate*. After describing the first kind of "Catholic truth," namely, those things contained in scripture and those that must necessarily be deduced from scripture, he continued with three more kinds of Catholic truths: "Secundum genus est earum veritatum, quae ab ipsis Apostolis ad nos per successionem revelationum vel scripturas fidelium pervenerunt, licet in sacris Scripturis non inveniantur inserta, nec ex solis eis necessario argumento possint concludi, de compositione symboli per Apostolos et de verbis additis in consecratione calicis super ea quae in

evangelio continentur" (fol. 132v); "Tertium genus est earum veritatum quas habemus in fide dignis coronicis et historiis et relationibus fidelium invenimus . . . Sub hoc genere sunt ea que continentur in legendis canonizata, quoniam in huiusmodi canonizationibus Ecclesia non potest errare" (fol. 133r); "Quartum genus est earum veritatum, quae ex veritatibus primi generis et secund. simili modo, vel ex eis seu alterius earum una cum veritatibus tertii generis possunt manifeste et necessario concludi. Ad hoc quartum genus reducuntur ea quae in decretis aut in constitutionibus decretaliam aut in generalibus conciliis determinata sunt" (fol. 133r). I am grateful to Professor Klaus Reinhardt for giving me a copy of a transcription of this text, which greatly facilitated my reading of the manuscript. He told me it had been in his file cabinet for a long time, and that he had once planned to do an edition of this with someone else, but now there were other projects and he would probably not get to it. I have since learned from Jesse Mann that he, too, has a copy of a transcription of this text, and that it was given to him by Benigno Hernández Montes. Since Reinhardt and Hernández Montes collaborated on several projects, I think that Hernández Montes probably contributed to this transcription, and I wish to recognize his (likely) contribution here.

159. Mann, "Ockham Redivivus or Ockham Confutator?" 198–99 including n. 53. For Mann's exploration of Segovia's use of scripture in one of these later works, see chapter 2 of his dissertation, "The Historian and the Truths."

160. This work occupies folios 181–193r in MS 128 in the cathedral library in Córdoba. The text appears in two columns on every page. In subsequent references to this work, I will include folios and A or B to designate the column. This work is described briefly in Hernández Montes, *Obras*, 271–72 (#3).

161. Juan de Segovia, *Repetitio de fide catholica*, fol. 184r A: "Ad declarandum igitur quid proprie sit fides prenotandum est qualis sit doctrina fidey infuse et acquisite et videtur inter ceteras assignari posse quatuor doctrinas Prima ex parte cause efficientis. Et quidem infusa a solo deo causatur, acquisita vero a deo simul et per exercicium nostrum. Secunda ex parte cause obiectalis sive nature, nam acquisita potest esse de uno, duobus, aut pluribus articulis etiam si non sit de omnibus, infusa autem non enim aliquo nisi universaliter credat sive implicite aut explicite omnia que tenet fides catholica. Tertia ex parte finis. Acquisita enim principaliter invititur miraculo raciocinationi aut persuasioni fame vel auctoritati, et si credit auctoritatibus in sacra scriptura contentis, propterea credit . . . Non sit autem fides infusa sed nititur principaliter divine illustrationi per quam credit in fide contenta esse a deo revelata. Est quarta doctrina formalis qualibet magnam in se habeat dificultatem tamen sine periudicio melioris finem sic declarari potest."

162. Juan de Segovia, *Repetitio de fide catholica*, fol. 182v A: "utraque pars elicitur ex auctoritate apostolici quam magister pro sua aducit confirmatione."

163. Juan de Segovia, *Repetitio de fide catholica*, fol. 184v B: "Ex dictis facili deductione manifestari potest diffinicio fidey assignata ab apostolo paulo in epistula ad he. xi. c., fides est substantia sperandum rerum, argumento non apparencium." Hebrews 11:1: "Now faith is the assurance of things hoped for, the conviction of things not seen."

164. Juan de Segovia, *Repetitio de fide catholica*, fol. 184v B: "donum spiritus sancti a deo gratis infusum cuius illustratione firma adhesione assentit mens humana hiis que supra facultatem suam sunt, veritatibus a deo revelatis in sacra scriptura."

165. Juan de Segovia, *Repetitio de fide catholica*, fol. 188v B: "Nunc igitur si auditis que in promptu dixero vobis, quilibet vestrum asserat fidem nostram que in sacra scriptura continetur semper ab inicio mundi et maxime post aductum christi, esse confirmatam miraculis que solus deus facere potest, satis me putabo probasse minorem premissam supra positi argumenti, videlicet quod fidem quam predicat religio christiana deus per se et suos nuncios revelavit."

166. Juan de Segovia, *Repetitio de fide catholica*, fol. 188v B: "xii fundamenta super que fundatus est murus civitatis, scilicet militantis ecclesie de quibus Apoc 12 est." Revelation 21:14 reads, "And the wall of the city has twelve foundations, and on them are the twelve names of the twelve apostles of the Lamb."

167. Juan de Segovia, *Repetitio de fide catholica*, fols. 188v B–189r A: "Quantum ad primum scilicet de prophetica denunciatione manifestum est quod futura simpliciter contingencia soli deo sunt nota. Si ergo alius enunciat futurum contengens et ita evenit certum est hoc non posse per se [189r A] ipsum, sed dumtaxat scire ex divina revelatione."

168. Juan de Segovia, *Repetitio de fide catholica*, fol. 189r A: "Si duo sint ceci et quilibet eorum conformiter iudicat de colore habitus intranseunte de quo prius nichil audierant certum est hoc ipsos habere ex divina revelatione. Sic igitur cum ad veritates quas prophete predixerunt non potuissent attingere per naturam sui intellectus et tamen in diversis temporibus et locis."

169. Juan de Segovia, *Repetitio de fide catholica*, fol. 189r B: "Et si alius dicat non esse libros scriptos ab hiis qui in eis narrantur, sed ab aliis mendacibus qui fabulose ista conposuerunt, hoc non potest stare. Nam aut libri sacre scripture sunt istorum auctorum quorum esse dicuntur aut non."

170. Juan de Segovia, *Repetitio de fide catholica*, fol. 189r B: "Nullo modo est verisimile eos fuisse mentuos ut scriberent, hec dicit dominus deus si deus illis non fuisset locutus."

171. Juan de Segovia, *Repetitio de fide catholica*, fol. 189v A: "Item ut apropriate loquar qui scripserunt ebbangelia et epistolas pauli aut fuerunt christiani aut non. Si christiani cum eorum scripta dapnent mendacium conarentur, ipsi mendacium non scribere. Si autem non fuerunt christiani

sed iudei vel sarraceni aut pagani quo modo est verissimille quod extranei tantam adhiberent diligenciam in tam auctentice scribendo et magnificando ea que facerent contra sectam eorum. Item quilibet circuspiciens percipere clare potest ad hec non posse sufficere ingenium humanum ut tam ordinate componeret factum in quo totum vetus testamentum apparet completum."

172. Juan de Segovia, *Repetitio de fide catholica*, fol. 190r B: "9o etiam fidem nostram confirmat racionalitas contentorum. Primo quam ad agenda. Et quidem continet illud quo nichil racionabilius inveniri potest, scilicet nostrum creatorem et benefactorem diligere ex toto corde ex proximi ad quod et propter quod nos ipsos Matthei 22 diliges etc. et subditur in hiis duobus pendent leges et prophete. Item illud racionabilissimum Matthei 7 quecumque vultis ut faciant vobis homines et vos facite illiis."

173. Juan de Segovia, *Repetitio de fide catholica*, fols. 190 B–190v A: "xi fidem catholicam confirmat ecclesie stabilitas. Et quidem inter multas tirranorum persecutiones et hereticorum fallacias ipsa semper ecclesia inmobilis perseverat quod certissimum est testimonium opus et fidem ecclesie specialiter ex deo. Unde in exordio nascentis ecclesie suprascriptus gamaliel de ea dixit ad iudices, actis 5 c, si ex hominibus est consilium hoc autem opus dissolvetur si vero ex deo est non poteritis dissolvere ne forte et deo repugnare inveniamini. Item [190v A] lucis 22, dominus ait petro, Ego pro te rogabo ut non deficiat fides tua. Similiter Matthei, ultis ego nobiscum sum omnibus diebus usque ad consumationem seculi."

174. Juan de Segovia, *Repetitio de fide catholica*, fol. 191 A: "Sequar docrinam augustini de civitate dei, Tria incredibilia hic ponuntur coram occulis nostris, primum quod christus, homo mortalis et mortuus, resurrexit et in celum ascendit. 2m incredibile quod istam rem tam incredibilem mundus tam firmiter credit. 3m quod homines tam imperiti secundum scilicet sicut fuerunt apostoli potuerunt facere quod mundus istam rem tam incredibilem tam efficaciter crederent."

175. Juan de Segovia, *Repetitio de fide catholica*, fols. 191r B–191v A: "quod homines rudes ingenio, piscatores, subito sunt reple[191v A]ti sciencia et loquebantur omnia ydiomata, cecos illuminabant, demones expellebart, non solum manu apposita sed sudario transmisso sanabant infirmos, et quos usque eorum umbra tangeret sanabantur a quacumque detinebantur infirmitate, de hiis omnibus ad plenum in actis apostolorum."

176. Mann, "Ockham Redivivus or Ockham Confutator?" 199.

177. See the discussion in Dahan, *Les intellectuels chrétiens et les juifs au moyen âge*, 386, and Pick, *Conflict and Coexistence*, chap. 4.

178. See Griffith, "Arguing from Scripture."

179. This page is fol. 74v in MS 246 at the Biblioteca Universitaria de Salamanca.

180. Hernández Montes, *Obras*, p. 327, #78.

181. See the discussion of this volume in Hernández Montes, *Biblioteca*, 184–91.

182. Augustine, *The City of God*, 883.

183. Juan de Segovia, *Repetitio de fide catholica*, fol. 189r A: "Si duo humani intellectus in eandem scilicet consenciant, certum est non a se ipsis cognitionem habere sed a superiori causa ipsorum mentes illustrante."

184. Juan de Segovia, *Repetitio de fide catholica*, fol. 189r A: "Sic igitur cum ad veritates quas prophete predixerunt non potuissent attingere per naturam sui intellectus et tamen in diversis temporibus et locis idem predixerunt. . . . Hoc autem non sic videmus in philosophis quilibros doctrinales composuerunt. Et enim posteriores in multis suis prioribus contradicunt et adhuc etiam quam ad principia ita ut totaliter destruant eorum doctrinam. Talis autem repugnancia non reperitur inter prophetas."

185. Juan de Segovia, *Repetitio de fide catholica*, fol. 192v A: "Que sit causa propter quam divina providencia tam multitudinem populi permittat perire: non spectat ad praesens et quidem est alterius speculationis sufficit declarare solam fidem quam predicat religio christiana a deo esse revelatam salutis viam, et quod ista racionabile et certissimum habet fundamentum ut manifesta ratione possit convinci ad obtinendam beatitudinem quae finis est humane nature per hanc solam rectos dirigi, calles alias vero quaslibet sectas esse oberraciones quasdam a via recta."

186. Juan de Segovia, *Repetitio de fide catholica*, fol. 192v B: "Equidem esset manifestissimum signum negligencie et incurie de sua propria salute si quamcumque simplex christianus ignoraret articulum trinitatis cum omni die se habeat per illud signare" (having been marked with the sign of the cross, as in baptized).

187. Smith, "The Use of Scripture in Teaching at the Medieval University," 230.

188. Roest, *A History of Franciscan Education*, 130.

189. ASV Reg. Suppl. 123, fol. 37v, *Bulario* II, #580: "cathedrae biblicae in tertiis tunc vacantis pro anno Domini millesimo quadringentesimo undecimo."

190. ASV Reg. Suppl. 124, fols. 123v–124, *Bulario* II, #581. In a footnote, Beltrán de Heredia noted that this document was barely implemented because the university received the new constitutions from Martin V in 1422.

191. ASV Reg. Suppl. 121, fol. 166, *Bulario* II, #574: "necnon dignum sit et rationi consonum ac consentaneum quod in sacra theologia, quae vinea est dominica et apex ac aliarum mundanarum scientiarum regina, laborantes et ipsius cathedras regentes deterioris conditionis non existant, ac aliquibus muneribus et gratiis favorabiliter sint prosequendi."

192. Hernández Montes, *Biblioteca*, 126.

193. Ryan, *The Apostolic Conciliarism of Jean Gerson*, 49.

194. Juan de Segovia, *Donatio*: "Et quantum ad theologie studium id profecto uerbum, quod, sicut relacione multorum et alias per meipsum intellex, in ecclesia latina tanta fortassis opportunitas non est proficiendi in audiendo ordinarias cotidianasque tres magistrales cathedralesque lecciones" (81); "Has profecto ad oculum demonstrat et uicessimus quinarius numerus cathedrarum salariatarum perenni stabilimento fundatus" (82); "Demonstrant item excellenciam ejus edificata sumptuosius insignissima auditoria et seorsum ac duplicate dictarum facultatum" (83); "Quod uero Uniuersitatem ipsam singulari candore perlustrat, quia regularis obseruancie dictarum disciplina gradibus tam baccalaureatus quam licenciature et doctoratus tanto libratis pondere, ut reformacione minime egeat. Unde ad gloriam Studii ejus singularem, pleno liberoque sermone, pluries annunciaui justiciam suam in ecclesia magna dum Basilee erat [synodus] legitime constituta et tractabatur de reformacione Generalium Studiorum" (83); "Taceo autem de singularissimo in tempore breui profectu ibidem studencium, conferentibus ad hoc permultum magno ingenii splendore et agili ac firma capacitate memorie, de quibus apud ceteras naciones plurimum yspani laudantur, graduatis quoque ejus, uiris quoque illustribus in orbe reputatis, id ipsum demonstrantibus eorum accionibus preclaris promocioneque ad dignitates sublimiores" (83). See also the discussion in Hernández Montes, *Biblioteca*, 30–33.

195. Hernández Montes, *Biblioteca*, 30.

196. Bull of Eugene IV, January 25, 1441, ASV Reg. Lat. 359, fol. 114, *Bulario* II, #987: "tum vero commendamus ex corde vestram devotionem, quae firmata est supra petram, adversus errores eorum qui in viam sathanae abierunt. . . . Itaque cooperante eo qui novit aspera deducere in vias planas, a certo tenemus quod illud Basiliense monstrum, in Dei contumeliam, in opprobium fidei, in sancalum christianorum, in animarum interitum per filios perditionis erectum, confringet virtus altissimi, qui nunquam in se sperantes delinquit. . . . Summam enim consolationem in Domino suscepimus ex vestris litteris; quas tam devote, tam reverenter scribitis ad nos, condolentes de iis quae contra nos per Basiliensium impietatem facta sunt in desolationem Ecclesiae sanctae Dei et ipsius miserabilem scissuram. Sentitis et scribitis recte ac vere, prout decet vestram prudentiam, et multum laetamur studia vestra bonum fructum tulisse in nobis."

Chapter Two. Contact, Conversations, and Conversion

1. Cabanelas Rodríguez, *Juan de Segovia y el problema islámico*, 141, citing BAV Vat. Lat. 2923, fol. 180.

2. BAV Vat. Lat. 2923, fol. 179v: "cum illo vero amore quem de vobis suscepi pro vestris nobilibus et excellentibus virtutibus domini generosi." *Domini generosi* should be understood as genitive. There is no reason to read it as a plural vocative. There is no mention of anyone else here other than Juan. Folio 180: "et tamen, sicut dixi, propter vestras nobiles virtutes, quas audivimus, sum obligatus ad faciendum quantum de me ordinaveritis." This letter is published in Cabanelas Rodríguez, *Juan de Segovia y el problema islámico*, appendix 2. His transcription and mine are the same. In his *Islamic Literature in Spanish and Aljamiado*, Gerard Wiegers offers a transcription and translation of this letter on pp. 230–35. He understood this phrase the way I have, as referring to Juan's own virtues.

3. See, for example, Echevarría Arsuaga, *Fortress of Faith*, 38.

4. As Wiegers notes (*Islamic Literature in Spanish and Aljamiado*, 12), Castilian archives offer much less documentation on Mudéjars than Aragonese archives.

5. Tapia Sánchez, *La comunidad morisca de Avila*, 45–51.

6. Tapia Sánchez, *La comunidad morisca de Avila*, 54.

7. Tapia Sánchez, *La comunidad morisca de Avila*, 55.

8. Tapia Sánchez, *La comunidad morisca de Avila*, 56.

9. Tapia Sánchez, *La comunidad morisca de Avila*, 56.

10. For a detailed discussion of the king's efforts to raise money from cities in the early fifteenth century, see Valdeón Baruque, "Las cortes de Castilla y las luchas del s. XV."

11. Tapia Sánchez, *La comunidad morisca de Avila*, 57; Echevarría Arsuaga, *Catalina de Lancaster*, 141–56.

12. Ladero Quesada, *Las guerras de Granada*, 21–23.

13. Echevarría Arsuaga, *Catalina de Lancaster*, 109–12.

14. See the excellent discussion of these developments in Echevarría Arsuaga, *Catalina de Lancaster*, 148–52. On Ferrer's preaching in Castilian, see Cátedra, "La predicación castellana de San Vicente Ferrer."

15. Tapia Sánchez, *La comunidad morisca de Avila*, 57; Echevarría Arsuaga, "Política y religión frente al Islám," 46.

16. Hernández Montes, *Biblioteca*, 260.

17. Juan de Segovia, Letter to Guillielmus de Orliaco (Guillaume d'Orlyé), BUS MS 202, fol. 182r, cited in Mann, "Juan de Segovia's 'Epistola ad Guillielmum de Orliaco,'" 185–86: "Hoc [daily Bible reading] certe ab inicio adolescencie sue exercicium fuit sancti Vincencii ordinis Predicatorum et predicatoris magni, cuius presentibus alligatum mit<t>o Tractatum consolatorium de temptationibus fidei, quem habui dum per annum vel amplius minimus fui disciplorum suorum." Mann notes (186n41) that Ferrer's authorship of this work is a matter of some dispute among scholars. See also Hernández Montes, *Obras*, 322–23.

13. The reference to the *Tractatus consolatorius* appears in Juan de Segovia, *Donatio*, 91; the commentary by Hernández Montes is on 181–82. The sermons appear in the *Donatio* in *Biblioteca*, 101, commentary on 259–60.

19. Juan de Segovia, *Historia*, MC 2:750: "episcopus Foroiuliensis, ambasiator regis Ludiuici Cecilie, surgens dicebat attendendum fore, quoniam principes forte non consentirent in clausula determinante Iudeis baptizandis manere bona sua, que prius habebant; etenim dominus suus rex Cecilie, quandocumque conuertebantur, illa haberet, sed et pluries liberalem faciebat eis donacionem, ideoque non esset statuendum illud sub pena anathematis in decreto contenta, sed fieri possent exhortaciones. Huic legatus respondebat reges non eo ipso fore dominos bonorum, que subditi sui habent, ut possint de eis ad nutum disponere, quare, si remanentibus Judeis in iudaismo non tellerentur bona, quanto minus ad Christum conuersis; in hiis preterea, que fidei erant, ecclesia non ad commoda principum, sed attendere debebat ad fidei incrementum, et quoniam, si tollerentur bona eis, manifeste cedebat in retraccionem a suscepcione fidei, oportebat ecclesiam prouidere. Magister vero Johannes de Segobia premittens, quoniam ex proposicione dicti episcopi videbantur notari principes christiani, dicebat, quantum ipse cognosceret de rege Castelle, ex dicta causa formam decreti mutari non debere, quoniam in regnis suis, cum Iudei conuertebantur ad fidem, necdum non tollerentur eis bona, sed ex magnis donariis eorum multi diuites fierent; et cum sancte memorie magister Vincencius circa annos domini mccccxii, coram rege predicasset, multipharie suadens Iudeorum conuersionem, ut in maiori multitudine conuerterentur, concesserat omnibus baptizandis libertatem ab omni exaccione regalium debitorum per x annos, et ita fuerat illis obseruatam."

20. Meyerson, *A Jewish Renaissance*, 59.

21. Ruiz, *Spain's Centuries of Crisis, 1300–1474*, 160. In his important *Crusade and Mission*, Benjamin Kedar noted that this lack of attention to missions to the Muslims was a characteristic of the general Christian approach to Islam until the rise of the mendicants, and that even then the efforts were not as frequent and intense as it might seem on first glance. See his discussion on 3–6 and 143–46.

22. Meyerson, *A Jewish Renaissance*, 59.

23. Juan de Segovia, Letter to Jean Germain, Dec. 18, 1455, fol. 97: "Quod ergo pavescent doctrina catholice fidei irrisionem formidans infidelium quasi documenta eius sint leves racioncinationes et raciones puerorum quando de se ipsa certissime agnovit probacionem suam multo preciosiorem esse auro quod per ignem probatur. Equidem non semel sicut aurum sed iam a mille quadringentis plusquam persepe examinata est veritas fidei catholic disputacionibus primo cum iudeis stephano superante rabinos quinque synagogarum qui surrexerunt tanquam aliis fortiores disputare eo paulo vero per synagogas fiducialiter predicante continue ihesum. Cum gentibus

autem persepe ut Ephesi posquam per tres menses in synagoga cum fiducia loquebatur de regno dei disputans Ita ut omnes qui habitabant in Asia audirent verbum domini. Quid igitur Corinthio et [97v] antiochie ubi primo vulgatum est nomen christianorum. Quid aliis locis Rome presertim biennio toto ad iudeos et grecos predicans regnum dei et docens ea que sunt de domino ihesu christo cum omni fiducia quamvis autem non sic auctenctice liber canonis testimonium de aliis apostolis ferat alie tamen scripture plenopere similia eos fecisse narrant. Ab inde examinata est tempore martirum. Denique post tempora persecucionem cum hereticis difficilibus ad vincendum quoniam fuere domestici hostes. Et quid dicendum post fundatus universitates generalium studiorum quorum precipuum exercitium est publice disputaciones de misterio trinitatis incarnacionis sacramenti eucharistie aliisque veritatibus fide utique et si non dixisset propheta regnis experiencia hactenus semper quoque magistris in dies demonstrat quod eloquia domini eloquia sunt casta argentumque igne examinatum probatum terre purgatum septuplum. Siquidem eloquia domini examinata sunt igne ipseque dominus protector est omni sperancium in se."

24. Adeline Rucquoi has written that Ferrer's preaching campaign did not produce the same hostility toward Valladolid's Muslims as it did for this city's Jews, and that Muslims continued to be well integrated into urban life. There is every reason to suspect that the same may have been true in Segovia. See her *Valladolid au Moyen Age*, 583.

25. Cuéllar, Archivo de la Comunidad, n. 29 (Sept. 5, 1390). Published in Ubieto Arteta, *Colección diplomática de Cuéllar*, #140.

26. López Martínez, "Sínodos burgalenses del siglo XV," 290.

27. ASV Reg. Vat. 365, fol. 202v.

28. Wiegers, *Islamic Literature in Spanish and Aljamiado*, 77.

29. Ruíz, *Spain's Centuries of Crisis, 1300–1474*, 145. For a fascinating exploration of this complexity, see Nirenberg, "Conversion, Sex, and Segregation."

30. Escorial 75-VI-15, Book 3, Section 130. I am grateful to José María Soto Rábanos for telling me about this text and for loaning me his photocopy of it. There are other manuscripts of this work in the Escorial as well. For a discussion of Clemente Sánchez's career and writings, see García y García, "Nuevas obras de Clemente Sánchez."

31. See the discussion in Wiegers, *Islamic Literature in Spanish and Aljamiado*, 145–49.

32. BAV Vat. Lat. 2923, fol. 179v, published in Wiegers, *Islamic Literature in Spanish and Aljamiado*, 234.

33. Yça Gidelli, *Breviario Sunni*, 250.

34. Yça Gidelli, *Breviario Sunni*, 251.

35. Yça Gidelli, *Breviario Sunni*, 297.

36. Yça Gidelli, *Breviario Sunni*, 283.

37. Yça Gidelli, *Breviario Sunni*, 253.

38. Yça Gidelli, *Breviario Sunni*, 370.

39. Yça Gidelli, *Breviario Sunni*, 302.

40. Archivo de la Real Chancillería de Valladolid, Reales Cartas Ejecutorias, caja 39-6. I am grateful to Ana Echevarría for providing me with her transcription of this document, which she has since published as an appendix in Echevarría Arsuaga, "Las aljamas mudéjares castellanas en el siglo XV," 105–12.

41. Echevarría Arsuaga, "Las aljamas mudéjares castellanas en el siglo XV," 93–94.

42. Concerning this family, see, for example, Molénat, "Une famille de l'élite mudéjare," 771; "A propos d'Abrahen Xarafi," 175; and "La question de l'élite mudéjare."

43. AGS, Escribanía Mayor de Rentas, Quitaciones de Corte (EMR, QC) leg. 1, 50. See the discussion where this is cited in Echevarría Arsuaga, "De cadí al alcalde mayor," part 1, 155–56.

44. Echevarría Arsuaga, "De cadí al alcalde mayor," part 2, 283; "Las aljamas mudéjares castellanas en el siglo XV," 100–101.

45. This letter is in BAV Vat. Lat. 2923, folios 41–136v. See the discussion on Germain and Juan's response to his arguments in Cabanelas Rodríguez, *Juan de Segovia y el problema islámico*, chap. 6 (pp. 191–223).

46. BAV Vat. Lat. 2923, fol. 98v: "Attestantur hec non esse verisimilia sed impossibilia magis. Quod ut inquit ostenditur ex simili nam in hyspaniis sarraceni tenent officia publica et magnam partem terre inhabitant et omni die possunt instrui de fide. Et tamen vix incentum annis potest reduci unus. Re vera ego nondum vixcentum annis, sed in adolescencia mea decem annis quibus in ea fui de inhabitantibus civitatem qua sum oriundus plures vidi conversos numero tunc ipsorum Sarracenorum vix attingente quinquiginta habitatorum. Nec recolo me vidisse unquam in regno Castelle sarracenos tenere officia publica super christianos. Sunt autem boni artifices manuales et velut servos decet nimium obsequiosi unde quia ex necesitate facientes virtutem velut id ipsum agant sponte a pluribus preiudeis sunt dilecti."

47. Juan de Segovia, Letter to Jean Germain, Dec. 18, 1455, fol. 57v: "De hiis vero que facta sunt in hyspania cum hyspano loquitur dominacio vestra, qui a plus xlª annis dicere valeo de bellis indictis contra sarracenos deque in preterito actis cum multa legerim audierimque. Sed consideratis omnibus a plurimo iam tempore visum michi fuit via pacis et doctrine intendendum esse ad eorum conversionem." Cabanelas discusses this passage in Cabanelas Rodríguez, *Juan de Segovia y el problema islámico*, 210.

48. See Fletcher, *Moorish Spain*, 157–60.

49. One scholar who has examined the *repetitios* is Mann in his "Ockham Redivivus or Ockham Confutator?"

50. See Biechler, "A New Face Toward Islam," 189. For Cusa's own account of his efforts to obtain copies of the Qur'ān and other books on Islam, see the prologue to his *Cribratio Alkorani*, in Hopkins, *Nicholas of Cusa's "De pace fidei" and "Cribratio Alkorani,"* 75–76. He mentioned leaving a volume containing the Qur'ān and several other works with Juan de Segovia before journeying to Constantinople.

51. Juan de Segovia, *Repetitio de superioritate*, fols. 144v–145: "Utrum autem infideles et gentiles ad hanc pertineant potestatem, videtur dicendum quod sic, cum etiam oves Christi nominentur, Joh 10, Alias oves habeo quae non sunt de hoc ovili, et illas oportet me adducere. Unde, si gentilis vel paganus vel barbara quaevis alia natio, etsi non habeant legem naturae, si tamen contra legem naturae faciat, licite per papam potest punir. Sic legimus sodomitas, qui contra legem naturae peccaverunt, fuisse punitos a Deo, Gen 19; sic et omnes idololatras punire potest, cum naturale sit unum Deum credere et eum solum adorare, ad Rom 1; similiter infideles, qui in terris suis non admittunt evvangelii praedicatores, cum omnis creatura rationalis facta sit ad laudandum Deum, Psalm 116 laudate Dominum omnes gentes, et verum omnis spiritus laudet Dominum. Unde pro ista causa iustum bellum indicere potest."

52. Juan de Segovia, *Repetitio de superioritate*, fol. 159r: "Ad primum dicendum quod unum subici alteri contingit dupliciter, vel propter meritum humilitatis aut propter debitum obligationis. Primo modo, anima omnis debet se humiliari omni humanae creaturae in quantum in ea relucet imago Deo."

53. Juan de Segovia, *Repetitio de superioritate*, fol. 160v: "Tertio ne si regnum accepisset, fides catholica personae humanae adscriberet, sicut lex Machometi, quae per potentiam gladii incoepit et per eum tenetur."

54. Juan de Segovia, *Repetitio de fide catholica*, fol. 182r A: "in quo magister declarare intendit fidei sufficientiam univerali sermone non referens ad personarum specialem statum."

55. Juan de Segovia, *Repetitio de fide catholica*, fol. 182v A: "patet nunquam enim quis obtinuit eternam salutem qui no haberet in presenti vita fidem spem et karitatem sed spes est certa expectatio eterne beatitudinis."

56. Juan de Segovia, *Repetitio de fide catholica*, fol. 183r B: "Comuniter est de rebus quae natura sui excedunt facultatem intellectus humani. Ita quod humanus intellectus non potest ad illa attingere cognoscendo per se ipsam."

57. Juan de Segovia, *Repetitio de fide catholica*, fol. 183r B: "Unde voluntas informata per rationem tali rei esse credendum imperat intellectui quod assenciat rey."

53. Juan de Segovia, *Repetitio de fide catholica*, fol. 184v A: "Ex predictis pa:ere potest quanta sit differentia fidey infuse ad acquisitam et quod fides acquisita non sufficit ut quis vere dicatur fidelis."

59. Juan de Segovia, *Repetitio de fide catholica*, fol. 184v A–B: "Videtur dicendum quod fides in nobis quae fideles facit est virtus quedam spiritualis sive donum spiritus sanctus a deo gratis infusum cuius illustratione firma adhesione assentit mens humana hiis quae supra facultatem suam sunt veritatibus a deo revelatis in sacra scriptura."

60. Juan de Segovia, *Repetitio de fide catholica*, fol. 184v B: "illuminacio mentis ad sumam veritatem."

61. Juan de Segovia, *Repetitio de fide catholica*, fol. 184v B: "Fides est substantia sperandarum rerum argumento non apparencium."

62. Juan de Segovia, *Repetitio de fide catholica*, fol. 185r A: "fundamentum totius spiritualis edifficii, id est, omnium virtutum quae ordinantur ad eternam beatitudinem consequendam."

63. Juan de Segovia, *Repetitio de fide catholica*, fol. 185r A: "Unde claret quod prima omnium virtutum sit fides."

64. Juan de Segovia, *Repetitio de fide catholica*, fol. 183v B: "Puer iudeus aut alius quilibet infidelis inter christianos nutritus si talis instruatur de credibilibus et persuadeatur illi de credendo ita credet quemadmodum si esset baptizatus et fidelis."

65. Juan de Segovia, *Repetitio de fide catholica*, fol. 183v B: "Manifestum est quod multa quisque in se ipso firmiter credit etiam si illa numquam viderit nec ad illa umquam habuerit evidenciam rationis unde credit quilibet talem esse suum patrem ex multorum relatione similiter hodie multi credunt esse civitatem Hierusalem et sanctum sepulcrum etiam si numquam viderit et hoc non ob aliud quam ex eo quod id referentes homines credunt esse veraces."

66. Juan de Segovia, *Repetitio de fide catholica*, fol. 184r A: "Acquisita enim principaliter innititur miraculo raciocinationi aut persuasioni fame vel auctoritati et si credit auctoribus in sacra scriptura contentis propterea credit quod sui patres ita crediderunt qualem hodie crudelitatem videntur habere iudei. Unde dicunt se velle mori in lege patrum suorum."

67. Juan de Segovia, *Repetitio de fide catholica*, fol. 188v B: "xii fundamenta super que fundatus est murus civitatis." As mentioned in the previous chapter, he listed only eleven and then apparently did not notice that he had no number eight.

68. Juan de Segovia, *Repetitio de fide catholica*, fol. 189v B: "Et enim si Iudeus interogaretur excepta sua quam ex affectione estimat veram fidem quam veriorem reputat, scilicet christi aut machometi sectam non dubito respondebit christianam religionem et quidem aliam reputat velit nichil et fabulosam esse hoc idem multo ferventiori animo assesereret sarracenus si

comparando iudicet legem christi ad legem moysi. Item et valida ratione hoc patet enim iudeus aut alius quilibet infidelis ultimo cogitur examine ut deserat sectam suam aut mortem subeat constat magis velle suscipere fidem christi."

69. Juan de Segovia, *Repetitio de fide catholica*, fol. 190r A: "Si quis ex infidelibus propter dei reverenciam conetur in quam possit evitare opera mala et cothidie secreta oratione deprecetur deum ut dignetur illustrare animum suum et ostendere quam debeat sequi fidem non durabit tempore multo quin ex dei inspiratione quam ipse in suo corde presenciat libera mente suscipiat fidem catholicam et sicut ad recipendum inspirat deus ita adhoc ut semper in ea firmiter perseveret."

70. Juan de Segovia, *Repetitio de fide catholica*, fol. 190r B: "Et hodie etiam apparet de secta machometi quae laxat frenum concupiscencie carnalis ad vicia multa et post mortem ponit suam felicitatem in carnalibus ac fetidis delectationis. Similiter si quis Iudeorum legat secreta ibi repperit deum flere cothidie propter destructionem templi et suis lacrimis mare repleri, cum pueris ludere et alia multa racioni contraria."

71. Segovia typically used "law of nature" not in way the scholastics referred to the natural law, but rather in the way associated with Joachim of Fiore, who divided history into three eras: nature, scripture, and grace. Thus the law of nature was the state of affairs before any direct revelation of God's will had taken place.

72. Juan de Segovia, *Repetitio de fide catholica*, fol. 192r A: "Et adhuc tamen christianorum multi has sequntur delectationes carnales, non igitur miraculis opus erat ad confirmandam illam doctrinam quae carnales sequentibus delectationes promium promittit quas multi etiam cominato supplicio student summopere adimplere. Non sicut autem de religione christiana quae in multis ut declaratum est enim legi nature contraria."

73. Juan de Segovia, *Repetitio de fide catholica*, fol. 192r A: "homines bestiales in desertis morantes, omnis doctrine divine prorsus ignari."

74. Juan de Segovia, *Repetitio de fide catholica*, fol. 192r A–B: "Et quemadmodum inicium habuit per violencia armorum ita precepit ut cum ultimo positi examini de veritate legis impeteretur non racionibus miraculis vel auctoritate sed gladio legem defenderent."

75. Juan de Segovia, *Repetitio de fide catholica*, fols. 192r B–192v A: "ipse machometus in lege sua fabulosa narratione depravat omnia documenta novi et veteris testamenti et astuto consilio libros novi et veteris testamenti suis sequentibus non reliquit legendos ne per eos de falsitate sua secta redargueretur." See the classic exploration of Western perceptions of Islam: N. Daniel, *Islam and the West*. The entire volume explores these themes, but see especially chap. 5, "The Place of Self-Indulgence in the Attack on Islam," 93–99 on the witness of miracles and 145–50 on the charge that Islam spread by violence and relied on it for its sustenance.

75. Juan de Segovia, *Repetitio de fide catholica*, fol. 192r B: "Et tunc Machometus videns inter orientales et romanos ortam discordiam surrexit fingens se a deo missum pro liberatione eorum a Iugo romani imperii."

77. See the discussion in Meserve, *Empires of Islam*, 157–79.

78. Krey, "Nicholas of Lyra and Paul of Burgos on Islam," 159.

79. Alfonso de Toledo, *Invencionario*, 112. This is in Title II, Chapter 13.

80. Juan de Segovia, *Repetitio de fide catholica*, fol. 188r B: "Dico autem sola ram cum ut comuniter omnis secte in aliquo conveniant et in aliquo differant sic tamen differunt quod diversitas est respectu unius vel plurium."

81. Juan de Segovia, *Repetitio de fide catholica*, fol. 188r B: "Lex moysi et religio fidey christiane licet conveniunt in hoc quod est credere unum deum creatorem gobernatorem et differunt tamen in articulo de redemptore quia venturum credunt illi nos autem venisse."

82. Juan de Segovia, *Repetitio de fide catholica*, fol. 188r B: "Sequitur quod si probabitur viam obtinende salutis eterne quam religio christiana predicat esse adeo revelatam cum alie sint contrarie concluditur in sola christiana religione esse contentam viam salutis esse."

33. Juan de Segovia, *Repetitio de fide catholica*, fols. 191v B–192 A: "Aut tam multus populus ab inicio sine miraculis credidit et hoc videtur maxime incredible aut credidit per miracula sic videtur verum fuisse quod credidit."

34. Juan de Segovia, *Repetitio de fide catholica*, fol. 192 A: "Non igitur miraculis opus erat ad confirmandam illam doctrinam quae carnales sequentibus delectationes promium promittit quas multi etiam cominato supplicio student summopere adimplere."

85. See Schwartz, *All Can Be Saved*.

86. Schwartz, *All Can Be Saved*, 53.

87. Schwartz, *All Can Be Saved*, 3–4.

88. Schwartz, *All Can Be Saved*, 12.

89. Juan de Segovia, *Repetitio de fide catholica*, fol. 192r A: "Et adhuc tamen christianorum multi has sequuntur delectationes carnales."

90. Juan de Segovia, *Repetitio de fide catholica*, fol. 191v B: "Legitur quod antichristus mirabilia operabitur ad confirmationem sue doctrine et tum constat eam falsam esse. Respondeo iam hec in lege nostra scripta sunt sic fieri debere et tamen nichilominus suam falsam esse doctrinam."

91. Juan de Segovia, *Repetitio de fide catholica*, fol. 192v A: "Que sit causa propter quam divina providencia tam multitudinem populi permittat perire: non spectat ad presens et quidem est alterius speculationis sufficit declarare solam fidem quam predicat religio christiana a deo esse revelatam salutis viam, et quod ista racionabile et certissimum habet fundamentum ut manifesta ratione possit convinci ad obtinendam beatitudinem quae finis est humane nature. Per hanc solam rectos dirigi calles vero quaslibet sectas esse oberaciones quadam a via recta."

92. Juan de Segovia, *Repetitio de fide catholica*, fol. 192v B: "Sic in fide ab inicio est ad salutem via universalis quod dei providencia confitendo salvi fuerint gentiles."

93. Juan de Segovia, *Repetitio de fide catholica*, fol. 192v A: "Labia sacerdotis custodiunt scienciam et legem requirent ex ore eius"; "Parati semper ad satisfacionem omni poscenti nos rationem reddere de ea quae in vobis est fide."

94. Juan de Segovia, *Repetitio de fide catholica*, fol. 192v B: "Patet equidem esset manifestissimum signum negligencie et incurie de sua propria salute si simplex christianus ignoraret articulum trinitatis cum omni die se habeat per illud signare. Similiter articulum nativitatis passionis resurrectionis et ascensionis cum de hiis fiant tam preclare sollemntates in ecclesia universali."

95. Beltrán de Heredia, "El Convento de San Esteban," 106. The text of a treatise for use by priests, authored by Alba and promoted and diffused at this synod, is published in García y García, *Synodicon Hispanum IV*. The Latin version appears on pages 48–174, a Castilian version on 174–291.

96. Juan de Segovia, Letter to Jean Germain, Dec. 18, 1455, fols. 78r–78v: "Occurrit vero pro hoc momento memorie scriptoris cum de Anno xxx. Cordube constitutus auctoritate Martini pape v certam inquisicionem facerem magistrum quemdam in theologia, Calcidanensis episcopum, Augusto et Septembrio mensibus cum fuerit apud me pro examinacione computorum suorum . . . exeunte eo in civitate Thunicii ubi christiani mercatores aut milites vel aliis operarii seorsum a sarracenis inhabitant de quibus ipse curam tunc gerebat animarum dum certo anno de que ad presens non memoror pluvia deficiente in dies cresceret fames omnibus vero pactis cerimoniis suis iuxta ritum sarracenorum nulla de celo pluvia descendente nec ad hoc visa disposicione fuisse requisitum ex parte regis quod iuxta legem suam christiani facere deberent oraciones ut pluvia daretur de celo. Cum vero respondisset quod eo casu ituri essent processionaliter cruce erecta per medium civitatis ad campos ubi missa celebraretur. Illi primo responderant velle pocius sustinere famem quam videre crucem christi erectam transire per medium civitatis. Post paucos vero dies media urgente forcius, iterato requisiverant, de cruce et ceri[78v]moniis christianorum dato consensu. Et tunc indicto Ieunio christianis per dictum episcopum triduo factis confessionibus restitucionibus et reconciliacionibus inter eos cum erecta cruce exmissent in campos letaniam cantantes ut moris celebrata missa exauditi fuissent a deo pluvia habundantissime de celo descendente."

97. Juan de Segovia, Letter to Jean Germain, Dec. 18, 1455, fol. 78v: This is a difficult construction: "Affirmabat autem dictus episcopus cum de hac re sermo fieret coram rege quare pocius christiani quam sarraceni exauditi fuissent. Rege ipso [which, it seems, must be taken as dative] et quibusdam ex suis ut astantibus apparuit ex eorum sermone velut titubantibus elatere,

dixisse unum ex astucioribus Sarracenorum ex ea re pocius sectam confirmari Mahumeti, deo in hoc mundo christianis providente in temporalibus quia in alio quemadmodum sarracenis daturus non erat premium eternum."

98. Juan de Segovia, Letter to Jean Germain, Dec. 18, 1455, fol. 78v: "Unde cum liber ipse alchoran in quam pluribus locis Sarracenis promittat pro bonis operibus eternam beatitudinem, scienti librum legis eorum, difficultas predicta minime urgere videtur."

99. Juan de Segovia, Letter to Jean Germain, Dec. 18, 1455, fol. 77v: "Arguitur preterea in xvii difficultate quod ex huiusmodi communicacione per viam doctrine accreescet fortasse contumelia maior et non pugnacio quia sarraceni, percipientes tam gloriosas monarchias mundi suscepisse, fidem christianam et christianos sarracenis periciores esse in omni arte et doctrina et bello fortissimos quod omni die dubitant de nullitate secte sue et magni aliquid existimantes de catholica fide."

100. Juan de Segovia, Letter to Jean Germain, Dec. 18, 1455, fol. 78v: "Quinimmo et roborare avisamentum quia si maiores se et excellenciores christianos esse arbitruntur, prompciores reddant se ut audiant verbum de pace tractanda utrimque perpetuo."

101. Juan de Segovia, Letter to Jean Germain, Dec. 18, 1455, fols. 135r–135v: "Verum est autem quod in diebus adolescencie mee, audivi de quocam in partibus de quodam in partibus ultramarinis apostatasse uxoremque iam et filios habente et cum benedictum xiii in sua obediencia nuncupatum parte eius tractaretur eum velle redire si fieret securus de nulla penitencie imposicione, quod attendens honorem ecclesie Benedictus ille non assensit."

102. A worthwhile study of them is Courbage and Fargues, *Christians and Jews under Islam*.

103. Juan de Segovia, Letter to Jean Germain, Dec. 18, 1455, fol. 100: "Quodque sunt omnes christiani cotidie conversantes cum superioribus afris. Et amen quod paternitas vestra nec audivit conversionem Maurorum de ulteriori Africa neque Thuniciorum ymmo neque Granatorum qui omni die, ut inquit, cum hyspanis conversantur. Quantum ad hoc cum yspania sim natus et aliquando moram traxi prope confines Sarracenorum regni Granate dicere possum conversationem huiusmodi, si qua et aliquando est, minime fore ordinatam ut sarraceni de fide christianorum instruantur. Conversatione hac existente quantum ad aliqua ex minoribus mercinioniis eorum portitoribus, de christi lege vel Mahumeti secta parum aut minime doctis ita ut alios instruere possint."

104. Ladero Quesada, *Las guerras de Granada*, 29–35.

105. Juan de Segovia, Letter to Jean Germain, Dec. 18, 1455, fols. 64r–64v: "Etenim cum rex Castelle victoria obtenta in bello campali de Sarracenis rediers de mensi Julii anno xxxi. Et cum eo frater quidam regis Granate cum

multis centenariis equorum in armis regi ipsi adherens Cordubam introisset principalem de curia infantis militem rogabam quantenus verbum habere possem cum aliquo ex sapientibus suis. Respondenti vero quod ille non audⁱ eret in terra christianorum loqui cum replicassem circa hoc teneri posse [64v] modum quia secreto in camera unius ex nobis vel in campis ubi nullus audiret loqueremur. Ultimo ille dixit quamvis in societate eorum quales christiani capellanos habent ad cantandum in ecclesia plures essent nullus tamen qui loqui sciret de lege." This incident is discussed in Cabanelas Rodríguez, *Juan de Segovia y el problema islámico*, 100–102. Although Cabanelas reported that Yūsuf later became the emir of Granada, and I have elsewhere relied upon his report, this is inaccurate, as Ladero Quesada explains in his *Las guerras de Granada* that Yūsuf was executed by his rival in late April, 1432, and that his most prominent followers fled to Castile.

106. Juan de Segovia, *De mittendo gladio*, fols. 18v–20 (Consideration IV). See appendix 2 in this volume. On the dating of this manuscript, see Hernández Montes, *Obras*, 311–12.

107. Juan de Segovia, *De mittendo gladio*, fols. 19–20v, pages 241–47 in appendix 2 in this volume. This series of discussions is described in Cabanelas Rodríguez, *Juan de Segovia y el problema islámico*, 102–7.

108. Juan de Segovia, Letter to Nicholas of Cusa, Dec. 2, 1454, BAV Vat. Lat. 2923, fol. 32v: "Expertus id novi in collationibus habitis cum ambassiatore supra mentionato regis Granate, obiciente, magno cum improperio, quod christiani comederent Deum suum et a peccatis absolverent in Deum commissis."

109. Juan de Segovia, Letter to Nicholas of Cusa, Dec. 2, 1454, BAV Vat. Lat. 2923, fol. 32v: "Unde tunc intellixi in isto aliisque multis, quam magna ignorantia divini iuris laboret tota multitudo abhominantur animoque vilipendunt christianos."

110. Edwards, "*Reconquista* and Crusade in Fifteenth-Century Spain," 168–69.

111. Goñi Gaztambide, "Presencia de España en los concilios generales," 80.

Chapter Three. The Basel Years

1. See, for example, the partial list in *Cartulario* I, 366.

2. I have also not included in this tally a sermon on the Epiphany (no. 44 in Hernández Montes, *Obras*); a collection of the decrees of the Council of Constance, which he made at Basel's request; nor the glosses and notations in his and others' works, which Hernández Montes listed as a sepaⁱ

rate work (no. 81). See the list by theme in *Obras*, 269, which shows that the overwhelming majority of his works were related to intraecclesial matters (presidency of the council, authority in the church, etc.). Other topics he addressed as part of his participation in the council were the discussions with the Greeks and Hussites and the controversy surrounding the immaculate conception.

3. The date for the *Historia* is uncertain, but it is likely that he began it during the council and continued to work on it for a few years after, probably with interruptions. In any case, he left it incomplete. The last events recorded were those in the spring of 1444. Hernández Montes thought that this was probably one of the projects that Segovia abandoned upon hearing the news of the fall of Constantinople; see his discussion in *Obras*, 307–8, no. 51. The *Historia* has been published in *Monumenta Conciliorum Generalium*, s. XV, vols. 2–4 (Vienna, 1873–1935). As Jesse Mann has noted, a new edition is sorely needed; see his "The Devilish Pope," 187n15. The most extensive study of the *Historia* is Fromherz, *Johannes von Segovia*. Hernández Montes argued convincingly (in "En busca de manuscritos de la donación de Juan de Segovia") that volume e I 8 at the Escorial, the first of a two-volume set containing this history, was one of the volumes in Juan's own library and part of his donation to the University of Salamanca. The volume, which I have examined, contains marginal notes in Juan's hand. It is not known how or when it arrived at the Escorial.

4. A. Black, *Council and Commune*, 2.

5. Piccolomini, *De Gestis Concilii Basiliensis Commentariorum*, 141.

6. See the discussion of these years in Housley, *The Later Crusades*, 80–83.

7. See, for example, the 1436 decrees in the Archivo General de Simancas (AGS), Estado, Francia, Legajo K-1711, fols. 40v–42r and 8r–12r, summaries of which are in Álvarez Palenzuela, *La situación europea*, documents 82 and 83, pp. 321–22.

8. Hay, *Europe in the Fourteenth and Fifteenth Centuries*, 282. See the discussion in Bisaha, *Creating East and West*, 23–25.

9. Hay, *Europe in the Fourteenth and Fifteenth Centuries*, 239–41 and 344–52. For more on the conflict in Bohemia, see the helpful discussion and notes in Housley, *Religious Warfare in Europe*, chap. 2 (pp. 33–61).

10. Juan de Segovia, Letter to Jean Germain, Dec. 18, 1455, fol. 56r: "Scio cum de anno xxviii° Io. pulchri nepotis subdyaconis pape Martini et ego fuerimus missi ad hyspanie reges et prelatos exhortandos ac requirendos pro collectione decime tunc imposite in subsidium fidei contra persecutionem Bohemorum dum redeunte illo ad curiam Romanam remansi pro execuendis literis quibusdam apostolicis super quibus agere specialiter debui

cum prelatis quod indetractionem impositionis illeus fuit michi dictum viam belli congruam minime esse ad hereticorum reductionem. Porro quam congrua fuerit via tractatus pacis et doctrine in facto Bohemorum et aliam viam minime profuisse."

11. Hay, *Europe in the Fourteenth and Fifteenth Centuries*, 300–305.

12. On the implications of considering Constance legitimate, see the excellent article by Oakley, "The 'New Conciliarism' and Its Implications." For a historical perspective on the status of Constance, see Izbicki, "Papalist Reaction to the Council of Constance."

13. Hay, *Europe in the Fourteenth and Fifteenth Centuries*, 305–7.

14. For an illuminating discussion on the favors Martin V bestowed on Spaniards who had been instrumental in his election, see Goñi Gaztambide, "Recompensas de Martín V a sus electores españoles." The article is followed by the transcriptions of fourteen documents from the Vatican registers.

15. A. Black, *Council and Commune*, 17; Hay, *Europe in the Fourteenth and Fifteenth Centuries*, 306–9. The decrees remain controversial. The issue is whether they were meant as emergency measures, valid only at that time or in the case of future schisms, or instead were intended as binding and lasting dogmatic decrees on the authority of a council over a pope. Scholars who have argued the former view include Franzen, especially in "Das Konzil der Einheit," esp. 103–110, and Baumer, "Die Interpretation und Verbindlichkeit." Those who argue that the council meant these decrees to have dogmatic status and to be enduringly valid include Oakley in "The 'New Conciliarism' and Its Implications"; Vooght, "Le conciliarisme aux conciles de Constance et de Bâle," in Botte et. al, and "Le conciliarisme aux conciles de Constance et de Bâle," *Irenikon*; Stieber, *Pope Eugenius IV*, 6–8; and Küng, *Structures of the Church*.

16. A. Black, *Council and Commune*, 18.

17. The Council of Pavia-Siena has received significantly less attention from scholars than Constance or Basel. For a recent assessment of it and an argument that it deserves more study, see Ferguson, "The Council of Pavia-Siena and Medieval Conciliarism."

18. Ferguson, "The Council of Pavia-Siena and Medieval Conciliarism," 13; Stieber, *Pope Eugenius IV*, 11. On the reform agenda at Constance, see Stump, *The Reforms of the Council of Constance*.

19. Minnich, "Councils of the Catholic Reformation," 313.

20. Minnich, "Councils of the Catholic Reformation," 313.

21. Ourliac, "Martin V, Eugène IV et le Concile de Bâle," 272.

22. *Cartulario* I, 371.

23. Some 1300 by a count done in 1985 by Meuthen, *Das Basler Konzil*, 5. The best annotated bibliography remains the one in Stieber, *Pope Eugenius IV*, 378–404, but see Helmrath, *Das Basler Konzil*, for more recent works.

24. Christianson, "Aeneas Sylvius Piccolomini and the Historiography of the Council of Basel," 157.

25. Oberman, *The Dawn of the Reformation*, 30–31.

26. *Cartulario* I, 363. I think fall of 1431 is more likely, since the first in a string of several bulls containing concessions to Segovia was dated Dec. 17. This is published in *Bulario* II, #832.

27. *Cartulario* I, 363–64.

28. A. Black, *Council and Commune*, 38. These delegates included, most notably, Jean Beaupère, a theologian and former colleague of Jean Gerson (d. 1429), the former chancellor of Paris and leading theorist of conciliarism who had been at Pisa and Constance. Other delegates to Basel from Paris were theologians Nicholas Lamy, Thomas Courcelles, and Denis Sabrovois.

29. Stieber, *Pope Eugenius IV*, 12.

30. A. Black, *Council and Commune*, 27.

31. On Segovia's esteem for Cesarini, see Fromherz, *Johannes von Segovia*, esp. 101–19. On Cesarini's career in the council and the scholarly discussion concerning what to make of the contradictions evident there, see Christianson, *Cesarini*.

32. Fromherz, *Johannes von Segovia*, 103.

33. From April 1432 to April 1433, the number of incorporated members went from 81 to about 420. See the chart in A. Black, *Council and Commune*, 32.

34. Stieber, *Pope Eugenius IV*, 12–18.

35. A. Black, *Council and Commune*, 119; Fromherz, *Johannes von Segovia*, 24.

36. Juan de Segovia, *Donatio*, 82: "Et id singulare censui munus, quia ejusdem Studii unicus fui orator deputatus ad interessendum generali, que celebrari tunc incipiebat, Basiliensi synodo, in qua, tanquam talem incorporari distuli, donec insignissima affuit ambassiata regia; et tunc locum obtinui inmediatum ambassiatoribus studii Parisiensis."

37. Hernández Montes, *Biblioteca*, 142–43.

38. Some authors, among them Nicolás Antonio, J. Haller, and Werner Krämer, have assumed that he was, but see the convincing refutation of this idea in Hernández Montes, *Biblioteca*, 142–45. The reports and correspondence of Juan II's delegation are in AGS, Estado, Francia, Legajo K-1711, and my own study of this compilation revealed that Juan de Segovia's name does not appear even once in this large volume.

39. See, for example, his description of Juan's 1436 *repetitio* in Hernández Montes, *Obras*, 271, and his discussion of a likely date for Juan's *Tractatus decem avisamentorum ex Sacra Scriptura de sanctitate ecclesiae et generalis concilii auctoritate* (275), where Hernández Montes argued against one

suggestion of 1433 on the grounds that Juan did not have such strongly conciliar views that early.

40. Stieber, *Pope Eugenius IV*, 12, 444–45.

41. A. Black, *Council and Commune*, 119.

42. This work has also had the title *Relatio in deputatione fidei super
materia bullarum praesidentia*. Juan was asked to publish it, so several manuscript copies exist. There is also a published edition: P. Ladner, "Johannes von
Segovias Stellung zur Präsidentenfrage des Basler Konzils," *Zeitschrift für
Schweizerische Kirchengeschichte* (*Revue d'Histoire ecclésiastique suisse*) 62
(1968): 1–113. See Hernández Montes, *Obras*, #6, pp. 273–74, and A. Black,
Council and Commune, 119.

43. Rucquoi, "Democratie ou monarchie," 252–55.

44. A. Black, *Council and Commune*, 16.

45. A. Black, *Council and Commune*, 119.

46. These phrases appear in his *Tractatus de tribus veritatibus fidei*,
fol. 95v. This work remains unpublished. See Hernández Montes, *Biblioteca*, 223.

47. Stieber, *Pope Eugenius IV*, 78.

48. Eugene IV's bull praising the *studium* for severing its ties with Juan
de Segovia as representative was dated January 25, 1441. ASV Reg. Vat. 359,
fol. 114, in *Bulario* II, #987.

49. This man is identified as the abbot of Saint Martin's, a designation
inconsistent with any of the other documentation related to "my" Juan. In
Cartulario I, 362, Beltrán de Heredia noted that there were numerous men
named Juan Alfonso and Juan de Segovia. Although Juan's full name was
Juan Alfonso de Segovia, which I have already discussed in chapter 1, I think
this abbott of Saint Martin's is simply another man with the same name. See
the excellent discussion in Hernández Montes, *Biblioteca*, 143, and the version he was countering in Suárez Fernández, *Castilla, el cisma y la crisis conciliar*, 112, and Serrano, *Los conversos don Pablo de Santa María y don Alfonso
de Cartagena*, 134–35. In his *La situación europea*, Álvarez Palenzuela repeated the two-delegation theory of Suárez Fernández, his teacher.

50. Stieber, *Pope Eugenius IV*, 20; Álvarez Palenzuela, *La situación europea*, 53.

51. AGS, Estado, Francia, Legajo K-1711, fols. 445r–445v.

52. Álvarez Palenzuela noted this and yet persisted in following Suárez
Fernández in assuming that the earlier group from Castile represented the
Crown. See Álvarez Palenzuela, *La situación europea*, 55.

53. ASV Reg. Vat. 370, fol. 124v, contains a bull from Eugene IV to
Juan II in which the pope expressed his surprise at hearing that the king intended to send representatives to Basel even though the council had been

"revoked" by Eugene himself, and that Juan had not consulted him. He asked and exhorted (*requirimus et hortamur*) that the king direct those delegates to go to Rome first, and that he send them to Bologna, where the pope intended to convene a council. This was dated Jan. 30, 1433. It is published in *Bulario* II #858 and Súarez Fernández, *Castilla, el cisma y la crisis conciliar*, 338–39. The pope also wrote to Alvaro de Luna making the same point (RV 370, 125r–125v, Jan. 30, 1433, in Suárez Fernández, 340), and to the bishops of Spain directing them to impede the departure of delegates from Juan II to Basel (RV 370, fol. 125v, Feb. 1, 1433, in Suárez Fernández, 342–43).

54. AGS, Estado, Francia, Legajo K-1711, fols. 218r–220v.

55. AGS, Estado, Francia, Legajo K-1711, fols. 510r–511r (both letters). See Álvarez Palenzuela, *La situación europea*, 291, and Jedin and Dolan, *Handbook of Church History*, 4:483.

56. Still, it must be noted that when Juan II finally sent a delegation, he placed Alfonso Carrillo, a prelate not exactly deferential to papal authority, at the head of it. Carrillo was in a dispute with the pope over the office of vicar in the region of Avignon, where he had been active in various endeavors, and where the local people had requested him as vicar. Ignoring custom, Pope Eugene IV gave this office and several others, traditionally all held by different people, to his nephew. The Avignonese appealed to the council, which in its fourth session issued a decree naming Carrillo to the position. This was well before Carrillo and his delegation arrived at the council. The pope would later complain to the king about Carrillo's betrayal. See the account in Álvarez Palenzuela, *La situación europea*, 29–30, 35–37.

57. Hernández Montes (*Obras*, 280) compared this work to the *Concordantiae maiores* of Hugh of St. Cher and Conrad of Halberstadt, who listed the declinable words.

58. A. Black, *Council and Commune*, 120. The writings listed in this paragraph, including whether any extant manuscripts or published editions exist, are discussed in Hernández Montes, *Obras*, and they are respectively nos. 15 (*Excerptum ex "Summa in quaestionibus armenorum"*), 17 (*Tractatus de processione Spiritus Sancti a Patre et Filio*), 19 (*Allegationes quod communio sub utraque non est de necessitate divini praecepti quantum ad plebem*), 20 (*Allegationes utrum licita communio Eucharistiae sit sub altera tantum specie*), 16 (*Concordantiae dictionum indeclinabilium Bibliae*). Hernández Montes listed another text, the *Tractatus de profunda speculatione emanationis divinarum personarum* (#18), which might have originated in this period, but could have been later. Segovia also wrote on some other topics during these years, such as in defense of the immaculate conception (against the Dominicans, who were arguing that it was an unfounded belief), also as part of his work on the faith committee.

59. Nicholas argued against the Hussite demand that everyone be allowed to receive communion under both species, bread and wine, in a treatise that has been recently translated. See Nicholas of Cusa, "To the Bohemians: On the Use of Communion," in Izbicki, *Nicholas of Cusa*, Text 1 and the introductory notes on ix–x.

60. Juan de Segovia, *Historia*, Escorial e I 8, fol. 1r: "Sed et hussitarum armata heresis que in regno Bohemie a tempore finiti concilii Constanciensis presertim in profundum veniens peccatorum arma susceperat infelicibus continue aucta crementes semper ac magis vexabat ecclesiam acerrima persecucione non tam verbo dogmatizans quam igne et gladio necdum regni illius civitates et oppida, sed etiam regiones per cicuitum suis erroribus non assencientes devastans." This history, which ends in the spring of 1444, has no certain date. See the discussion in Hernández Montes, *Obras*, 307–8, where he agreed with earlier scholars who had suggested that most of the work was done after 1450, although Hernández Montes believed that Segovia likely began to plan the work during the council. At least twelve copies of this work exist, and it was published in the *Monumenta Conciliorum Generalium saeculi XV*, vols. 2–4 (Vienna, 1873–1935). These lines appear in this edition, vol. 2, Book I, Chapter 2, p. 2.

61. Juan de Segovia, *Historia*, MC 1:5. This wording is from part of the title he gave to this chapter: "De insultacionibus hereticorum Bohemorum contra fidem et ecclesiam."

62. Juan de Segovia, *Historia*, MC 1:5: "Qui si haberent viam rectam et diuinam caritatem, accipientes libro diuine scripture, venirent ad eos quomodo apostoli ad paganos cum armis verbi diuini, et hoc erat eorum desiderium, quod si in spiritu lenitatis, vt inquit apostolus, episcopi et sacerdotes probarent se iustos esse et eos iniustos, si nollent recipere informacionem, tunc possent in adiutorium recipere reges, principes, dominos et ciuitates imperiales."

63. Juan de Segovia, *Historia*, MC 1:11: "quo accinctos se esse gloriabantur, gladio diuini verbi recte intellecti suarum caput heresum a corpore separaretur."

64. Hernández Montes, "En busca de manuscritos de la donación de Juan de Segovia," 59.

65. Juan de Segovia, *Historia*, Escorial e I 8, fol. 26v. In the normal body of the text: "Item conmemorarent de literis missis ad regem polonie et ducem lithuanie quo modo concilium vellet interponere vices suas ad eorum pacem quia timendum erat ne heretici alteri parti adhererent." In the margin: "Similiter et turci in desolacionem maximam totius christianitatis." The lines cited here from the body of the *Historia* appear in MC 1:90.

66. Hernández Montes, *Obras*, 305.

67. Juan de Segovia, *Liber de magna auctoritate*, 381: "Id vero unum silencio preterire nequimus, cum iam ab annis trecentis pluries et permaxime expediciones exercituum christianorum adversus Sarracenos tam per terram quam per mare facte sint et paululum profuere quantum ad eam, que intendebatur, terre sancte liberacionem [f. 104r] et exterminacionem Machometice suorumque sectatorum."

68. Juan de Segovia, *Liber de magna auctoritate*, 382: "ut via belli plurimum difficilis censeatur, quod inutile atque inconsultum forte non esset alium temptare modum reduccionis eorum. Non enim semper gladio, sed aliis multis sepe modis vincitur inimicus illaque permaxima esset victoria: operam dare ad salvandas eorum animas. Nempe vidimus diebus nostris, quod adversum Hussitas aliosque hereticos regni Bohemie igne et gladio universa in circuitu vastantes parum invaluere multi et maximi exercitus fidelium. Sed quando ad ecclesie exhortacionem acquieverunt, ut raciocinacione publica differencie examinarentur, notissimum est cessasse eos ab ea, quam primo adversus confines suorum errorum ob causam inferebant persecucionem."

69. Christianson, *Cesarini*, 23–24.

70. Juan de Segovia, Letter to Jean Germain, Dec. 18, 1455, fol. 69r: "sed scio me audivisse a Reverendissimo domino Juliano, concilii presidente, quod dum exercitu congregato pro cinctus ipse, ingredi volens aut ingressus bohemie regnum, literas mandasset procopio Capitaneo Thaboritarum ad ea que pacis exortans. Respondisse illum, 'Cum gladio evaginato ad me venis et pacem petis,' unde postea attenciori considerans mente Julianus mutato animo alter effectus, ut dicebat, recognovit alium esse tendendum modum convenientem magis pro reductione bohemorum quam per modum vindicte intendere ad eorum extermina[69v]cionem. Sicut et fecit destinata ad eos epistola sinodali omni humilitate et christiana caritate que ut notissimum tunc fuit hodieque illis est qui gesta noverunt multo profuit amplius ad eorum conversionem quam multi potentissimi excercitus christianorum qui regnum illud ingressi turpi fuga rediere et cum permaximis dampnis."

71. Christianson, *Cesarini*, 23.

72. The text is in Juan de Segovia, *Historia*, MC 2:109–17. See the discussion in Christianson, *Cesarini*, 45–51.

73. Juan de Segovia, Letter to Jean Germain, Dec. 18, 1455, fol. 55v: "Hiis a ligatam destino epistolam magni Iuliani apostolici in Basiliensis concilio presidentis papam acerrime informantis quam licitum meritoriumque utileque ac necesarium fuit intendere ad Bohemorum reductionem per viam tractatus pacis et doctrine."

74. Christianson, *Cesarini*, 26.

75. Juan de Segovia, *Historia*, MC 2:431–32, excerpted in Crowder, *Unity, Heresy and Reform*, 158.

76. Jedin and Dolan, *Handbook of Church History*, 4:476; Stieber, *Pope Eugenius IV*, 117. These Compacts made it possible for Sigismund, a Catholic king, to gain control of Bohemia. Stieber explained that because the status and acceptance of the Compacts depended upon the legitimacy of Basel, these negotiations made Sigismund a stakeholder in the success of the council.

77. Juan de Segovia, *Historia*, MC 2:894: "Sancta synodus in die sancti Jacobi cum diuina celebrarentur, recepit litteras oratorum suorum in Bohemiam destinatorum de finali concordia et pace habita cum Bohemis; vnde post missam fuit decantatus ymnus Te Deum laudamus in iubilo vocis et organis. Eiusmodi litterarum sub data Iglauie vᵃ huius effectus erat, vt exultaret et iubilaret synodus sacrosancta altissimo depromens graciarum acciones, quoniam desideratus ecce dies adveniset, quo laborum suorum meterent fructus in area dominica plenos reportaturi manipulos."

78. Jedin and Dolan, *Handbook of Church History*, 4:476.

79. Christianson, *Cesarini*, 31, 45.

80. Juan de Segovia, *Historia*, MC 2:432, excerpted in Crowder, *Unity, Heresy and Reform, 1378–1460*, 159.

81. Juan de Segovia, *Historia*, MC 2:753: "Vnde et aliam rei publice christiane Deo propicio vtilitatem accrescere confidimus, quoniam ex hac unione, cum facta fuerit, plurimos ex nefanda Machometi secta ad fidem catholicam conuerti sperandum est."

82. Stieber, *Pope Eugenius IV*, 35–39.

83. Setton, *The Papacy and the Levant*, 2:53.

84. Setton, *The Papacy and the Levant*, 2:537.

85. Stieber, *Pope Eugenius IV*, 36–37.

86. Bull of Eugene IV (*Doctoris gencium*), Sept. 18, 1437, document 29 in Crowder, *Unity, Heresy and Reform*, 161.

87. Stieber, *Pope Eugenius IV*, 39. Segovia also recognized this as a turning point and devoted considerable space to these developments in his history of the council. For his discussion of the events surrounding this vote, see his *Historia*, MC 2:950–92. The atmosphere at Basel surrounding the transfer to Ferrara was even more soured by the fact that the pope's main representative at Basel, the archbishop of Taranto, stole the official seal of the council, used it to falsely certify the minority opinion as the decision of the council, and sent it to the pope.

88. Stieber, *Pope Eugenius IV*, 39; Hay, *Europe in the Fourteenth and Fifteenth Centuries*, 310.

89. See the extensive discussion in Christianson, *Cesarini*, 149–80.

90. Fromherz, *Johannes von Segovia*, 119; Juan de Segovia, *Historia*, MC 2:1319. See Genesis 38 for the story of Tamar.

91. A. Black, *Council and Commune*, 120.

92. A. Black, *Council and Commune*, 120.

93. Hernández Montes, *Obras*, 284.

94. Izbicki, *Nicholas of Cusa*, vii–viii. For an extended examination of Nicholas of Cusa's switch in allegiance, see Biechler, "Conciliar Movement."

95. Nicholas of Cusa, Oration at the Diet of Frankfurt, §17, p. 183.

96. Juan de Segovia, Letter to Nicholas of Cusa, Dec. 2, 1454, BUS 19, fol. 169r: "Etenim cum vestra concessione librum ipsum alchoran habuerim anno xxxvii sepe que in eo legeram et errores excerperam." See the discussion in Hernández Montes, *Biblioteca*, 172. There was also a chained copy that he examined in a library in Germany that same year. Juan de Segovia, *Prefacio in translationem*, fol. 188v: "Et ex tunc multorum percepi relatione, idque ipse agnovi, quod paucissimi christianorum librum ipsum tenent quodque in paucissimis reperitur librariis, de quarum una, in Germania, librum incathenatum habui, anno XXXVII [1437] copiarique feci."

97. Stieber, *Pope Eugenius IV*, 42. Stieber criticized Gill (*The Council of Florence*) for failing to consider the fact that Florence had such little representation from church leaders outside Italy or from traditionally respected faculties of theology, such as Paris.

98. Stieber, *Pope Eugenius IV*, 173–83.

99. Stieber, *Pope Eugenius IV*, 35–39. He was deposed for being a heretic (because Basel had by then declared *Haec sancta* and *Frequens* to be articles of faith), for mismanagement of his office, and for opposition to ecclesiastical reform. See Stieber's discussion on 44–56.

100. Juan de Segovia, *Historia*, in MC 3:406: "et vnanimi deliberacione omnium sacrarum deputacionum nominati et electi sunt Thomas abbas de Scocia, Iohannnes de Segobia et Thomas de Corcellis pro electoribus summi pontificis, data eis plenaria facultate, si vellent, assumendi secum vnum, duo uel res alios."

101. Piccolomini, Letter to Francesco Pizzolpaso, Oct. 29, 1439, 122.

102. In the museum at the Grand Seminaire de Maurienne, formerly the bishop's palace in St. Jean Maurienne, one can see a hat Segovia was allegedly wearing on that trip.

103. Stieber, *Pope Eugenius IV*, 190. See the colorful account of the papal coronation festivities in Piccolomini, Letter to Juan de Segovia, August 13, 1440, 125–31.

104. Nicholas of Cusa, Oration at the Diet of Frankfurt, §§46–47, pp. 235–36.

105. Juan de Segovia, *Historia*, MC 3:427: "Post prandium autem circa horam terciam, ruptis cum securibus fenestris supra ostium conclauis posita cruce in media fenestra, stantibus prelatis in pluuialibus et mitris, aliisque electoribus in suis habitibus, Arelatensis ex fenestra ad multitudinem populi

alta voce clamuit dicens: Annuncio vobis gaudium magnum. Summarie post hoc referens de eleccione facta in personam ducis breuissime autem virtutes eius commemorans contestabatur eleccionem hanc esse ad gloriam Dei, ecclesie vtilitatem, consolacionem concilii et ciuitatis Basiliensis, cuius prudenti regimine tamdiu in ea tanta libertate concilium permanserat. Interpretacione denique facta theutonico ydeomate per decanum Basiliensem intonante Arelatensi cantatum est *Te deum laudamus* per electores adhuc constitutos in conclaui, a quo, resonante produccius pulsacione campanarum tocius ciuitatis, exierunt hora quarta, recipiente eos processione concilii et omnium collegiorum ciuitatis armatorumque multitudine, circa conclaue et in platea sistente, proutque in ingressu, bini et bini intrarunt ecclesiam."

106. A. Black, *Council and Commune*, 121.

107. Stieber, *Pope Eugenius IV*, 190–91, 343–47.

108. Stieber, *Pope Eugenius IV*, 147–48, 156, 185, 224–30, 237–40, 250; A. Black, *Council and Commune*, 120–22.

109. Piccolomini, *De Gestis Concilii Basiliensis Commentariorum*, 23 and 25. Panormitanus was one of the participants at Basel whose views could change from one occasion to the next. A canonist who tried to bring more theology into legal discussions of church matters, he was in fact one of Basel's leaders, despite his intervention against deposing the pope in 1439. See the discussion in A. Black, *Council and Commune*, chap. 6, esp. 94–95.

110. Juan's works from this period (1437–49) are too numerous to list here, but see Hernández Montes, *Obras*, nos. 22–48, and the discussion of the dating of these works in Kathrin Utz, "Zur Chronologie der kirchenpolitischen Traktate." Also see Mann's criticisms of Utz's article in his "The Historian and the Truths."

111. Mann, "The Historian and the Truths," 174. For further discussion and examples of texts Juan recycled, see pp. 252–53 and 272.

112. Mann, "The Historian and the Truths," 151.

113. Stieber, *Pope Eugenius IV*, 223; Mann, "The Historian and the Truths," 252–53.

114. Stieber, *Pope Eugenius IV*, 227.

115. Stieber, *Pope Eugenius IV*, 228.

116. Stieber, *Pope Eugenius IV*, 228.

117. Mann, "The Historian and the Truths," 271; Stieber, *Pope Eugenius IV*, 228–29. This work is #32 in Hernández Montes, *Obras*.

118. Mann, "The Historian and the Truths," 272.

119. Juan de Segovia, *Explanatio*, §2, 308–9: "ut omnibus catholicis evidenter constet, quam racionabiliter sancta sinodus eum iudicavit hereticum et quam necesse sit ad conservacionem religionis christiane prefatam acceptari sentenciam ipsumque Gabrielm devitari ab omnibus tamquam hereticum" (fol. 220v). The English translation is in Mann, 194.

120. Juan de Segovia, *Explanatio*, §3, 309–10.

121. Juan de Segovia, *Explanatio*, §10 and §11, 315–17.

122. These are discussed at length in the *Explanatio*. See Mann's discussion in "The Historian and the Truths," 201–232.

123. See Mann, "William of Ockham, Juan de Segovia, and Heretical Pertinacity," 67–88.

124. Mann, "Historian and the Truths," 28–30; Stieber, *Pope Eugenius IV,* 56; Helmrath, *Das Basler Konzil*, 474. For Nicholas of Cusa's argument against this line of reasoning, see his Oration at the Diet of Frankfurt, esp. §§34–42, pp. 208–27.

125. Mann, "The Historian and the Truths," 197–98.

126. Mann, "The Historian and the Truths," 197.

127. See, for example, A. Black, *Council and Commune*, 128–32; Hernández Montes, *Biblioteca*, 60–62.

128. Juan de Segovia, *Explanatio,* §48, 349: "Est enim Sacra Scriptura fundamentum omnium veritatum catholicarum. Veritas autem de potestate concilii est de re spirituali et fundatur in evangelio, Mt. XVIII: Ubi sunt duo vel tres congregati in nomine meo, ibi ego sum in medio eorum" (fols. 231r–231v).

129. Juan de Segovia, *Explanatio*, §48, 349: "Secundo in eodem capitulo: Amen dico vobis, quecumque ligaveritis super terram etc. Tercio Io. XXI: Quorum remiseritis peccata, remissa erunt, et quorum retinueritis, retenta sunt etc." (fol. 231v).

130. A. Black, *Council and Commune*, 129–30.

131. Juan de Segovia, *Explanatio*, §48, 349: "Quarto, Lc. X; Qui vos audit, me audit, et qui vos spernit, me spernit" (fol. 231v).

132. Juan de Segovia, *Explanatio,* §48, 349–50: "Fundatur eciam in quampluribus locis Actuum Apostolorum et specialiter I, VI, XV, XX et XXI capitulis, ubi expresse habetur de celebracione plurium conciliorum sive plurium accionum eiusdem continuati concilii temporibus suis" (fol. 231v).

133. Juan de Segovia, *Explanatio*, §10, 315–16: "Unde quia vix aut nullum maius periculum in christiana religione assignari potest quam libere inficiens erronea doctrina, consequenter dicendum est, quod resistere pape heretico est summe meritorium, quia non solum eius, sed et anime multorum secum abberancium resistendo eidem salvantur a morte, Iac. V: Fratres mei, si quis ex vobis erraverit a veritate et converterit quis eum, scire debet quoniam, qui converti fecerit peccatorem ab errore vie sue, salvabit animam eius a morte et operi<e>t multitudinem peccatorum" (fol. 222v).

134. Juan de Segovia, *Explanatio*, §10, 316: "Quando arguit Petrum, qui summus pontifex erat, a veritate fidei deviare allegans, quod suo exemplo alios cogeret ad imitandum, resistit ei in faciem, dicendo expresse quod erat reprehensibilis, quia non ambulabat ad veritatem evangelii quodque nec per

unam horam cessit, quin eidem resisteret" (fol. 222v). See Galatians 2:11–14. See Mann's discussion of Juan's use of this verse on 159, where he suggests that Segovia might have been influenced by Ockham's treatment of it in the *Dialogus*.

135. Juan de Segovia, *Explanatio*, §10, 316: "Item, ut docet ipse Petrus, quoniam adversarius noster diabolus tamquam leo rugiens circuit querens quem devoret, catholici ei resistere debent maxime fortes in fide. Leo autem precipue rugit in christiana religione, quando papa hereticus nititur involvere suo errori omnem populum [fol. 223r] fidelem" (fols. 222v–223r).

136. Juan de Segovia, *Explanatio*, §20, 325: "Hii autem specialiter declarantur ad Tit. III c.: Hereticum hominem post primam et secundam correccionem devita, quia subversus est, qui eiusmodi est, et deli<n>quit proprio iudicio condempnatus" (fol. 225r). See also Mann's discussion on 159.

137. Juan de Segovia, *Explanatio*, §11, 316: "Sicut ergo maxime meritorium est resistere pape heretico, ita non resistere errori pape heretici manifesti aut notorii, maxime ei, qui verbo, exemplo aut facto potuit predicare et defendere veritatem fidei, est plenum omni dampnacione, Iac. IV: Scienti bonum facere et non facienti peccatum est illi" (fol. 223r).

138. For a general discussion of the sources in this work, see Mann, "The Historian and the Truths," 157–93.

139. Mann, "The Historian and the Truths," 156; A. Black, *Council and Commune*, 128. See also Hernández Montes, *Biblioteca*, 60–62.

140. See Tierney, *Foundations of Conciliar Theory*.

141. A. Black, *Council and Commune*, 10–11, 44.

142. This was the case, for example, with Panormitanus, a canon lawyer at Basel who represented contradictory views due to the various mandates he held. See the discussion in Watanabe, "Authority and Consent in Church Government."

143. Ryan, *The Apostolic Conciliarism of Jean Gerson*, 44; Helmrath, *Das Basler Konzil*, 417–20. Bentley has also noted the lack of attention by scholars to later medieval exegesis. See the discussion in his *Humanists and Holy Writ*, 21–22.

144. Nicholas of Cusa, Oration at the Diet of Frankfurt, §19, p. 187.

145. Nicholas of Cusa, Oration at the Diet of Frankfurt, §20, p. 189.

146. Ryan, *The Apostolic Conciliarism of Jean Gerson*, 49.

147. See, for example, the discussion in Ryan, *The Apostolic Conciliarism of Jean Gerson*, 40–77, and Flanagin, "God's Divine Law."

148. Leff, "The Apostolic Ideal in Later Medieval Ecclesiology," 71.

149. Ryan, *The Apostolic Conciliarism of Jean Gerson*, 40.

150. Leff, "The Apostolic Ideal in Later Medieval Ecclesiology," 72.

151. See Leff, "The Apostolic Ideal in Later Medieval Ecclesiology," 81–82, and "The Making of the Myth of a True Church."

152. Leff, "The Making of the Myth of the True Church," 1.

153. Hendrix, "In Quest of the *Vera Ecclesia*," 348.

154. Hendrix, "In Quest of the *Vera Ecclesia*," 349.

155. Leff, "The Making of the Myth of the True Church," 3.

156. Bentley, *Humanists and Holy Writ*, 70–74.

157. Bentley, *Humanists and Holy Writ*, 124.

158. See Stieber, *Pope Eugenius IV,* 322–30, for the events surrounding the closure, in which Charles VII of France played an important role.

159. Herández Montes, *Obras*, 308.

160. Fromherz, *Johannes von Segovia*, 150.

161. Juan de Segovia, *Liber de magna auctoritate,* 224: "Ex qua unitate capitis sequatur—necesse est—unitas corporis, quia sicut unum caput duo corpora vivificare non potest, ita nec corpus unum duplici capite gubernari. Si iam monstruosum non fuerit, quando aliquando visum est in corpore uno duo fuisse capita."

162. Juan de Segovia, *Liber de magna auctoritate,* 225: "Cuius caput unicum est Dominus noster Ihesus Christus Paulo id attestante frequentissime in epistolis suis, propter quod ipsa unitas capitis ecclesiam, que huius capitis corpus est, unicam reddit et indivisam."

163. Tierney, *Church Law and Constitutional Thought*, ix, 253.

164. Nicholas of Cusa, Oration at the Diet of Frankfurt, §34, p. 209.

165. Juan de Segovia, *Liber de magna auctoritate,* 225: "Eadem proinde pariter racione secta Mahometi ab ecclesia substancialiter differt plus Mahometo quam credere Christo volens nec enim fieri potest, ut sint unum corpus membra renuencia subesse capiti uno."

166. If so, he was not alone in using the example of the Muslims to criticize Christians. One Basel colleague, John-Jerome of Prague, wrote that the Hussites' destruction of Christian abbeys made them worse than the Saracens because at least the Saracens attacked out of ignorance. See Hyland, "Abbot John-Jerome of Prague," 28. In a 1398 poem containing a dream-vision written as a social commentary, entitled *Apparicion Maistre Jehan de Meun*, Honorat Bovet put the most stinging criticism of Christian society in the dialogue lines of a Saracen nobleman. See the discussion by Michael Hanly in the introduction to his *Medieval Muslims, Christians, and Jews in Dialogue*, 55–56.

Chapter 4. *Converting Fellow Christians*

1. N. Daniel, *Islam and the West*, 307.

2. Tolan, *Saracens*, 276.

3. Cabanelas Rodríguez, *Juan de Segovia y el problema islámico*, 93.

4. Bisaha, *Creating East and West*, especially chaps. 1–2.

5. Bisaha, *Creating East and West*, 144.

6. Gros, *Histoire du diocèse de Maurienne*, 2:131. Gros did not cite an archival record giving this information, and my own explorations in the Archives Départementales de Savoie in Chambery did not yield such a find. However, this is consistent with information contained in a booklet dated 1680 with the title *Historia ecclesiae, episcoporum et diocesis Maurianensis, a reverendo Jacobo Dumé, maurianensi canonico*. This is Chambery, ADS, 3G, item 184. A history of Maurienne's bishops begins on fol. 23v. Juan appears on fol. 26v. In contrast to much longer descriptions of the episcopates of Louis de La Palud and Guillaume d'Estouteville, Segovia's entry fills less than four lines and reads simply, "Joannes de Segovia sti callixti qui obiit Eytone fuit provisus a Nicolas v de Episcopatu maurianensi quem postea idem Summus pontifex retraxit provisionem allasi [?] Joannis de Archiepiscopatu cesariensi et de nro sequanti ut constat ex bulla provisionis in lib. Citato fol. 44." The cited book was Michaelis Boissonis, *Cathalogus e maurieanensium episcoporum*. A booklet dated 1741 (Chambery, ADS, 3G, item 185) entitled *Brieve notice du Diocese de Maurienne* fails to mention Juan de Segovia at all in its list of bishops. It lists Louis de la Palud for the year 1450 and Guillaume d'Estouteville for 1460.

7. Gros, *Histoire du diocèse de Maurienne*, 2:129.

8. He was given a pension to reside at the Aiton priory by Nicholas V on April 3, 1451. This document is in Chambery, France, at the Archives Départementales de Savoie, 3G Maurienne 30, fols. 16r–22r. It was published as Document V in *Mémoires et Documents,* 2nd series, vol. 52 (1912), pp. 187–91. There is no editor listed. The 3G designation is apparently a more recent classification. From p. 188 of the *Mémoires et Documents* edition: "nec non Cardinalis in Ethonis duos, et abbas predicti in Fricteripe prioratibus hujusmodi unum monachos manute[ne]rent." See the discussion of the history of this establishment in chapter 13, "Jean de Segovie," in Gros, *Histoire du diocèse de Maurienne*, esp. 2:131–32.

9. Juan de Segovia, *Donatio*, 80: "Ad obtinendos uero libros major utique affuit sollicitudo, ab eo presertim tempore quo, in alciorem assumptus statum, quemadmodum consueueram uisitare commode non potui librarias communes; alia demum superexcrescente racione: a ciuitatibus et oppidis in quibus librarie habentur communes quem incolo prioratu distante longius, et propterea quinque aut quatuor apud me continuo residentibus scriptoribus, plures quam argenti marchas libros aggregaui."

10. Piccolomini, *De Europa*, par. 153, p. 174: "Ioannes Segobiensis, homo hispanus moribus et doctrina illustris, qui cum summos theologie preceptores doctrina equaret, ab Amedeo, dum se papam dixit, cardinalatus emi-

nentiam acceperat, et diende unioni consentiens a Nicolao pontifice maximo cardinalatus dimisso titulo cesariensi ecclesie prefectus fuerat, uocatis ex Hispania legis arabice magistris librum, quem uocant Alchoranum et in quo Maumethis pseudoprophete non tam mysteria quam deliramenta continentur, in nostram linguam de nouo conuertit et ineptias eius ueris ac uiuis rationibus et argumentis explosit."

11. Cabanelas Rodríguez, *Juan de Segovia y el problema islámico*, 93–94.

12. ASV Reg. Suppl. 388, fol. 81, dated January 26, 1443. In *Bulario* II, #1027: "Cum autem, pater sancte, dictus Joannes de Segobia, diabolico spiritu seductus, schismaticus sit effectus dictoque privilegio non immerito sit indignus: supplicat s. v. dictus card. quatenus dictum Joannem de Segobia de praefato libro cancellariae abradere, delere et amovere, necnon illius loco devotum vestrum Joannem Gundisalvi de Piñera, . . . scribi, nominari et reputari cuad similem effectum dicto privilegio gaudendi concedere et mandare dignemini de gratia speciali."

13. Juan de Segovia's reply is in BUS MS 202, fols. 172r–184r. It has received little attention from scholars. For a convincing argument regarding the identity of Guillielmus de Orliaco, previously unknown, and what this reveals about Segovia's regional connections, see Mann, "Juan de Segovia's 'Epistola ad Guillielmum de Orliaco.'"

14. Gros, *Histoire du diocèse de Maurienne*, 2:122.

15. See the report of an ecclesiastical visitor from 1592 in *Acta Sanctorum*, vol. 27, June 25th.

16. *Chronica latina Sabaudiae*, in *Monumenta Patriae*, t. III (Scriptorum t. I), column 615a–b.

17. These are bundled together in Chambery, ADS, 3G, item #68.

18. Juan de Segovia, Letter to Nicholas of Cusa, Dec. 2, 1454, BUS 19, fol. 168r.

19. Juan de Segovia, Letter to an unknown friend, April 18, 1458, fol. 196v. In Cabanelas Rodríguez, *Juan de Segovia y el problema islámico*, 338. Cabanelas gives 1457 as the year for this letter, but it is not clear why, since the manuscript does not provide one. I agree with Hernández Montes, who put the date at 1458 (*Obras*, 324n72) because in it Segovia says that two years and five months had passed since he had written to Jean Germain. That letter was dated Dec. 18, 1455.

20. Schwoebel, *The Shadow of the Crescent*, 3.

21. Schwoebel, *The Shadow of the Crescent*, 9.

22. Juan de Segovia, Letter to an unknown friend, April 18, 1458, fols. 196v–197r: "Sed ut veritatem fatear, antea pluribus iam annis illud visum fuerat prout testis est liber De magna auctoritate episcoporum in sinodo generali, per me editus et mandatus Yspalim Reverendissimo domino meo Ostiensi

[Cervantes]. At cum post flebilem direptionem constantinopolitanam, calamo dato operi ut cogitatus meos copiosius illi explicarem, scripta oblaturus felicis recordationis Nicolao [fol. 197] pape V°, percepta notitia passagii indicti, in continuando scripta elanguit manus, in prosequendo vero amplius multo." Folio 197r: "qui finis, initium mediumque laborum est meorum: Via pacis et doctrine plusquam igne et gladio procedendum fore ad exterminationem exinanitionemve secte vanissime sarracenorum." In Cabanelas Rodríguez, *Juan de Segovia y el problema islámico*, 338–39.

23. Hernández Montes, *Obras*, p. 311, no. 53. *De gladio* is preserved in Seville, Colombina, MS 7-6-14, folios 1–110v. Hernández Montes wrote that this manuscript is the original that Juan sent to Seville, but see Álvarez Márquez (*Manuscritos localizados de Pedro Gómez Barroso y Juan de Cervantes*, 89), who argues that this volume pertained instead to the library of Hernando Colombus. The *Liber de praeclara noticia* is no longer extant, but Juan sent a summary of its contents to Aeneas Sylvius Piccolomini in May 1458, and this is contained in BAV Vat. Lat. 2923, fols. 164r–178r.

24. *De magna auctoritate* dates to sometime after February 1449 but before the fall of Constantinople. See the discussion in Hernández Montes, *Obras*, pp. 305–6, no. 49. See also Juan de Segovia, *Liber de magna auctoritate*.

25. Cervantes' rejection of Segovia may not have been heartfelt in the first place, and if so, Segovia could have known this. It is difficult to know. Unlike Segovia's, Cervantes' positions in the pope-council struggle vacillated, from his strong defense of the papacy at the Council of Siena, to his early robust support for the council at Basel, to his later renunciation of this support. See the discussion in Goñi Gaztambide, "Presencia de España en los concilios generales," 80.

26. Bull of Nicholas V, Document 45 in Housley, *Documents of the Later Crusades*, 138–39.

27. Juan de Segovia, Letter to Nicholas of Cusa, Dec. 2, 1454, in Cabanelas Rodríguez, *Juan de Segovia y el problema islámico*, 307: "Erubescerem utique, Reverendissime Pater, tandiu protraxisse calamum, nisi fiducia consolaretur agnoscentem me Vestram Metuendissimam Dominationem in hiis que sui Patris sunt, ut oportet, esse velle semper." Cabanelas transcribed this from BAV Vat. Lat. 2923, fol. 31v.

28. Juan de Segovia, Letter to Nicholas of Cusa, Dec. 2, 1454, in Cabanelas Rodríguez, *Juan de Segovia y el problema islámico*, 307: "Celeri quippe sermone vulgatum est de vestra operatione studiosa ad reformationem in Germanie partibus, utque moris est perfectorum, mentem vestram magna delectare et ardua; habet nempe hoc optimum in se generosus animus, quod concitatur ad honesta." Cabanelas transcribed this from BAV Vat. Lat. 2923, fol. 31v.

29. See the discussion in Hernández Montes, *Obras*, pp. 314–15, no. 56. Several copies are extant: BUS 19, fols. 168r–184r; BUS 55, fols. 126r–138v and 140r–155r; BAV Vat. Lat. 2923, fols. 4r–35r. Excerpts are published in Cabanelas Rodríguez, *Juan de Segovia y el problema islámico*, 303–10. The copy sent to Germain may be Paris BN cod. lat. 3659. Juan might also have sent this work to Piccolomini. He mentioned having received encouragement from the future pope to circulate his translation of the Qur'ān and his refutation of this text (*reprobatione Alkurani*). This is in his May 1458 letter to Piccolomini, BAV Vat. Lat. 2923, fols. 1r–3v, published in Cabanelas Rodríguez, *Juan de Segovia y el problema islámico*, 343–49. Though this refutation could refer to the preface to the Qur'ān, it is a more apt description of the letter to Cusa, which he had already sent to others as well, than it is of that preface.

30. Nicholas of Cusa, Letter to Juan de Segovia, Dec. 29, 1454, in Cabanelas Rodríguez, *Juan de Segovia y el problema islámico*, 311: "Reverendissime in Christo pater, domine et amice singularissime: Post recommendationem; recepi litteras vestras, michi utique gratissimas, quas legi et relegi, et de multis maximam recepi complacentiam; in primis, quia nexum veteris inter nos amicitie, non tantum vidi integrum, sed potius glutino compactum, quod iocundissime intellexi, maxime autem huius ostensio michi patuit quando secretiora michi primum revelastis et, ut paucis utar, hec stet sentencia: nos et esse et manere semper amicos affectibus atque operibus id ipsum attestantibus." A translation of this letter into Spanish is available in Sanz Santacruz, *La paz de la fe*, 91–98.

31. Nicholas of Cusa, Letter to Juan de Segovia, Dec. 29, 1454, in Cabanelas Rodríguez, *Juan de Segovia y el problema islámico*, 313: "De aliis vero duobus punctis, Reverendissima Paternitas Vestra, doctior et prudentior, non eget instructore; sed ne videar, iusta posse, nolle complacere, quam breviter tangam que occurrunt." Cabanelas transcribed this from BAV Vat. Lat. 2923, fol. 36v.

32. Nicholas of Cusa, Letter to Juan de Segovia, Dec. 29, 1454, in Cabanelas Rodríguez, *Juan de Segovia y el problema islámico*, 313–14: "Visum est michi omnino ita agendum cum infidelibus uti [314] placere conspitio Reverendissime Paternitati Vestre, et de hoc scripsi libellum parvulum, quem nominavi *De pace fidei*." Cabanelas transcribed this from BAV Vat. Lat. 2923, fol. 36v.

33. Nicholas of Cusa, Letter to Juan de Segovia, Dec. 29, 1454, in Cabanelas Rodríguez, *Juan de Segovia y el problema islámico*, 314: "quia si iuxta doctrinam Christi processerimus, non errabimus, sed spiritus eius loquetur in nobis, cui non poterunt omnes adversarii Christi resistere; sed, si invasionis gladio aggresionem elegerimus, formidare habemus ne, gladio pugnantes,

gladio pereamus. Unde sola defensio sine periculo est christiano." Cabanelas transcribed this from BAV Vat. Lat. 2923, fol. 36v.

34. Some examples are Norman Daniel, *Islam and the West*, 307; Bisaha, *Creating East and West*, 144–47; Izbicki, "The Possibility of Dialogue with Islam"; and Biechler, "A New Face Toward Islam."

35. Nicholas of Cusa, *De pace fidei*, paragraph 2, p. 4.

36. Biechler made the same observation in "A New Face Toward Islam," 196. See also Izbicki, "The Possibility of Dialogue with Islam."

37. The likely challenges Christians would face in talking with Muslims about the Trinity, the Incarnation (which he thought would be harder), paradise, the cross, and the Eucharist receive a few sentences each in his letter. These paragraphs appear on pp. 314–17 in Cabanelas Rodríguez, *Juan de Segovia y el problema islámico*.

38. Biechler and Bond, *Nicholas of Cusa on Interreligious Harmony*, xxvi.

39. Biechler and Bond, *Nicholas of Cusa on Interreligious Harmony*, xxx.

40. Nicholas of Cusa, *De pace fidei*, § 9, p. 10.

41. Nicholas of Cusa, *De pace fidei*, § 9, p. 10.

42. Nicholas of Cusa, *De pace fidei*, § 68, p. 62.

43. Nicholas of Cusa, *De pace fidei*, § 68, pp. 62–63.

44. Nicholas of Cusa, *Cribratio Alkorani*, Prologue, §4, p. 76.

45. Hopkins, *Nicholas of Cusa's "De pace fidei" and "Cribratio Alkorani,"* 14.

46. Nicholas of Cusa, *Cribratio Alkorani*, Book II, §158, p. 149.

47. Nicholas of Cusa, *Cribratio Alkorani*, Book III, Chapter 9, §184, pp. 161–62.

48. These works are newly available in English in Izbicki, *Nicholas of Cusa.*

49. See, for example, Hopkins, *Nicholas of Cusa's "De pace fidei" and "Cribratio Alkorani,"* 14.

50. Hernández Montes, *Obras*, p. 317, no. 61. This is in BUS 55, fols. 158v–159, and BAV Vat. Lat. 2923, fols. 39r–40v. Published in Cabanelas Rodríguez, *Juan de Segovia y el problema islámico*, 319–23.

51. This work is in BAV Vat. Lat. 2923, fols. 146r–147r. See Hernández Montes, *Obras*, p. 316, no. 59. For a helpful treatment of traditional Islamic belief about Adam and his sin, see Murata and Chittick, *The Vision of Islam*, 142–44.

52. Hernández Montes, *Obras*, p. 316, no. 60. This work is found is Seville, Colombina 7-6-14, fols. 111r–114v, and BAV Vat. Lat. 2923, fols. 157v–164r.

53. This document is in BUS 55, fols. 161r–212r, and BAV Vat. Lat. 2923, fols. 41r–136v. Two small sections of the letter-treatise are in Cabanelas Rodríguez, *Juan de Segovia y el problema islámico*, 331–35. Along with this long reply, Juan sent a brief letter acknowledging receipt of Germain's correspondence. This shorter cover letter is in BUS 55, fols. 159r–160r, and BAV Vat. Lat. 2923, fols. 184r–185r. It is published in Cabanelas Rodríguez, *Juan de Segovia y el problema islámico*, 325–28.

54. Juan de Segovia, Letter to Jean Germain, Dec. 18, 1455, fol. 47: "Quia igitur intentionis mee fuit estque ad p. v. velud ad magistrum loqui discipulum suum tenere amantem necesaria minime fuit exhortacio in prima litera vestra scripta manu dure me non accepturum fore si r. p. v. per me conceptam viam non amplexa fuisset via tractatuum pacis et doctrine collacione mutua ad sarracenorum conversionem intendendum fore quoniam iam diu prout ex scriptis eus sencio ab annis xii eidem fuerat visum magis quod vi armorum super quo longam epistolam misisset fe. re. Nicolao pape v. Necnon regibus francie Anglie et Aragonum ac per Germanos."

55. Paviot, "Burgundy and the Crusade," 71–72.

56. Echevarría Arsuaga, *Fortress of Faith*, 7–8.

57. Paviot, "Burgundy and the Crusade," 72.

58. Schwoebel, *The Shadow of the Crescent*, 107–8.

59. Juan Germain, extracts from an oration before King Charles VII of France in 1451 in Housley, *Documents of the Later Crusades*, 140–41. Although its original editor gave this homily the date of 1452, it has been redated. See the bibliography on this in Housley, 143n1.

60. Paviot, "Burgundy and the Crusade," 76.

61. Paviot, "Burgundy and the Crusade," 73.

62. See the discussion in Hernández Montes, *Obras*, p. 318, no. 63.

63. Cabanelas Rodríguez, *Juan de Segovia y el problema islámico*, 223.

64. This work is in the BUS MS 202, fols. 172r–184v. The entry describing it is in Hernández Montes, *Obras*, 321n16, where the author suggests that this version is a copy of the original manuscript.

65. Mann, "Juan de Segovia's 'Epistola ad Guillielmum de Orliaco,'" 184.

66. This letter is in BAV Vat. Lat. 2923, fols. 196v–198, published in Cabanelas Rodríguez, *Juan de Segovia y el problema islámico*, 343–49. For a discussion of the dating, see above, note 19.

67. Juan de Segovia, Letter to an unknown friend, April 18, 1458, fol. 196v (in Cabanelas Rodríguez, *Juan de Segovia y el problema islámico*, 338): "Amantissime frater mi, si collegas sibi optarunt viri sancti predicti aliique plurimi ad consummationem operis sibi iniuncti a Deo, vel tanti suo ex genere boni quod omnium iudicio laudabile foret, quid igitur agendum michi erat in alium suadenti finem opus quod tota fere christiana religio prosequebatur?"

68. Juan de Segovia, Letter to an unknown friend, April 18, 1458, fol. 196v (in Cabanelas Rodríguez, *Juan de Segovia y el problema islámico*, 338): "Sed ut veritatem fatear, antea pluribus iam annis illud visum fuerat prout testis est liber *De magna auctoritate episcoporum in sinodo generali*, per me editus et mandatus Yspalim Reverendissimo domino meo Ostiensi [Cervantes]. At cum post flebilem direptionem constantinopolitanam, calamo dato operi ut cogitatus meos copiosius illi explicarem, scripta oblaturus felicis recordationis Nicolao [fol. 197r] pape Vo, percepta notitia passagii indicti, in continuando scripta elanguit manus, in prosequendo vero amplius multo."

69. Juan de Segovia, Letter to an unknown friend, April 18, 1458, fols. 197–197v (in Cabanelas Rodríguez, *Juan de Segovia y el problema islámico*, 339): "Desiderio desideravi vestrum interpellare consilium, et super scriptorum substantia et de modo quo in palam fiat; id profecto auxilium vestri [fol. 197v] dignum laborare, qui a primevo iuventutis flore studio semper vacastis Scripture sancte magnisque admodum operibus inexigue conferentibus illi."

70. Juan de Segovia, Letter to an unknown friend, April 18, 1458, fol. 197r (in Cabanelas Rodríguez, *Juan de Segovia y el problema islámico*, 339): "finis, initium mediumque laborum est meorum: Via pacis et doctrine plusquam igne et gladio procedendum fore ad exterminationem exinanitionemve secte vanissime sarracenorum."

71. See text in Cabanelas Rodríguez, *Juan de Segovia y el problema islámico*, 340–41.

72. The manuscript does not supply a year, only the month and day. Cabanelas offered the year of 1457, but I agree with Hernández Montes (*Obras*, 324) in thinking that 1458 is more likely due to the fact that the letter mentions that he replied to Germain two and a half years earlier, and that reply was sent in December 1455.

73. Juan de Segovia, Letter to Aeneas Sylvius Piccolomini, May 1458, fol. 1r (in Cabanelas Rodríguez, *Juan de Segovia y el problema islámico*, 343): "Illud autem est, cum significatur quatenus faciam ut opus super translatione et reprobatione Alkurani quam primum in utilitatem reipublice exeat, rogatione accedente vestra, que michi ut arbitror, salutare mandatum est, et quod michi gracie amplioris, quia id ipsum exposcente."

74. Juan de Segovia, Letter to Aeneas Sylvius Piccolomini, May 1458, fol. 1r (in Cabanelas Rodríguez, *Juan de Segovia y el problema islámico*, 344): "Videns igitur me gravissima egritudine laborantem, diebus ultimis vite mee, sic quod vix queam calamum notule huius imprimere, pro insignissima gratia Reverendissime Paternitatis Vestre habeo incitamentum, ut quod talentum accepi non paciar absconditum manere sub sabulo. Quocirca, scripta quedam meum concernencia propositum, super quibus cum duobus contuli magnis viris, Vestre Metuendissime Dominationi transmitto."

75. See, for example, Piccolomini's letters to Segovia dated Aug. 13, 1440, and June 6, 1444.

76. Piccolomini, Letter to Giovanni Peregallo, April 18, 1444, 188.

77. Nicholas of Cusa, Letter to Juan de Segovia, Dec. 29, 1454, fol. 38v (in Cabanelas Rodríguez, *Juan de Segovia y el problema islámico*, 318): "Scio quod Sanctissimus dominus noster libentissime videbit. Utinam posset vos Sanctitas Sua audire loquentem potius, nam infirmitas non sinit eum legere, et libenter confert. Testis sum ego, quia sepe audivi, ipsum diligere et cum affectu personam Reverendissime Paternitatis Vestre et multum ad ipsam inclinari."

78. Juan de Segovia, Letter to Nicholas of Cusa, Dec. 2, 1454, BAV Vat. Lat. 2923, fols. 32v–33r (in Cabanelas Rodríguez, *Juan de Segovia y el problema islámico*, 309–10): "Et si ego meritus non fuerim in oculis vestris tanti gratiam beneficii quod huiusmodi scripta, multis quamvis referta ineptiis et in-[fol. 33r]solentiis, Reverendissima Paternitas Vestra videre dignabitur desuperque donare responsum; quoniam autem consilium humillime posco et ante consultationem putem non decere hanc rem in publicam deferre notionem, habens vero singularissimam confidentiam, primum volui communicare Reverendissime Pater-[p. 310]nitati Vestre labores meos ut ipsius perficiantur auxilic consulatque an publicari debeant."

79. Nicholas of Cusa, Letter to Juan de Segovia, Dec. 29, 1454, fol. 38v (in Cabanelas Rodríguez, *Juan de Segovia y el problema islámico*, 318): "Perficiat igitur Reverendissima Paternitas Vestra; ita pro Dei reverentia supplico, et requiro ut communicetis, primo, Sanctissimo domino nostro, deinde michi et ceteris: erit enim de melioribus Ecclesie thesauris."

80. Nicholas of Cusa, Letter to Juan de Segovia, Dec. 29, 1454, fol. 38v (in Cabanelas Rodríguez, *Juan de Segovia y el problema islámico*, 318): "ubi quidam doctus frater Dyonisius vivens, laboravit, scribendo opus parvum contra errores Mahumeti; sed non est comparatio ad volumen illud gloriosum vestre compilationis."

81. Izbicki, Christianson, and Krey, *Reject Aeneas, Accept Pius*, 49.

82. Juan de Segovia, Letter to Aeneas Sylvius Piccolomini, May 1458, fol. 1v (in Cabanelas Rodríguez, *Juan de Segovia y el problema islámico*, 345): "Quoniam vero quanto communius tanto opus divinius est, et inter evangelica precepta mandatum illud communius generaliusque esse videtur quod Apostolis in ultimis verbis suis Salvator iniuncxit, dicens: Euntes in mundum universum, docete omnes gentes, Evangelium predicturi omni creature, ut doctrina hec, que basis fundamentumque est Sancte Catholice Ecclesie, continua in prelatis ac doctoribus esset exercitatione."

83. Juan de Segovia, Letter to Aeneas Sylvius Piccolomini, May 1458, fols. 3–3v: "Et sedens rex ille cogitabat si cum decem millibus occurrere

posset regi cum XX millibus [fol. 3v] venienti adversus eum, aut legationem mittere, que pacis sunt rogaturam; evangelico verbo isto nobis exemplum dante, ut cum maior communiter multitudo sarracenorum quam christianorum, multis ex causis, lege sua id magnopere hortante, concurrat ad corporea bella, Ecclesia sancta Dei, cui Christus suam reliquit pacem suamque pacem donavit, pacem inquirat et persequatur eam." In Cabanelas Rodríguez, *Juan de Segovia y el problema islámico*, 349.

84. Juan de Segovia, Letter to Aeneas Sylvius Piccolomini, May 1458, fol. 1r: "Illud autem est, cum significatur quatenus faciam ut opus super translatione et reprobatione Alkurani quam primum in utilitatem reipublice exeat, rogatione accedente vestra, que, ut arbitror, salutare mandatum est, et quod michi gratie amplioris, quia id ipsum exposcente." In Cabanelas Rodríguez, *Juan de Segovia y el problema islámico*, 343.

85. Piccolomini, *De Europa,* par. 153, p. 174: "uocatis ex Hispania legis arabice magistris librum, quem uocant Alchoranum et in quo Maumethis pseudoprophete non tam mysteria quam deliramenta continentur, in nostram linguam de nouo conuertit et ineptias eius ueris ac uiuis rationibus et argumentis explosit."

86. Piccolomini, *Commentariorum*, Book I, Chapter 27, paragraph 4, p. 1:135.

87. Bisaha, "Pope Pius II and the Crusade," 41.

88. Bisaha, "Pope Pius II and the Crusade," 42.

89. Bisaha, "Pope Pius II and the Crusade," 52. Also see the discussion in Izbicki, Christianson, and Krey, *Reject Aeneas, Accept Pius*, 50–53.

90. Bisaha, "Pope Pius II and the Crusade," 41–52.

91. For a helpful review of scholars' debates on how to interpret this puzzling letter, see Bisaha, "Pope Pius II's Letter," 183–85.

92. Piccolomini, *Epistola ad Mahometem II*, §121, p. 65.

93. Piccolomini, *Epistola ad Mahometem II*, §136, p. 70.

94. Bisaha, "Pope Pius II's Letter," 189.

95. Bisaha, "Pope Pius II's Letter," 196.

96. Bisaha, "Pope Pius II's Letter," 198–99.

97. Juan de Segovia, Letter to Nicholas of Cusa, Dec. 2, 1454, BUS 19, fol. 174r: "Quam vero id notissimum est quod christiani cum sarracenis super re temporali acturi inexpectato quod deus per se vel angelos illis de super loquatur, iuxta magnitudinem rerum agendarum plus minus ve solempnes, suos legatos vel nuncios mortales homines ad eos mittunt, inducturos eos ad faciendumque pestulant, magnum profecto dignique attentione gravi offertur ante oculos nostros avisamentum. Si dum pertractandum est de pace tocius populi christiani deque sarracenorum salute, sed et de gloria dei gentibus annuncianda tuenda christi innocencia honoreque ecclesie ac totius christiane

religionis, christi fidelis per se ipsos non intendant sed expectent a deo fieri miracula."

98. Juan de Segovia, Letter to Nicholas of Cusa, Dec. 2, 1454, BUS 19, fol. 174r: "Virtus quippe angelica adeo naturam humanam excellit ut humane non sit coaptata iugi conversationi. Siquidem ut Daniel de se ipso testator in angeli visione pretimore eius compages hominis dissolvuntur nichilque in eo remaneret virium sed intercluditur anhelitus. Quocirca apparentes angeli hominibus dicunt ut comuniter primo sermone quod nolint timere."

99. Juan de Segovia, Letter to Nicholas of Cusa, Dec. 2, 1454, BUS 19, fol. 173v: "Sic enim paulus testatur de tempore legis nature patres quidem carnis nostre habuimus eruditores et reverebamur eis. Tali quippe modo adam dei voluntatem notificavit filiis suis. Sic noe sic Abraham sic ysaac sic Iacobi. Tempore vero scripture id manifestius constat quia per moysem samuelem, david, ysaiam, Jeremiam, aleosque prophetas revelavit deus pertinencia ad salutem populi illius, unde dicit quod misit ad eos omnes servos, suos prophetas, per diem consurgens diluculo et mittens. . . . Intempore autem legis gracie plus quam satis est testimonium illud quod cum multiphariam multisque modis olim deus locutus fuerit patribus in prophetis novissime locutus est nobis in filio suo qui ut per omnia fratribus assimilaretur cum in forma dei esset exinanivit se ipsum, formam servi accipiens, habitu inventus ut homo. Et sicut missus a patre est ut homo factus hominibus predicaret. Ita et ipse non quidem angelos sed discipulos suos misit in universum mundum."

100. See Wolf, "Precedents and Paradigms," 150–51; Madrigal Terrazas, *El proyecto eclesiológico de Juan de Segovia*, esp. 73–85; Mann, "The Devilish Pope."

101. Keck, *Angels and Angelology*, 156–57.

102. Keck, *Angels and Angelology*, 201.

103. See the discussion in Tolan, *Saracens*, 231–32.

104. Juan de Segovia, Letter to Nicholas of Cusa, Dec. 2, 1454, BUS 19, fol. 179r: "Propter quod modus ille non iuderetur sufficiens si formam habentes mercatorum mitterentur plures viri docti christo specialiter devoti predicaturi sarracenis evangelicam veritatem. Etenim cum diu ignis latere non posset, suspicione habita via facti provideretur ne umquam proficere possent propterea quod penes ipsos est temporale dominium."

105. Juan de Segovia, Letter to Jean Germain, Dec. 18, 1455, fols. 60v–61r: "Et de lege Mahumeti [61] parum aut nichil scientes doctos quippe suos apostolos fecit christus priusquam mitteret eos predicaturos inter gentes. Nec enim iuxta doctrinam pauli sufficit zelum habere dei sed zelum servi scienciam id vero in fine huius racionis subiunctum quod sanctus dominicus ingressus arabiam ad predicandum non profecit sed secuta est via belli sine qua nichil."

106. Izbicki, Christianson, and Krey, introduction to *Reject Aeneas, Accept Pius*, 7–8.

107. Hobbins, *Authority and Publicity*, 107–8.

108. Juan de Segovia, Letter to Nicholas of Cusa, Dec. 2, 1454, BUS 19, fol. 182v: "cum finem accepisset, opusculum meum, cuius initium, medium, finisque est ut pacis magis quam belli via intendatur ad conversionem sarracenorum."

109. Juan de Segovia, Letter to Nicholas of Cusa, Dec. 2, 1454, BAV Vat. Lat. 2923, fol. 32v: "Quocirca et michi fiducia simper excrescit habunde cum res ista natura sui contingat precordia catholice fidei."

110. Housley, *The Later Crusades*, 389–97.

111. Juan de Segovia, Letter to Nicholas of Cusa, Dec. 2, 1454, BUS 19, fol. 182r: "audivi quod a tempore apostolorum de nullo legeretur eius causa labore ve tot millia infidelium ad fidem conversa fuisse sicut de Ladislao pleo [pleno?] dierum mortuo polonie rege. De conversione quoque regni ungarie ad fidem legitur racione inrationii unius de regno quoque anglie quomodo ad fidem venerit notissimum est. Maxima quoque germanie pars Bonifacio Maguntino episcopo verbi divini tunc predicatore."

112. Juan de Segovia, Letter to Nicholas of Cusa, Dec. 2, 1454, BUS 19, fol. 182: "a principio christiane religionis in prosecucione quoque terreni gladii non legimus populos multos ad fidem conversos quoniam fides, ut vera sit, voluntatis est, non neccesitatis cum sit voluntaria firmaque adhesio rebus creditis sive auditis ob auctoritatem dicentis."

113. Juan de Segovia, *De mittendo gladio*, fol. 22r: "Experientia denique multipliciter iam habita est quamvis Sarracenorum terre occupentur teneri non posse per christianos."

114. Juan de Segovia, Letter to Nicholas of Cusa, Dec. 2, 1454, BUS 19, fol. 174r: "Yspani autem de hoc plenum habent exemplum in continuatis per eos guerris experimento probantes sarracenos malle interfici quam timore gladii ad fidem converti sed et tot iam facta passagia noticiam pleniorem de super hiis dedere."

115. Juan de Segovia, *De mittendo gladio*, fols. 101v–102r: "Etenim cum de tempore concilii Constanciensis post condempnacionem errorum Io. Voutzleph et Io. Huss combustionemque Io. Huss et Jeronimi de Praga totum fere Regnum Bohemie sicut ab Eccesie unitate ita recesserat ab obediencia Romani Imperii Regisque sui naturalis Sigismundi. Constat hiis qui suis viderunt oculis auribusque sive legerunt annales, quam plures potentissimos armatorum exercitus Centum aliquando autem Centum quinquaginta milium [102r] equorum et eo amplius parte fidelium ut Bohemos ipsos ad unitatem fidei et obedencie reducerent vel eos exterminarent introisse regnum eorum nullo ab inde aut vix aliquo secuto fructu qui sperabatur quin aliquando turpi fuga

quasi fugeret impius nemine persequente retrocesserunt. Tantusque timor Bohemos ipsos extulerat invaseratque vicinos timor eorum ut quamplurimos vehemens temptacio agitaret de componenda cum eis pace susceptis eorum articulis prout ipsi intelligebant erroneis. Legatus vero apostolice sedis qui adversus illos crucem predicaverat et potenti exercitu congregato intraverat Regnum eorum, manifeste agnoscens quod via belli frequentius ordinata nullathenus proficeret, pedes suos direxerit in viam pacis, quatenus eius amicabili tractatu interveniente Bohemi ipsi illuminarentur in tenebris sedentes in umbra mortis. Et hoc summum et unicum putavit remedium."

116. N. Daniel, *Islam and the West*, 156.

117. Juan de Segovia, *De mittendo gladio*, fol. 24v: "Hec sane cum sit lex gracie cui proprie proprium est omnibus gentibus annunciare propinquans esse regnum dei iubet discipulis suis quamcumque intraverint domum eam primum salutent dicentes pax huic domui, pacem namque eis reliquit."

118. Juan de Segovia, *De mittendo gladio*, fol. 24v: "In lege quippe nature profundum malicie Cayn in Abel exercuit quando nulla eidem insinuata mali operis causa sed rogato illo fortassis ut a conspectu patris et matris cum eo egrederetur dum essent in agro soli consurrexit adversus eum et interfecit. Lex preterea scripture ut pax primo offerretur anmonuit, dicens Cum accesseris ad expugnandum civitatem offeres ei primum pacem. Et si lex Moysi in qua dicebatur oculum pro oculo, dentem pro dente, pacem primum offerri iubet, quid lex Evangelii in qua mandatur ut percucienti maxillam prebeatur et altera tollentique pallium ut et tunica dimittatur."

119. Juan de Segovia, Letter to Nicholas of Cusa, Dec. 2, 1454, BUS 19, fol. 176r: "Hanc certe pacem relictam a christo, quam mitttere in terram venit, decet ecclesiam catholicam procurare omnibus infidelibus ut cum eam acceptaverint pax illis adveniat data Christi discipulis insufflante eo accepturis spiritum sanctum. Siquidem qualem christus in terram misit talem utique gladium omnibus christifidelibus presidibus ecclesie permaxime et doctoribus fidei catholice mittere licet in sarracenos."

120. Juan de Segovia, *De mittendo gladio*, fol. 25: "Itaque pacem habere volens cum omnibus hominibus, nulli malum pro malo reddere debet, sed accendere in eum ignem amoris bonorum exhibicione operum."

121. Juan de Segovia, *De mittendo gladio*, fol. 25r: "Ath verba hoc doctrine apostolice eciam si preclare virtutis excellentiam demonstrent in eisdem vix explicatur evangelica perfectio quam christus docuit ut fideles sui inimicos suos diligant benefacturi hiis qui oderunt eos oraturi quoque pro persequentibus et calumpmantibus ut sint perfecti sicut pater celestis eorum qui solem suum oriri facit super bonos et malos."

122. Juan de Segovia, Letter to Jean Germain, Dec. 18, 1455, fol. 51v: "Lex nempe christiana in hoc differt ab omni quacumque alia secta propterea

quod in ea non est accepcio personarum ubi apostolo teste. Non est masculus et femina, gentilis et Iudeus, circumcisio et prepucium, Barbarus et Scitha, servus et liber, sed omnia in omnibus christus."

123. Juan de Segovia, Letter to Nicholas of Cusa, Dec. 2, 1454, BUS 19, fol. 176v: "Sic enim christus, sic apostoli sui, sic eorum posteri intenderunt ut ex iudeis ac gentilibus fieret populus unus christianus, unde paulus inquit in christo ihesu per evangelium, Ego vos genui quos per evangelium deus vocavit in acquisicionem glorie ihesu Christi."

124. Juan de Segovia, Letter to Jean Germain, Dec. 18, 1455, fol. 51v: "Christus non horum illorum ve sed omni fuit redemptor."

125. Juan de Segovia, *De mittendo gladio*, fol. 25: "Si licitum christianis est uti Sarracenis ut servis cum hii rationales sint creature beatitudinis eterne capaces. Ille certe usus magis convenire videretur operam dari per christianos non quod descendant in infernum viventes sed ut eorum anime salve fiant salutari suscepta doctrina."

126. Juan de Segovia, *Repetitio de superioritate*, fols. 134r–134v: "Hoc etiam et quarto patet per auctoritates Apostoli, in quibus probatur quod sacra Scriptura sufficiens sit nec dum ad determinandum [fol. 134v] veritates catholicas, sed etiam ad reprobandum haereses contrarias, 2 Tim 3 omnis scriptura divinitus inspirata utilis est ad docendum, ad arguendum, ad corrigendum, ad erudiendum in iustitia, ut perfectus sit homo Dei et ad omne opus bonum instructus."

127. Juan de Segovia, Letter to Jean Germain, Dec. 18, 1455, fol. 51: "est enim dei sermo et efficax et penetrabilior omni gladio ancipite et pertingens usque ad divisionem anime et spiritus compagum quoque et medullarium et discretor cogitacionum et intencionum cordis."

128. Juan de Segovia, Letter to Nicholas of Cusa, Dec. 2, 1454, BUS 19, fols. 182r–182v: "Sperandum igitur est ut, si sancte dei ecclesie ita videatur pacis modo intendendum fore ad conversionem sarracenorum, quod opus bonum qui incipiet deus [fol. 182v] ipse perficiet pace dei que omnem exsuperat sensum."

129. Juan de Segovia, Letter to Nicholas of Cusa, Dec. 2, 1454, BUS 19, fol. 171r: "Ecce ego vobiscum sum omnibus diebus usque ad consumacionem seculi. Itaque quamdiu erunt in mundo gentes evvangelium predicandum et illis." Matthew 28:19–20: "Go therefore and make disciples of all nations, baptizing them in the name of the Father and of the Son and of the Holy Spirit, and teaching them to obey everything that I have commanded you. And remember, I am with you always, to the end of the age."

130. A modern edition of this work was recently published with a German translation: *De gladio divini spiritus in corda mittendo Sarracenorum*, 2 vols., edited by Ulli Roth, Corpus Islamo-Christianum, Series Latin, Band 7

(Altenberge, Germany: CIS-Verlag, 2012). Unfortunately, this work appeared too late to inform this book.

131. Juan de Segovia, Letter to Nicholas of Cusa, Dec. 2, 1454, BUS 19, fol. 178v: "Quia vero cuilibet christianorum preceptum a deo est ut inquirat pacem et persequatur eam consideracione propterea dignum est quomodo ecclesiam decet non solum oblatam attendere sed inquirere et persequi magnum profecto verbum est, cum divinus ait sermo *Inquire pacem et eam prosequere.* Etenim siqui invenit thesaurum abstenditum in agro pro quo non laboravit in inquirendo vendit omnia que habet et emit illum. Nec exigui valoris est pax populi christiani." Matthew 13:44: "The kingdom of heaven is like treasure hidden in a field, which someone found and hid; then in his joy he goes and sells all that he has and buys that field."

132. Juan de Segovia, Letter to Nicholas of Cusa, Dec. 2, 1454, BUS 19, fol. 176r: "Siquidem qualem christus in terram misit talem utique gladium omnibus christifidelibus presidibus ecclesie permaxime et doctoribus fidei catholice mittere licet in sarracenos, eosque velut petro mandatum extitit gladio isto occidere et manducare, separando animas gentilium apectati corpore et traiciendo in corpus ecclesie."

133. Juan de Segovia, Letter to Nicholas of Cusa, Dec. 2, 1454, BUS 19, fol. 176v: "Quorum principatus ut in sua integritate permaneat armis utitur sub apostolo designatis lorica iusticie, scuto fidei, salutis galea et gladio spiritus, quod est verbum dei."

134. Juan de Segovia, Letter to Nicholas of Cusa, Dec. 2, 1454, BUS 19, fol. 182r: "ignem quoque apponentibus divini amoris quem in terram mittere venit voluitque ut accenderetur semper." Luke 12:49: "I came to bring fire to the earth, and how I wish it were already kindled."

135. Juan de Segovia, Letter to Nicholas of Cusa, Dec. 2, 1454, BUS 19, fol. 176r: "Hic enim cibus est quem discipulis christus dixit se manducaturum . . . in hoc voluntatem faciens patris sui qui non vult mortem peccatorum sed ut convertatur et vivat."

136. Juan de Segovia, *De mittendo gladio*, fol. 4v: "quam oportunum sit per modum tractande pacis intendere ad conversionem Sarracenorum severitati parcendo ob multitudinem eorum ignoranciamque [word written above line: quorum?] instruendo. Et sic noticia veritatis uniendo animos violenta pace numquam firma manente. Cum vero eadem sint principia essendi et conservandi quamviter [?] hoc mahumeti secta non servat quod decet religionem christianam uti originem accepit per verbum dei vivi sic semet ipsam continuare et sibimet subdere orbis naciones talibus armis sibi concessis."

137. A. Black, *Council and Commune*, 143–44.

138. Juan de Segovia, *Tractatus super presidentia*, in the critical edition by P. Ladner, ed., "Johannes von Segovias Stellung zur Präsidentenfrage des Basler

Konzils," *Zeitschrift für Schweizerische Kirchengeschichte* (*Revue d'Histoire ecclésiastique suisse*) 62 (1968): 1–113, pp. 36–37, as quoted in A. Black, *Council and Commune*, 144. In Hernández Montes, *Obras*, this work is described on 273–74 and bears the title *Relatio in deputatione fidei super materia bullarum de praesidentia.* The work originated with Segovia's participation in the *deputatio fidei* in March 1434. Several manuscripts of it exist.

139. Juan de Segovia, Letter to Nicholas of Cusa, Dec. 2, 1454, BUS 19, fol. 177v: "sicut agnoscitur differentem fuisse nativitatem ita agnoscatur differentem utrique competere conservacionem. Ecclesie quidem Christi per semen verbi divini quod nisi dominus reliquisset, quasi Sodoma fuissemus et similes gomorre hoc est gladium spiritualem. Secte autem sarracenorum per materialem [in margin: gladium] et prolis multiplicationem. Et sicut istam hoc est prolem multam habere cupiens minime dubitat crebro effundere suum semen cum vix contingat quartam eius partem cadere in terram bonam. Nec continuo illa reddit fructum sed speratur in tempore opportuno. Et rursus quanto experimur quod secta sarracenorum mititur pro incremento robore que sui materiali gladio. Non minus decet ecclesiam intendere ut gladium suum spiritualem quem sibi eius sponsus reliquit pro sua conservatione."

140. Hernández Montes, *Biblioteca*, 276.

141. Avilés, "La teología española en el siglo XV," 500–501.

142. Hernández Montes, *Biblioteca*, 276. The mention of this work appears in the text of the *Donatio* on p. 105. See also the text (and accompanying brief study) of a proposal by Benedict XIII in 1415 for ending the schism in Linehan, "Papa Luna in 1415," esp. 96.

143. Siberry, *Criticism of Crusading*, 190.

144. Tolan, *Saracens*, 261. This is from Llull's *Llibre de contemplació en Déu*, one of his early works.

145. For a reassessment of this aspect of his reputation, see Iogna-Prat, "The Creation of a Christian Armory against Islam."

146. Bisaha, *Creating East and West*, 137.

147. Kedar, *Crusade and Mission*, 138–41.

148. Siberry, *Criticism of Crusading*, 18.

149. Siberry, *Criticism of Crusading*, 19.

150. Siberry, *Criticism of Crusading*, 207. The citation is to *Opus maius*, iii. 120–22.

151. One example is in Juan de Segovia, Letter to Nicholas of Cusa, Dec. 2, 1454, BUS 19, fol. 172r: "Sed et consideracio minus quam distemperancia calidarum regionum occidentalibus non est dispositio salutaris quantum exhaurietur religio christiana multitudine virorum fortium quando non semel aut bis sed continuo gentes novas mittere necesarie foret ad lucrandum sine acquisita custodiendum. Legitur namque de Constantino impera-

tore quod sepcies sarracenos a Ihrusalima expulsit tociens que illis recupera-
vere. Donec Karolus magnus vocatus per Imperatorem ipsum victoriam per-
fectam obtinuit contra illos. Set et illud palam omnibus est lucrata quecumque per christianos in oriente vix aut minime permanissa, nec solum illa
devenisse postea ad manus sarracenorum sed quasi continue [fol. 173r] eos
plurima occupare de novo."

152. Juan de Segovia, *De mittendo gladio*, fol. 25r: "Ille certe usus magis
convenire videretur operam dari per christianos non quod descendant in infernum viventes sed ut eorum anime salve fiant salutari suscepta doctrina."

153. Juan de Segovia, Letter to Nicholas of Cusa, Dec. 2, 1454, BUS 19,
fol. 174v: "Quod vero officit quinymmo omne prestat impedimentum ad
conversionem eorum est quem si ex instructione bellorum in ipsos sarracenis
super excrescit in christianos odium multo utique maiori ac velud incompa-
rabil. incremento super excrescit in christum arbitrantur namque prout veritas habet quod christiani omnes pro eius pugnant honore in ducem protec-
toremque suum habentes eum. Nec id possunt ignorare videntes pugnatores
omnes crucesignatos christi. Unde sicut contingit principem cuius sit guerra
mandato per militibus suis odio per hostes suos magis haberi. Ita sarracenorum odia in bellorum extratione exardescunt in christum potius. Ad huc
etiam nullo in ipsos instructo bello per christianos ad odium christi aspirant
exagitante illos invidie livore odio propterea ipsa livore roborato magis."

154. See the discussion of Bacon in Tolan, *Saracens*, 225–29.

155. Kedar, *Crusade and Mission*, 180.

156. Iogna-Prat, "The Creation of a Christian Armory against Islam,"
326, 334.

157. In Germain's *Dialogue du crestien et du sarrasin*, described in
Echevarría Arsuaga, *Fortress of Faith*, 109.

158. Echevarría Arsuaga, *Fortress of Faith*, 106–8.

159. Juan de Segovia, Letter to Nicholas of Cusa, Dec. 2, 1454, BUS 19,
fol. 176v: "Quorum principatus ut in sua integritate permaneat armis utitur
sub apostolo designatis lorica iusticie, scuto fidei, salutis galea et gladio spiritus. quod est verbum dei."

160. Echevarría Arsuaga, *Fortress of Faith*, 106.

161. Echevarría Arsuaga, *Fortress of Faith*, 119.

162. Tolan, *Saracens*, 159.

163. Tolan, *Saracens*, 241.

164. Siberry, *Criticism of Crusading*, 18; Kedar, *Crusade and Mission*,
138–43.

165. Webster, "Conversion and Co-existence," 176.

166. Juan de Segovia, *Historia*, MC 2:11: "Erat quoque ipsis fidelibus
spes firma, vt in concilio generali, quemadmodum illorum antiquorum ita et

Hussitarum suo, quo accinctos se esse gloriabantur, gladio diuini verbi recte intellecti suarum caput heresum a corpore separaretur."

167. Juan de Segovia, Letter to Jean Germain, Dec. 18, 1455, fol. 47v: "Nemini e quidem extra domum quam inhabito comunicavi nisi per secretarium meum illi Reverendissimo domino ad quem litera plenior destinabatur et vestre prestantissime dominacioni."

168. Juan de Segovia, Letter to Nicholas of Cusa, Dec. 2, 1454, fol. 33r: "Proinde, magna cum humilitate exoro ne ante consilium suum, michi notificandum, aliis manifested; ideo namque cum proprio nuntio antiquiori quo habeo familiari transmitto. Est etiam quedam particularis ratio de qua ad partem scribo et decree videtur, ymmo exigi, quod ante accessum illius non publicetur opus, adhuc corrigendum" (in Cabanelas Rodríguez, *Juan de Segovia y el problema islámico*, 310); Letter to Jean Germain, Dec. 18, 1455, fol. 136r: "Mea tum repetita supplicacione ne in publicum quod etiam vestra censet paternitas principale feratur intentum meum."

169. Setton, *The Papacy and the Levant*, 2:168, 272.

170. Setton, *Western Hostility to Islam*, 20.

171. The council's ambassador to Constantinople wrote back to Basel on Sept. 16, 1436, relating, among other things, that the power of the Turks was growing. He advised the council to tell the emperor to put the kingdom of Hungary on alert. There is a copy of this letter in AGS, Estado, Francia, Legajo K-1711, fols. 383r–385r, and a summary in Álvarez Palenzuela, *La situación europea*, 330. See pp. 334–35 and 342–43 for more letters from Ragusa on the Turkish threat.

172. R. Black, *Benedetto Accolti and the Florentine Renaissance*, 226–34.

173. Helmrath, "The German *Reichstage* and the Crusade," 53.

174. Helmrath, "The German *Reichstage* and the Crusade," 58–60.

175. D. Lalande, ed., *Le Livre des fais du bon messire Jehan le Maingre, dit Boucicaut*, Document 3, pp. 105–8, in Housley, *Documents on the Later Crusades*, 106–7.

176. Bisaha, *Creating East and West*, 62.

177. His name has been rendered with various spellings, including Jacopo or Jacques Tedaldi. There are several manuscript versions of his account, which do not agree. See the discussion in Philippides, *Mehmed II the Conqueror*, 21–26. This volume contains both the Latin and the French texts.

178. Tetaldi, *Tractatus de Expugnatione Urbis Constantinopolis*, Chapter 2, par. 1, p. 139. For a discussion of the cannon's origin and role in the siege, see Philippides, "Urban's Bombard(s)."

179. Tetaldi, *Tractatus de Expugnatione Urbis Constantinopolis*, Chapter 6, par. 2, p. 159.

180. Schwoebel, *The Shadow of the Crescent*, 4–5. The manuscript version that Schwoebel used is "Informations envoyées, tant par Francisco de

France, à tres-reverend père en Dieu monseigneur le cardinal d'Avignon, que par Jehan Blanchin et Jacques Edadly [sic] marchant Florentin, de la prinse de Constantinople par l'empereur Turc le xxix. jour de May MCCCCLIII. à la quelle ledit Jacques estoit personnellement," in E. Martène and U. Durand, *Thesaurus novus anecdotorum* I (Paris, 1717), cols. 1819–1825. On the violence that followed the fall of the city, see also Runciman, *The Fall of Constantinople*, chap. 11.

181. Master Henry of Soemmern: The Fall and Sack of the City of Constantinople, in Philippides, *Mehmed II the Conqueror*, par. 5, p. 125.

182. Schwoebel, *The Shadow of the Crescent*, 13; Meserve, *Empires of Islam*, 65–70.

183. Schwoebel, *The Shadow of the Crescent*, 8, citing "Citazione del G. M. de Lastic a' Cavalieri del Priorato d'Alvernia, imponendo loro l'accorrere alla difesa di Rodi, minacciata dall' Ottomanno" in S. Pauli, ed., *Codice diplomatico del sacro militare ordine Gerosolimitano* II (Lucca, 1737), no. cvi, 31–32.

184. Tetaldi, *Tractatus de Expugnatione Urbis Constantinopolis*, Chapter 23, par. 1, p. 209.

185. On Isidore's long and illustrious ecclesiastical career and his efforts to achieve union between the West and the East, see Setton, *The Papacy and the Levant*, 2:3n5.

186. Schwoebel, *The Shadow of the Crescent*, 7, citing O. Raynaldus, *Annales eccesiastici post Baronium ab anno 1198 usque ad annum 1565*, ad an. 1453, nos. 5, 6; Isidore's letter from Crete to Nicholas V, August 15, 1453, in N. Iorga, *Notes et extraits pour servir à l'histoire des croisades au xve siècle* II (Bucharest, 1915–16), 522–24.

187. Juan de Segovia, Letter to Jean Germain, Dec. 18, 1455, fol. 65v. Germain's letter is not extant, but Juan wrote, "Verum nec michi difficultas esse videtur designata xiiii° puncto quod etiam si cetera concurrerent infra tres annos non posset practicari infra quos Thurcus posset multa conquirere ymmo Romani et ytalias."

188. A copy of this letter is in AGS, Estado, Francia, Legajo K-1711, fols. 96v–99r, and a summary is in Álvarez Palenzuela, *La situación europea*, 334–35. Ragusa also wrote that the patriarchs of Alexandria, Antioch, and Jerusalem were reportedly requesting the sultan's permission to attend Basel personally. Another letter from Ragusa (dated Feb. 13, 1437) informed the council that the sultan had denied them permission to go, threatening to kill all the Christians under their leadership. Furthermore, he wrote, the council should give serious thought to the defense of Hungary, since the Turks already possessed Greece, Romania, and Bulgaria, and the Albanians were already reduced to tribute. This letter is in AGS, Estado, Francia, Legajo K-1711, fols. 124v–125r, summarized in Álvarez Palenzuela, *La situación europea*, 342–43.

189. Setton, *The Papacy and the Levant*, 2:2.

190. See the discussion in Housley, introduction to *Documents on the Later Crusades*, 7–10.

191. Stieber, *Pope Eugenius IV*, 200–202.

192. This letter was dated March 8, 1456. It is quoted at length in Stieber, *Pope Eugenius IV*, 338–39.

193. Stieber, *Pope Eugenius IV*, 341–42.

194. Setton, *The Papacy and the Levant*, 2:235.

195. Bisaha, *Creating East and West*, 23–24.

196. Bisaha, *Creating East and West*, 58–59, 69.

197. Bisaha, *Creating East and West*, 62.

198. See the discussion in Bisaha, *Creating East and West*, 174–87.

Chapter Five. Converting Muslims

1. Cabanelas Rodríguez, *Juan de Segovia y el problema islámico*, 118.

2. Southern, *Western Views of Islam*, 91. Rudolf Haubst had also drawn connections among three of these thinkers in "Johannes von Segovia im Gespräch mit Nikolaus von Kues und Jean Germain," 118.

3. Biechler, "A New Face Toward Islam," 190.

4. Juan de Segovia, Letter to Nicholas of Cusa, Dec. 2, 1454, BUS 19, fol. 179v, see appendix 3 in this volume, lines 7–9.

5. Juan de Segovia, Letter to Nicholas of Cusa, Dec. 2, 1454, BUS 19, fol. 179v, appendix 3 in this volume, lines 6–9, and Letter to Jean Germain, Dec. 18, 1455, fol. 52v: "Quoniam vero prout in suis obiectionibus conmemorat d. v. quam plures doctorum et ministrorum christi conati sunt singuli seorsum obtinere apud sarracenos locum audiencie illis verbum dei predicaturi nec obtinere potuerunt id certe in eo exili iudicio videbatur quatenus huiusmodi audiencia publica interveniente ecclesie auctoritate obtineretur sub forma tractande pacis inter has maiores mundi tocius comunitates duas christianorum et sarracenorum legacionesque pro ea re tam insignes tamque magnifice forent ut a sarracenis contempni non possent."

6. Juan de Segovia, Letter to Nicholas of Cusa, Dec. 2, 1454, BUS 19, fol. 179v, appendix 3 in this volume, lines 12–15.

7. Juan de Segovia, Letter to Nicholas of Cusa, Dec. 2, 1454, BUS 19, fol. 179v, appendix 3 in this volume, lines 18–21.

8. Southern, *Western Views on Islam*, 91.

9. Biechler, "A New Face Toward Islam," 190. This is in BAV Vat. Lat. 2923, fol. 3v: "et haudubie materiam praebituro quatenus contraferencia assit de legum differencia."

10. Juan de Segovia, Letter to Jean Germain, Dec. 18, 1455, fol. 100v: "Si autem aliquando fuit contraferencia illa certe fuit dumtaxat inter latinos et greccs."

11. Juan de Segovia, *Historia*, MC 3:401: "Siquidem in Pysano concilio sentencialiter depositis contendentibus de papatu Benedicto XIII et Gregorio XII sic nominatis decimo sequenti die cardinales intrarunt conclaue pro eleccione futuri pastoris. In sancta vero Constanciensi synodo ingressus conclauis dilacionem accepit, sed nec tantam, vt in Basiliensi, propter contrafeencias tunc magnas, si per cardinales dumtaxat, aut per eos aliosque per concilium deputatos fienda esset eleccio."

12. Cabanelas Rodríguez, *Juan de Segovia y el problema islámico*, 118.

13. Juan de Segovia, Letter to Nicholas of Cusa, Dec. 2, 1454, BUS 19, fols. 179v–180r, pp. 252–57 in appendix 3 in this volume.

14. Juan de Segovia, Letter to Nicholas of Cusa, Dec. 2, 1454, BUS 19, fol. 179v, appendix 3 in this volume, lines 23–25.

15. Juan de Segovia, Letter to Nicholas of Cusa, Dec. 2, 1454, BUS 19, fol. 179v, appendix 3 in this volume, lines 12–15.

16. Juan de Segovia, Letter to Nicholas of Cusa, Dec. 2, 1454, BUS 19, fol. 180r, appendix 3 in this volume, lines 39–41.

17. Juan de Segovia, Letter to Nicholas of Cusa, Dec. 2, 1454, BUS 19, fol. 179v, appendix 3 in this volume, lines 17–18.

18. Juan de Segovia, Letter to Nicholas of Cusa, Dec. 2, 1454, BUS 19, fol. 179v, appendix 3 in this volume, lines 30–32.

19. Juan de Segovia, Letter to Nicholas of Cusa, Dec. 2, 1454, BUS 19, fol. 180r, appendix 3 in this volume, lines 55–77.

20. Juan de Segovia, Letter to Nicholas of Cusa, Dec. 2, 1454, BUS 19, fol. 181v: "et quanta audacia roborabuntur armati exercitus dum intelligent vel nolle audire legacionem christianorum ex parte de pace locuturam vel qucd nolunt edicere belli causas quod continue in christianos exercent vel qucd pudet ipsos omninoque renuunt ut de veritate legis in eorum presencia cum sapientibus suis conferendo videatur in quibus ipsi cum christianis conveniunt aut differunt super que differenciis pertractetur modus quo de medio auferantur."

21. Juan de Segovia, Letter to Nicholas of Cusa, Dec. 2, 1454, BUS 19, fol. 173v.

22. Juan de Segovia, Letter to Jean Germain, Dec. 18, 1455, fol. 67r: "Quod autem difficultari uidetur de lapsu trium annorum priusquam via pacis et doctrine practicari posset utinam in triginta annis compleretur effectus illius. Siquidem practicavit christus viam predicacionis plusquam per tres annos. . . . Transierunt denique ccc anni priusquam lex christi pacifice reciperetur in orbe. . . . Et si iam a quadringentis quin pocius ab octingentis

annis practicata est via belli de novoque licet eam resumere, via utique doc-trine triennio coartanda non est, quam practicari christus voluit usque ad mundi consummacionem."

23. Kedar, *Crusade and Mission*, 157.

24. On this visit and the memory of it, see Tolan, *Saint Francis and the Sultan*.

25. Tolan, *Saracens*, 215.

26. Tolan, *Saracens*, 219–22.

27. Juan de Segovia, Letter to Nicholas of Cusa, Dec. 2, 1454, BUS 19, fol. 178v: "Cum per illos maxima facta fuisset strages christianorum in un-garia, polonia, et moravia Innocencius papa quartus Anno domini M⁰ ii^c xlv miserit fratres Joannem de piano carpini et benedictum polonum ordinis mi-norum ad tartorum imperatorem [179r] Fratrem autem Guilielmum et alios tres predicatores. Ad primum quem reperiissent capitaneum illorum. Lega-cio autem contenta in litteris apostolicis hec erat quod placebat pape qui dominus et pater christianorum erat ut christiani omnes amicis essent pacem habituri cum tartaris, desideransque in celo esse magnos monebat ut christi fidem reciperent quem aliter salvari non possent, quodque miraretur de ho-mini occisione maxime christianorum ac potissime ungarorum moravorum et polonorum subiectorum pape facta per ipsos tartaros cum in millo ledere attemptassent eos. Et quia super hoc graviter deus erat offensus moneret ut de cetero caverent a talibus et penitentiam agerent. Scripta hec ubi supra tangen-cia parte christiane religionis pacem tartaris oblatam fuisse aut sarracenis. Non sic ille refert de prosecucione ad pacem oblatam consequenter se habente, sed quod per ipsum Innocencium quartum fuit passagium indictum." Actually, William of Rubruck was sent by Louis IX of France, not by Innocent IV. See the discussion in Tolan, *Saracens*, 222. John of Plano Carpini may not have been the best support for a peaceful approach to anyone. His *History of the Mongols* detailed the great threat he thought this empire posed and called for a multinational European force to fight them. See Nederman, *Worlds of Differ-ence*, 54.

28. See Kedar, *Crusade and Mission*, chap. 5, esp. 159–69.

29. Juan de Segovia, *De mittendo gladio*, fol. 22r: "Experientiaque sepe monstraverit dum aliqui singulares, zelo ducti fidei, ad predicandum veri-tatem Sarracenos adeunt, quod eos audire nolunt. Aliquando etiam nec oc-cidere, ut de sancto francisco contigit. Si vero occidantur, non propterea, ut martyrum tempore, multitudinem illorum ad fidem converti, quod pro au-dientia pertinetetur alio habenda modo instandum videretur."

30. Juan de Segovia, Letter to Jean Germain, Dec. 18, 1455, fol. 100v: "Si autem aliquando fuit contraferencia illa certe fuit dumtaxat inter latinos et grecos."

31. This appears in BAV Vat. Lat. 2923, fol. 3v, and was noted in Biechler, "A New Face Toward Islam," 190. I have not noted this term's appearance anywhere else in his writings to refer to this meeting he proposed with Muslim leaders.

32. Juan de Segovia, Letter to Jean Germain, Dec. 18, 1455, fol. 98r: "Et quamvis post acceptam pacem ecclesie et unitatem adhuc quedam remanserint pristini erroris reliquie Id nichilominus actum est interveniente pacis tractatu. Et per instructionem ecclesie cum primo ipsorum bohemorum dogma non solum heresis sed heresis armata diceretur quod illico arma deposuit nec terrori est quomodo primo fuit toti [98v] germanie nacioni eorum capite. . . . An vero perdiderit nomen heresis id certum est quod multitudo catholicorum non de illa ut primo loquitur nec ecclesia circa eius extirpacionem ut primo occupatur. Ut nam et utinam aliquando incipiat cum universitate Sarracenorum vel similis pacis tractatus ut concesso eis quidquid divine legi non repugnet, etiam si iuri positivo pacem et unitatem ecclesie suscipere vellent."

33. Juan de Segovia, Letter to Jean Germain, Dec. 18, 1455, fol. 97r: "Quod ergo pavescent doctrina catholice fidei irrisionem formidans infidelium quasi documenta eius sint leves racioncinationes et raciones puerorum quando de se ipsa certissime agnovit probacionem suam multo preciosiorem esse auro quod per ignem probatur. Equidem non semel sicut aurum sed iam a mille quadringentis plusquam persepe examinata est veritas fidei catholic disputacionibus primo cum iudeis stephano superante rabinos quinque synagogarum qui surrexerunt tanquam aliis fortiores disputare eo paulo vero per synagogas fiducialiter predicante continue ihesum. Cum gentibus autem persepe ut Ephesi posquam per tres menses in synagoga cum fiducia loquebatur de regno dei disputans Ita ut omnes qui habitabant in Asia audirent verbum domini. Quid igitur Corinthio et [97v] antiochie ubi primo vulgatum est nomen christianorum. Quid aliis locis Rome presertim biennio toto ad iudeos et grecos predicans regnum dei et docens ea que sunt de domino ihesu christo cum omni fiducia quamvis autem non sic auctenctice liber canonis testimonium de aliis apostolis ferat alie tamen scripture plenopere similia eos fecisse narrant. Ab inde examinata est tempore martirum. Denique post tempora persecucionem cum hereticis difficilibus ad vincendum quoniam fuere domestici hostes. Et quid dicendum post fundatus universitates generalium studiorum quorum precipuum exercitium est publice disputaciones de misterio trinitatis incarnacionis sacramenti eucharistie aliisque veritatibus fide utique et si non dixisset propheta regnis experiencia hactenus semper quoque magistris in dies demonstrat quod eloquia domini eloquia sunt casta argentumque igne examinatum probatum terre purgatum septuplum. Siquidem eloquia domini examinata sunt igne ipseque dominus protector est omni sperancium in se."

326 Notes to Pages 184–186

34. Juan de Segovia, Letter to Nicholas of Cusa, Dec. 2, 1454, BUS 19, fol. 180r: "tam diucius erraverant, existimantes christianos adoratores esse participum dei et sociorum. Sed et si hoc taceant christiani audacissima constancia inferre poterunt christianos nullatenus incredulos fore illos per suam legem reputatos adoratores participum dei et sociorum." For the surrounding lines, see appendix 3 in this volume, lines p. 256.

35. Juan de Segovia, *De mittendo gladio*, fol. 20v: "Audita resolucione qua utitur comunis scola theologorum, anmiratus verba hec dixit in effectu Et per deum nullus est inter christianos qui sciat hec declarare nisi vos solus. Cui Responsum est non credatis christianam religionem tam defectuosam in litteratis viris quia eciam hodie in hoc opido sunt xx persone scientes ista declarare." For the full account of this encounter, see appendix 2 in this volume.

36. Nicholas of Cusa, Letter to Juan de Segovia, Dec. 29, 1454, in Cabanelas, *Juan de Segovia y el problema islámico*, 314: "Spes est quod omnes Teucri acquescerent fidei Santissime Trinitatis ex rationibus tactis in scripto Reverendissime Paternitatis Vestre, quas et alias Basilee audivi a vos quando michi Richardum de Sancto Victore laudastis. Possunt et plures alie formari que ostenderent sufficientere fidem Trinitatis ad summam notitiam unius Dei accedere." This section appears in BAV Vat. Lat. 2923, fol. 37r.

37. Nicholas of Cusa, Letter to Juan de Segovia, Dec. 29, 1454, in Cabanelas, *Juan de Segovia y el problema islámico*, 314–15: "Expertus sum, tam apud iudeos quam ipsos Teucros non esse difficile persuadere Trinitatem in unitate substantie; sed circa unionem ypostaticam, in qua principaliter, ultra unum Deum colentes, nostra fides consistit, non minus difficile erit nunc quam semper ab initio." BAV Vat. Lat. 2923, fol. 37r.

38. Nicholas of Cusa, Letter to Juan de Segovia, Dec. 29, 1454, in Cabanelas, *Juan de Segovia y el problema islámico*, 315: "Ista pars erit, uti semper fuit, difficilis valde, quam no legi in hiis scriptis vestris nunc ad me missis elucidatam." BAV Vat. Lat. 2923, fol. 37r.

39. Juan de Segovia, Letter to Nicholas of Cusa, Dec. 2, 1454, BUS 19, fol. 180r: "Et hoc unum est ex maximis bonis quod non solum efficere sed perficere posset in sui principio pacis tractatus veritatem hanc iuris et facti parte religionis christiane publice notificando deum esse tantum unum et ita plusquam firmissime omnis credere christianos. Itaque nulla belli est causa in ipsos tanquam plurium sint adoratores deorum." See also appendix 3 in this volume.

40. Juan de Segovia, Letter to Nicholas of Cusa, Dec. 2, 1454, BUS 19, fol. 180r: "Lex quippe eorum iniungit eis . . . facere lites et bella, dicens quod . . . est utile et iustum facere contra non invocantes deum unum tanum quales reputant christianos omnes a lege ipsa per totum fere vocatos incredulos." See also appendix 3 in this volume.

41. Juan de Segovia, Letter to Nicholas of Cusa, Dec. 2, 1454, BUS 19, fol. 180r: "Ex quo alia etiam non exilis infamia aboleri posset quod christiani

adorent sicut deum sacerdotes suos presumptuosos, ut lex eorum inquit, indignantes."

42. Juan de Segovia, Letter to Nicholas of Cusa, Dec. 2, 1454, BUS 19, fols. 180r–180v: "Unde et si tales non sunt apud [180v] christianos, intelligere igitur ipsi possunt alios esse quam christianos quibus lex sua hoc imponit."

43. Juan de Segovia, Letter to Nicholas of Cusa, Dec. 2, 1454, BUS 19, fol. 183r: "Expertus id novi in collationibus habitis cum ambassiatore supra mentionato regis Granate, obiciente, magno cum improperio, quod christiani comederent Deum suum et a peccatis absolverent in Deum commissis."

44. Juan de Segovia, Letter to Nicholas of Cusa, Dec. 2, 1454, BUS 19, fol. 183r: "Unde tunc intellixi in isto aliisque multis, quam magna ignorantia divini iuris laboret tota multitudo abhominantur animoque vilipendunt christianos."

45. See Bisaha, *Creating East and West*, esp. chap. 2.

46. Juan de Segovia, Letter to Nicholas of Cusa, Dec. 2, 1454, BUS 19, fol. 181r: "Nec legis lator eorum talis reputandus erit quando tot tantaque falsa asseruit in illa." Also see Juan de Segovia, Letter to Jean Germain, Dec. 18, 1455, fol. 54v: "Hoc igitur avisatur ut ostendatur sarracenis non esse verum quod de christo lex testatur eorum. Et per consequens eam falsissimum dicere testimonium in isto et aliis quam plurimis quatenus ex ipsorum ostensione agnoscere occulariter valeant non esse eam legem [55r] dei."

47. Juan de Segovia, *Prefacio in translationem*, fol. 188v: "Sunt etenim, ut memorari michi videor, XXIX anni quod, Rome constitutus, rogatus fui a Patriarcha Constantinopolitano, quoniam in Ytalia haberi nescirem, in Hispaniam me scribere pro illo habendo. Et ex tunc multorum percepi relatione, idque ipse agnovi, quod paucissimi christianorum librum ipsum tenent quodque in paucissimis reperitur librariis, de quarum una, in Germania, librum incathenatum habui, anno XXXVII [1437] copiarique feci. Sed de hoc certissimum perhibere queo testimonium, translationem predictam in quamplurimis deviare a textus arabici continentia; et quod permultum gravat, cum multi doctrum catholicorum aliique etiam non doctores vixque docti, multos libellos multosque ediderint tractatus ad secte [fol. 189r] huius impugnationem, quorum multos perlegi multosque etiam penes me habeo, multi certe aut paucissimi vixque unus reperitur qui, prout Alchuranus continet dictaque patefacit translatio, testimonia vera referant ex quibus redarguere nituntur sectam eorum; sed persepe grossa quedam recitant nimis distantia a virili ratione, velut bestialia, puerilia quoque, pro lege teneant." In Cabanelas Rocríguez, *Juan de Segovia y el problema islámico*, 286.

48. Juan de Segovia, Letter to Nicholas of Cusa, Dec. 2, 1454, BUS 19, fol. 169r: "Etenim cum vestra concessione librum ipsum alchoran habuerim anno xxxvii sepe que in eo legeram et errores excerperam." See the discussion in Hernández Montes, *Biblioteca*, 172.

49. Juan de Segovia, *Prefacio in translationem*, fol. 189v: "Quocirca Basileam destinavi pro alchurano quem videram in libraria predicatorum Constantinopoli scriptum sed hic confirmis erat meo correcte tamen scriptus." As Hernández Montes noted (*Biblioteca*, 172), this work appears in Cabanelas Rodríguez, but that version omits the word Basileam.

50. Hernández Montes, *Biblioteca*, 171. There were also two others: one Arabic copy and the trilingual version that resulted from Gidelli's work in Aiton.

51. His name has also been rendered Yça or Isa or Hice or Içe de Gidelli or Gidelli or Jedih. See Wiegers, *Islamic Literature in Spanish and Aljamiado*, 82–89. For an explanation of the role and responsibilities of the *alfaquí* (*faqīh* in Arabic) and other leaders in the Mudéjar community, see 143.

52. Juan de Segovia, *Prefacio in translationem*, fol. 190r: This translation appears in Wiegers, *Islamic Literature in Spanish and Aljamiado*, 71. The original reads, "Cum regio abinde facto mandato uni ex alphaquinis maioribus regni Castelle, ille transferre se non posse, et quia nesciret et quia adhuc nec possibile fore[t], respondisset, placuit divine pietati ut desiderium meum, ad gloriam ordinatum nominis eius, adimpleretur; et a parentibus amicisque meis securitate reddita de indempnitate persone salarioque votive pro suis obtinendo laboribus, die quinto decembris, anno lv locum hunc mei incolatus prioratus Eythonis, dyoces[is] Maurianensis, applicuit fame qui celebrioris inter Sarracenos regni Castelle, Yca Gidelli, Alfaquinus Segobiensis, secte sue habens comitem." I agree with Wiegers's comment that the *fame* here should be translated as from *fama*, not *fames*. Cabanelas Rodríguez (*Juan de Segovia y el problema islámico*, 145) treated it as the latter, which led him to some unwarranted conclusions about Yça.

53. Gidelli's letter notifying Juan that he had changed his mind and was willing to make the journey if needed is an interesting document. A later copy of this letter (with unknown amounts simply left out—the scribe put "et cetera" three times) is contained in BAV Vat. Lat. 2923, fols. 178v–180r, and is published in Cabanelas Rodríguez, *Juan de Segovia y el problema islámico*, 273–77, and Wiegers, *Islamic Literature in Spanish and Aljamiado*, 230–32. Wiegers offered an English translation on 232–35. He also wrote (71) that the existing copy is a Latin translation of the letter, presumably in Castilian, that Gidelli sent to Segovia. Cabanelas commented (140n2) that the letter is curious for its "Castilianized" Latin sprinkled with awkward wording that reveals the peculiarities of the Muslim's means of expressing himself in Latin. The explanation given by Wiegers seems more likely: that he wrote his letter in Castilian (we know that Segovia wrote to *him* in Castilian—see Hernández Montes, *Obras*, 320) and that original letter was translated by someone into the version in BAV Vat. Lat. 2923.

54. Wiegers, *Islamic Literature in Spanish and Aljamiado*, 83–84.

55. Juan de Segovia, Letter to an unknown friend, April 18, 1458, fol. 198: "Cum vero die uno ministratum ei fuerit de porrea pisorum, ut moris modico preparata vino, notitia habita die sequenti, panem in vispera solum comedit velut penitentiam agens." In Cabanelas Rodríguez, *Juan de Segovia y el problema islámico*, 340.

56. This preface is contained in BAV Vat. Lat. 2923, fols. 186–196 (this version published in Cabanelas Rodríguez, *Juan de Segovia y el problema islámico*, 279–302), and a much later copy (eighteenth century?) is in Biblioteca Nacional, MS 9250, fols. 107–121v. Some have argued that Toledo, Biblioteca Pública, MS 235 is a later copy of Yça's Spanish translation of the Qur'ān. See the discussion by Wiegers, *Islamic Literature in Spanish and Aljamiado*, 110–14, and López-Morillas, "'Trilingual' Marginal Notes."

57. Juan de Segovia, *Prefacio in translationem*, fol. 190v: "Ipso autem magistro, qui uxorem noviter nuptam dimiserat, ad recessum hinc festinante et secum translationem per eum scriptam reportare volente, quoniam ille qui iuxta arabicum in alia columpna translationem in vulgari hispanico scribebat, litera grossa et formata, non valebat eque cito complere opus, ut copia maneret; alium scriptorem fuit habere necesse." In Cabanelas Rodríguez, *Juan de Segovia y el problema islámico*, 290.

58. Juan de Segovia, *Prefacio in translationem*, fols. 191–191v: "Completa, autem, ut predictum est, translatione, magnopere insteti quatenus per alics menses duos magister ille mecum permaneret ut in notitiam proficerem arabici ydeomatis, quod velut sillabicando legere incipiebam, agnitis literis, nec tamen signis aut caracteribus [fol. 191v] omnibus accentum tantumve significantibus vel in alium sensum trahentibus dictiones, utque etiam in materia legis mutuo conferremus." In Cabanelas Rodríguez, *Juan de Segovia y el problema islámico*, 291.

59. Juan de Segovia, *Prefacio in translationem*, fol. 191v: "Sed dum recessit, salarii recepta conferta atque coagitata mensura, promisit acturum se ut frater eius, qui alphaquinus etiam erat nec uxore ligatus, venturus ad me foret, docturus me usque ad perfectum arabicum ydeoma." In Cabanelas Rodríguez, *Juan de Segovia y el problema islámico,* 292.

60. Juan de Segovia, *Prefacio in translationem*, fol. 191v: "Conductore autem ex Hyspania redeunte, etiamsi id facere promiserat, ille non venit, animo sibi deficiente, quia ubi timor non erat, trepidanti timore [Ps. 13:5], equidem Magnificencia ducalis salvumconductum concesserat, sub protectione sua constituens ex sarracenorum secta ad me venientes, stantes et recedentes." In Cabanelas Rodríguez, *Juan de Segovia y el problema islámico*, 292.

61. Echevarría Arsuaga, "Las aljamas mudéjares castellanas en el siglo XV," 101.

62. Juan de Segovia, *Prefacio in translationem*, fol. 191v: "habere eum cupiens, experimento previo si cum eo essem profecturus, per destinatum sibi psalmum unum, literis scriptum arabicis interpretationemque eius latinam seorum, responsum accepi ut expensis parcerem." In Cabanelas Rodríguez, *Juan de Segovia y el problema islámico*, 292.

63. Juan de Segovia, *Prefacio in translationem*, fols. 191v–192: "Rationem autem reddidit non scientie sue, properea quod, sicut inter christianos [fol. 192r] aliud ydeoma vulgare est aliud latinum, sic etiam inter sarracenos, scripturamque per me ad eum destinata illa esset arabice lingue sicut latine, cuius paucissimi, etiam inter sarracenos, conscii forent." In Cabanelas Rodríguez, *Juan de Segovia y el problema islámico*, 293.

64. Juan de Segovia, *Donatio*, 108n100: "Responsio ad litteram alphaqueni Segobiensis, interpretis Alcurani, putantis se loqui excelsa de unitate Dei et ultimi finis; eciam in pergameno et uulgari."

65. Juan de Segovia, Letter to an unknown friend, April 18, 1458, fol. 98: "Retrahere nequirem manum, secretiora aperire volens legis eorum; id autem dixero, quoniam retinere eum non potui, collaturus super continentia legis. Rogatu pleniori meo, dum in Yspania fuit, xii dubia exposuit michique transmisit, retrahentia, ut inquit, sarrecenos omnes a confessione catholice fidei, requisita a me de illis satisfactione. Evangelicam igitur attendens doctrinam fidelem omni petenti tribuendam, intermisso alio ichoato opere, dum in Yspania trasmittere volui, ad aratrum misi manum, sed intercidentibus multis, precipue autem infirmitate, que a mensibus xix in tibiis primum, sed iam ab anno medio in epate sita, in dies totum debilitat corpus animique vires; ut cupio, intendere nequeo labori manibus languidatis." Published in Cabanelas Rodríguez, *Juan de Segovia y el problema islámico*, 341. Here I must disagree with the translation offered by Wiegers, *Islamic Literature in Spanish and Aljamiado*, 74. He translated "Evangelicam igitur attendens doctrinam fidelem omni petenti tribuendam" as "Following the doctrine of the Gospel that one should seek to satisfy any believer who asks for something." But the *fidelem* is accusative and goes with the *doctrinam*, not the *petenti*, and should be taken as something like "the trustworthy Gospel teaching." It would be striking, indeed, if Segovia had referred to Gidelli as a believer.

66. These two are numbers 99 and 100 in Hernández Montes, *Biblioteca*, 108–9. This account of these works differs from that offered by Cabanelas, who based his on Julio González's edition of Segovia's *Donatio*. The difference resulted from punctuation of the manuscript and from a supposed reference to a work in another of Juan's writings. This is one of the ways in which Hernández Montes's edition improved upon the earlier one by González. See the discussion in Hernández Montes, *Obras*, 319–20, numbers 66 and 67.

67. Wiegers argued (see *Islamic Literature in Spanish and Aljamiado*, 112–14) that a copy of this exists in the Municipal Library of Toledo (MS T235), but see López-Morillas, "Lost and Found?" for a convincing challenge to this.

68. See the discussion in Burman, *Reading the Qur'ān in Latin Christenaom*, 181–83.

69. Juan de Segovia, Letter to Nicholas of Cusa, Dec. 2, 1454, BUS 19, fol. 178v: "Dicit namque 'non sitis contemptores sed pacem diligite eamque vocate quem vos digniores et potenciores existitis unde vobiscum deus de beneficiis vestris nichil diminui permittit.' Cum igitur lex iubeat eorum ut sarraceni diligant pacem eamque vocent nulla repulsa timenda est quod ad ipsam invitati que pacis sun audire nolint."

70. Juan de Segovia, Letter to Nicholas of Cusa, Dec. 2, 1454, BUS 19, fol. 178v: "Sed et si hodie prevenientes ipsi christianos vocarent ad pacem ambasiatam ecclesie catholice desuper destinantes nemo certe christianorum aut quis ille esset tante audacie responsurus actendere nolle."

71. Juan de Segovia, Letter to Jean Germain, Dec. 18, 1455, fol. 61v: "[Q]uarta vero difficultas affirmans in lege Mahumeti expresse caveri quod non disputent de fide sua contra christianos ideoque daturi non essent salvumconductum invititur cum dicto plurimorum de hiis que non viderunt perhibentium testimonium. Siquidem de materia disputacionis liber Alchoran in pluribus locis pro modo non conmemorandis mencionem facit. Sed in azoara xxxviii § iiiiº inquit auctor secte illius ad Mahumetum, 'Omnes homines legum preter malos honestis verbis disputando semper alloquere et confitere et semper te in deum credere et preceptis sibi missis parere cum deus suus sit tui deus et omnium omnibus adorandus.' Non minus loquitur etiam de via pacis per sectatores suos diligenda atque vocanda."

72. Juan de Segovia, Letter to Jean Germain, Dec. 18, 1455, fol. 72v: "Nec in uno solum sed in quam multis passibus affirmatur librum alchoran celitus esse missum."

73. Juan de Segovia, Letter to Jean Germain, Dec. 18, 1455, fol. 72r: "Denique si illud noviter factum est nisi iam combusti forent omnes libri legis eorum ubicumque in mundo habenture et quod illa nova composicio ubique habeatur ipsimet testimonio essent illud opus noviter editum non esse [72v] legem datam per angelum Gabrielem ut Alchoran inquit Mahumeto prophete suo." Grammatically, this sentence suggests that Segovia was saying that Muhammad was Gabriel's prophet, but he certainly knew otherwise and expressed as much explicitly earlier on this folio. This genitive must be taken to refer to God's prophet, picking up this earlier reference.

74. Juan de Segovia, Letter to Jean Germain, Dec. 18, 1455, fol. 72v: "Si igitur, ut inquit liber ipse de de ipso, testimonium perhibens celitus datus est,

qua temeritate ve a pauco citra tempore ausi sunt alterare. Aliud quippe est de uno ydeomate in aliud transferre, aliud transmutare modum loquendi."

75. Juan de Segovia, Letter to Jean Germain, Dec. 18, 1455, fol. 72v: "Adhuc et si omnes libri penes sarracenos consistentes combusti forent combusti non essent quos habent christiani."

76. Juan de Segovia, Letter to Jean Germain, Dec. 18, 1455, fol. 72r: "Etenim, cum tota summa secte huius redignatur quasi ad ista duo quod deus est unus et Mahumetus nuncius propheta atque legatus eius eo ipso quod confiterentur verba legis eorum non esse verba dei sed quod a suis sapientibus lex eorum composita est per inquisicionem et discursum scientificum."

77. Juan de Segovia, Letter to Jean Germain, Dec. 18, 1455, fol. 73v: "Ita quod huiusmodi nova composicio sit ad formam dyalogi vel discipulo magistrum interrogante aut econverso vel per modum questionum profecto collaturis cum ipsis sarracenis magnopere gaudendum esset quin ex interrogaciones et responsione materia et extensionem recipiit et clarificationem sicut in operibus scolasticorum doctorum editis quasi ab aniis iii^c quorum [74v] modus est posita questione argumentis pro et contra factis diffinere questioni et argumentis incontrarium respondere."

78. Juan de Segovia, Letter to Jean Germain, Dec. 18, 1455, fol. 74r: "qui moderni sunt sapientes sarracenorum quia ipsi non fuerunt auctores composicionis illius ipsimet confiterentur se non intelligere legem suam et sic defendere non posse aut dubia eius declarare."

79. Burman, *Reading the Qur'ān in Latin Christendom*, 181.

80. See the discussion in Burman, *Reading the Qur'ān in Latin Christendom*, 182–83, and the full text of this document contained in Cabanelas Rodríguez, *Juan de Segovia y el problema islámico*, 279–302.

81. Juan de Segovia, *Liber de magna auctoritate*, 223.

82. Juan de Segovia, *Liber de magna auctoritate*, 224.

83. Juan de Segovia, Letter to Nicholas of Cusa, Dec. 2, 1454, BUS 19, fol. 170v: "Referre pudet alia pudenda absurda quoque non modica secte illius obvoluta certe vel proxime antecedentibus vel sequentibus immediate magnarum virtutum moralium divinarum que sentenciis gravibus. Hiisque et illis poetice dulcedinis et insignis eloquencie perfusis nitore."

84. N. Daniel, *Islam and the West*, 172–76.

85. Juan de Segovia, Letter to Nicholas of Cusa, Dec. 2, 1454, BUS 19, fol. 172r: "Set quia imponunt eidem multiplex falsum testimonium in derogacionem catholice fidei et secte eorum confirmationem. Attestante hac christum marie filium dixisse O filii israhel, Ego vobis adeo missus sum nuncius quod de testamento meis in est manibus affirmo vobis que bonum nuncium affero denuncio post me venturum esse cui nomen mahumetus. Alibi etiam dicit quod eius nomen in testamento et evangelo continetur."

86. Juan de Segovia, *De mittendo gladio*, fol. 15r: "Intuenti namque legem Sarracenorum Alchoran vocatam, notum existit quod plus centum locis libri prefati mentio fiat de hiis qui dei loco adorant seu invocant in auxilium quos appellat socios dei atque participes seu pares. Magna de illis facta irrisione cum deus nisi unus non sit. . . . Hec similiaque multa dicit propter christianos, quos incredulos sepissime vocat quoniam adorant filium et spiritum sanctum, auxilium eorum sicut et dei invocantes. . . . Quo circa vocat eos associatos quia adoratores sociorum et participum dei, girovagos quoque et ventilantes. Et in quam pluribus locis appellans mendacissimos et inscios vocat eos tamquam falsum imponentes deo quod peccatum dicit irremissibile."

87. Juan de Segovia, Letter to Nicholas of Cusa, Dec. 2, 1454, BUS 19, fol. 176v: "Hoc enim ut sermo preexposuit pro fundamento habet sarracenorum secta velud domus supra arenam fundata quod minus attenta observatione legum gratie et scripture servanda sit lex nature Abrahe temporibus permanens. In reductione hac posterioris ad legem priorem"; fol. 177r: "Sic igitur Mahumetus reiectis lege gracie et scripture observari precepit legem nature ut quomodo ante tempora diluvii [in margin: sic] stadium sarracenorum sic abusus plurimarum illis concessus mulierum quatenus crescent et multiplicent terram repleturi."

88. Juan de Segovia, Letter to Nicholas of Cusa, Dec. 2, 1454, BUS 19, fol. 170v: "quod certe ex lege Mahumeti videtur Belzebuth demoniorum principem quimendax est et pater mendacii fuisse legis ipsius datorem."

89. Juan de Segovia, Letter to Nicholas of Cusa, Dec. 2, 1454, BUS 19, fol. 175v: "Timet quidem spiritus rector, magis autem subversor eorum, incitare sarracenos ut dumtaxat pro causa fidei occidant christi predicatores singulariter transeuntes ad eos."

90. Juan de Segovia, *De mittendo gladio*, fol. 4v: "xxxvi[ra] multipharia ratiocinatione arguit Sarracenos adoratores esse principis mundi huius, cuius nuncios fuit Mahumetus."

91. Tolan, *Saracens*, 156.

92. N. Daniel, *Islam and the West*, 51. Note that this contradicts Tolan's statement (*Saracens*, 226) that "Bacon, unlike so many earlier Christian authors, does not describe Muhammad as inspired by the devil."

93. Juan de Segovia, *Prefacio in translationem*, fol. 187v: "Siquidem, multis attenta pensatis meditatione, non quidem a me primo, sed a multis progenitoribus meis, secta huiusmodi bestia illa est descripta in Apocalipsi a Johanne, que de terra ascendens, fecit, facit, et faciet, sed diu in suo permanebit vigore, terram et omnes inhabitantes in ea, terrenos videlicet homines, adorare bestiam primam de mari ascendentem, *ut quicumque non adoraverit ymaginem bestie occidatur aut quod habeat caracterem in dextera manu aut in fronte sua* [Rev. 13:15–16], confitendo publice eius dogma perversum aut solvendo tributum;

experimento utique demonstrante quod maior semper accepit crementum in dies, ut nisi in Galliarum et Hispanie partibus, ab octingentis annis confinia sua dilataverit continuo fere super dominia christianorum." In Cabanelas Rodríguez, *Juan de Segovia y el problema islámico*, 283–84.

94. See, for example, Biechler, "A New Face Toward Islam," 189–93; Izbicki, "The Possibility of Dialogue with Islam," 183; Bisaha, *Creating East and West*, 144–47. In *Saracens*, John V. Tolan wrote that from 1300 until the Enlightenment, there was little development in European thinking about Muslims, with occasional exceptions, among whom Juan de Segovia was the most significant (276).

95. Hopkins, *Nicholas of Cusa's "De pace fidei" and "Cribratio Alkorani,"* 19.

96. Nicholas of Cusa, *Cribratio Alkorani*, Book II, Chapter 13, par. 124, p. 132.

97. Nicholas of Cusa, *Cribratio Alkorani*, Book II, Chapter 19, par. 158, p. 149.

98. See the helpful discussion in Hopkins, *Nicholas of Cusa's "De pace fidei" and "Cribratio Alkorani,"* 21–29.

99. Nicholas of Cusa, *Cribratio Alkorani*, Book II, Chapter 18, pars. 150–52, pp. 145–46: "Nevertheless, there are those who allege, by way of excusing the writer of the Koran, the consideration that he wanted to persuade the uneducated Arabs (in order that they would believe in one Creator, who gave them life in this temporal age) that in the everlasting, future age the Creator was also going to give them a life without deficiency—la lifel much better than this present one. Moreover, Ithey allegel that to this end (as is read in the Koran) the writer introduced many likenesses, which he nonetheless did not explain; rather, he left them as known to the wise. Furthermore, las is alleged,I unless in foretelling of the joyfulness of the future life he had taken examples from this sensible life, Ithe Arabsl would not have understood and would not have been moved, because what was promised would have been unknown to them. . . . [par. 151] And so, at the place in Chapter 1 where Ithe writerl says that those who are good will enter into Paradise, where they will possess forever very fresh waters, many kinds of fruit, various vegetables, very lovely and very pure women, and every good, we must take note of that which he says: 'And they will possess forever . . . every good.' Surely, [p. 146] this good is none other than God. . . . [par. 152] And so, in the last analysis, IMuhammadl does not seem to contradict the Gospel, which asserts that the Paradise of the intelligent and wise is the vision of God and of His Wisdom (i.e., of Christ)." Ramón Llull had also thought that Christianity and Islam were quite close in their beliefs. See the discussion and references in Garcías Palou, *Ramón Llull*, 401–5.

100. Juan de Segovia, Letter to Nicholas of Cusa, Dec. 2, 1454, BUS 19, fol. 170v: "Sarracenica vero paradisus talis describitur qualis a gente illa inerudita arabum in hoc desideratur mundo: Set et mencio non sit de illa quod in hoc mundo dum vixerint multiplicatissimis preceptis illis iubetur ut pugnatu vadant atque predatu, magis autem quod accubabunt in stratis sericeis, eruntque eis rivorum genera quatuor subtus fluencium a quarum meri, lactis, et mellis despumati condicione beatitudinis huius actionum manifestante apercius quanta debeant securitate [in margin with insert mark: sarraceni sperare a] credere in lege talia promittente suas animas salvare posse."

101. Juan de Segovia, Letter to Nicholas of Cusa, Dec. 2, 1454, BUS 19, fol. 170v: "Referre pudet alia pudenda absurda quoque non modica secte illius obvoluta certe vel proxime antecedentibus vel sequentibus inmediate magnarum virtutum moralium divinarumque sentenciis gravibus. Hiisque et illis poetice dulcedinis et insignis eloquencie perfusis nitore."

102. Juan de Segovia, Letter to Jean Germain, Dec. 18, 1455, fol. 87r: "Ut namque in prima emanacione respectus originis verbi preintelligitur ei quod est cognitum sine intuitum esse. Ita et in 2ª respectus passive spiracionis ad complacencium sine complacitum esse. Sed hoc explicare longiorem tractatum requireret. Verum est autem quod non hiis terminis dicere et dici sed usitaciori certe sermone quem divina scriptura nobis insinuat, lex utitur Mahumeti in pluribus locis vocando christum verbum dei. Ex qua appellacione magnum utique auxilium confertur doctoribus christianis de trinitatis misterio collaturis cum sapientibus sarracenorum."

103. Juan de Segovia, *De mittendo gladio*, fol. 4v: "xxxiiª consideracio respondetur quatuor ex vii rationibus ultimo allegatis quare secta Mahumeti continuo mansit in maiori propagatione. Et quod magna dignum est anmiracione quomodo id sit factum absque gloria martyrii christianorum inter rationes alias quia putatum est non contrariari doctrine evangelice quam pre ceteris Sarraceni odio habent."

104. Juan de Segovia, Letter to Nicholas of Cusa, Dec. 2, 1454, BUS 19, fol. 169v: "spiritus mahumeti pseudo magister."

105. Juan de Segovia, Letter to Nicholas of Cusa, Dec. 2, 1454, BUS 19, fol. 170r: "impudentissime spiritus."

106. Juan de Segovia, Letter to Nicholas of Cusa, Dec. 2, 1454, BUS 19, fol. 170v: "Ex lege Mahumeti videtur Belzebuth demoniorum principem qui mendax enim et pater mendacii fuisse legis ipsius datorem." Also Juan de Segovia, *De mittendo gladio*, fol. 4r: "quod spiritus Machumetum alloquens fuit Beelzebuth."

107. Hopkins, *Nicholas of Cusa's "De pace fidei" and "Cribratio Alkorani,"* 29.

108. Tolan, *Saracens*, xiii–xv.

109. Tolan, *Saracens*, 137.
110. Tolan, *Saracens*, 137–52.
111. Tolan, *Saracens*, 137–53.
112. Tolan, *Saracens*, 157–58.
113. Juan de Segovia, *Prefacio in translationem*, fol. 186r: "errantes in vera fide, erroneos, hereticos ac perfectos hereticos et supra omnes qui hactenus fuerunt." In Cabanelas Rodríguez, *Juan de Segovia y el problema islámico*, 279.
114. Juan de Segovia, Letter to Nicholas of Cusa, Dec. 2, 1454, BUS 19, fol. 173r: "Rationeque prolis multiplicatione necdum illis fore gentes satis ad custodiendum sed habundare ut continuo exerceantur ad prelium lege sua que multiplicatissima dedit mandata pugne permittente illis multitudinem uxorem aliarumque mulierum ut eorum numerositas semper augeatur."
115. Juan de Segovia, *De mittendo gladio*, fol. 16r: "Cumque scriptura sacra ve te de cuius ystoriis in Alchoran mentio sepe sit notificet belli iusti xii causas iuxta Sarracenorum creditum adversus christianos incredulos vocatos ab."
116. Juan de Segovia, Letter to Nicholas of Cusa, Dec. 2, 1454, BUS 19, fol. 177v: "via utraque armorum, scilicet violencia et seductione."
117. Juan de Segovia, Letter to Nicholas of Cusa, Dec. 2, 1454, BUS 19, fol. 173r: "Quod experimento patuit quando centesimo anno post introductam sectam suam tam prole habundavit sarracenorum communitas quod ad centena millia transierint in yspaniam obtinuerint que maximam illius et partem magnam galliarum, ut autem affirmat petrus abbas Cluniacensis, qui anno domini Mcxliii de arabico in latinum librum alchoran fecit transferri Sarracenorum, tunc adeo maxima gens erat ut dimidia pars mundi posset reputari."
118. Juan de Segovia, Letter to Nicholas of Cusa, Dec. 2, 1454, BUS 19, fol. 173r: "Spiritus vero Mahumeti ad roborandam sectam sarracenorum quod dare non potuit feminas atque viris videlicet quod fieret prolis multiplicatio naturali lege servata inrationii viro carnem suam in plures non dividente hoc est quod una unius dumtaxat viri esset uxor virque unius solum uxoris vir, sed quod uno concepto plures filii generarentur quem hoc efficere non potuit gratia vel natura supplere voluit ex culpa."
119. Qur'ān, Sura 2, 221–27, trans. Cragg, *Readings in the Qur'ān*, 316. Juan de Segovia, Letter to Nicholas of Cusa, Dec. 2, 1454, BUS 19, fol. 170r: "Expresse permittente lege sua preter uxores quatuor, illarumque pro voluntate triuum repudium cum ancillis cum ompticiis omnibusque subiectis mulieribus arandis a natura sua ubi voluerint."
120. European writers dedicated so much attention to this verse that Norman Daniel remarked that it must be "the verse most often translated in all the Middle Ages" (*Islam and the West*, 351). He thought their treatment

of it such an important feature of the evolution of the West's image of Islam that he included an appendix (Appendix E, 351–53) on this verse alone.

121. Juan de Segovia, Letter to Nicholas of Cusa, Dec. 2, 1454, BUS 19, fol. 176v: "Qualis autem sit nobisque pateat conservatio et incrementium secte sarracenorum qui longius ab eis distant intelligere possunt, sed qui inhabitant prope experiuntur et senciunt. Experiuntur equidem bellorum continuacione, sentiunt autem in omni multiplicacione prolis quia terra vix illis ad inhabitandum sufficiente vicinas replent." Note that this contrasts with what he said about Jews who entered Palestine after the Egyptian enslavement. He explained that these Jews multiplied quickly because they married young (fol. 173: "quomodo in prima contigit etate ut feminas haberent quibus nutere possent").

122. Juan de Segovia, *Repetitio de fide catholica*, fol. 190r B: "Et hodie etiam apparet de secta machometi que laxat frenum concupiscencie carnalis ad vicia multa et post mortem ponit suam felicitatem in carnalibus ac fetidis delectationis."

123. Juan de Segovia, Letter to Nicholas of Cusa, Dec. 2, 1454, BUS 19, fol. 176v: "Hiisque et illis poetice dulcedinis et insignis eloquencie perfusis nitore Sarracenica vero paradisus talis describitur qualis a gente illa inerudita arabum in hoc desideratur mundo . . ."

124. N. Daniel, *Islam and the West*, 176. See his discussion on Christian commentators' treatment of the Qur'ānic paradise (172–76) and also the rest of this chapter (chap. 5, "The Place of Self-Indulgence in the Attack on Islam," 153–85), which treats other features of Islam's alleged moral laxity.

125. Mirrer, *Women, Jews, and Muslims*, 48–50 and 57. But see all of chap. 3, "Muslim Men in the Ballad."

126. Weissberger, *Isabel Rules*, 109–10.

127. Weissberger, *Isabel Rules*, 104–14.

128. It is interesting that, as Tolan notes (*Saracens*, 146), accusations of sexual depravity were also commonly levelled at heretics. In Le Mans, chroniclers accused Henry of Lausanne of seducing both boys and women and engaging in lewd acts, which their writings report in detail. Jerome accused Simon Magus and Priscillian of sexual depravity.

129. This concern on the part of Christian writers to show that Islam was not a religion oriented toward spiritual things also played a role in their discussions of the Qur'ānic paradise. See N. Daniel, *Islam and the West*, 172.

130. Juan de Segovia, Letter to Nicholas of Cusa, Dec. 2, 1454, BUS 19, fol. 176r: "enim circumcisio apud eos servetur hoc non reperitur in Mahumeti secta preceptum, sed forte observant ex primo patre eorum ysmaele circumcisus qui fuit, et per hoc reputant se agregatos eorum communitati cuius non est velut proprium signum."

Notes to Pages 203–204

131. Juan de Segovia, Letter to Nicholas of Cusa, Dec. 2, 1454, BUS 19, fol. 176v: "Namque illo permaxime utuntur iudei ex ysaac semine descendentes cui non vero ysmaeli dei ex parte fuit statutum, pactum, et phedus. Ex hoc patescente causa quare sacras litteras sarraceni non venerantur in hoc aliisque plurimis expressum contra eorum legem dantes testimonium. Unde sicut ex verbo vite non acceperunt originem. Ita minime apreciantur hunc divinum sermonem quem abrahe locutus est deus cuius gloriantur se legem tenere gloriantur vero in eo per quod originem acceperunt in corporea videlicet generatione et pugna gladii."

132. Ryan, *The Apostolic Conciliarism of Jean Gerson*, 143–44.

133. See, for example, Juan de Segovia, *De mittendo gladio*, fol. 4v: "quam oportunum sit per modum tractande pacis intendere ad conversionem Sarracenorum severitati parcendo ob multitudinem eorum ignoranciamque [word written above line: quorum?] instruendo. Et sic noticia veritatis uniendo animos violenta pace numquam firma manente. Cum vero eadem sint principia essendi et conservandi quamviter hoc mahumeti secta non servat quod decet religionem christianam uti originem accepit per verbum dei vivi sic semet ipsam continuare et sibimet subdere orbis naciones talibus armis sibi concessis."

134. N. Daniel, *Islam and the West*, 93–99.

135. Juan de Segovia, Letter to Jean Germain, Dec. 18, 1455, fol. 48v: "Lex autem Mahumeti gloriatur quod non ambiguum sed quod racione constans dicit ideoque eius lator non venerit cum miraculis."

136. Juan de Segovia, Letter to Nicholas of Cusa, Dec. 2, 1454, BUS 19, fol. 170v: "Ath de miraculis quare per Mahumetum ipsum non fierent, ad susceptionem legis sue decem tribuit excusationes, quedam vero in libro recitata vel tam confuse exprimuntur ut intelligencia haberi non valeat, vel dumtaxat mira sunt." Also Juna de Segovia, *De mittendo gladio*, fol. 15r: "Unde Azoara lxxxi de semet ipso loquens Machumetus ait, Michi divinitus missum est quod homines dyabolici auscultando dicebant Nos Alchoran mirabilem auditu, viam rectam edocentem credimus."

137. Peter the Venerable, Book 1 of *Liber contra sectam sive haeresim saracenorum*, in Kritzeck, *Peter the Venerable and Islam*, 233: "non solum natura rationales, sed et ingenio et arte rationabiles." For this quote and the next, I have quoted the translation that appears in Tolan, *Saracens*, 161.

138. Peter the Venerable, Book 1 of *Liber contra sectam sive haeresim saracenorum*, in Kritzeck, *Peter the Venerable and Islam*, 234: "aliquis studiosorum secularem scientiam amantium."

139. Tolan, *Saracens*, 161 and 251.

140. Tolan, *Saracens*, 254.

141. Tolan, *Saracens*, 254.

142. Hopkins, *Nicholas of Cusa's "De pace fidei" and "Cribratio Alkorani,"* 2.

143. Juan de Segovia, Letter to Nicholas of Cusa, Dec. 2, 1454, BUS 19, fol. 180r: "quod sarraceni ipsi ita credere compellentur dum audient rationes divine unitatis seriosius eis coram exponendas quatenus evidentissime percipiant quam longissime distat christianorum fidei, nec solum credere sed vel leviter plures estimare deos esse scientes probare ad oculum hoc esse maximum omnium impossibilium, sicut deum esse unum maximum est omnium necesitatorium quodque ita hoc clarissime sciunt esse verum deum esse dumtaxat unum quod longissime quinymmo omnino distat ab eorum fide credere aliquos esse dei socios atque participes quoniam tale asserere divine repugnat unitati. Cumque ipsi hoc intelligent, eciam si christiani id aperte non dicerent sarracenos ipsos necesse est de sua cogitare lege."

144. See, for example, Llull's *Libre de contemplació en Déu,* chapter 112, and the discussion in Garcías Palou, *Ramón Llull,* 55. I have argued elsewhere (Wolf, "Juan de Segovia and Western Perspectives on Islam in the Fifteenth Century," 200–201) that Segovia and Llull departed significantly in aspects of their thought beyond these broad similarities.

145. Tolan, *Saracens,* 251.

146. Jesse Mann has acknowledged this in his "Truth and Consequences."

147. Biechler, "A New Face Toward Islam," 189–93; Izbicki, "The Possibility of Dialogue with Islam," 183.

148. See Hernández Montes, *Biblioteca,* 248, and Mann, "The Historian and the Truths," 180.

149. Peter is mentioned in Juan de Segovia, Letter to Nicholas of Cusa, Dec. 2, 1454, BUS 19, fols. 173 and 181, and in Juan de Segovia, *Prefacio in translationem,* fol. 188v (and in Cabanelas Rodríguez, *Juan de Segovia y el problema islámico,* 285). Raymond Llull is mentioned in Segovia, Letter to Jean Germain, Dec. 18, 1455, fol. 61, where he referred to having seen Llull's *De arte bellandi* thirty years earlier.

150. Juan de Segovia, *Prefacio in translationem,* fols. 188v–189: "Sed de hoc certissimum perhibere queo testimonium, translationem predictam in quamplurimis deviare a textus arabici continentia; et quod permultum gravat, cum multi doctorum catholicorum aliique etiam non doctores vixque docti, multos libellos multosque ediderint tractatus ad secte [189] huius impugnationem, quorum multos perlegi multosque etiam penes me habeo, multi certe aut paucissimi vixque unus reperitur qui, prout Alchuranus continet dictaque patefacit translatio, testimonia vera referant ex quibus redarguere nituntur sectam eorum; sed persepe grossa quedam recitant nimis distantia a virili racione, velut bestialia, puerilia quoque, pro lege teneant." Published in Cabanelas Rodríguez, *Juan de Segovia y el problema islámico,* 286.

151. Juan de Segovia, Letter to Jean Germain, Dec. 18, 1455, fol. 184r: "cum ex multis suscepta michi foret interpretatio libri Alchoran quem latine scriptum penes me habeo a xviii iam annis, persepe in Castelle mandavi pro interpretatione in vulgari hyspanico ut de vera continentia haberem noticia. Aliquando autem destinatus est michi pro libro Alchoran liber unus, invectivam in eum magis quam eius designans tenorem, et quamplurima illi falso imponens." Published in Cabanelas Rodríguez, *Juan de Segovia y el problema islámico*, 326.

152. Juan de Segovia, *Prefacio in translationem*, fols. 189v–190: "Et licet plurimum ac persepe literas pro habenda vera translatione in Hyspaniam destinassem, magno iam edito volumine in confirmationem catholice fidei et in illius secte confutationem, ne in vacuum currerem aut cucurrissem [Gal. 2:2], alia referendo [fol. 190] pro aliis, quomodo fecisse agnoveram alios permultos tractatores, proprio nuntio ad hoc bis transmisso, qui desuper duobus fere stetit annis, nomine editum N. episcopi Gienensis, in reprobationem dicte secte, quam, ut inquit, didicerat cum apud sarracenos multo tempore captivus fuisset, multa utique secte huiusmodi, que in libro Alchurani non habentur, imponentem." Published in Cabanelas Rodríguez, *Juan de Segovia y el problema islámico*, 288–89.

153. Pick, *Conflict and Coexistence*, chap. 4 (pp. 127–81).

154. Pick, *Conflict and Coexistence*, 134.

155. Peter the Venerable, *Epistola domini Petri*, 213–14: "Nam licet hoc perditis illis ut aestimo prodesse non possit, responsionem tamen condignam sicut contra alias hereses, ita et contra hanc pestem, Christianum armarium habere deceret. . . . Quod si hinc errantes conuerti non possunt, saltem infirmis ecclesiae qui scandalizari uel occulte moueri leuibus etiam ex causis solent, consulere et prouidere, doctus uel doctor si zelum habet iusticiae, non debet negligere." I have quoted the translations of these lines that appear in Kritzeck, 44–45.

156. Tolan, *Saracens*, 160.

157. Bisaha, "Pope Pius II's Letter," 198.

158. Juan de Segovia, *Prefacio in translationem*, fols. 188v–189: "Sed de hoc certissimum perhibere queo testimonium, translationem predictam in quamplurimis deviare a textus arabici continentia; et quod permultum gravat, cum multi doctorum catholicorum aliique etiam non doctores vixque docti, multos libellos multosque ediderint tractatus ad secte [fol. 189] huius impugnationem, quorum multos perlegi multosque etiam penes me habeo, multi certe aut paucissimi vixque unus reperitur qui, prout Alchuranus continet dictaque patefacit translatio, testimonia vera referant ex quibus redarguere nituntur sectam eorum; sed persepe grossa quedam recitant nimis distantia a virili ratione, velut bestialia, puerilia quoque, pro lege teneant. Et permaxi-

man in hoc sarraceni ipsi contumeliam reputant, retrahentes se propterea ne sane doctrine aures suas inclinent; nichil etenim officit magis ad reductionem hereticorum quam illis circa dicta sua falsum imponere testimonium, data pro hoc illis occasione ut nullatenus acquiescant doctorum catholicorum doctrine, quos in suis propriis dictis experiuntur alia referre pro aliis." In Cabanelas Rodríguez, *Juan de Segovia y el problema islámico*, 286.

159. Juan de Segovia, Letter to Nicholas of Cusa, Dec. 2, 1454, BUS 19, fol. 174v: "Quod vero officit quinymmo omne prestat impedimentum ad conversionem eorum est quem si ex instructione bellorum in ipsos sarracenis super excrescit in christianos odium multo utique maiori ac velud incomparabili incremento super excrescit in christum arbitrantur namque prout veritas habet quod christiani omnes pro eius pugnant honore In ducem protectorem que suum habentes eum. Nec id possunt ignorare videntes pugnatores omnes crucesignatos christi."

160. Juan de Segovia, Letter to Nicholas of Cusa, Dec. 2, 1454, BUS 19, fol. 173v: "Ad huc etiam si christus post resurrectionem suam per dies xl^{ta} apparuerit discipulis suis locutus de regno dei evangelia magis continent que docuit dum vineret in carne mortali. Etenim quia sine fide homines convivere non possunt sed necesse est ut sibi invicem credant et etiam [?] de occultis que ratione vel oculo mostrari non possunt, voluit deus ut homines mortales alter alteri credat in hiis que ad dei cognitionem sueque anime pertirent salutem sicut non solum per nam sed magnam adhibent fidem In hiis que pertinere arbitrantur ad sanitatem corporis vel substantie utilitatem. Quod autem gravius quia etiam in hiis que ad anime dampnationem suadentibus namque malum aliquando facile credunt. . . . [fol. 174] Ex quo manifeste percipi potest si quamdiu videbunt eos tali di[174v]spositione si doctoribus christianis credent predicaturis fidei catholice veritate. Iure dictante nature ut de suo inimico non confidat homo. Iure quoque testante divino dum ait labiis suis intelligitur Inimicus cum in corde tractaverit dolos quando submiserit vocem suam ne credideris ei quoniam septem nequicie sunt in corde illius. Alio item loco, Non credas inimico tuo ineternum sicut enim eramentum eruginat nequicia illius. Et si humiliatus vadat curvus abice animum tuum et custodi te ab illo. Lege igitur nature sistente affirmante quoque divino eloquio quod inimico non creditur sed amico ut sarraceni christianis credant animarum suarum salutem procuraturis dignum est quod agnoscant christianos evangelicam attendere doctrinam de dilectione inimicorum principientem utque benefaciant hiis qui oderunt, quatenus in bono vincentes malum carbones ignis ingerant super capita eorum. Maxime quippe importancie est verbum diligite."

161. Rouhi, "A Fifteenth-Century Salamancan's Pursuit of Islamic Studies," 26.

162. Yça Gidelli, Letter to Juan de Segovia, April 24, 1454, fols. 178r–180r, trans. in Wiegers, *Islamic Literature in Spanish and Aljamiado*, 231. This letter, which exists only in a Latin translation of what was probably a Spanish original, appears in its entirety in Wiegers, 230–32, and also in Cabanelas Rodríguez, *Juan de Segovia y el problema islámico*, 273–77.

163. Gros, *Histoire du diocèse de Maurienne*, 2:123.

164. Rouhi, "A Fifteenth-Century Salamancan's Pursuit of Islamic Studies," 35.

165. Tolan, *Saracens*, 154.

166. Echevarría Arsuaga, *Fortress of Faith*, 167.

167. Echevarría Arsuaga, *Fortress of Faith*, 162–64.

168. Juan de Segovia, Letter to Jean Germain, Dec. 18, 1455, fol. 98v: "Sunt autem boni artifices manuales et velut servos decet nimium obsequiosi unde quia ex necesitate facientes virtutem velut id ipsum agant sponte a pluribus preiudeis sunt dilecti."

169. Juan de Segovia, Letter to Jean Germain, Dec. 18, 1455, fol. 51v: "Non est masculus et femina, gentilis et Iudeus, circumcisio et prepictium, Barbarus et Scitha, servus et liber, sed omnia in omnibus christus. Non enim de lege christi dicitur quod de lege moysi. Non fecit taliter omni nacioni, et iudicia sua non manifestavit eius . . . christus non horum illorum ve sed omni fuit redemptor."

170. Juan de Segovia, Letter to Nicholas of Cusa, Dec. 2, 1454, BUS 19, fol. 171r: "Certum vera est divina intuenti eloquia et condicionem homini in mundo [171v] hodie sistencium gentium nomine Non tam christianos tam aut iudeos sed proprie magis intelligi sarracenos aut tartaros."

171. Juan de Segovia, Letter to Jean Germain, Dec. 18, 1455, fol. 63r: "Quid igitur de miserandis sarracenis qui per totam vitam suam non audierunt. Et fortasse in maiorum presencia iam per octingentos annos rarissime vix aut nunquam predicata seu declarata illis fuit minima caritas qua deus sic mundum dilexit ut filium suum unigenitum traderet pro eius salute."

172. For a fascinating study of Augustine's views and his impact on subsequent thinkers, along with the shift away from his perspective in the eleventh and twelfth centuries, see Cohen, *Living Letters of the Law*.

173. MacKay, *Spain in the Middle Ages*, 184–85.

174. Documents mentioning Reina: Archivo Catedral de Salamanca, Actas Capitulares 1, fol. 100 (in Vicente Baz, *Los libros de actas capitulares*, #234, pp. 171–72) and Actas Capitulares 1, fol. 107v (in Vicente Baz, *Los libros de actas capitulares*, #247, p. 176). Mentioning Alfonso Rodríguez: Actas Capitulares 2, fol. 55v (in Vicente Baz, *Los libros de actas capitulares*, #404, p. 221).

175. On Abraham: Archivo Catedral de Salamanca, Actas Capitulares 2, fol. 121v (in Vicente Baz, *Los libros de actas capitulares*, #569, p. 260). On

Jacob: Actas Capitulares 1, fol. 153 (in Vicente Baz, *Los libros de actas capitulares*, #323, p. 199). On Yuçe Cohen: Actas Capitulares 2, fol. 54 (in Vicente Baz, *Los libros de actas capitulares*, #399, p. 220). On Samuel Cohen: Actas Capitulares 2, fol. 79 (in Vicente Baz, *Los libros de actas capitulares*, #458, p. 236).

176. Echevarría Arsuaga, *Fortress of Faith*, 110–14.

177. I have discussed his approach to the reading of scripture in Wolf, "Precedents and Paradigms." See esp. 158–59.

178. See E. Daniel, *The Franciscan Concept of Mission in the High Middle Ages*.

179. See Phelan, *The Millennial Kingdom of the Franciscans*.

180. West and Kling, *The "Libro de las profecías" of Christopher Columbus*, 8.

181. West and Kling, *The "Libro de las profecías" of Christopher Columbus*, 30–34. See the list of medieval authors quoted by Columbus on p. 23. One of these was Pierre d'Ailly, a colleague of Gerson's in Paris. Columbus cited his *Libro de legibus et sectis*, Chapter 4.

182. Juan de Segovia, Letter to Jean Germain, Dec. 18, 1455, fol. 46v: "Si via pacis et doctrine opportuna magis ad conversionem sarracenorum in sacramenta catholice fidei quam via belli, nullam equidem prefigit mensuram temporis qua id ipsum operis inchorari prosequi debeat aut finiri ut namque divina ait sapiencia, Qui crediderit non festinet et non turbetur ponam in pondere iudicium et iusticiam in mensura."

183. Juan de Segovia, Letter to Nicholas of Cusa, Dec. 2, 1454, BUS 19, fol. 182v: "Siquidem spiritus anxietatis nimis replevit cor meum videns innumerabilem hominum multitudinem perire sub errore heresis illius tam insane [183r] quodque paciatur christiana religio ne illis in faciem ostendat falsa omninoque a veritate distancia fore testimonia que lex imponit eorum salvatori domino nostro Ihesu christo sacerdotibus quoque eius et generaliter omnibus christianis eisdem imposito adoratores esse participum dei et sociorum eius. Et si hec in lege continentur eorum profecto quam multa alia obloquuntur de religione christiana arbitrantes nos absurdissima credere et per hec se ipsos iustificantes quia non sunt de societate talia pro fide tenentium. Expertus id novi in collacionibus habitis cum ambasiatore supra mencionato regis Granate obiciente magno cum improperio quod christiani comederent deum suum et a peccatis absolverent in deum commissis."

184. Juan de Segovia, *Repetitio de fide catholica*, fol. 192v A: "Que sit causa propter quam divina providencia tam multitudinem populi permittat perire: non spectat ad presens et quidem est alterius speculationis sufficit declarare solam fidem quam predicat religio christiana a deo esse revelatam salutis viam, et quod ista racionabile et certissimum habet fundamentum ut

manifesta ratione possit convinci ad obtinendam beatitudinem quae finis est humane nature. Per hanc solam rectos dirigi calles vero quaslibet sectas esse oberaciones quadam a via recta."

185. Juan de Segovia, Letter to Jean Germain, Dec. 18, 1455, fol. 63r: "Quid igitur de miserandis sarracenis qui per totam vitam suam non audierunt. Et . . . iam per octingentos annos rarissime vix aut nunquam predicata seu declarata illis fuit minima caritas qua deus sic mundum dilexit ut filium suum unigenitum traderet pro eius salute."

186. Juan de Segovia, Letter to Nicholas of Cusa, Dec. 2, 1454, BUS 19, fol. 171r: "Ita eternum dedit mandatum de predicando illis evangelio, cum dixit Euntes docete omnes gentes, Ecce ego vobiscum sum omnibus diebus usque ad consumacionem seculi . . . Si igitur obligatur ecclesia predicare gentibus verbum dei, attendatur si factura est diligencia posse tot ut audiencia prestetur."

187. Juan de Segovia, Letter to Nicholas of Cusa, Dec. 2, 1454, BUS 19, fol. 176r: "in hoc voluntatem faciens patris sui, qui non vult mortem peccatorum, sed ut convertatur et vivat."

188. Juan de Segovia, Letter to Jean Germain, Dec. 18, 1455, fol. 51v: "Lex nempe christiana in hoc differt ab omni quacumque alia secta propterea quod in ea non est accepcio personarum ubi apostolo teste. Non est masculus et femina, gentiles et Iudeus, circumcision et prepucium, Barbarus et Scitha, servus et liber . . . quando christus non horum illorum ve sed omni fuit redemptor."

189. Juan de Segovia, Letter to Jean Germain, Dec. 18, 1455, fols. 51v–52r: "Et id certissimum est quod quam plurimos ipsorum gentilium Paulus convertit, nullam primo auctoritatem, veteris aut novi testamenti recipientes. Multo revera gentilibus ipsis qui nec deum unum confitebantur amplius differentibus a christiana fide pre sarracenis in libro Alchoran deum unum firmissime confitentibus, multos [fol. 52r] quoque sacre scripture libros, ita enim dicit spiritus ad Mahumetum, Tu ergo fidem creatoris illis predica penitus persuade ut libris tibi divinitus missis abraheque et ysmaeli et ysaac atque iacob et tribubus legibusque moysis et christi ceterorumque prophetarum nullis parte segregatis firmam fidem adhibeant. Rursus de evangelio atque psalterio inquam plurimis locis mencionem facit."

190. See the discussion by Carrete Parrondo, "Judíos, moros y cristianos."

191. "Tertium. Tam israelitas quam gentiles per sacri baptismatis ianuam ad fidem catholicam ingredientes non duos populos aut duas gentes divisas manere sed ex utrique ventientibus unum populum novum creari." Cited from the outline of this work provided in López Martínez, "Teología española de la convivencia a mediados del siglo XV," 157.

192. Izbicki, "Juan de Torquemada's *Defense of the Conversos*," 203. On the participation of Lope de Barrientos in the debate about the *conversos*, see Martínez Casado, *Lope de Barrientos*, 49–54. See also Martínez Casado, "La situación jurídica de los conversos según Lope de Barrientos," which contains facing Latin and Castilian editions of Lope's *Responsio* (*Respuesta a una duda*) to a question brought to him by the bachiller Alfonso González de Toledo concerning the *converso* question. The Latin is from BUS 2070, fols. 65r–70v (a sixteenth-century manuscript), and the Castilian is from Madrid BN 1181, fols. 128v–154r (a fifteenth-century manuscript). It is interesting that in the final paragraphs of this work (Martínez Casado, 62–63) Barrientos cited a decree from the Council of Basel stipulating that converted Jews were to enjoy all the privileges and immunities that other Christians did. Martínez Casado gave the work a probable date of October 1449.

193. "Non enim vocantur chaldaei, persae vel graeci, romani nec hispani, judaei vel gentiles, sed quodam generali nomine, scilicet, christiani a Christo omnium redemptore, qui *ex altatus fuit a terra ut omnia traheret ad se ipsum*, ut ipse dicit in Joh [12:32]; *in quo* ut ait Apostolus, *non est masculus et femina, gentilis et judaeus, circumcisio et praeputium, barbarus et scytha, servus et liber, sed omnia in omnibus Christus*, ad Col cap. 3 [Col. 3:11]." This anonymous sermon is in MS 14 in the cathedral library in Oviedo, fols. 120r–127v. It was edited by Blázquez in "Sermón anónimo pro judíos conversos." This quote is on pp. 267–68, fols. 124–124v.

194. Blázquez, "Sermón anónimo pro judíos conversos," fol. 127v (p. 273): "Compescite ergo, per illos, iustissime rex, ministerio enim Deo estis, divisionem in sancta Ecclesia, in regno vestro rebellionem et proditionem, fidei catholicae iacturam nullatenus permittentes; sed sitis *solliciti servare unitatem spiritus in vinculo pacis*, ut vos et omnes regnicolae vestri per unionem fidei et caritatis in praesenti mereamini pervenire ad illam gloriosam et consummatam caritatem in futuro, ubi pax felicitas, ubi vita aeternitas, ubi dignitas sanitas, quam nobis omnibus praestare dignetur ipse Dei Filius qui cum Deo et Spiritu Sancto vivit et regnat per infinita saecula saeculorum, amen."

195. For a brief account of Torquemada's and Cartagena's participation at Basel, see Goñi Gaztambide, "Presencia de España en los concilios generales," 81–86. For more extensive information, see Álvarez Palenzuela, *La situación europea*, and Suárez Fernández, *Castilla, el cisma y la crisis conciliar*.

196. Martínez Casado, *Lope de Barrientos*, 17–21.

197. See the discussion in chap. 2 in this volume, 65–68.

198. Housley, "A Necessary Evil?" 273.

199. Housley, "A Necessary Evil?" 271.

200. Housley, "A Necessary Evil?" 273–74.

201. Housley, "A Necessary Evil?" 261–63.

202. Housley, "A Necessary Evil?" 275. For another helpful examination of the complexities of Erasmus's views on the Turks and just war, see Musto, "Just Wars and Evil Empires."

203. Christianson, *Cesarini*, 1.

204. Bisaha, *Creating East and West*, 187.

205. Bisaha, *Creating East and West*, 186.

206. See the discussion in Burman, *Reading the Qur'ān in Latin Christendom*, 181–83.

Epilogue

1. This visit and the tomb description are recorded in chapter 10 ("Les Prévots et les autres dignitaires de la collégiale") in *Mémoires et Documents*, 2nd series, vol. 29 (1890), part 2, 412–13. The author of this chapter, whose name I could not find, wrote that he saw this document in the Chambery archive, Series C, 727. The Archives Départementales de Savoie in Chambery still employ that cataloguing system, but I could not find this document in Series C, volume 727.

2. Archives Départementales de Savoie, Chambery, Series 3G, 184, fol. 26v. The title of this document is *Historia ecclesiae, episcoporum et diocesis Maurianensis, a reverendo Jacobo Dumé, maurieanensi canonico, a. 1680.*

3. Archives Départementales de Savoie, Chambery, Series 3G, 187, folios not numbered. This is an account of the bishops of Maurienne and notes extracted from their archives. It is not dated, but the hand is the same throughout, and the last bishop included entered the office in 1792.

4. *Chronica latina Sabaudiae*, in *Monumenta Patriae* t. III (Scriptorum t. I), column 615a–b. This chronicle begins with the reign of Amadeus VIII and ends in 1487. I am not sure when it was written originally. The relevant text reads, "Huius Amedei tempore duo secum fuerunt cardinales, unus videlicet, Ludouicus Alamandi de Arbeuco legdunensis diocesis arelatensis archiepiscopus et cardinalis, qui in maiori ecclesia arelatense sepultus maximis et quotidianis claret miraculis. Alius Ioannes de Segovia sacre theologie doctor profundissimus hispanus, qui in prioratu Oytonis mauri-annensis diocesis sepultus euidentissimus claret miraculis. Hii duo cardinales ipsi Amedeo in papatu et post semper adhererunt durante scismate, et post horum sanctissima vita fecit, et in sempiternun gloriosa memoria, quos vite sanctitas et innumero miracula multipliciter decorant."

5. Piccolomini, Letter to Jordan Mallant, August 13, 1447, 275.

6. Piccolomini, Letter to Jordan Mallant, August 13, 1447, 276.

7. See the discussion of this gradual change in Izbicki, Christianson, and Krey, *Reject Aeneas, Accept Pius*, esp. pp. 22–50.

8. Izbicki, Christianson, and Krey, *Reject Aeneas, Accept Pius*, 51.

9. Pius II, *Execrabilis*, in Izbicki, Christianson, and Krey, *Reject Aeneas, Accept Pius*, 392.

10. Izbicki, Christianson, and Krey, *Reject Aeneas, Accept Pius*, 52.

11. Edwards, "*Reconquista* and Crusade in Fifteenth-Century Spain," 170.

12. Edwards, "*Reconquista* and Crusade in Fifteenth-Century Spain," 170

13. See Echevarría Arsuaga, "Enrique IV de Castilla, un rey cruzado."

14. Edwards, "*Reconquista* and Crusade in Fifteenth-Century Spain," 173.

15. Juan de Segovia, *Donatio*, 79: "Pari utique modo circa custodiam librorum euenit, ut qui penes priuatas custodiuntur personas facile transmutentur et facile pereant distraccione, donacione aliisque multifariam mutacionibus a persona in personam, a loco in locum, a regione—nacione quoque—una in aliam, sicut passeres in monte ab arbore in arborem facile transmigrantes."

16. There has been some discrepancy in how scholars have counted these works. On the different approaches, see Hernández Montes, *Biblioteca*, 37–42.

17. Hernández Montes, *Biblioteca*, 30. The corresponding section of the *Donatio* appears on 114.

18. Hernández Montes, *Biblioteca*, 43.

19. Juan de Segovia, *Donatio*, 109.

20. Juan de Segovia, *Donatio*, 78.

21. Hernández Montes, *Biblioteca*, 121.

22. See the discussion of these loans in Hernández Montes, *Biblioteca*, 28n14.

23. Hernández Montes, *Biblioteca*, 48–49.

24. Hernández Montes, *Biblioteca*, 47. Hernández Montes noted that the wording of this bull also extended the required silence to other places (*quibusvis aliis*), which prompted him to wonder if the pope also appropriated the books destined to Valladolid (that city's Cabildo de la Colegiata and the Convento de la Merced). He noted that the two volumes intended for the Convento de la Merced would have been especially attractive to the pope, since they both dealt with Islam. This bull is published in *Bulario* III, 95.

25. Hernández Montes, *Biblioteca*, 28n13.

26. Hernández Montes, *Biblioteca*, 47.

27. Hernández Montes, *Biblioteca*, 50.

28. BN MS 3999, fol. 7r: "letra antiqua de mano."
29. BN MS 3999, fol. 7r.
30. BN MS 3999, fols. 12–18.
31. BN MS 3999, fol. 13v.
32. BN MS 3999, fols. 15r–16r.
33. BN MS 3999, folio 14v.
34. BN MS 3999, fol. 12v: "Natales ignorant: sed neque obscuros, neque ignobiles fuisse"; 16v: "At qua tandem aetate, quo funere, quo monumento Ioannes obierit, ignoramus."
35. RAH 9/1024, folio 22r.
36. A. Black, *Council and Commune*, 2.

Bibliography ⎯⎯⎯

Manuscripts Consulted

Córdoba, Biblioteca de la Catedral, MS 128
Escorial, Real Monasterio de San Lorenzo de El Escorial, MS e I 8
Madrid, Biblioteca Nacional, MS 3999
Madrid, Real Academia de historia, MS 9/1024
Salamanca, Biblioteca Universitaria de Salamanca, MS 19
Salamanca, Biblioteca Universitaria de Salamanca, MS 246 fol. 74v
Seville, Biblioteca Colombina, MS 7-6-14
Simancas, Archivo General de Simancas, MS Estado, Francia, Legajo K-1711
Simancas, Archivo General de Simancas, Patronato Real, 60-174
Valladolid, Biblioteca de Santa Cruz, MS 89
Vatican City, Biblioteca Apostolica Vaticana, Codex Vaticanus latinus 2923

Primary Sources

Acta Sanctorum quotquot toto urbe coluntur: Vel a catholicis scriptoribus cele-brantur. Vol. 27. Paris: V. Palmé, 1863–.
Alfonso de Toledo (El Madrigal/El Tostado). *Invencionario*. Edited by Philip O. Gericke. Madison, Wis.: Hispanic Seminary of Medieval Studies, 1992.
Augustine. *The City of God Against the Pagans*. Edited and translated by R. W. Dyson. Cambridge: Cambridge University Press, 1998.
Beltrán de Heredia, Vicente, ed. *Bulario de la Universidad de Salamanca (1219–1549)*. Vols. 1–3. Salamanca: Universidad de Salamanca, 1966.
———. *Cartulario de la Universidad de Salamanca (1218–1600)*. Vol. 1. Salamanca: Universidad de Salamanca, 1970.
Blázquez, J., ed. "Sermón anónimo pro judíos conversos." *Revista española de teología* 34 (1974): 257–73.

Castro Toledo, Jonas. *Colección diplomática de Tordesillas, 909–1474*. Valladolid: Diputación Provincial de Valladolid, 1981.

Chronica latina Sabaudiae, in *Monumenta Patriae* t. III (Scriptorum t. I). Edited by Regis Caroli Alberti. Turin: E. Regio Typographeo, 1840.

Cragg, Kenneth. *Readings in the Qur'ān*. 3rd ed. London: Harper Collins, 1991.

Crowder, C. M. D., ed. *Unity, Heresy and Reform, 1378–1460: The Conciliar Response to the Great Schism*. New York: St. Martin's Press, 1977.

Esperabé Arteaga, Enrique, ed. *Historia pragmática e interna de la Universidad de Salamanca*. Salamanca: Francisco Núñez, 1914.

García y García, Antonio, ed. *Synodicon Hispanum IV (Ciudad Rodrigo, Salamanca, Zamora)*. Latin text on 48–174, Castilian on 174–291. Madrid: Biblioteca de Autores Cristianos, 1987.

Housley, Norman, ed. and trans. *Documents on the Later Crusades, 1274–1580*. London: Macmillan Press, 1996.

Jean Germain. Extracts from an oration delivered before Charles VII of France in 1451. Edited and translated in Housley, *Documents on the Later Crusades*, Text 46, pp. 139–44.

Juan de Segovia. *De mittendo gladio divini Spiritus in corda sarracenorum* (1454). Seville, Colombina 7-6-14, fols. 1r–110v. Excerpts in Cabanelas Rodríguez, *Juan de Segovia y el problema islámico*, 265–72, under title *De gladio divini Spiritus in corda mittendo sarracenorum*. A modern edition and German translation was published after this book was written: Ulli Roth, ed. *De gladio divini spiritus in corda mittendo Sarracenorum*. Corpus Islamo-Christianum, Series Latin, Band 7. Altenberge, Germany: CIS-Verlag, 2012.

———. *Donatio inter vivos*. In Hernández Montes, *Biblioteca*, 75–115.

———. *Explanatio de tribus veritatibus fidei*. In Mann, "The Historian and the Truths," 306–565.

———. *Historia gestorum synodi Basiliensis*. Escorial e I 8. Also in *Monumenta Conciliorum Generalium, s. XV*, vols. 2–4, under title *Historia gestorum generalis synodi Basiliensis*. Vienna, 1883–1935.

———. Letter to Aeneas Sylvius Piccolomini, May 1458. Vatican City, Biblioteca Apostolica Vaticana, Codex Vaticanus latinus 2923, fols. 1r–3v. Also in Cabanelas Rodríguez, *Juan de Segovia y el problema islámico*, 343–49.

———. Letter to an unknown friend, April 18, 1458. Vatican City, Biblioteca Apostolica Vaticana, Codex Vaticanus latinus 2923, fols. 196v–198. Also in Cabanelas Rodríguez, *Juan de Segovia y el problema islámico*, 337–41.

———. Letter to Jean Germain, December 18, 1455. Vatican City, Biblioteca Apostolica Vaticana, Codex Vaticanus latinus 2923, fols. 41r–136v. Excerpts in Cabanelas Rodríguez, *Juan de Segovia y el problema islámico*, 325–28.

————. Letter to Nicholas of Cusa, December 2, 1454, Salamanca, Biblioteca Universitaria de Salamanca, MS 19, fols. 168r–184r, and Vatican City, Biblioteca Apostolica Vaticana, Codex Vaticanus latinus 2923, fols. 4r–35r. Excerpts in Cabanelas Rodríguez, *Juan de Segovia y el problema islámico*, 303–310.

————. *Liber de magna auctoritate episcoporum in concilio generali*. Edited by Rolf de Kegel. Freiburg, Switzerland: Universitätsverlag, 1995.

————. *Liber de substantia ecclesiae*. Edited by Santiago Madrigal Terrazas. Madrid: Universidad Pontifícia Comillas, 2000.

————. *Prefacio in translationem noviter editam ex Arabico in latinum vulgareque hyspanum libri Alchorani*. Vatican City, Biblioteca Apostolica Vaticana, Codex Vaticanus latinus 2923, fols. 186–96. Also in Cabanelas Rodríguez, *Juan de Segovia y el problema islámico*, 279–302.

————. *Repetitio de fide catholica* (1427). Córdoba, Biblioteca de la Catedral, MS 128, fols. 181v–193r.

————. *Repetitio de superioritate et excellentia supremae potestatis ecclesiasticae et spiritualis ad regiam temporalem* (1426). Valladolid, Biblioteca de Santa Cruz, MS 89, fols. 130r–165v.

Mémoires et Documents publiés par la Société Savoisienne d'Histoire et d'Archéologie, 2nd series. Vols. 29 (1890) and 52 (1912).

Nicholas of Cusa. *Cribratio Alkorani*. In Hopkins, *Nicholas of Cusa's "De pace fidei" and "Cribratio Alkorani,"* 75–193.

————. *De pace fidei*. In Biechler and Bond, *Nicholas of Cusa on Interreligious Harmony*.

————. Letter to Juan de Segovia, December 29, 1454. Vatican City, Biblioteca Apostolica Vaticana, Codex Vaticanus latinus 2923, fols. 35v–38v. Also in Cabanelas Rodríguez, *Juan de Segovia y el problema islámico*, 311–18. A translation of this letter into Spanish is available in Sanz Santacruz, *La paz de la fe*, 91–98.

————. Oration at the Diet of Frankfurt (1442). Translated in Izbicki, *Nicholas of Cusa*, Text 4, pp. 162–259.

Peter the Venerable. *Epistola domni Petri abbatis ad domnum Bernardum Claraevallis abbatem, de translatione sua qua fecit transferri ex Arabico in Latinum sectam siue heresim Sarracenorum*. In Kritzeck, *Peter the Venerable and Islam*, Text 3, pp. 212–14.

————. *Liber contra sectam sive haeresim saracenorum*. In Kritzeck, *Peter the Venerable and Islam*, Text 6, pp. 220–91.

Piccolomini, Aeneas Sylvius. *Commentariorum Pii Secundi Pontificis Maximi Libri XIII (The Commentaries of Pius II, Pontifex Maximus, in Thirteen Books)*. Edited and translated by Margaret Meserve and Marcello Simonetta. 2 vols. Cambridge, Mass.: Harvard University Press, 2003.

———. *De Europa*. Edited by Adrian Van Heck. Vatican City: Biblioteca
Apostolica Vaticana, 2001.

———. *De Gestis Concilii Basiliensis Commentariorum*. Edited and translated by Denys Hay and W. K. Smith. Oxford: Clarendon Press, 1967;
reissued with corrections, 1992.

———. *Epistola ad Mahomatem II*. Edited and translated by Albert R. Baca.
New York: Peter Lang, 1990.

———. Letter to Francesco Pizzolpaso, Oct. 29, 1439. In Izbicki, Christianson, and Krey, *Reject Aeneas, Accept Pius,* Letter 16, pp. 122–23.

———. Letter to Giovanni Peregallo, April 18, 1444. In Izbicki, Christianson, and Krey, *Reject Aeneas, Accept Pius,* Letter 43, pp. 187–89.

———. Letter to Jordan Mallant, August 13, 1447. In Izbicki, Christianson,
and Krey, *Reject Aeneas, Accept Pius*, Letter 69, pp. 274–86.

———. Letter to Juan de Segovia, August 13, 1440. In Izbicki, Christianson,
and Krey, *Reject Aeneas, Accept Pius,* Letter 19, pp. 125–31.

Sanz Santacruz, Víctor, ed. and trans. *La paz de la fe: Carta a Juan de Segovia*. Pamplona: Cuadernos de Anuario Filosófico, 1996.

Tetaldi (Tedaldi). *Tractatus de expurgnatione urbis Constantinopolis*. In
Philippides, *Mehmed II the Conqueror,* 133–217.

Ubieto Arteta, Antonio, ed. *Colección diplomática de Cuéllar*. Segovia: Diputación, 1961.

Vaca, Angel, and José Bonilla. *Salamanca en la documentación medieval de
la Casa de Alba*. Salamanca: Caja de Ahorros y Monte de Piedad, 1989.

Valero García, Pilar, and Manuel Pérez Martín, eds. *Constituciones de Martín
V*. Salamanca: Ediciones de la Universidad de Salamanca, 1991.

Vicente Baz, Raúl. *Los libros de actas capitulares de la Catedral de Salamanca
(1298–1489)*. Salamanca: Publicaciones del Archivo Catedral de Salamanca, 2008.

Yça Gidelli [Gebir]. *Breviario Sunni*. In *Memorial Histórico Español*,
5:247–421. Madrid: Real Academia de Historia, 1853.

———. Letter to Juan de Segovia, April 24, 1454. BAV Vat. Lat. 2923, fols.
178v–180. In Cabanelas Rodríguez, *Juan de Segovia y el problema islámico*, 273–77.

Secondary Sources

Aguadé Nieto, Santiago, ed. *Universidad, cultura y sociedad en la Edad
Media*. Alcalá de Henares: Servicio de Publicaciones, 1994.

Alonso Getino, Luis G. *Vida y obras de fray Lope de Barrientos*. Salamanca:
Estab. tip. de Calatrava, 1927.

Alonso Romero, María Paz. *Universidad y sociedad corporativa: Historia del privilegio jurisdiccional del estudio salmantino.* Madrid: Editorial Tecnos, 1997.

Álvarez Márquez, María del Carmen. *Manuscritos localizados de Pedro Gómez Barroso y Juan de Cervantes, arzobispos de Sevilla.* Alcalá de Henares: Servicio de Publicaciones and Sevilla Diputación Provincial, 1999.

Álvarez Palenzuela, Vicente Ángel. *La situación europea en época del concilio de Basilea: Informe de la delegación del reino de Castilla.* León: Centro de Estudios e Investigación "San Isidoro," Archivo Histórico Diocesano, 1992.

Asenjo González, María. *Segovia: La ciudad y su tierra a fines del medievo.* Segovia: Diputación Provincial de Segovia, 1986.

Avilés, Miguel. "La teología española en el siglo XV." In Melquíades Andrés, *Historia de la teología española,* 1:495–577.

Barrio Gonzalo, Maximiliano. "La iglesia de Segovia durante el pontificado de Arias Dávila (1461–1497): Instituciones y poder económico." In Galindo García, *Arias Dávila,* 77–97.

Baumer, R. "Die Interpretation und Verbindlichkeit der konstanzer Dekrete." *Theologisch-praktische Quartalschrift* 116 (1968): 44–53.

Beceiro Pita, Isabel. "Educación y cultura en la nobleza (siglos XIII–XV)." *Anuario de Estudios Medievales* 21 (1991): 571–89.

Beltrán de Heredia, Vicente. "El Convento de San Esteban en sus relaciones con la iglesia y la Universidad de Salamanca durante los siglos XIII, XIV y XV." *Ciencia tomista* 84 (1957): 95–116.

———. "La cancillería de la Universidad de Salamanca." *Salmanticensis* 1 (1954): 5–49.

Bentley, Jerry H. *Humanists and Holy Writ: New Testament Scholarship in the Renaissance.* Princeton: Princeton University Press, 1983.

Biechler, James. "Conciliar Movement: A Humanist Crisis of Identity." *Church History* 44:1 (1975): 5–21.

———. "A New Face Toward Islam: Nicholas of Cusa and John of Segovia." In *Nicholas of Cusa in Search of God and Wisdom. Essays in Honor of Morimichi Watanabe by the American Cusanus Society,* edited by Gerald Christianson and Thomas M. Izbicki, 185–202. Leiden: Brill, 1991.

Biechler, James E., and H. Lawrence Bond, ed. and trans. *Nicholas of Cusa on Interreligious Harmony: Text, Concordance and Translation of "De pace Fidei."* Lewiston, N.Y.: Edwin Mellen Press, 1990.

Bisaha, Nancy. *Creating East and West: Renaissance Humanists and the Ottoman Turks.* Philadelphia: University of Pennsylvania Press, 2004.

———. "Pope Pius II and the Crusade." In Housley, *Crusading in the Fifteenth Century,* 39–52.

————"Pope Pius II's Letter to Sultan Mehmed II: A Reexamination." *Crusades* 1 (2002): 183–200.

Black, Antony. *Council and Commune: The Conciliar Movement and the Fifteenth-Century Heritage.* Shepherdstown, W. Va.: Patmos Press, 1979.

————. "Political Languages in Later Medieval Europe." In *The Church and Sovereignty, c. 590–1918*, edited by Diana Wood, 313–28. Oxford: Basil Blackwell, 1991.

————. *Political Thought in Europe, 1250–1450.* Cambridge: Cambridge University Press, 1992.

————. "What Was Conciliarism? Conciliar Theory in Historical Perspective." In *Authority and Power: Studies in Medieval Law and Government*, edited by Brian Tierney and Peter Linehan, 213–24. Cambridge: Cambridge University Press, 1980.

Black, Robert. *Benedetto Accolti and the Florentine Renaissance.* Cambridge: Cambridge University Press, 1985.

Bonmann, Ottokar. "De testamento librorum Iohannis de Segovia (Num Segoviensis ex Ordine Minorum fuerit?)." *Antonianum* 29 (1954): 209–16.

Burman, Thomas E. *Reading the Qur'ān in Latin Christendom, 1140–1560.* Philadelphia: University of Pennsylvania Press, 2007.

Burns, Robert I. "Christian-Islamic Confrontation in the West: The Thirteenth-Century Dream of Conversion." *American Historical Review* 76 (1971): 1388–91.

————. *Muslims, Christians, and Jews in the Crusader Kingdom of Valencia.* Cambridge: Cambridge University Press, 1984.

Cabanelas Rodríguez, Darío. *Juan de Segovia y el problema islámico.* Madrid: Universidad de Madrid, Facultad de Filosofía y Letras, 1952; repr. Granada: Universidad de Granada, 2009.

Camillo, Ottavio Di. *El humanismo castellano del siglo XV.* Valencia: Fernando Torres, 1976.

Cantelar Rodríguez, Francisco. "Luces y sombras en un 'speculum' del siglo XV." *Revista española de derecho canónico* 54 (1997): 9–36.

Cantera Burgos, Francisco. *Alvar García de Santa María y su familia de conversos.* Madrid: Instituto Arias Montano, 1952.

Carabias Torres, Ana María, ed. *Historia de la Universidad de Salamanca hecha por el maestro Pedro Chacón.* Salamanca: Universidad, 1990.

Carlé, María de Carmen. *Una sociedad del siglo XV: Los castellanos en sus testamentos.* Buenos Aires: Universidad Católica de Argentina, Facultad de Filosofía y Letras, 1993.

Carrete Parrondo, Carlos. "Judíos, moros y cristianos: La Castilla interconfesional de los Arias Dávila segovianos." In *Arias Dávila: Obispo y mecenas; Segovia en el siglo XV*, edited by Ángel Galindo García, 141–59. Salamanca: Publicaciones Universidad Pontifícia de Salamanca, 1998.

Cátedra, Pedro. "La predicación castellana de San Vicente Ferrer." *Boletín de la Real Academia de Buenas Letras de Barcelona* 39 (1983–84): 235–309.

Catlos, Brian. *The Victors and the Vanquished: Christians and Muslims of Catalonia and Aragon, 1050–1300.* Cambridge: Cambridge University Press, 2004.

Christianson, Gerald. "Aeneas Sylvius Piccolomini and the Historiography of the Council of Basel." In *Ecclesia militans: Studien zur Konzilien- und Reformationsgeschichte Remigius Bèaumer zum 70. Geburtstag gewidmet*, edited by Walter Brandmüller, 157–84. Paderborn: Ferdinand Schèoningh, 1988.

———. *Cesarini: The Conciliar Cardinal; The Basel Years, 1431–1438.* St. Ottilien: EOS-Verlag, 1979.

Cohen, Jeremy. *Living Letters of the Law: Ideas of the Jew in Medieval Christianity.* Berkeley: University of California Press, 1999.

Colmenares, Diego de. *Historia de la insigne ciudad de Segovia y conpendio de las historias de Castilla.* Segovia: Academia de Historia y Arte San Quirce, 1969. Orig. pub. Madrid, 1640.

———. *Vida y escritos de escritores segovianos.* Segovia: Academia de Historia y Arte San Quirce, 1975.

Courbage, Youssef, and Philippe Fargues. *Christians and Jews under Islam.* Translated by Judy Mabro. London: I. B. Tauris Publishers, 1997.

Courtenay, William J. "The Institutionalization of Theology." In *Learning Institutionalized: Teaching in the Medieval University*, edited by John Van Engen, 245–56. Notre Dame, Ind.: University of Notre Dame Press, 2000.

Cragg, Kenneth, trans. *Readings in the Qur'ān.* 3rd ed. London: Harper Collins, 1991.

Cruz Hernández, Miguel. *El pensamiento de Ramón Llull.* Madrid: Editorial Castalia, 1977.

Cuenca Muñoz, Paloma. *El "Tractado de la Divinança" de Lope de Barrientos: La magia medieval en la visión de un obispo de Cuenca.* Cuenca: Ayuntamiento de Cuenca, Instituto Juan de Valdés, 1994.

Dahan, Gilbert. *Les intellectuels chrétiens et les juifs au moyen âge.* Paris: Editions du Cerf, 1990.

Daniel, Emmett Randolph. *The Franciscan Concept of Mission in the High Middle Ages.* Lexington: University Press of Kentucky, 1975.

Daniel, Norman. *Islam and the West: The Making of an Image.* Oxford: Oneworld Publications, 1993.

Diener, H. "Zur Persönlichkeit des Johannes de Segovia: Beitrag zur Methode der Auswertung päpstlicher Register des späten Mittelalters." *Quellen und Forschungen aus Italienischen Archiven und Bibliotheken* 44 (1964): 289–365.

Echevarría Arsuaga, Ana. "Las aljamas mudéjares castellanas en el siglo XV: Redes de poder y conflictos internos." *Espacio, tiempo y forma: Serie III-Historia Medieval* 14 (2001): 93–121.

———. *Catalina de Lancaster, Reina Regente de Castilla (1372–1418).* Hondarribia, Guipúzcoa, Spain: Nerea, 2002.

———. "De cadí a alcalde mayor: La elite judicial mudéjar en el siglo XV." *Al-Qantara* 24:1 (2003): 139–68 and 24:2 (2003): 273–89.

———. "Enrique IV de Castilla, un rey cruzado." *Espacio, tiempo y forma*: *Serie III-Historia Medieval* 17 (2004): 143–56.

———. *The Fortress of Faith: The Attitude towards Muslims in Fifteenth Century Spain*. Leiden: Brill, 1999.

———. "Política y religión frente al Islám: La evolución de la legislación real castellana sobre musulmanes en el siglo XV." *Qurtuba* 4 (1999): 45–72.

Edwards, John. "*Reconquista* and Crusade in Fifteenth-Century Spain." In Housley, *Crusading in the Fifteenth Century*, 163–81.

Ferguson, Thomas. "The Council of Pavia-Siena and Medieval Conciliarism." *Journal of Religious History* 25:1 (Feb. 2001): 1–19.

Flanagin, David Zachariah. "God's Divine Law: The Scriptural Founts of Conciliar Theory in Jean Gerson." In *The Church, the Councils, and Reform: The Legacy of the Fifteenth Century*, edited by Gerald Christianson, Thomas Izbicki, and Christopher Bellitto, 101–121. Washington, D.C.: Catholic University of America Press, 2008.

Fletcher, Richard. *Moorish Spain*. Berkeley: University of California Press, 1992.

Franzen, A. "Das Konzil der Einheit: Einigungsbemühungen und konziliare Gedanken auf dem Konstanzer Konzil; Die Dekrete "Haec sancta" und "Frequens" in das Konzil von Konstanz." In *Das Konzil von Konstanz: Beiträge zu seiner Geschicte und Theologie*, edited by A. Franzen and W. Müller, 69–112. Freiburg: Herder, 1964.

Fromherz, Uta. *Johannes von Segovia als Geschichtsschreiber des Konzils von Basel*. Basler Beiträge zur Geschichtswissenschaft 81. Basel: Helbing und Lichtenhahn, 1960.

Galindo García, Ángel, ed. *Arias Dávila: Obispo y mecenas; Segovia en el siglo XV*. Salamanca: Publicaciones Universidad Pontifícia de Salamanca, 1998.

García y García, Antonio. "The Medieval Students at the University of Salamanca." *History of Universities* 10 (1991): 93–115.

———. "Nuevas obras de Clemente Sánchez, arcediano de Valderas." *Revista española de teología* 34 (1974): 69–89.

———. "Terminología universitaria de Salamanca." *Bulletin du Cange* 48–49 (1988–89): 144–68.

Garcías Palou, Sebastián. *Ramón Llull y el Islám*. Palma de Mallorca: Impresos Lope, 1981.

Gill, Joseph. *The Council of Florence*. Cambridge: Cambridge University Press, 1969.

Gómez Caneda, Lino. *Un español al servicio de la Sante Sede: Don Juan de Carvajal, Cardenal de Sant' Angelo, legado en Alemania y Hungría (1399?–1469)*. Madrid: Consejo Superior de Investigaciones Científicas, 1947.

Goñi Gaztambide, José. "Presencia de España en los concilios generales del siglo XV." In González Novalín, *Historia de la iglesia en España*, vol. 3-1, 25–114.

———. "Recompensas de Martín V a sus electores españoles." *Hispania Sacra* 11 (1958): 259–97.

González García, Manuel. *Salamanca: La repoblación y la ciudad en la Baja Edad Media*. Salamanca: Centro de Estudios Salmantinos, 1973.

González Novalín, José Luís, ed. *Historia de la iglesia en España*, vol. 3-1, *La iglesia en la España de los siglos XV y XVI*. Madrid: Biblioteca de Autores Cristianos, 1980.

Goodman, Anthony, and Angus MacKay, eds. *The Impact of Humanism on Western Europe*. New York: Longman, 1990.

Goodwin, Jason. *Lords of the Horizons: A History of the Ottoman Empire*. London: Chatto & Windus, 1998.

Griffith, Sidney H. "Arguing from Scripture: The Bible in the Christian/ Muslim Encounter in the Middle Ages." In *Scripture and Pluralism: Reading the Bible in the Religiously Plural Worlds of the Middle Ages and Renaissance*, edited by Thomas J. Heffernan and Thomas E. Burman, 29–58. Leiden: Brill, 2005.

Gros, A. *Histoire du diocèse de Maurienne*, vol. 2, *Du XIVe siècle à la Revolution*. Chambery: Imprimeries Réunies, 1948.

Hanly, Michael. *Medieval Muslims, Christians, and Jews in Dialogue: The "Apparicion Maistre Jehan de Meun of Honorat Bovet"; A Critical Edition with English Translation*. Tempe: Arizona Center for Medieval and Renaissance Studies, 2005.

Haubst, Rudolf. "Johannes von Segovia im Gespräch mit Nikolaus von Kues und Jean Germain über di göttliche Dreieinigkeit und ihre Verkündigung vor den Mohammedanern." *Münchener Theologische Zeitschrift* 2 (1951): 115–29.

Hay, Denys. *Europe in the Fourteenth and Fifteenth Centuries*. 2nd ed. Essex: Pearson Education, 1989.

Helmrath, Johannes. *Das Basler Konzil (1431–1449): Forschungsstand und Probleme*. Köln: Böhlau, 1987.

———. "The German *Reichstage* and the Crusade." In Housley, *Crusading in the Fifteenth Century*, 53–69.

Hendrix, Scott H. "In Quest of the *Vera Ecclesia*: The Crises of Late Medieval Ecclesiology." *Viator* 7 (1976): 347–78.

Hernández Montes, Benigno. *Biblioteca de Juan de Segovia: Edición y comentario de su escritura de donación.* Madrid: Consejo Superior de Investigaciones Científicas, Instituto "Francisco Suárez," 1984.

———. "En busca de manuscritos de la donación de Juan de Segovia: Tres manuscritos segovianos en El Escorial." *Revista española de teología* 34 (1974): 35–68.

———. *Obras de Juan de Segovia: Repertorio de Historia de las Ciencias Eclesiásticas en España*, vol. 6, *Siglos I–XVI.* Salamanca: Universidad Pontificia, 1977.

Herrera, María Teresa, ed. *Historia de los Reyes Magos: Manuscrito 2037 de la Biblioteca de la Universidad de Salamanca (anónimo).* Salamanca: Universidad, 1993.

Hobbins, Daniel. *Authorship and Publicity before Print: Jean Gerson and the Transformation of Late Medieval Learning.* Philadelphia: University of Pennsylvania Press, 2009.

Hopkins, Jasper, ed. *Nicholas of Cusa's "De pace fidei" and "Cribratio alkorani": Translation and Analysis.* Minneapolis: Arthur J. Banning Press, 1994.

Housley, Norman. *The Later Crusades, 1274–1580: From Lyons to Alcazar.* New York: Oxford University Press, 1992.

———. "A Necessary Evil? Erasmus, the Crusade, and War against the Turks." In *The Crusades and Their Sources*, edited by John France and William G. Zajac, 259–79. Brookfield, Vt.: Ashgate, 1998.

———. *Religious Warfare in Europe, 1400–1536.* Oxford: Oxford University Press, 2002.

———, ed. *Crusading in the Fifteenth Century: Message and Impact.* New York: Palgrave Macmillan, 2004.

Hyland, William P. "Abbot John-Jerome of Prague: Preaching and Reform in Early Fifteenth-Century Poland." *Analecta Praemonstratensia* 80:1–4 (2004): 5–42.

Iogna-Prat, Dominique. "The Creation of a Christian Armory against Islam." In *Medieval Religion: New Approaches*, edited by Constance Hoffman Berman, 325–46. New York: Routledge, 2005.

Izbicki, Thomas M. "Juan de Torquemada's *Defense of the Conversos.*" *Catholic Historical Review* 85:2 (1999): 195–207.

———. *Nicholas of Cusa: Writings on Church and Reform.* Cambridge, Mass.: Harvard University Press, 2008.

————. "Papalist Reaction to the Council of Constance: Juan de Torquemada to the Present." *Church History* 55:1 (1986): 7–20.

————. "The Possibility of Dialogue with Islam in the Fifteenth Century." In *Nicholas of Cusa in Search of God and Wisdom*, edited by Gerald Christianson and Thomas M. Izbicki, 175–83. Leiden: Brill, 1991.

Izbicki, Thomas M., Gerald Christianson, and Philip Krey, trans. *Reject Aeneas, Accept Pius: Selected Letters of Aeneas Sylvius Piccolomini (Pope Pius II)*. Washington, D.C.: Catholic University of America Press, 2006.

Jedin, Hubert, and John Dolan. *Handbook of Church History*. New York: Herder and Herder, 1970.

Kaplan, Gregory B. *The Evolution of Converso Literature: The Writings of the Converted Jews of Medieval Spain*. Gainesville: University Press of Florida, 2002.

Karras, Ruth Mazo. *From Boys to Men: Formations of Masculinity in Late Medieval Europe*. Philadelphia: University of Pennsylvania Press, 2003.

Keck, David. *Angels and Angelology in the Middle Ages*. New York: Oxford University Press, 1998.

Kedar, Benjamin. *Crusade and Mission: European Approaches toward the Muslims*. Princeton: Princeton University Press, 1984.

Krey, Philip. "Nicholas of Lyra and Paul of Burgos on Islam." In *Medieval Christian Perceptions of Islam*, edited by John Victor Tolan, 153–74. New York: Routledge, 1996.

Kritzeck, James. *Peter the Venerable and Islam*. Princeton: Princeton University Press, 1964.

Küng, Hans. *Structures of the Church*. Translated by Salvator Attanasio. New York: T. Nelson, 1964.

Ladero Quesada, Miguel-Ángel. *Las guerras de Granada en el siglo XV*. Barcelona: Editorial Ariel, 2002.

Lawrence, Jeremy. "Humanism in the Iberian Peninsula." In Goodman and MacKay, *The Impact of Humanism on Western Europe*, 220–58.

Leff, Gordon. "The Apostolic Ideal in Later Medieval Ecclesiology." *Journal of Theological Studies* 18 (1967): 58–82.

————. "The Making of the Myth of a True Church in the Later Middle Ages." *Journal of Medieval and Renaissance Studies* 1 (1971): 1–15.

Linehan, Peter. "Papa Luna in 1415: A Proposal by Benedict XIII for the Ending of the Great Schism." *English Historical Review* 113:450 (Feb. 1998): 91–98.

López Martínez, Nicolás. "Sínodos burgalenses del siglo XV." *Burgense* 7 (1966): 211–406.

————. "Teología española de la convivencia a mediados del siglo XV." *Burgense* 8 (1967): 149–62.

López-Morillas, Consuelo. "Lost and Found? Yça of Segovia and the Qur'ān among the Mudejars and Moriscos." *Journal of Islamic Studies* 10 (1999): 277–92.

———. "'Trilingual' Marginal Notes (Arabic, Aljamiado and Spanish) in a Morisco Manuscript from Toledo." *Journal of the American Oriental Society* 103:3 (1983): 495–504.

MacKay, Angus. *Spain in the Middle Ages: From Frontier to Empire, 1000–1500.* London: Macmillan Press, 1993.

Madrigal Terrazas, Santiago. *El proyecto eclesiológico de Juan de Segovia (1393–1458): Estudio del "Liber de substantia ecclesiae"; Edición y selección de textos.* Madrid: Universidad Pontifícia Comillas, 2000.

Mann, Jesse D. "The Devilish Pope: Eugenius IV as Lucifer in the Later Works of Juan de Segovia." *Church History* 65:2 (1996): 184–96.

———. "Duns Scotus, Juan de Segovia, and Their Common Devil." *Franciscan Studies* 52 (1992): 135–64.

———. "The Historian and the Truths: Juan de Segovia's *Explanatio de tribus veritatibus fidei.*" Ph.D. dissertation. University of Chicago Divinity School, 1993.

———. "Juan de Segovia's 'Epistola ad Guillielmum de Orliaco': Who Was Guillielmus de Orliaco?" *Archivum Fratrum Praedicatorum* 62 (1992): 175–93.

———. "Ockham Redivivus or Ockham Confutator? Juan de Segovia's *Repetitio de superioritate* Reconsidered." *Annuarium historiae conciliorum* 24:1 (1992): 186–200.

———. "Truth and Consequences: Juan de Segovia on Islam and Conciliarism." *Medieval Encounters* 8:1 (2002): 79–90.

———. "William of Ockham, Juan de Segovia, and Heretical Pertinacity." *Medieval Studies* 56 (1994): 67–99.

Marcos Rodríguez, Florencio. *Extractos de los libros de claustros de la Universidad de Salamanca, siglo XV (1464–1481).* Salamanca: Universidad de Salamanca, Acta Salmanticensia, 1964.

Martínez Casado, Ángel. *Lope de Barrientos: Un intelectual de la corte de Juan II.* Salamanca: Editorial San Esteban, 1994.

———. "La situación jurídica de los conversos según Lope de Barrientos." *Archivo Dominicano* 17 (1996): 25–63.

McDermott, Peter L. "Nicholas of Cusa: Continuity and Conciliation at the Council of Basel." *Church History* 67:2 (1998): 254–73.

Melquíades Andrés, D., ed. *Historia de la teología española*, vol. 1, *Desde sus orígenes hasta fines del s. XVI.* Madrid: Fundación Universitaria Española, 1983.

Meserve, Margaret. *Empires of Islam in Renaissance Historical Thought.* Cambridge, Mass.: Harvard University Press, 2008.

Meuthen, E. *Das Basler Konzil als Forschungsproblem der europäischen Geschichte*. Opladen: Westdeutscher, 1985.

Meyerson, Mark. *A Jewish Renaissance in Fifteenth-Century Spain*. Princeton: Princeton University Press, 2004.

Minnich, Nelson. "Councils of the Catholic Reformation (Pisa I to Trent): An Historiographical Survey." *Annuarium Historiae Conciliorum* 32 (2000): 303–37.

———. "The Voice of Theologians in General Councils from Pisa to Trent." *Theological Studies* 59:3 (1998): 420–41.

Mirrer, Louise. *Women, Jews, and Muslims in the Texts of Reconquest Castile*. Ann Arbor: University of Michigan Press, 1996.

Molenat, J. P. "A propos d'Abrahen Xarafi: Les alcaldes mayores de los moros de Castille au temps des Rois Catholiques." In *Actas del VII Simposio Internacional de Mudejarismo*, 175–84. Teruel: Instituto de Estudios Turolenses, 1999.

———. "Une famille de l'élite mudéjare de la Couronne de Castille: Les Xarafi de Tolède et d'Alcalá de Henares." In *Mélanges Louis Cardaillac*, edited by I. Zaghouan, 1:765–72. Tunis: FTERSI, 1995.

———. "La question de l'élite mudéjare dans la Péninsule Ibérique Médiévale." Conference paper presented at "Elites e redes clientelares na Idade Media: Problemas metodológicos." Évora, June 2000.

Murata, Sachiko, and William C. Chittick. *The Vision of Islam*. St. Paul, Minn.: Paragon House, 1994.

Musto, Ronald. "Just Wars and Evil Empires: Erasmus and the Turks." In *Renaissance Society and Culture*, edited by John Monfasani and Ronald G. Musto, 197–216. New York: Italica Press, 1991.

Nader, Helen. *The Mendoza Family in the Spanish Renaissance, 1350–1550*. New Brunswick, N.J.: Rutgers University Press, 1979.

Nederman, Cary J. *Worlds of Difference: European Discourses of Toleration, c. 1100–c. 1550*. University Park: Pennsylvania State University Press, 2000.

Nederman, Cary, and John Christian Lauren. *Difference and Dissent: Theories of Toleration in Medieval and Early Modern Europe*. New York: Rowman and Littlefield, 1996.

Nicol, Donald. *The Last Centuries of Byzantium, 1261–1453*. 2nd ed. Cambridge: Cambridge University Press, 1993.

Nieto Soria, José Manuel. *Un crimen en la corte: Caída y ascenso de Gutierre Álvarez de Toledo, Señor de Alba (1376–1446)*. Madrid: Sílex Ediciones, 2006.

———. "Franciscanos y franciscanismo en la política en la corte de la Castilla Trastámara (1369–1475)." *Anuario de estudios medievales* 20 (1990): 109–28.

Nirenberg, David. *Communities of Violence: Persecution of Minorities in the Middle Ages*. Princeton: Princeton University Press, 1996.

————. "Conversion, Sex, and Segregation: Jews and Christians in Medieval Spain." *American Historical Review* 107:4 (Oct. 2002): 1065–93.

Novikoff, Alex. "Between Tolerance and Intolerance in Medieval Spain: An Historiographic Enigma." *Medieval Encounters* 11:1–2 (2005): 7–36.

Oakley, Francis. "The Conciliar Heritage and the Politics of Oblivion." In *The Church, the Councils, and Reform: The Legacy of the Fifteenth Century,* edited by Gerald Christianson, Thomas Izbicki, and Christopher Bellitto, 82–97. Washington, D.C.: Catholic University of America Press, 2008.

————. "The 'New Conciliarism' and Its Implications: A Problem in History and Hermeneutics." In *Natural Law, Conciliarism and Consent in the Late Middle Ages,* article VIII. London: Variorum Reprints, 1984. Orig. pub. *Journal of Ecumenical Studies* 8 (1971): 815–40.

Oberman, Heiko. *The Dawn of the Reformation.* Grand Rapids, Mich.: Eerdmans Publishing Company, 1992.

————. *Forerunners of the Reformation: The Shape of Late Medieval Thought Illustrated by Key Documents.* Philadelphia: Fortress Press, 1981.

————. *The Harvest of Medieval Theology.* Durham, N.C.: Labyrinth Press, 1983.

Ourliac, Paul. "Martin V, Eugène IV et le Concile de Bâle." In *Histoire de l'Eglise depuis les origines jusqu' à nos jours,* vol. 14, *L'Eglise au temps du Grand Schisme et de la crise conciliaire (1378–1449),* edited by Etienne Delaruelle, Edmond-René Labande, and Paul Ourliac, 201–293. Paris: Bloud & Gay, 1962–64.

Paviot, Jacques. "Burgundy and the Crusade." In Housley, *Crusading in the Fifteenth Century,* 70–80.

Phelan, John Leddy. *The Millennial Kingdom of the Franciscans in the New World.* 2nd rev. ed. Berkeley: University of California Press, 1970.

Philippides, Marios. *Mehmed II the Conqueror and the Fall of the Franco-Byzantine Levant to the Ottoman Turks: Some Western Views and Testimonies.* Tempe: Arizona Center for Medieval and Renaissance Studies, 2007.

————. "Urban's Bombard(s), Gunpowder, and the Siege of Constantinople (1453)." *Byzantine Studies/Etudes Byzantines,* n.s., 4 (1999): 1–67.

Phillips, William D. *Enrique IV and the Crisis of Fifteenth-Century Castile, 1425–1480.* Cambridge, Mass.: Medieval Academy of America, 1978.

Pick, Lucy K. *Conflict and Coexistence: Archbishop Rodrigo and the Muslims and Jews of Medieval Spain.* Ann Arbor: University of Michigan Press, 2004.

Rashdall, Hastings. *The Universities of Europe in the Middle Ages,* vol. 1, repub. and ed. by F. M. Powicke and A. B. Emden. Oxford: Oxford University Press, 1987. Orig. pub. 1958.

Reilly, Bernard. *The Medieval Spains*. Cambridge: Cambridge University Press, 1993.

Roest, Bert. *A History of Franciscan Education (c. 1210–1517)*. Leiden: Brill, 2000.

Rouhi, Leyla. "A Fifteenth-Century Salamancan's Pursuit of Islamic Studies." In *Under the Influence: Questioning the Comparative in Medieval Castile*, edited by Cynthia Robinson and Leyla Rouhi, 21–42. Leiden: Brill, 2005.

Rucquoi, Adeline. "Contribution des *studia generalia* à la pensée hispanique médiévale." In *Pensamiento medieval hispano: Homenaje a Horacio Santiago-Otero*, edited by José María Soto Rábanos, 737–70. Madrid: Consejo Superior de Investigaciones Científicas, 1998.

———. "Democratie ou monarchie : Le discours politique dans l'université castillane au XVe siècle." In *El discurso político en la Edad Media*, edited by Nilda Guglielmi and Adeline Rucquoi, 223–55. Buenos Aires: Programa de Investigaciones Medievales, Consejo Nacional de Investigaciones Científicas y Técnicas, 1995.

———. "Éducation et société dans la Péninsule ibérique médiévale." *Histoire d'Education* 69 (Jan. 1996): 3–26.

———. "Valladolid, pôle d'immigration au XVe siècle." In *Les Communications dans la Péninsule Ibérique du Moyen Age*, 179–89. Paris: CNRS, 1981.

———. *Valladolid au Moyen Age, 1080–1480*. Paris: Editions Publisud, 1993. Also published in Spanish as *Valladolid en la Edad Media*. Junta de Castilla y León: Consejería de Educación y Cultura, 1997.

Ruiz, Teofilo. *Spain's Centuries of Crisis, 1300–1474*. Malden, Mass.: Blackwell Publishing, 2007.

Runciman, Steven. *The Fall of Constantinople: 1453*. Cambridge: Cambridge University Press, 1965.

Ryan, John J. *The Apostolic Conciliarism of Jean Gerson*. Atlanta: Scholars Press, 1998.

Santamaría Lancho, Miguel. "El cabildo catedralicio de Segovia como aparato de poder en el sistema político urbano durante el siglo XV." *Studia Histórica: Historia Medieval* 8 (1990): 47–77.

Santiago Otero, Horacio, and José María Soto Rábanos. "Los saberes y su transmisión en la península ibérica (1200–1470)." *Medievalismo* 5:5 (1995): 215–56.

Schwartz, Stuart. *All Can Be Saved: Religious Tolerance and Salvation in the Iberian Atlantic World*. New Haven: Yale University Press, 2008.

Schwoebel, Robert. *The Shadow of the Crescent: The Renaissance Image of the Turk (1453–1517)*. New York: St. Martin's Press, 1967.

Seidenspinner-Núñez, Dayle. "Inflecting the *Converso* Voice: A Commentary on Recent Theories." *La Corónica* 25:1 (1996): 6–18.

Serrano, L. *Los conversos don Pablo de Santa María y don Alfonso de Carta-gena*. Madrid: Consejo Superior de Investigaciones, 1942.

Setton, Kenneth. *The Papacy and the Levant*. 4 vols. Philadelphia: American Philosophical Society, 1978.

————. *Western Hostility to Islam and Prophecies of Turkish Doom*. Phila-delphia: American Philosophical Society, 1992.

Siberry, Elizabeth. *Criticism of Crusading, 1095–1274*. Oxford: Clarendon Press, 1985.

Smith, Lesley. "The Use of Scripture in Teaching at the Medieval University." In *Learning Institutionalized: Teaching in the Medieval University*, ed-ited by John Van Engen, 229–43. Notre Dame, Ind.: University of Notre Dame Press, 2000.

Soto Rábanos, José María. "Consideraciones jurídico-morales sobre la guerra en la obra de un canonista español anónimo del siglo XV." In *Moral and Political Philosophies of the Middle Ages*, edited by Bernardo C. Bazàn, 1720–31. Proceedings of the Ninth International Congress of Medieval Philosophy. New York: Legas, 1995.

————. "La ignorancia del pueblo llano como obstáculo para el diálogo in-terreligioso." In *Diálogo filosófico-religioso entre cristianismo, judaísmo e islamismo durante la edad media en la península ibérica*, edited by Horacio Santiago-Otero, 99–116. Turnhout: Brepols, 1994.

Southern, Richard W. *Western Views of Islam in the Middle Ages*. Cambridge, Mass.: Harvard University Press, 1962.

Stieber, Joachim. *Pope Eugenius IV, the Council of Basel and the Secular and Ecclesiastical Authorities in the Empire: The Conflict over Supreme Au-thority and Power in the Church*. Leiden: Brill, 1978.

Strand, A. A. "Studia Piccolomineana: Vorarbeiten zu einer Geschichte der Bibliothek der Päpste Pius II und III." In *Enea Silvio Piccolomini, Papa Pio II: Atti del Convegno per il quinto Centenario della morte e altre scritti raccolti a Domenico Maffei*, edited by Domenico Maffei, 295–390. Siena: Accademia senese degli intronati, 1968.

Stump, Philip H. *The Reforms of the Council of Constance, 1414–1418*. New York: Brill, 1994.

Suárez Fernández, Luís. *Castilla, el cisma y la crisis conciliar (1378–1440)*. Madrid: Consejo Superior de Investigaciones Científicas, 1960.

Tapia Sánchez, Serafín de. *La comunidad morisca de Avila*. Salamanca: Uni-versidad de Salamanca, 1991.

Tierney, Brian. *Church Law and Constitutional Thought in the Middle Ages*. Aldershot: Variorum, 1979.

————. *Foundations of Conciliar Theory: The Contribution of the Medieval Canonists from Gratian to the Great Schism*. London: Cambridge Uni-versity Press, 1968.

Bibliography *365*

Tolan, John V. *Francis and the Sultan: The Curious History of a Christian-Muslim Encounter*. New York: Oxford University Press, 2009.
———. *Saracens: Islam in the Medieval European Imagination*. New York: Columbia University Press, 2002.
Utz, Kathrin. "Zur Chronologie der kirchenpolitischen Traktate des Johannes von Segovia." *Annuarium Historiae Conciliorum* 9 (1977): 302–14.
Vadeón Baruque, Julio. "Las cortes de Castilla y las luchas del s. XV." *Anuario de estudios medievales* 3 (1966): 293–326.
Val Valdivieso, María Isabel del. "Universidad y luchas urbanas en la Castilla bajomedieval." *Mayurqa* 22:1 (1989): 213–37.
———. "Universidad y oligarquía en la Castilla bajomedieval." In *Universidad, cultura y sociedad en la Edad Media*, edited by Santiago Aguadé Nieto, 131–46. Alcalá de Henares: Servicio de Publicaciones, 1994.
Van Liere, Katherine Elliot. "Humanism and Scholasticism in Sixteenth-Century Academe: Five Student Orations from the University of Salamanca." *Renaissance Quarterly* 53:1 (2000): 57–107.
Vázquez Janeiro, Isaac. "En torno a la biblioteca de Juan de Segovia (+ 1458)." *Antonianum* 60 (1985): 670–88.
———. "Historia de la iglesia y ciencias sagradas en la Segovia del siglo XV." In Galindo García, *Arias Dávila*, 257–72.
———. *Tratados castellanos sobre la predestinación y sobre la Trinidad y la Encarnación, del Maestro Fray Diego de Valencia O.F.M. (siglo XV): Identificación de su autoría y edición crítica*. Madrid: Consejo Superior de Investigaciones Científicas, Instituto "Francisco Suárez," 1984.
Voogt, P. "Le conciliarisme aux conciles de Constance et de Bâle." In *Le concile et les conciles*, edited by B. Botte et al., 143–81. Chevetogne: Éditions Chevetogne, 1960.
———. "Le conciliarisme aux conciles de Constance et de Bâle: Compléments et précisions." *Irenikon* 36 (1963): 61–75.
Watanabe, M. "Authority and Consent in Church Government: Panormitanus, Aeneas Sylvius, Cusanus." *Journal of the History of Ideas* 33 (1972): 217–36.
Webster, Jill R. "Conversion and Co-existence: The Franciscan Mission in the Crown of Aragon." In *Iberia and the Mediterranean World of the Middle Ages. Essays in Honor of Robert I. Burns S.J.*, edited by P. E. Chevedden, D. J. Kagay, and P. G. Padilla, 163–77. Leiden: Brill, 1996.
Weissberger, Barbara F. *Isabel Rules: Constructing Queenship, Wielding Power*. Minneapolis: University of Minnesota Press, 2004.
West, Delno C., and August Kling. *The "Libro de las profecías of Christopher Columbus."* Gainesville: University of Florida Press, 1991.
Wiegers, Gerard. *Islamic Literature in Spanish and Aljamiado: Yça of Segovia (fl. 1450), His Antecedents and Successors*. Leiden: Brill, 1994.

Williams, George Davis. "Governance at the University of Salamanca, 1200–1500." Ph.D. dissertation, University of Denver, 1970.

Wolf, Anne Marie. "Juan de Segovia and Western Perspectives on Islam in the Fifteenth Century." Ph.D. dissertation, University of Minnesota, 2003.

———. "Precedents and Paradigms: Juan de Segovia on the Bible, the Church, and the Ottoman Threat." In *Scripture and Pluralism: Reading the Bible in the Religiously Plural Worlds of the Middle Ages and Renaissance*, edited by Thomas J. Heffernan and Thomas E. Burman, 143–60. Leiden: Brill, 2005.

Index —⚬—

Al-Andalus, historical background, 6

A_ba, Gonzalo de, 85

Á_varez de Toledo, Gutierre Gómez (founder of House of Alba), 18

Amadeus VIII of Savoy (duke, Pope Felix V): elected pope at Basel, 119–20; miracles associated with tomb, 224

a¬gels, and conversion of Muslims, 152–53

Antichrist: in argument that Christianity is affirmed by miracles, in *De fide catholica*, 84; Muslims as precursors of in Christian polemic, 214

Apocalypse, in Christian thought about Islam: 215

Augustine: influence on *De fide catholica*, 51, 54–57, 78, 80; saw Jews as beneficial to Christian society, 212–13

Bacon, Roger, compared to Juan de Segovia, 163–64

Barrientos, Lope de: defender of *conversos*, 218; at Salamanca, 18

Basel, Council of: colleagues from as later recipients of letters

from Juan de Segovia, 135; conclusion of, 127; deposition of Eugene IV, 119; election of Amadeus VIII of Savoy as Pope Felix V, 119; and growing strength of Turks, 166, 170; Juan II and, 106–7; Juan de Segovia incorporated at, 104; legitimacy of in Juan de Segovia's arguments, 122–24; not well studied, 100–101; origins, 100; Salamanca and, 106; transferred to Ferrara and then Florence, 115–18, 127

Beelzebub, as spirit that inspired Qur'ān, 195, 198

"being and conserving," principles of: Bible as Christianity's, 160; contrasting in Islam and Christianity, 203; origins in conciliarists' thought, 160; showing Christians correct path for dealing with Islam, 204

Benedict XIII (pope): favors to university at Salamanca, 20; *Sincerae devotionis*, 27. *See also* Pedro de Luna

Bible: Augustine and reliability of, 57; Christianity's "being and conserving," 160; conciliarists' emphasis on, 124–26; *Concordantiae dictionum indeclinabilium*, 108; not corrupted by Christians or Jews, as Muslims charge, appendix 3, lines 108–12; and end of the world calculations, 215; and Erasmus, 220; Muhammad prohibiting followers from reading, 80, appendix 1, lines 57–62; not respected by Muslims, 202–3; parallels with the Qur'ān, appendix 2, lines 126–79; as source of Juan de Segovia's thought, 23, 50–58, 157–61; as sword of the Spirit, 165; use of in proposed dialogues with Muslims, appendix 3, lines 98–116

canon law, 28; used to defend power of pope, 43, 124–25
Cartagena, Alonso de: colleague of Juan de Segovia at Basel, 214; *converso*, 214; student at Salamanca, 17; treatise opposing discrimination against *conversos*, 218
Cartagena, Pablo de. *See* Santa María, Pablo de
Catalina de Lancaster (queen, regent for Juan II), 65
Catholic truths: sources for other than scripture, 274n158; outline of in *Repetitio de superioritate*, 50; scripture as foundation for, 123
Cervantes, Juan de: *De mittendo gladio, Liber de praeclara*

noticia, and *Liber de magna auctoritate* written for, 135; Juan de Segovia *familiar* of, 104; Juan de Segovia learning of fall of Constantinople from *familiar* of, 132; led crusade against Muslims, 135–36; petition to remove Juan de Segovia from his *familiares*, 133
Cesarini, Giuliano: abandoning Basel for Ferrara, 116–17; crusade at Varna, 103; delegate of Eugene IV to Basel, 103; leading troops against Bohemia, 110–11; letter to pope advocating dialogue with Hussites, 112; peace proposal to Hussites, 157; refusal to accept bull of dissolution, 103
circumcision: in Islam, Juan de Segovia on, 202; linked Islam and Judaism in Alsonso de Espina's thought, 212
conciliarists: in Castile, 32–33; and fiscal reforms, 171; goals of, 101, 125–26; and principles of "being and conserving," 160; prominence of scripture in thought of, 96, 124–25; similarities between aims of and 1422 constitution for Salamanca, 45, 106
Concordantiae dictionum indeclinabilium, 108
Constance, Council of: Castile's loyalties during, 31–33; ending schism and providing the impetus for Basel, 98–99; increased Salamanca's library, 30; Salamanca faculty participating in, 19, 30

Constantinope, fall of: described
by Juan de Segovia and
contemporaries, 134;
eyewitness accounts of siege,
168–69; as loss for Europe,
168; losses prior to, 167; as
punishment for Greeks by
God, 172

contraferentia, 177: as term for
historical interreligious
dialogue, 178; Juan de
Segovia's choice of term, 182.
See also delegation

conversos: defined, 213; increasing
numbers, 213; and Juan de
Segovia's attitude toward
Muslims, 219; social tensions
surrounding and defenses of,
218–19

crusades: in Castile against Granada,
226–27; exhortation to as
common rhetorical exercise,
166; explanations for failures
of, 162; idealization of in
later Middle Ages, 155;
ineffectiveness of, 155–56;
Innocent IV and, 181–82; as
inspiration in address before
court of Burgundy, 143; linked
to strong papacy, 172; resistance
to tax levies for, 171–72

Cusa, Nicholas of (Cusanus):
correspondent of Juan de
Segovia, 136–37; Cribratio
Alkorani, 140–42; De pace fidei,
138–39; at Diet of Frankfurt
(1442), 125; differences with
Juan de Segovia in approach
to Islam, 138–41; encouraged
Juan de Segovia to share ideas,
148; left Basel for Ferrara, 118;
loaned Juan de Segovia copy of

Qur'ān at Basel, 62; opponent
of Juan de Segovia at Diet of
Mainz (1441), 121; shared belief
with Juan de Segovia that
Muslims were rational, 204

De fide catholica, 51; references to
Jews and Muslims in, 78–84

delegation (proposed by Juan de
Segovia to hold discussions
with Muslims), 176–84,
appendix 3

De mittendo gladio divini Spiritus
in corda Sarracenorum:
military imagery in title,
164; paradoxical title, 26

disputations: Christianity tested
and proven by, 68, 183; as
combat and model of
masculinity, 25; as means
of bonding, 26; as part of
progress toward Salamanca
degree, 25; at Tortosa, 68

Donatio, 191; stipulations
concerning Juan de Segovia's
books, 227–28; translations
of the Qur'ān in Juan de
Segovia's possession, 188;
Vincent Ferrer in, 66

Duns Scotus, 47–48

Enrique IV (king): exempted
Muslims of Segovia from
jurisdiction of alcalde mayor,
72; Salamanca men in his
service, 17–18; and Salamanca's
retraction of authorization of
Juan de Segovia, 60

Erasmus, compared to Juan de
Segovia, 219–20

Espina, Alonso de, on armor that
Christians need, 164–65

Eugene IV (pope): and crusade for
    Balkans (1443), 171; described
    by Juan de Segovia as heretic,
    122–24; issued bull dissolving
    Basel, 102–3
*Explanatio de tribus veritatibus
    fidei*, 121

faith: acquired and infused,
    77–78; as assent to contents
    of Bible, 52–53, 78; church
    leaders encouraged to
    foster, 85; defined by
    Christian thinkers, 77–78;
    defined by Juan de Segovia,
    52; questions on whether
    Christian faith is only path
    to salvation, 81
Felix V (pope). *See* Amadeus VIII
    of Savoy
Fernando de Antequera
    (Fernando I, king of Aragon):
    power indirectly exercised in
    Castile, 34–35; renewal of war
    with Granada, 65
Ferrer, Vincent: chaplain to
    Benedict XIII, 65; and Juan
    de Segovia, 66–67; preaching
    in Castile in 1411, 65; and
    schism, 161
Francis, Saint, missions of, 180–82
Franciscans: influence on Juan
    de Segovia, 47–50; and
    millenarianism, 215; as possible
    inspiration for Juan de Segovia,
    180–81; school of thought,
    48–50
Frequens: affirmed by Basel after
    bull of dissolution from pope,
    104; reason Basel was
    convened, 99–100

Germain, Jean: correspondent of
    Juan de Segovia, 142–46; fear
    of Turks conquering Italy, 170;
    proponent of crusading,
    143–44; use of military
    analogies, 164
Gerson, Jean: admired by Juan de
    Segovia, 31, 106, 125; in devel-
    opment of principles of "being
    and conserving," 160; possible
    inspiration for organization of
    De mittendo gladio, 154
Gidelli, Yça: adoption of Christian
    terminology, 72; *Breviario
    Sunni*, 71–72; connections to
    elite families, 73; correspon-
    dence with Juan de Segovia
    after leaving Aiton, 191, 225;
    letter to Juan de Segovia
    agreeing to travel to Aiton,
    62, 188–89, 210; role among
    Castile's Muslims, 70–71,
    189; translation of Qur'ān,
    188–90, 210
Greeks: disputes over location
    for negotiations with,
    115–16; hopes for reunion
    with at Basel, 115; hoping for
    western help against Turks,
    116; Juan de Segovia involved
    in discussions with, 108;
    reunion with important to
    Juan de Segovia, 115; wary of
    council, 116

Haec sancta, 99, 104
*Historia gestorum synodi
    Basiliensis*, 95; autographic
    marginal notes in Escorial
    copy, 110; Cesarini as central
    figure in, 103; election of

Amadeus VIII (Felix V) as
pope, 120; language used to
describe Hussites, 109;
negotiations with Greeks in,
115; on Vincent Ferrer's
preaching in Castile and
aftermath for Jews, 67
humanists: and crusading rhetoric,
166; and Islam, 172–73;
Italian response to fall of
Constantinople, 130; legacy
of their writing on the Turks,
221; secular outlook, 187
Hussites, 97–98; Compacts of
Prague (or Basel), 113;
compared by Cartagena to
those wanting to discriminate
against *conversos*, 218; dialogue
with as parallel to situation
with Muslims, 156–57, 182–83,
217; Nicholas of Cusa active at
Basel on question of, 108;
references to in *Historia*, 108–9

Islam, rise of: early Christian
writings on, 198–99; as
liberation from yoke of Roman
oppression, 80–81; Juan de
Segovia's explanations for,
199–200, appendix 1, lines
25–62; as new heresy, 199

Jews, 6–7, 64–65; in *De fide
catholica*, 78; disputations at
Tortosa, 68; faith lacking
reason, 79, 82; interactions with
Christians, 69; Juan de Segovia
not interested in converting,
211–14; Vincent Ferrer's
preaching and subsequent
conversions, 66–67

John of Ragusa, 117, 170
Juan II (king): accession to throne
and challenge from *infantes*
of Aragon, 28, 34; delegation
to Basel, 106–7; request for
easier absolution for subjects
aiding Muslims, 69; Salamanca
men serving him, 17–18;
struggle for influence over
Salamanca, 21–22; tax
exemptions for converting
Jews, 67

law of nature, 76, 152, 209; vs. law
of grace, 80, 158; appendix 1,
lines 1–24
letter-treatises, as genre, 154
*Liber de magna auctoritate
episcoporum in concilio
generali*; 135–36, 146: advising
against war, 110; Muslims in,
127–28
library, Juan de Segovia's, 227–28
Llull, Ramón: approach to Muslims
compared to Juan de Segovia's,
162; believed Muslims were
rational, 204
love: Christians called to love
enemies, 158, 209–10; Muslims
could come to know love
Christians have for them,
179, appendix 3, lines 43–47;
tragedy that Muslims had
not heard of the love of
God, 216–17, appendix 2,
lines 187–93

maestrescuela, 15, 20, 35; conflict
concerning authority over the
university, 40–41, 99–100
Martí, Ramón, 164

Martin V (pope): and conflict over constitutions for Salamanca, 42; elected at Constance, called Basel, 99–102; favors granted to Salamanca, 20; Juan de Segovia traveling as delegate for, 86

Martínez de Covarrubias, Pedro, 102

Mendoza, Lope de, 38–39

miracles: associated with Juan de Segovia's tomb, 224; foundation of Christian faith, 54–55; Islam lacking support from, 80, 82, appendix 1, lines 20–23 and 34; Juan de Segovia arguing that Christians should not wait for, 152; Muhammad's lack of, 204

Montecroce, Riccoldo da, 198, 204

Moro, Ibo, 42

Mudéjars (Muslim population of Castile), 63–65, 68–74; Juan de Segovia's general impressions of, 74–75; new research on, 72–73; Yça Gidelli's advice to, 71–72

Muhammad (prophet): bearer of Qur'ān, 193; coming predicted in Bible, need to refute, 195, appendix 3, lines 101–16; Juan de Segovia and Nicholas of Cusa on, 197–98; Juan de Segovia echoing standard polemic about, 80–81, 192; as liberator from Romans, appendix 1, lines 43–50; Nicholas of Cusa on in *Cribratio Alkorani*, 141; placed above Christ by Muslims, 128; as portrayed by Western Christian writers, 199, 214

Muslims: badly informed about Christianity, 183–86, 205, appendix 2, lines 193–99; beliefs about whether they were rational, 158, 163, 204; hopes at Basel for conversion of, 115; influence of on Juan de Segovia's thought, 175–76, 184, 186, 216; Juan de Segovia's conversations with in 1431, 88–93, appendix 2

Nicholas V (pope): crusading bull against Granada, 226; Juan de Segovia not confirmed as cardinal by, 131; succeeded Eugene IV, recognized by Basel, 127

Nicopolis, 143, 167–68

Oleśnicki, Zbigniew, 171

d'Orlyé, Guillaume (Guillielmus de Orliaco), 47, 133, 146, 231

de La Palud, Louis, 131, 133, 211, 224

Panormitanus, 120

paradise: in Qur'ān, discussed by Juan de Segovia, 142, 197, 200; in Qur'ān, discussed by Picco-lomini, 151; in standard Western polemic against Islam, 199

Paris (university), 19; delegates from at Basel, 102; Juan de Segovia seated next to delegates from, 18, 104; and schism, 105, 161

peace: seeking it as imitation of Christ, 177; fluidity of concept in Juan de Segovia's writings, 178–79; Innocent IV sending delegation to Tartars to seek, 181; preaching gospel meant

preaching peace, 157–58;
Qur'ān calling Muslims to, 192
Pedro de Luna: delegate to Castile
for Avignon Pope Clement VII,
32; plans for ending schism,
161. *See also* Benedict XIII
(pope)
persuasion: as means of promoting
Christian faith, 58, 87; Juan de
Segovia sensitive to psychology
of, 208–10
Peter the Venerable: on Islam and
Muslims, 162–64, 199, 204;
polemical works as way to
strengthen Christians' faith,
207
Philip the Good (duke of
Burgundy), 143–45
Piccolomini, Aeneas Sylvius:
appropriation of Juan de
Segovia's library, 228; as
correspondent of Juan de
Segovia, 147–49; and crusading,
148–51, 167, 172; *Execrabilis*,
226; history of the council, 230;
on Juan de Segovia's retirement
to Aiton, 132; praise for Juan
de Segovia, 120, 147; recanting
earlier conciliar pursuits, 225
Pius II (pope). *See* Piccolomini,
Aeneas Sylvius
polemic, religious: against Islam,
standard themes in, 194–202,
205–6, 214; military imagery in,
164–65; role and purpose of,
7–8, 206–8; usually against
both Judaism and Islam, 211–12
Prague, Compacts of (or Compacts
of Basel), 113
Preface (to trilingual translation of
Qur'ān), 190–95, 199, 206, 208

Qur'ān: contents opposed to
reason, appendix 1, lines
70–72; distorts Old and
New Testaments, appendix 1,
lines 57–58; in *Donatio*, 228;
excusing followers from
following earlier religions,
appendix 2, lines 99–115; false
things imputed to Christians
in, appendix 3, lines 64–89;
Juan de Segovia's efforts to
find a good translation,
187–89, 206; Juan de Segovia's
interest in how Muslims
read, 193–94; Juan de Segovia's
notes on "errors" in, 142; as
miracle, 204; need to prove as
false, 187, 193; Nicholas of
Cusa on, 140, 196; Pedro
Pascual's translation, 206;
Piccolomini on, 149; quotes
from (Latin translation),
appendix 2, lines 136–57;
trilingual edition prepared
by Juan de Segovia and Yça
Gidelli, 190; urging Muslims
to fight unbelievers, 186, 200,
appendix 3, lines 83–89; urging
Muslims to seek peace, 192,
appendix 3, lines 22–26

Reichstage, 166–67
Repetitio de superioritate: context
and meaning of, 35–45;
references to Muslims in,
76–77; use of Ockham in, 48
Ruíz, Antón, 35

St. Jean Maurienne (in Savoy),
2, 131, 133, 166, 189, 211, 224
Salamanca (city), 15–16

Salamanca (university): and
Council of Constance, 31–32;
curriculum determined in
Sincerae devotionis, 25; in early
fifteenth century, 16–19; Juan
de Segovia's praise for, 59–60;
Juan de Segovia's studies at,
26, 28; library as intended
recipient for most of Juan
de Segovia's books, 227–29;
in power struggle between
popes and kings, 20–21;
retracting authority for Juan
de Segovia to represent it at
Basel, 60
Salamanca, Álvaro de, 59
Sánchez de Arévalo, Rodrigo, 17
Santa María, Pablo de (Pablo de
Cartagena, Pablo de Burgos):
commentary on Nicholas of
Lyra on Apocalypse, 81;
influenced Castile's loyalties
during schism, 32
Savoy, 3, 146, 191; chronicles of,
224; duke of chosen as pope by
Basel, 119, 224; Juan de Segovia
as bishop there, 131
sexual appetites in Christian
polemic on Islam, 199–202; in
De fide catholica, 79, 82, 84,
appendix 1, lines 2–11 and
31–36
Sigismund (emperor): and Bohemia
and Hussites, 97, 111, 156,
182; and conciliar efforts,
98, 103
sword: *De mittendo gladio*, 26,
164; impediment to peace
negotiations, 111; Islam spread
by, 77, 80, 203, appendix 1,
lines 25–36; of the Spirit

(evoked by Erasmus), 220;
swordfighting used as image
of disputation, 25; vs. way of
peace, 110, 146; of the word
of God, 109, 159, 165

theology: advocates for dignity of as
a discipline, 59; Benedict XIII's
Sincerae devotionis and study
of at Salamanca, 27; choice to
study it, 26–28; conciliarist
leanings of theologians
(vs. canonists), 124; Juan
de Segovia holding all three
chairs of, 29
Toledo, Alfonso de, 81
tolerance, among common people
of Iberia, 83
Torquemada, Juan de, 218–19
Tractatus super presidentia, 105,
160
Trinity (Divine Unity): Juan de
Segovia explaining to Muslims,
90, appendix 2, lines 26–80;
debunking Muslim belief that
Christians were polytheists,
142, 179–80, 184–86, 204–5,
appendix 3, lines 51–89;
Muslims marveling at
Christians' disagreements
over *filioque*, 170; need for
Christians to know teaching
on, 58, 85; Nicholas of Cusa
on importance of in dialogues
with Muslims, 139, 185
Tudeschi, Nicolò de'. *See*
Panormitanus
Turks: as ascendant power, 97,
166–70; Basel delegates in
eastern Mediterranean alarmed
about, 170; Constantinople,

siege on, 168–69; crusading plans negatively affected by popes' declining influence and revenues, 171; humanists' portrayal of, 130, 173; Jean Germain arguing for crusading against, 144; as minor threat compared to others Christianity had faced, 171; *Türkenrade* and *Türkenkriegsrede*, 166–67

twelve foundations of Christian faith: in *De fide catholica*, 53–58, 78–80; Islam lacking, appendix 1, lines 51–53

Varna, 97, 165, 167–68, 171: defeat as God's punishment, 220–21

via pacis et doctrinae, 75, 134, 177; Jean Germain previously favoring, 142–43; possibly modelled after proposals at Paris for ending schism, 161; vs. war as means of conversion, 98, 147, 155, 157–58, 215

violence, in Islam. *See* sword

William of Ockham: apostolic church as inspiration for, 126; influence on Juan de Segovia's thought, 48–50, 124

Anne Marie Wolf

is associate professor of history at the University of Maine at Farmington.